corePerson
Krishna Sāṁkhya

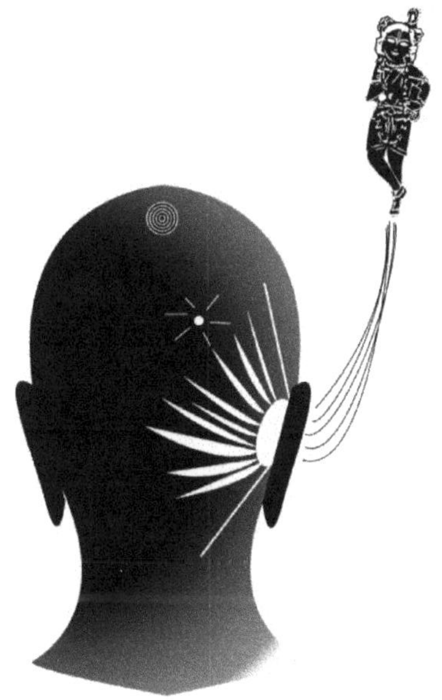

Michael Beloved

Correspondence

Michael Beloved

19311 SW 30TH ST

Miramar, FL 33029

USA

Email

axisnexus @gmail.com

ISBN paperback **9781942887539**

ISBN epub **9781942887546**

LCCN **2022912941**

Scheme of Pronunciation

Consonants

Gutturals:	क	ख	ग	घ	ङ	
	ka	kha	ga	gha	ṅa	
Palatals:	च	छ	ज	झ	ञ	
	ca	cha	ja	jha	ña	
Cerebrals:	ट	ठ	ड	ढ	ण	
	ṭa	ṭha	ḍa	ḍha	ṇa	
Dentals:	त	थ	द	ध	न	
	ta	tha	da	dha	na	
Labials:		प	फ	ब	भ	म
		pa	pha	ba	bha	ma

Semivowels:

य र	ल	व
ya ra	la	va

Numbers:

०	१	२	३	४	५	६	७	८	९
0	1	2	3	4	5	6	7	8	9

Sibilants:	श	ष	स
	śa	ṣa	sa

Aspirate: ह

ha

Vowels:

अ आ	इ	ई	उ	ऊ	ऋ	ॠ
a ā	i	ī	u	ū	ṛ	ṝ
ए औ	ओ	औ	ळ	ॣ	<	⍰
e ai	o	au	lṛ	lṝ	ṁ	ḥ

Apostrophe ऽ

Table of Contents

Introduction ***7***
Chapter 1 corePerson ***8***
Chapter 2 Bhagavad Gītā Evidence ***24***
Chapter 3 Sāṁkhya Theory of Creation* ***253***
Index ***286***
About the Author ***295***
Publications ***297***

English Series **297**
Meditation Series **299**
Explained Series **301**
Commentaries **302**
Specialty **304**
inVision Series **306**

Online Resources ***310***

How to use this book:

Make a casual reading initially.

Make a second reading while pausing and considering topics of interest.

Make a third reading while observing the main themes in the discourse.

Finally, make an indepth study of the entire text.

A note on the diacritical marks and pronounciation:

Names like Krishna and Arjuna are accepted in common English usage. Their English spellings occur in the translation without diacritical marks.

Here are some hints on how to use the diacritical marks for near-exact pronunciation:

Letters with a **dot** under them, should be pronounced while the tongue touches and is released curling slightly at the top of palate.

The s sound for **ś** carries an h with it and is said as the **sh** sound in **she**.

The s sound for **ṣ** carries an h with it and is said as the **sh** sound in **shun**.

The h sound for **ḥ** carries an echoing sound of the vowel before it, such that **oḥ** is actually **oho** and **aḥ** is actually **aha**.

In many Sanskrit words the **y** sound is said as an **i** sound, especially when the y sound preceeds an a. For instance, prāṇāyāma should be praa-**nai**-aa-muh, rather than praa-naa-**yaa**-muh.

The **a** sound is more like **uh** in English, while the **ā** sound is like the a sound in **far**.

The **ṛ** sound is like the **ri** sound in **ridge**.

The **ph** sound is never reduced to an f sound as in English. The **p sound** is maintained.

Whenever **h** occurs after a consonant, its integrity is maintained as an air forced sound.

If the h sound occurs after a vowel and a consonant, one should let the consonant remain with the vowel which preceeds it and allow the h sound to carry with the vowel after it, such that Duryodhana is pronounced with the d consonant allied to the o before it and the h sound manages the a after it. Say Dur-**yod-ha**-na or Dur-**yod-han**. Do not say Dur-yo-**dha**-na. Separate the d and h sounds to make them distinct. In words where you have no choice and must combine the d and h sound, as in the word dharma. Make sure that the **h sound** is heard as an **air sound pushed out from the throat**. Dharma should never be mistaken for darma. But adharma should be **ad-har-**ma.

The **c** sound is **ch,** and the **ch** sound is **ch-h**.

Introduction

This is a continuation of the argument for the reality of person. This argument was conducted in the *Upanishads* as well as in the Buddhist literature. Most of the *Upanishads* tilt for the feature of *brahman,* which is defined as the ultimate energy. It tags *atma* or self as being a trivial part of the *brahman* ultimate force. Even though the term *paramatma* appears, that is not given the same significance as *brahman*. *Paramatma* denotes the supreme or superior *atma* or self. Hence there is this idea that regardless of if someone is rated as an *atma* or *paramatma*, still whatever it is, it fades into *brahman* which is the real ultimate.

After the *Upanishads* issued these challenges to the idea of a lasting personSelf, the *Advaita Vedanta* arguments of *Shankara* and others wiped away the idea of an enduring self. It ridiculed any idea of a relationship between selves as being fundamental. It points to *brahman* as the ultimate real feature with other aspects like *atma, jivatma*, being trivial. The solution given is that the self or the so-called self, should renounce itself practically by giving itself over to *brahman*, so that there is no self but only *brahman*.

This literature, *corePerson ~ Krishna Sāṁkhya*, establishes the personSelves as a continuous reality and not as a mere passing phase. It is a feature of the ultimate substance, but it endures in its subjective phase. When it can contrast itself with anything in its surroundings, it requires support for the manifestation of its objective condition.

In the *Bhagavad Gītā* and *Uddhava Gītā,* Krishna explained the enduring person. In this book his explanations are regarded. The philosophy which supports this is the *Krishna Sāṁkhya* information.

Chapter 1

corePerson

declaration of personSource

The two requirements for perception are person and environment. The person is subjective to itself but is objective to the environment when it has the means of sensual perception to describe what surrounds the self. Sensual perception includes bare attention without sensual aids like hearing, touching, seeing, tasting and smelling. When exercised, attention manifests as interest. When relaxed it manifests as feelings. Environment could be a medium which supplements the self or a medium which is parasitic to it.

The environment which someone discovers, may be of a similar psychic or physical material. It could be of a spiritual medium which is similar to that of the coreSelf. The environment cannot be of a higher spiritual level, because otherwise due to the transcendence value of that higher place, the person would have no way to perceive the location.

One can perceive what is the same, equivalent to or what is inferior to, one's corePerson. Whatever is higher cannot be perceived unless one is outfitted with a sensual adaptation through special grace of a deity. It is natural to descend, to perceive what is lower. It is unnatural to have access to what is higher. As with gravity going down is easy. Going up requires effort and is attained strenuously.

There is the aspect of perception whereby there is use of one or more of the five senses with the extrasensory perception which comes with the subtle body on that higher plane. It is easier to function in an environment which is lower than the self. This is the reason why a personSelf regularly finds itself in the physical or near-physical existences with sense perception which can be verified with one or more senses.

For instance, one may hear the bleating of sheep. Then one may verify this by touching the mouth of the animal. By using two senses, one may verify something. The easiest materials to detect and analyze are physical. This itself informs that it is difficult and unnatural to research what is psychic.

The requirements for self-research are:

- person
- environment

Of these the **person** is essential if there is to be perception of objects. The **environment** must be there, but the person is relevant. In a situation of personSelves, the environment is the surface or medium where action occurs.

Regarding self, considering person, the traditionalSelf, the social somebody, is a composite. To understand, one must sort the parts. Even if one cannot segregate it, still one should enter transcendence states to experience the fragments of the traditionalSelf.

This traditionalSelf has two main parts. One is the corePerson which is a radiance of awareness. The other part is the social adaptability energy and the skill which is developed by that energy. *Function! Function! Function!* Through acceptance of function from the sourceSelf, the deity, each person should have relationship and format.

The other relationships which the self has with anything and anyone who is not the sourceSelf, create personality formats for the self, where that self takes forms to suit the requirements of various persons and things in the physical and astral existence. The faces assumed are impositions which are unhealthy for the corePerson, and are discarded in the process of time.

The faceForm that happens when a self turns to face its corePerson is the desirable personality of that self. Environments are not the focus. And yet, for a yogi, environment takes priority when he/she is harassed in unwanted locations, and feels the need to exit such places in the hope of transferring to a paradise.

The environments are to a greater or lesser extent regulated by deities. The focus on the environments with the hope of being transferred to one, or to be an explorer and possessor, is an uncertain way to approach this. It is best to have a need to be relational to the deity of the desired environment, or to the deity even without knowing which environment that deity supervises.

The statement is that whatever is incongruous with the mind of the deity cannot be in his/her paradise environment. That statement may be contested using current evidence of the experiences we get in this physical place. There are contrary outcomes, uncertainties and unwanted features here. One may ask if a deity can have environments, where another person acts contrary to what the deity desires. Like for instance, someone may plan violence to the deity, or perform actions which are contrary to the deity's wish. Is that possible?

In this physical place, we find that good people are harmed, restricted and affected by others whose actions run contrary to social harmony.

The supreme deity of this physical place and of the related astral locations, parceled this place and assigned it to lesser deities. These lords are related to this place in a way whereby from the onset, they do not have full control of events. They supervise but it is not an absolute governance. Hence, we witness and hear of deviations and upsets in this location and in the corresponding astral situations.

We are here because of being under the auspices of a deity. We should tune to that sourcePerson and live with a behavior which is least obstructive to him/her. That will allow us to develop detachment from what happens here, from the evolutionary pressures which this place imposes. That in turn will allow us to have time to meditate so that we can contact the deity such that he/she would transfer one's existence to a place where nothing contrary to the deity takes place. It is not the individual limited personSelf, but it is rather the outlay of the deity and his/her requirements for living elsewhere in his/her full compliance environment.

Is it likely that a sub-deity, who services this environment along with other sub-deities, would select someone to be transferred to a paradise worthy of that spiritual official, such that the transferee would no longer exist in this place and would not have to endure a contrary social situation anywhere else?

I must admit that this is not likely. However, a yogi should make the effort to prepare for such a glorious transfer. In fact, the statement is that a yogi should strive continuously to qualify for such life.

It is suggested in the *Yoga Sutras* and *Bhagavad Gītā*, that a yogi should develop a nature what is similar to what is natural for a higher habitat. By that action, he/she is likely to be transferred, not otherwise.

Meditation is required to withdraw from the personFace or personFormat, one developed thus far in this creation. That formatFace alters from life to life as one moves from the astral existence to this physical place and then again when a body is no longer serviceable, and one subsides to the astral place, then develops an embryo and manifests as a physical being.

The personFaces one acts as currently should be erased by decreasing focus on the roles as a child of a parent, and as the parent of a child. One should relax the value of these faces so that they no longer are targets for one's focus and identity.

This relaxation of the social personFace, having to do with relationship in the physical and corresponding astral environment, will cause one to shift to the psychic side. Initially however this will be the experience of a blank personFace. But if one persists in the meditation on this blankSelf, in time, it will develop, that this changes to being a personRole which is useful to the personSource, the deity. That will cause a change where the blankSelf will assume a relationship form which is divine.

The retreat from social roles in this existence, leads to a temporary state of having no role. Some experience this as being a blankPerson, a faceless someone, a nothing, a reference-less something. That should not be a cause for discouragement where one ceases the practice of meditation or where one continues the practice with a no-self view of existence.

Patience! Patience! Patience!

That is required to complete this transformation from being a physically involved social self to shedding that role identity; then to being without social definition, being only a subjective spiritual radiance. Then at last to be a spiritual relationship self based only on relationship with a sourcePerson, a deity.

The occupation in many past lives was to be a socially useful or obstructive self. It resulted in a strenuous effort to break from the past and focus on shedding those numerous identities in various lives as this or that human, animal or insect or less. Now at last to relax that interest in the physical and its related astral levels. One should discover that for the time being, during the interim of being someone who craved physical existence to being someone who desires relationship usefulness to the sourcePerson, the self is faceless.

The realization that this physical existence and the role one plays, are problematic, is insufficient for getting exemption from having to continue here. The mere desire not to be here does not cause one to be exempt from this. One must direct all focus into the psyche, study its design, segregate its components, single out the core, and relate to it without accessories. It will be discovered as an open non-particular something.

There will be occasions during meditation, where the yogi gets instant transfer to a bliss consciousness. Then he/she experiences only a desirable environment and himself/herself. But these experiences are momentary, as the yogi is unable to make those locales respond to his willpower. However, in repeated attempts at deep meditation with the coreSelf transcending its adjuncts, the yogi will have experiences with deities. These will inspire more practice, until some definite contact occurs with a deity and with the deity's super-environment.

Transcendence is Illusive

From the onset of the current phase of creation, some billion years prior, the coreSelf did not have sufficient objectivity to track its emergence from a sourcePerson. This means that no personal proof was within reach. That leaves us with faith in a reliable source of information.

A child does not recall how it came to be from its mother's body. Its only resort is to rely on information from the lady. If she is truthful, the child will know. If she is untruthful, the child must be content with that. The demand for truth about everything is impractical.

I gave the information, that initially there was an emergence of the self from a sourcePerson. That self could not know how it emerged. It had no sense of pre-time. It could not figure its source because it did not have the means of doing so. Now at this stage, late in the creation, long, long, after its emergence as a self, only some questions can be answered by direct perception.

For one thing the subjective part of the self, will not allow an objective view or memory of everything that happened. Even if a yogi can learn how to be objective even in subjective states, his/her perception will be limited to his/her presence during the dawn of this creation. Those who were present subjectively but had no objective face at the time, have no recall capacity. They cannot retrogress into the condition because to do so requires some objective diving which one cannot do with a mere subjective condition.

At this time, one should follow the process of *ashtanga* yoga, as delineated by Patanjali, retracting one's interest into the coreSelf. Initially this will be done incorrectly because one does not know when one begins, where the coreSelf or its adjuncts are located. However, in time, painstakingly, one will realize the geography. One can correct the method, again study Patanjali, and better apply his recommendations.

The interest of the coreSelf must be recalled into the self, such that in meditation, it is no longer an active arm for grasping experiences relating to the interaction of objects in the physical and corresponding astral existence.

This recall will in time, cause the core to be self-obsessed. This will bring about a stabilizing condition where supernatural and spiritual perception and even subjective awareness, will develop. Through that, one will increase the chances of accessing the *chit akash* sky of consciousness, the great yogis and the deities. This is the turning away from this physical and astral situation which is contrary to wholesome identity and relationship.

Traditional Person

The traditional person is a temporary identity which is a placement in social negotiations. It is useful for physical existence, but it is problematic in the quest for spiritual discovery of the core. The traditional person brings to question the existence of a self. It is responsible for the doubts an ascetic harbors about a real identity.

Despite its condemnation by identity researchers and its appraisal by worldly people, the traditional person is the starting point of the research into the formation and breakup of identity. In the lifespan of a physical body, we address that form as a person. Some of us do so only in relation to human beings. Others include animals. Some others regard even vegetation as person. And yet, they are others who regard even inanimate objects, physical substance, as person.

For inSelf Yoga™, it is sufficient to regard the humans and animals as persons. The admittance however is that the human beings have the intellectual capacity to approach a self-inquiry into identity. The animals because of the limits of their brain capacity do not have the objectivity to do the internal mental investigation. In that sense, the search for a core identity is impractical in their case.

In dream states, the observational factor in consciousness operates using a psychic form, a subtle body. That subtle form, if observed repeatedly and keenly, causes one to realize that it separates from and unites with the physical body. When it is reunited with the physical system, that system awakens. When it separates, the physical body sleeps.

From the position of being a physical body which is respected as a single person, a yogi should understand that the subtle body's unification with and separation from the physical form explains that at the death of the physical body, the subtle body will again indulge in development of a new physical body which will again be regarded as a person.

That newly developed form will function socially for a time, then again that will die which will cause the subtle body to again indulge in the development of an embryo. This behavior will be repeated for as long as nature's system of reincarnation operates.

When as a sperm, the person begins in the father's body, it may be transferred into the mother's uterus. There it may develop into being an embryo. That may develop and be birthed as an infant. This child may develop as a juvenile, which in turn may develop as an adult. That adult may indulge and reproduce another child. All the while the adult will age. This aging process develops until that body dies. At that event, the subtle body loses its physical capacity. Then again it miraculously becomes a sperm. And the same process of physical body development happens with the same risks of dying at some stage or definitely dying due to old age.

But this traditional person is different in each life. Hence it cannot be said that as a physical body, the person of one life is the same person of a previous life. Even if two physical bodies of the supposed person look alike, still there will be incongruencies where one will admit that it is different.

According to the time and place, the subtle body is altered. It adjusts itself to its physical form in each life. Since it changes either in obvious or subtle ways, it cannot be tagged as being the same. It is an ever-changing form.

One cannot delve into the personality by gaging the physical body. One must investigate the subtle form to make sense of personality. Because the traditional personality alters in each physical body, an ascetic is faced with the task of delving into the subtle system which is the form of the psychological principles of the traditional person.

First one must realize that the traditional person is a composite. It is a functional but temporary combination of psychological and physical factors. The psychological features are:

- sensual energies
- intellect
- memories
- blinking witness (subjective/objective coreSelf)

What is regarded as a human or animal person is a composite of psychic factors which are a coreSelf surrounded by functional psychic adjuncts. This composite is the traditional person which is more than the basic self. It is a combination of a subtle body and physical system which is tagged as a person in human society.

The physical person, the traditional self, which is suitable in the physical world, must be de-configured, sorted and evaluated. For one thing, when the physical body dies, the physical system depreciates rapidly. The world which recognized it no longer accepts it. It no longer functions as a living somebody.

Death means that the subtle body no longer has privileges in the physical world as it used to experience when the physical body lived. After death, the person is everything it is, except for what its physical body provided. The traditional person, being dead, the self surfaces as a psychic presence only. It is such with no recognition from the physical senses of those who live in the physical world.

A yogi must meditate to realize this state of the subtle body when it is without the facilities of the physical one. This must be done first in the dream states by having firm dream recall. Later it must be done during meditation when using both bodies, whereby the traditional self is realized and is compared to the subtle body with no physical system.

Again, the yogi should research what would remain if the subtle body has no format as a ghost and instead interiorized its interests where it was only aware of the psychological functions within the subtle body.

What would remain as the self, if the subtle body was awake but with no participation in the subtle environment, with only its organs/functions which did not interact with objects in the astral environment.

The functional but temporary combination of psychological factors are:

- sensual energies
- intellect
- memories
- blinking witness (subjective/objective coreSelf)

Of these factors, the one of concern is the **blinking witness**. It consists of two factors.

- sense of identity
- coreSelf

The witness blinks because it does not remain objective to itself. By its very nature it has an involuntary function whereby it is switched from being objective to itself to being subjective to itself. This means that it cannot at all times and in all places, register or account for itself.

न त्वेवाहं जातु नासं
न त्वं नेमे जनाधिपाः ।
न चैव न भविष्यामः
सर्वे वयमतः परम् ॥२.१२॥

na tvevāhaṁ jātu nāsaṁ
na tvaṁ neme janādhipāḥ
na caiva na bhaviṣyāmaḥ
sarve vayamataḥ param (2.12)

na — no; tv (tu) — in fact; eva — alone; aham — I; jātu — ever; na — not; āsam — I did exist; na — nor; tvaṁ — you; neme = na — nor + ime — these; jana-adhipāḥ — rulers of the people; na — not; caiva — and indeed; na — nor; bhaviṣyāmaḥ — we will exist; sarve — all; vayam — we; ataḥ - from now; param — onwards

There was never a time when I did not exist, nor you nor these rulers of the people. Nor will we cease to exist from now onwards. (Bhagavad Gītā 2.12)

In that quote Krishna said that the self is perpetual. However, it cannot by itself verify that. It can assume that, but it cannot prove that to itself nor to anyone else. It is due to this that some ascetics state that there is no evidence for a self. Their proposal is flimsy because if something cannot check its perpetuity, that does not mean that it is insubstantial.

For the purpose of inSelf Yoga™, the statement of Krishna is given as evidence that the self is eternal. It is so but with sporadic objectivity. This means that it cannot remain objectively conscious unless it is supported by an environment which reinforces the objectivity. As soon as that support is unavailable, it continues to exist but with no method for verifying itself.

In this physical world, there are many objects which exists, but which have no way of asserting that. These are inanimate objects. There are rocks which existed for millions of years. They give no indication that they are aware of themselves. In contrast we have animate objects like the human and animals, where these demonstrate objectivity on occasion.

The **blink** of the witness is the change from being conscious of itself and then being unconscious of itself, being an observer and then being with no means of observation even in reference to itself.

The blinking neutral witness consists of two factors.

- sense of identity
- coreSelf

The **sense of identity** is a psychic urge to express an interest in anything which registers. The object may also have a physical impact, but we are concerned only with the psychic aspect because the sense of identity can only sense psychic reality. It cannot directly sense physical impacts.

This sense of identity surrounds the coreSelf. This core is a single iSelf, a single neutral witness. This is regarded as a personSelf in higher yoga. However, from the perspective of living as a traditional person in the physical world, this single neutral witness, is assessed as being a nothing, a non-registered reality. This is due to the fact that in comparison to physical substance, this neutral core of personality is not marked, positioned nor formatted in a physical tangible way. It is transcendental. It is inconceivable. It is space-less. It has no reference nor obvious border

The **coreSelf** is surrounded by the sense of identity. This happens on all sides of the core, spherically, such that if the core attempts to do anything, even if it attempts to do what it cannot directly handle, the sense of identity will provide a supplementary urge. Conversely if the sense of identity is attracted to anything besides the coreSelf, that impulsive interest is felt by the core which will notice that an attention interest is instantly generated in the sense of identity with a force to focus the core.

The blinking neutral interest has the personSelf as its core, but the yogi should meditate and allow himself/herself to experience only the personSelf. To do this the personSelf must retreat to the spiritual plane of existence which is higher than where the personSelf is fused to the sense of identity. When the personSelf shifts to the spiritual plane, it loses contact with the sense of identity. It stands alone without the facility of the sense of identity. By itself, it may rate itself, as a perpetual or nonperpetual reality. It should study itself to know its category.

Opinion of Yogeshwarananda

On the astral side of existence, I inquired about the issue of the person (*purusha*) in the *Upanishads*, as to why it was not dealt with, as to its avoidance and the prominence of *brahman* abstract spiritual reality. Yogeshwarananda said this.

> *"If anything, the word used there is* atma. Purusha *is person or rather character of someone as that is demonstrated in social interactions. That cannot be figured because there is the sleep phase where there is suspension of it, of that particular* atma *or pin spiritual force."*

I pressed for more answers. I said this.

"Even if one sticks with *atma* and does not use the character inclusive word of *purusha*, one is still left with a blank page where there should be a statement. *Atma* is illusive because it really means something which is there before this creation occurred, something which was there when there was nothing like this.

Saying that the *atma* is *brahman* or that it is simultaneously segregated from and connected into *brahman*, the reality energy, does not clear the issue because the said *atma* cannot guarantee that it was objectively conscious as itself or as the collective which is *brahman*.

"There is also the issue, or the vocabulary, where the word *param* challenges more inquiry. For instance, if there is *brahman* and then there is also *parambrahman*, why *param* or supreme or superior? In that case even requiring the word *param*, puts *brahman* to question."

In reply, Yogeshwarananda said this,

> *"I left* purusha *alone. The character phase of the* atma *is suspended time and again. That much we know. Therefore, it was avoided in the discussions in the* Upanishads *and also by some modern philosophers. During meditation there is always a phased-out state where one is suspended. Then one phases back in as a conscious being here or there. Some yogis did not admit and did not discuss the phasing in and phasing out states.*
>
> *"How did one know that one was the same when one phased back into being conscious even in instances where one did not have a memory or any way to identity that one was phased out?*
>
> *"Direct evidence that the individual who comes alive, or comes aware today, was some individual who existed yesterday, is hard to produce either by a witness or by self-knowing. Certainly, when someone becomes aware as a physical body and can remember what was one before falling asleep, that can be cited as proof, but it is flimsy proof because how do we know if the person switched and someone else accessed the memories and knowledge. There were yogis who entered someone's psyche and took information.*
>
> *"Two criminal yogis named* Madhu *and* Kaitabha *were listed in the* Puranas *with a plan to steal information from* Brahma's *mind. They were intercepted by* Vishnu. *He killed or rather displaced them.*
>
> *"It is an assumption and a necessary one where we assume that the same entity rises from bed each day after sleep. Still, that continuation of a self must be used as evidence that the individual's objectivity is repeatedly suspended, and activated by natural process.*
>
> *"Even* samadhi *transcendence absorption states are risky. The yogi cannot guarantee what will happen, as to if he will be displaced from one realm and shifted involuntarily to another favorable or unfavorable*

place, and must exist in that other place, just as currently one was an embryo with no choice in the matter, then one lives out the life of the body, and then when it dies, one is shifted somewhere.

"The writers of the Upanishad *overlooked or avoided the* purusha, *the personSelf. Why? That is the question. I feel it was because one must begin that discourse with a temporary self designation, where one begins life as the son or daughter of this or that parent. Thus, the license to be a person is installed initially in this life on a temporary shifting basis because the parents themselves are a temporary footing. It is like building a house on a shifty raft. What is the foundation? Water?*

"It begs the famous question of Ramana Maharshi. *Who am I?*

"The basis transcends the formatted self which has social usefulness. In this dimension, in the physical world, the foundation is absent. At least the house on the raft can claim a shifty situation on water which can be sensed and identified. The temporarily assigned person cannot do that because what it was before it became an embryo where social identity was assigned, cannot be shown. A sperm particle? And what was there prior to that? The more one retreats into it, the more one is baffled until one gives up because of the subtlety.

Originated from nothing? Is that the conclusion?

"To avoid the embarrassment, the writers of the Upanishad *used the term* brahman. *For them that concluded the inquiry."*

Traditional Person

In looking for a coreSelf, a sourcePerson, one must not be stymied by character additives and subtractions. The temporariness of the social formats which are willingly or unwillingly adapted, neither erase nor abolish a core. In fact, such variations adhere to the adjuncts which adhere to the core.

The traditional person is a composite of a core and character facets which make the person function aptly or inaptly in an environment. The readymade colorful features of the character serve to undervalue and underrate the core but in spiritual research, the converse is true where the yogi shifts the worth so that the core has value, and the acquired character features fade.

This leaves a neutral, transparent and non-assertive coreSelf which is self-evident. In meditation when the composite self internalizes, it is first challenged to define itself in terms of its outward going tendency and its thinking compulsions. When these are squelched, it is left with a radiant core and sense of interest.

With no environment other than the mind space, the core is left to wonder what it should do. Unless there are transcendental experiences with supernatural beings and places other than its mind space, it is likely that the coreSelf will consider itself as being of the fabric of nothingness or of somethingness but without features except for existence with or without bliss feelings

However, it does not remain in that state of being a neutral existence or being a blissful something. Rather, it resumes its traditional self and must meditate again to recover the free unfettered condition.

Some draw the conclusion that even if a yogi enters into a neutral self state and is compulsively made to resume the temporary character state, even so he will not have to be a temporary character after transiting through the death of his physical body. This idea is fancy only. Even if at death, the yogi enters that state, a question arises as to how long he will remain in the nothingness existential condition. Can he control when he will be in that condition and when he shifts to some other state in which a social relationship will cause the instant development of a temporary character identification in some other place?

In meditation, a yogi should practice turning his face away from the frontal part of the mind. This front area is the face of the subtle body. One other related practice is to pull one's interest from the frontal area. The core can remain centered in the subtle head. It may turn about and face the back of the subtle head or retract its interest from the front so that thoughts and ideas do not arise there.

The thoughts and ideas are reliant on the self's interest which shoot forward to and through the frontal part. If the expressions from the core ceases, the thoughts and ideas will stop instantly.

More and less, the energy which emanated from the core, should be retracted into itself, curled into itself for core perception, which is subjective viewing, a skill which is difficult to cultivate.

Around the coreSelf there is the sense of identity which shoots forward when there is interest in an idea. This sense of identity is a neutral energy but, on its surface, there are the character person formats which are suited to various social situations. The coreSelf which is neutral, involuntarily provides energy to energize one or many character formats, either for use in the physical environment or in a subtle level.

If it encounters a new environment, it uses a suitable identity which was already developed, or it develops a new identity then and there. It wields these for what it determines to be its best interest.

Reliance

The presentation that the limited self is absolute but is currently a shadow or mistaken something, and that after being liberated by some method, it will assume infinity or oneness with the absolute, is absurd.

Anything can improve in status but if one does not begin something with infinity, that factor cannot in the future attain an absolute condition. If something is not absolute, it must rely on one or more factors. That in itself puts it at a disadvantage. If it began in a reliant condition, its potential is not absolute.

Definitely the coreSelf should be what it is at its best but that does not imply that it is God or that it can exercise the power of being everything. Whatever is God must be God in any and every place, in lower or higher conditions. Variations in being God, where something begins as a relative something, then develops, then is attributed as having transformed itself in being God, is only a subject for fools.

The coreSelf needs an environment which supports it so that it experiences itself at its very best. Environment is important to it. Realizing that it is reliant on an environment is essential. Otherwise, the core will have the tendency to believe that it is a potential absolute something. Such a state of mind is nonproductive.

Objectivity and Subjectivity

Apart from the markings of experience and memory, the coreSelf should figure its subjective consciousness and its degree of objectivity. Beginning at birth of the body, when the entity first becomes aware of itself as an air breathing biological system, at that onset, there is no cohesive memory. The only facet present is experience and sensuality. At that time, the experience lacks clarity. The sensuality is not comprehensive. There is objectivity but with no reference, with whatever it experiences being shifty.

At birth of its body, the coreSelf finds itself to be a relatively unmarked something, not etched or scarred by specific experiences but with a brush mark, little streaks, on its subtle membrane. These were applied by its transit through the birth canal where its body was squeezed through the narrow opening which served as a door to physical existence.

With no access to former memory, either of the psychic or physical levels of existence, the self discovers itself as being clean of memorabilia but with a desire to experience so as to deposit memory markers which will give value to the self in the social setting.

In any event, of the two aspects, experience and memory, the memory is vital as a reference for person. However, the experience is necessary for objectifying the person and for adding to the memory. The person needs assurance of itself as having existed somewhere somehow prior to the event.

The idea of "I recently began to exist," is no cause for uncertainty but all the same, it means that the self did not have an objective estimation of itself as a person. It clung to experience to offset its insecurity and to establish a commencement which would itself be a marker in consciousness.

First there is experience, a beginning point of that. It must be sufficient to have a feeling of "*I exist*". This experience checks for memory. If it finds none, it will observe something, anything. It will log that, thus creating a marker. It will then check for more memory. If it finds nothing else, it will note the absence for future reference.

This results in objective awareness within the spread of consciousness. It will wonder how it will continue, as to if it may not exist or if it will lose objectivity due to a loss of control of its perspective.

Memory is eternal but access to it is not. This means that the self cannot estimate its duration unless it has the grasp on enough memory to be objective in an experience. If the self is part of an experience and nothing else, if it has no other reference, it cannot stake its claim on the experience. It will then be part of the experience as a subjective factor.

This is why it is important to give up the idea that the threat of full subjectivity is an indication that the self is a temporary something. Existence of an item, function or factor, does not rely merely on objective awareness of that principle. Not having absolute access to memory does not state that one is not perpetual.

Transcendence Authority

At some point in the research into the origin, duration and potential for perpetuity of the coreSelf, one has to conclude that due to one's limited access to objectivity, one must rely on a transcendence authority for information about the value of the coreSelf. This is value in terms of perpetual existence without objectivity. The coreSelf has value undoubtedly but it cannot, itself, estimate its worth because it does not have grasp on perpetual objectivity.

I present a prePerson who may or may not rely on a transcendent prePerson. This personSource may have numerous personSources who transcend, double transcend, triple transcend, quadruple transcend and multi-transcend him/her.

A particular self should investigate its core. Once it identifies and inFocuses into itself as its coreSelf, it should resume consciousness of only the core. From that, from repeated meditation on that, it is likely that it will meet the face of its sourcePerson, its preLord. It may also meet others who were produced from it. It would be the sourcePerson of those individuals.

However, that does not mean that it would have absolute control over anyone whom it emitted at the dawn of personTime. The agency of being someone's preLord is not an absolute factor. It functions as an emittance point with only limited control over what or who is produced. A limb emerging from the branch of a tree is not controlled absolutely by the branch. There is some control, but it is limited only.

Another important factor is the environment in which the self emerges or finds itself to be in at the onset of its individual awareness. The environment has some compelling factors. The environment is itself a profound influence. The self must submit to much of the pressure which it is subjected to in any given environment.

The objectivity and subjectivity of the self is regulated in part by the environmental influences. This self in part relies on the environment for support in sensual perception, memory access, consciousness reinforcement and many other psychic events which short circuit or energize what the self is.

It does not help to dismiss the self, the environment around it and the adjuncts which aid it, as illusion or as temporary existences. Everything is real but the issue is the value of each factor. What is the value when something is referenced to a self which is a fully subjective and partially objective reality?

In summary.

- There is a personSelf.
- It has a personSource.

This personSelf is perpetual but it can provide no evidence to proof that; neither to itself nor to someone else.

The personSource is another personSelf who is transcendent to the self.

The personSource may have a personSource which is its preLord.

Even though the personSelf is limited and does not have full grasp on its perpetuity, still it should have full confidence that it will persist existentially with or without objectivity.

Chapter 2

Bhagavad Gītā Evidence

Śrī Śrī Krishna-Arjuna - Artist Terri Stokes

Original Sanskrit text: Bhishma Parva, Mahābhārata
granted and permitted by John Smith, University of Cambridge,
Bhandarkar Oriental Research Institute

The verses below are extracted from the Bhagavad Gītā discourse between Lord Krishna and the warrior prince Arjuna. This supports the idea of a personSelf which is perpetual. It also presents a *mahapurusha*, supremeSelf. Carefully read this.

For the time being until there is direct or contradictory evidence, accept this at face value as evidence of a perpetual coreSelf. To be considered as a sourcePerson from whom the self emerged, that source may itself have a source.

There was some struggle and challenge to present this information. The reason being that since the time of the *Upanishad*, there was a discouragement energy for presenting the importance of the person and the personSource. *Atma* and *brahman* are extolled in the *Upanishads* but *purusha* is minimized and barely mentioned.

Later *atma* was stressed. The term *jivatma* was used. If *brahman* is sand on a beach, *atma* is one speck of such sand with no emphasis on its particularities. *Jivatma* is the mention that each speck has unique markings and shape. *Purusha* however is putting each sand grain under a high-resolution microscope.

On April 25, 2022, while composing this publication, I was uncertain as to if I could gather enough evidence and information to publish this. Suddenly behind me to my right, Lord Krishna appeared. With omniVision I saw him even though I did not turn about. I remembered that some years ago, he reminded me that his appearance to anyone at any time is rare. Rarer is his appearance even once in a lifetime, even once in any era. He transmitted energy in my psyche for the completion of this book.

That energy caused me to reference the Bhagavad *Gītā*. The result is this part of the book which delves into selected verses which bring to our attention the *purusha*, the personSelf. With that energy from Krishna, I was confident that I could complete this publication.

न त्वेवाहं जातु नासं
न त्वं नेमे जनाधिपाः ।
न चैव न भविष्यामः
सर्वे वयमतः परम् ॥२.१२॥

na tvevāhaṁ jātu nāsaṁ
na tvaṁ neme janādhipāḥ
na caiva na bhaviṣyāmaḥ
sarve vayamataḥ param (2.12)

na — no; tv (tu) — in fact; eva — alone; aham — I; jātu — ever; na — not; āsam — I did exist; na — nor; tvaṁ — you; neme = na — nor + ime — these; jana-adhipāḥ — rulers of the people; na — not; caiva — and indeed; na — nor; bhaviṣyāmaḥ — we will exist; sarve — all; vayam — we; ataḥ - from now; param — onwards

There was never a time when I did not exist, nor you nor these rulers of the people. Nor will we cease to exist from now onwards. (Bhagavad Gītā 2.12)

Analysis

This is a declaration by Lord Krishna to Arjuna who was dismayed when confronted by the army of his cousins. Arjuna wanted to turn away from the horrific scene. This was detailed in the *Mahabharata* literature.

Arjuna was afraid of the death scenes which would occur during the war. He lamented the potential for injury and death, feeling that his friends and relatives on both sides of the conflict, would be no more. His opinion was that it was better to allow everyone on the battlefield to live, rather than to engage in combat which would result in many deaths.

Krishna disagreed. He declared that there was no reason to figure anyone's death because only the physical body of the person could die. The person itself was incapable of dying. Due to its persistent nature, the personSelf could not be diminished even if its body was demolished.

Krishna declared life for the personSelf prior to an incidence, during the incidence and after the incidence. This use of life as the persistence of psychological parts of a physical person, is a novel view of social interaction of the physical body which we currently identify as and use.

Krishna's declaration does not include a license to kill a physical body, merely on the belief that some psychological aspects of the person will persists at death. The continuation of anyone who exists at this time, is a separate concern to the wounding and death of that person's physical body. A fatal action to someone's physical self is accountable. However, that does not mean that the physical self is more valuable than the psychological self which will exist after physical death.

This declaration should not be used as a justification for killing or fatally wounding someone's body. It is for the purpose of understanding that the self transcends the physical existence. In terms of endurance, it is more than the physical system which functions in this dimension as its self.

Three terms from the Sanskrit which must be considered are *atma*, *brahman* and *purusha*. *Atma* is a general term for self. It denotes a radiant something. *Brahman* indicates a massive energy which is persistent. It is said that the *atmas* or selves are individually or collectively *brahman*, massive spiritual energy.

The term *purusha* is person, the one who will persist with or without cultural markings. The system of consideration where the person is marked as being illusory or as being formulated by social forces, has validity. However, there is more to this. The formulated parts of the self adhere to the coreSelf which is perpetual.

Purusha in our usage is a distinct person, a coreSelf. Sand is sand, but one grain has specific marking and would show differently under high magnification. *Atma* is the term for the self as just a self. *Purusha* is for a specific self, a particular person.

The markings on each self which were formulated by social forces are temporarily assigned relational roles. There are other markings which are transcendental to normal itemizing. Those other features are perpetual. Later in the *Bhagavad Gītā*, Krishna stated that he recognizes the various individual selves even though other persons fail to identify him.

As one goes in, inner and inner and inner, as one transcends one's very self, one loses sensual distinction. The terrain becomes more and more subtle until one cannot objectify oneself. It is not that there is nothing as one goes in and in and in, but rather there are factors, but one is not equipped with the existential means of grasping what is present.

Comprehension of Bhagavad Gītā Verse 2.12

One cannot prove if one will continue to exist perpetually. The fact is that one's existence now, as a physical body with consciousness, proves conclusively that one is a factor in existence currently. It does not matter if one is a fantasy creation of somebody, or a natural development which occurred with no creative agency. It is sufficient to accept that one exists, and one cannot determine if one will continue as is in the future, especially after the physical body dies.

Krishna issued statements which may be accepted at face value. Much of his declarations cannot be proven. Still, for the sake of understanding his views, one should trust what he vouched for. He proposed that one believe that never was there a time when he, Krishna, did not exist, nor Arjuna nor the rulers of the people who were on the battlefield as depicted in the *Mahabharata*. Krishna declared further that neither he, nor Arjuna, nor any other warrior would cease to exist from then onward.

देहिनोऽस्मिन्यथा देहे
कौमारं यौवनं जरा ।
तथा देहान्तरप्राप्तिर्
धीरस्तत्र न मुह्यति ॥२.१३॥

dehino'sminyathā dehe
kaumāraṁ yauvanaṁ jarā
tathā dehāntaraprāptir
dhīrastatra na muhyati (2.13)

dehinaḥ — of the embodied soul; asmin — in this; yathā — as; dehe — in the body; kaumāraṁ — in childhood; yauvanam — in youth; jarā — in old age; tathā — so in sequence; deha — body; antara — another; prāptiḥ — acquirement; dhīraḥ — wise person; tatra — on this topic; na — not; muhyati — is confused

As the embodied soul endures childhood, youth and old age, so another body is acquired in sequence. The wise person is not confused on this topic. (Bhagavad Gītā 2.13)

Analysis

In each life of the same individual, there are additions and omissions made to the social format which develops. There is a coreSelf which remains the same but a particular self becomes known as its present social role which is added to that core and to instincts which adhere to the core.

The convention is that we accept the new format, which is developed around the core, to be the person, who is addressed initially as the son or daughter of this and that parents. Since these add-ons are temporary, since they end with the end of a body, we may consider the character identity of any self as being illusory, as being non-permanent and insubstantial.

However, the obvious feature which endures beyond the death of a body, is its dream format, its subtle body, which is experienced as other than the physical form, and which is experienced during the life of the physical body during sleep.

Normally we dismiss dreams as either imagination concocted by the mind or as illusions imposed on the mind. However, the reality is that we have one other aspect to consider which is a psychic world which is even more substantial than this physical existence.

Yes, the physical existence is temporary, and yet for the time being, even for millions of years, this physical existence is a force to contend with. It is real in the sense of the endurance of some of its materials which show very little change, if any, over thousands of years.

The same person may endure infancy, sexual maturity and senility. We know this because of the memory and skill demonstrated by the individual. That proves that it is one person who survives in a changing body. The body changes from year to year. The person whom we identify as the body, keeps his/her instincts, education and special skills through the years of the body. At least until the body is afflicted with a debilitating disease which affects memory and nerve functions.

Comprehension of Bhagavad Gītā Verse 2.13

Krishna stated that when this body is dysfunctional as a living mechanism, another body would be acquired in sequence

How so?

He used the example of someone who is a child, who develops and becomes a youth and who develops further and is afflicted with old age. As we regard a person as the same individual as he or she passes through these phases, so someone moves from one body to another and endures the natural process of psychic and biological alterations.

Once the physical body dies, the person seems to disappear as a living somebody. However according to Krishna's information, the person shifts to the dream world. From there, in the process of time, that person will again enter the lifeforce production system and become an embryo.

Usually no one gives information about the hereafter or about how a self transmigrates from a dying body to a pregnancy. Evidence about this is hard to acquire. Thus, why should one believe Krishna?

अविनाशि तु तद्विद्धि
येन सर्वमिदं ततम् ।
विनाशमव्ययस्यास्य
न कश्चित्कर्तुमर्हति ॥२.१७॥

avināśi tu tadviddhi
yena sarvamidaṁ tatam
vināśamavyayasyāsya
na kaścitkartumarhati (2.17)

avināśi — indestructible; tu — indeed; tad — that factor; viddhi — know; yena — by which; sarvam — all; idaṁ — this world; tatam — is pervaded; vināśam — destructible; avyayasyāsya — of the everlasting principle; na — no; kaścit — anyone; kartum - to accomplish; arhati — can

Know that indestructible factor by which all this world is pervaded. No one can accomplish the destruction of that everlasting principle. (Bhagavad Gītā 2.17)

Analysis

With just the physical body, with no scientific instruments, all detection made by a human being must be done through consciousness. As soon as there is sleep, coma or loss of objectivity in trance, the individual disconnects from his source of information which is physical awareness.

Some arise from sleep. Some do not. Some awaken with memory and skill from a coma. Others do not. Some regain objectivity while in trance. Some lack that and have no perspective.

Comprehension of Bhagavad Gītā Verse 2.17

Krishna proposes an everlasting principle, an indestructible factor. This cannot be verified or checked by a limited being. It certainly cannot be proven by someone who has no recall besides memories which were stored from the life of the current physical body.

य एनं वेत्ति हन्तारं
यश्चैनं मन्यते हतम् ।
उभौ तौ न विजानीतो
नायं हन्ति न हन्यते ॥२.१९॥

ya enaṁ vetti hantāraṁ
yaścainaṁ manyate hatam
ubhau tau na vijānīto
nāyaṁ hanti na hanyate (2.19)

ya — who; enaṁ — this embodied soul; vetti — concludes; hantāraṁ — the killer; yaścainaṁ = yas — who + ca — and + inam — this embodied soul; manyate — thinks; hatam — is killed; ubhau — both; tau — two viewers; na-not; vijānītaḥ-understood; nāyaṁ = na — not + ayam — this embodied soul; hanti — kill; na — nor; hanyate — can be killed

Both viewers do not understand, namely: He who concludes that the embodied soul is the killer and he who thinks that the embodied soul is killed. The embodied soul does not kill, nor can he be killed. (Bhagavad Gītā 2.19)

Analysis

There must be physical impact for the killing or death of a body. Superficially, we think that one man may kill another. We express that another man was killed and is dead. These ideas are the convention only.

The corePerson factor is so remote from physical existence that it is not possible for it to directly efface anything physical, nor can it be directly affected by a physical agency. Its interactions with physical reality must be done through attenuating agencies.

The attenuation or adaptation is done through adjuncts. Some are physical apparatus. Some are psychic equipment. These interact. Through psychic contact, there is interplay.

Comprehension of Bhagavad Gītā Verse 2.19

To understand Krishna's line of reasoning, much of what he declared should be accepted at face value. This is because one may not have the sensual access to deny nor verify each part of the information. Some of it is reasonable. Some of it is not.

The viewer mentioned in this verse is the person who kills a physical body or the one whose body is killed by some means. In either case, the concept which is impressive is that the body is the person. Thus, a detrimental action of a person is considered to be a reason to tag that person as an agent.

Conversely a physical body which is maliciously killed is tagged to be the death of the person who was known as that body. The misunderstanding is based on and supported by the way the senses of the physical body operate. The living physical form is more than physical. It is a physio-psychic mechanism, where it has both physical and psychic operations.

A dead physical body has everything physical which it had before except that the psychic functions cease for it. These psychic actions operate the physical limbs and senses. At death, those maneuvers cease.

Because one regarded the person as the physical actions of his body, the body's death results in the view that the person is finished. If otherwise he was violently struck and his physical system did not die, one considers that the offender only harmed him.

None of this is true but it is the conventional and practical way to deal with physical issues. The basic correction is a sensual one where one should train the mind to always realize that the living physical body is enlivened by psychic energy. The psychic feelings form as a subtle body which though not physical resembles the physical structure.

The subtle body does not die when the physical one can no longer be used. The subtle form continues. If anything, the person is the subtle body. It is certainly not the physical system. The person shifts into being the subtle body, when the physical one dies. While the physical body is alive, the subtle one enlivens it to such an extent that it seems that both forms are identical.

न जायते म्रियते वा कदा चिन्
नायं भूत्वा भविता वा न भूयः ।
अजो नित्यः शाश्वतोऽयं पुराणो
न हन्यते हन्यमाने शरीरे ॥२.२०

na jāyate mriyate vā kadā cin
nāyaṁ bhūtvā bhavitā vā na bhūyaḥ
ajo nityaḥ śāśvato'yaṁ purāṇo
na hanyate hanyamāne śarīre (2.20)

na — not; jāyate — is born; mriyate — dies; vā — either; kadācin — at any time; nāyaṁ = na — nor + ayam — this embodied soul; bhūtvā — having been; bhavitā — will be; vā — or; na — not; bhūyaḥ — again; ajo — birthless; nityaḥ — perpetual; śāśvataḥ — eternal; 'yaṁ = ayam- this; purāṇaḥ — primeval; na- not; hanyate — is killed; hanyamāne — in the act of killing; śarīre — in the body

This embodied soul is not born, nor does it die at any time, nor having existed will it not be. Being birthless, eternal, perpetual and primeval, it is not slain in the act of killing the body. (Bhagavad Gītā 2.20)

Analysis

It is important to keep in mind that the existence of something is not based on its objectivity, on its knowing that it exists, or even on it being able to distinguish itself from anything else.

Even a subjective view of itself is not required for anything to exist. Awareness may occur with no self-awareness.

If one thinks that self-awareness is necessary for perpetual existence, one will be closed-minded to many phases of reality and will be unable to research inSelf.

Statements or proclamations of Krishna which express ideas which we can neither prove conclusively nor disprove, should be accepted at face value but all the same it is more than a matter of trust in Krishna and a willingness to believe what he declares. We should be open to being gifted by him with the insight to perceive the reality.

Each and every yogi should be open to Krishna to learn about factors which are beyond one's mystic capacity.

Krishna discussed the embodied soul as if to say that the reference from this dimension is the physical body but to counter that he presents another reference which is the self which became known as its body. The body and self are different but for the time being, the convention is that one should accept the body as the self. Hence with that as a marker, one should regard that even though the body is treated as the self, that self transcends the body and will persists beyond it. How long will that self persist? Krishna said that it will do so indefinitely.

Comprehension of Bhagavad Gītā Verse 2.20

Whatever that person is besides its physical body, it is not born when the body is birthed from the mother. That self does not die when its physical body is no longer functional. Once it existed in any place, its continued existence is guaranteed. It is birthless, eternal, perpetual and primeval. It is not eliminated if someone kills its body. It is a psychic reality. It is not a physical principle, but it can be mistaken for something physical when somehow a physical body is developed as it.

In this physical world, the physical system represents the eternal self. But due to the irresistible attraction one has for physical things, one assumes that the self is its physical body.

वेदाविनाशिनं नित्यं
य एनमजमव्ययम् ।
कथं स पुरुषः पार्थ
कं घातयति हन्ति कम् ॥२.२१॥

vedāvināśinaṁ nityaṁ
ya enamajamavyayam
kathaṁ sa puruṣaḥ pārtha
kaṁ ghātayati hanti kam (2.21)

vedāvināśinaṁ = veda — knows + avināśinam — indestructible; nityaṁ — eternal; ya = yaḥ — who; enam — this; ajam — not born, birthless; avyayam — imperishable; kathaṁ — how; sa = saḥ — he; puruṣaḥ — person; pārtha — O son of Partha; kaṁ — whom; ghātayati — causes to kill; hanti — kills (directly); kam — whom

O son of Pṛthā, how can the person who knows this indestructible, eternal, birthless and imperishable principle, cause someone to be killed or even kill someone directly? (Bhagavad Gītā 2.21)

Analysis

The son of *Pṛthā* is Arjuna. He was challenged by Krishna. It is a challenge to each yogi to determine if it is possible to kill a self. If a self is other than its physical body, the death of that form, if anything, will superficially affect the self

The task for proof is with the yogi, to segment himself into being a physical and a psychic system combined for the time being, for as long as the physical body survives. During the life of the body, a yogi should research the psychic aspect of the self to know if that feature can and will survive without the physical body. If psychic aspects will persist after the death of the physical system, the yogi can be confident that he/she will not die when the physical system is ended.

The problem which confronts such a yogi is how to be more in tune with the psychic remnant which will survive, how to stress that, how to transfer priorities to that psychic energy.

Comprehension of Bhagavad Gītā Verse 2.21

Even though Lord Krishna challenged Arjuna about knowing of the eternal birthless and imperishable principle, that it cannot be killed, nor can it kill someone, still the convention is that someone as a physical body can be killed or can kill someone else who is a physical body.

Krishna's information however is useful in knowing that what happens when someone is killed or when someone kills, is that the assaulted person is displaced from his physical form, which is such a valuable possession, that people regard its death as the equivalent of the death of the person.

वासांसि जीर्णानि यथा विहाय नवानि गृह्णाति नरोऽपराणि । तथा शरीराणि विहाय जीर्णा:न्य् अन्यानि संयाति नवानि देही ॥२.२२॥	vāsāṁsi jīrṇāni yathā vihāya navāni gṛhṇāti naro'parāṇi tathā śarīrāṇi vihāya jīrṇāny anyāni saṁyāti navāni dehī (2.22)

vāsāṁsi — clothing; jīrṇāni — worn out; yathā — as when; vihāya — discarded; navāni — new; gṛhṇāti — takes; naro = naraḥ — person; 'parāṇi = aparāṇi — others; tathā — so; śarīrāṇi — bodies; vihāya — abandoned; jirṇāny = worn-out; anyāni — others; saṁyāti — encounters; navāni — new; dehī — the embodied soul

As when discarding old clothing, a person takes new garments, so the embodied soul abandons old bodies taking new ones. (Bhagavad Gītā 2.22)

Analysis

When someone discards old clothing, that person may be happy or somewhat sad about it. When someone loses or is displaced from his body, people who live on and who are related usually express sorrow about it.

The other factor is that the discarder of clothing is usually in control of the act while in the case of a body, the enduring self does not necessarily control its terminal illness. Even when there is suicide, the person may be distraught about committing the killing. He/She may have no idea of what will occur hereafter.

This analogy of Krishna gives some idea of his perception and point of reference. With this we may strive to shift value to the psychic body instead of the conventional stress on the physical form which one is accustomed to being.

Comprehension of Bhagavad Gītā Verse 2.22

According to Krishna, the embodied soul shifts from an old or damaged body to an embryo. He/She does this repeatedly. By the grace of psychic and physical reality, this happens. It is not dependent on the self knowing how it happens. The self is conveyed through this displacement from an old or damaged body, and to the assumption of a new embryo, in turn.

It is repetitive but it is not remembered by the self who endures it. This is the problem with Krishna's information. The experience of it, is hard to come by. Initially we should believe it. For a time however one may strive to realize it through meditation and keen observation of psychic events.

What we naturally ignore which is subtle activity, we should no longer neglect.

नैनं छिन्दन्ति शस्त्राणि
नैनं दहति पावकः ।
न चैनं क्लेदयन्त्यापो
न शोषयति मारुतः ॥२.२३॥

nainaṁ chindanti śastrāṇi
nainaṁ dahati pāvakaḥ
na cainaṁ kledayantyāpo
na śoṣayati mārutaḥ (2.23)

nainaṁ = na — not + enam — this; chindanti — pierce; śastrāṇi — weapons; nainaṁ = na — not + enam — this; dahati — burns; pāvakaḥ — fire; na — not; cainaṁ = ca — and + enam — this; kledayantyāpo = kledayanti — soak + āpo = āpaḥ — water; na — nor; śoṣayati — dry out; mārutaḥ — the wind

Weapons do not pierce, fire does not burn, and water does not wet, nor does the wind dry that embodied soul. (Bhagavad Gītā 2.23)

Analysis

Damage to the physical body is not direct damage to the psychic person who is regarded as the self. This does not mean that a damaged body is not problematic to the self. It certainly is but that is due to an indirect relationship between the feelings of the physical system and the psychic self.

So long as the physical body is indirectly connected to the self, pains of that physical system will indirectly affect the self but the death of the body, which is its ultimate negative condition, will not cause the death of the psychic self. When the physical body dies, the psychic self realizes itself as being without a physical means of action.

A dying or terminally diseased physical body has pains within it. These are indirectly felt by the psychic self. In any case, the death moment of the physical system is not felt by the self except as having lost its physical means of performance.

Comprehension of Bhagavad Gītā Verse 2.23

Assuming that Krishna is correct. The person has a psychic part which transcends the physical body which we know as that person. It is not affected directly by weapons, fire, water, or wind.

It does feel when the body is damage, burnt, drenched, or dried, but these feelings are indirect only. The physical system is directly affected but the psychic portion of the being may or may not be aware of what happened on the physical side.

अच्छेद्योऽयमदाह्योऽयम्
अक्लेद्योऽशोष्य एव च ।
नित्यः सर्वगतः स्थाणुर्
अचलोऽयं सनातनः ॥२.२४॥

acchedyo'yamadāhyo'yam
akledyo'śoṣya eva ca
nityaḥ sarvagataḥ sthāṇur
acalo'yaṁ sanātanaḥ (2.24)

acchedyaḥ — not to be pierced; 'yam = ayam — this; adāhyo = adāhyaḥ — not to be burnt; 'yam = ayam — this; akledyo = akledyaḥ — not to be moistened; 'śoṣya = aśoṣya — not to be dried; eva — indeed; ca — and; nityaḥ — eternal; sarvagataḥ — penetrant of all things; sthāṇuḥ — a permanent principle; acalo = acalaḥ — unmoving; 'yaṁ = ayam — this; sanātanaḥ — primeval

This embodied soul cannot be pierced, cannot be burnt, cannot be moistened and cannot be dried. And indeed, this soul is eternal. It can penetrate all things. It is a permanent principle and is stable and primeval. (Bhagavad Gītā 2.24)

Analysis

Even though, according to Krishna's information, this embodied soul cannot be pierced, burnt, moistened, or dried, this does not mean that the physical representation of the self, which is the material body, is not affected. It is. One may be liable for affecting someone by some means such as this.

This information does not cover the liability one may have for affecting someone's physical body. This information applies when determining oneself as being other than a physical body, but it does not remove the social complications any self would face for damaging the body of another person. The value of a human body is such that if one damages the body of some other person, one may face unfavorable consequences.

Hence realizing that the physical body is minor, and the subtle self is major, does not free one from the responsibility of being violent to a body.

Comprehension of Bhagavad Gītā Verse 2.24

The fact is that the conventional person, the normal animal self, the physical body, can be pierced, burnt, moistened, and dried. Hence one should take that into account in social dealings. Simultaneously, one should be aware that the enduring factor on which the physical system is based, is one which cannot be damaged in the physical way. Even though the animal self lives for the time being, it will be curtailed and terminated shortly, but on the other side, the psychic body, will continue with or without alterations. The psychological consequences for physical actions will be served to the psychic body either hereafter or when it adopts another physical body in the course of time.

The individual cannot stop the impact of physical acts on the enduring psychic body. This means that despite the uselessness of the physical system, still, the subtle body should be conscientious because acts committed by the physical system will impact the subtle body even after the physical system is destroyed in some natural or unnatural way.

अव्यक्तोऽयमचिन्त्योऽयम् अविकार्योऽयमुच्यते । तस्मादेवं विदित्वैनं नानुशोचितुमर्हसि ॥२.२५॥	avyakto'yamacintyo'yam avikāryo'yamucyate tasmādevaṁ viditvainaṁ nānuśocitumarhasi (2.25)

avyakto = avyaktaḥ — undisplayed; 'yam = ayam — this; acintyo = acintyah — unimaginable; 'yam = ayam — this; avikāryo = avikāryaḥ — unchanging; 'yam = ayam — this; ucyate — it is declared; tasmāt — therefore; evaṁ — thus; viditvainaṁ = viditva — knowing + enam — this; nānuśocitum = na — not + anuśocitum — to lament; arhasi — you should

This embodied soul is undisplayed, unimaginable, and unchanging. Therefore, knowing this, you should not lament. (Bhagavad Gītā 2.25)

Analysis

This is a description of the coreSelf which is a factor in the composite which is the physical body. It is undisplayed because it cannot register itself as a physical principle. It is unimaginable because the mind as it is utilized in a physical body does not have a reference through which it can be visualized. It is unchanging because as contrasted to the ever-changing environment which we can sensual perceived, it is a constant factor which is out of range.

Krishna challenged Arjuna to abandon the traditional self as the reference and shift to a plane of consciousness where the coreSelf is felt as the object of focus.

Comprehension of Bhagavad Gītā Verse 2.25

Normally one relies on physical existence. One operates in the world in reference to that. Even the portions of our mental or emotional actions which are hidden to physical viewing, are reference to the physical body. This means that we enjoy, are indifferent to, or become sad, about physical incidences.

Krishna wanted Arjuna to abandon that natural method and use a process which was native to Krishna, but which was unusual for Arjuna.

When trying to use this advice, one may be stymied because one may find that one cannot shift the point of reference from the physical level which one used from the birth of one's body from the mother.

We crave physical displays. We imagine based on what we experience in the physical world or what we hear off through physical speech. We observe the slow or rapid changes in the environment and in our bodies. This would be required to change so that the physical is not the reference.

An urgent challenge however is that if one attempted to follow this advice given to Arjuna, one would have to do introspection to discover afresh this undisplayed, unimaginable, and unchanging embodied self.

अथ चैनं नित्यजातं
नित्यं वा मन्यसे मृतम् ।
तथापि त्वं महाबाहो
नैनं शोचितुमर्हसि ॥२.२६॥

atha cainaṁ nityajātaṁ
nityaṁ vā manyase mṛtam
tathāpi tvaṁ mahābāho
nainaṁ śocitumarhasi (2.26)

atha — furthermore; cainaṁ = ca — and + enam — this; nityajātaṁ = nitya — continually + jātam — being born; nityam — continually; vā — or; manyase — you think; mṛtam — dying; tathā 'pi = tathā — so + api — also; tvam — you; mahābāho — strong-armed man; nainaṁ = na — not + enam — this; śocitum arhasi = śocitum — to mourn + arhasi — you can

And furthermore, if you think that this embodied soul is continually being born or continually dying, even so, O strong-armed man, you should not lament. (Bhagavad Gītā 2.26)

Analysis

If one cannot realize that there is an enduring factor which is psychic but which supports the physical body which is perishable, then Krishna pronounces that one can continue thinking in the usual way. It is natural to think that the physical body is the person which will die. Everyone is born with that mentality. However, Krishna added another feature which is that one should go a step further and think that maybe, perhaps, that dead person will somehow or the other miraculously come back into existence and will be born again as a physical system.

It happened before that someone was born and developed social value. Hence why not consider that after dying that someone will be reborn as a new person, as an infant of parents.

Comprehension of Bhagavad Gītā Verse 2.26

In the time of Krishna some people believed reincarnation, but the concept, differed from person to person. Some felt that one is born, then one dies, then there is nothing, no remnant of oneself. Then uneventfully, one comes again as an infant with no agency causing that to happen.

When one is born again, one feels as if one is a new being. One lives again for a time. Then one dies and there is no trace of oneself again. Then this is repeated.

जातस्य हि ध्रुवो मृत्युर्
ध्रुवं जन्म मृतस्य च ।
तस्मादपरिहार्येऽर्थे
न त्वं शोचितुमर्हसि ॥२.२७॥

jātasya hi dhruvo mṛtyur
dhruvaṁ janma mṛtasya ca
tasmādaparihārye'rthe
na tvaṁ śocitumarhasi (2.27)

jātasya — of that which is born; hi — infact; dhruvo = dhruvaḥ — certain; mṛtyur = mṛtyuḥ — death; dhruvaṁ — certain; janma — birth; mṛtasya — of that which is dead; ca — and; tasmādaparihārye = tasmāt — therefore + aparihārye — in what is unavoidable; 'rthe = arthe — in the assessment; na — not; tvaṁ — you; śocitum — to lament + arhasi — you should

In fact, of that which is born, death is certain; of that which is dead, birth is certain. Therefore, in assessing what is unavoidable, you should not lament. (Bhagavad Gītā 2.27)

Analysis

From a philosophical angle, life may be summarized as a series of certainties which no limited being can alter, and which everyone is subjected to in so far as one uses and is identified as a physical body.

While living, the conventional person is faced with the fact that death is certain. As a physical body, the person is sure to die. No matter what kind of life one has, if it is the best or the worse of the historic probabilities, still tragedy will be served. The body will end. Will it be done in an acceptable way? Will it be in a dishonorable circumstance? Who knows? It does not matter because a good death or a bad one results in loss of the body.

Krishna indicated to Arjuna that for whatever is born, death is certain and for whatever is dead, birth is certain. How can one verify that if one has no way of gaging if there is a psychic remnant of the person who died? If one cannot see the surviving portion, how can one verify that there is one?

We know that whatever dies is recycled gradually or radically. In that sense from the view of biology, whatever dies, a human body, a leaf or a section of skin, it will be recycled. In that sense its elements will exist somewhere somehow.

The physical reality is contained in space. Its only method of existing is constant alteration which is a process of recycling.

Comprehension of Bhagavad Gītā Verse 2.27

Krishna explained to Arjuna that the determination of a self is such that if it dies which means that it loses a physical body, it is sure to be born again. That is the unalterable course of nature.

A self came to be as a physical person because it is part of the roll out of time, which operates inexorably to bring beings into a manifestation and to have them be displayed while acting there, and then to terminate the form used there. This is a process which is beyond the control of a limited self. We should know that any person from the invisible existence who becomes aware of itself visibly in the physical world, will endure deterioration of the physical body which nature developed for it.

The body will malfunction, either shortly and in due course. It will die, then that person will no longer be active on the physical side. Then again as nature continues this history, that person will again find itself to be a physical person.

अव्यक्तादीनि भूतानि
व्यक्तमध्यानि भारत ।
अव्यक्तनिधनान्येव
तत्र का परिदेवना ॥२.२८॥

avyaktādīni bhūtāni
vyaktamadhyāni bhārata
avyaktanidhanānyeva
tatra kā paridevanā (2.28)

avyaktādīni = avyakta — undetected + ādīni- beginnings of a manifestation; bhūtāni — living beings; vyakta madhyāni = vyakta — visible + madhyāni — interim states; bhārata — O descendant of Bharata; avyakta nidhanāny eva = avyakta — undetected + nidhanāni — ends of a manifestation + eva — again; tatra — there; kā — what; paridevanā — complaint

The living beings are undetected in the beginning of a manifestation, visible in the interim stages, and are again undetected at the end of a manifestation. What is the complaint? (Bhagavad Gītā 2.28)

Analysis

The onset of the birth of anyone, any conventional person, is not within the reach of physical sensing. It is not a physical event. It is a psychic scene. Even its formation which is a biological event for the formation of sperm and ova is not comprehensible to the physical senses of a human being.

However, once a pregnancy shows as a distended abdomen, everyone can see that the formation indicates a baby. But again, at the end of the manifestation, at the death of the body, the psychic forces at work become invisible again because of losing their grasp on physical reality, not being in a position to make obvious history.

Krishna in a curt remark, asked Arjuna about his complaint of this natural process which is repeated again and again not just for human beings but for any species even for vegetation. Provided that nature accommodates a species, death is certain and so is the emergence of life. The psychological force continues during the life of a body. It becomes invisible after the body's death. Soon after, it emerges in a living way again.

Comprehension of Bhagavad Gītā Verse 2.28

To follow Krishna's explanation about the flow of life, we are required to accept some assumptions. Even though we have no proof of the sequences of rotary events, which Krishna described, we may endeavor to understand his perspective.

It is obvious that with human senses, no living being can detect the beginning of a manifestation of a body. The body begins as a sperm particle in the father's testes and as ovum in the mother's ovaries. If there is a psychic side, that is imperceptible. To us that is insensible. We have no physical means of detecting that.

Our evidence of a body begins during a pregnancy, and even that is not obvious to the full degree. However, once the infant is evicted from the mother's form, it becomes visible. It is perceptible to one's sense of touch. It may be heard. It is reasonable to draw the conclusion that the baby developed from a tiny life form, from a sperm which originated in the father's body. It then developed further in the mother's uterus. It was birthed. It reached sexual maturity. It aged. It had a terminal disease, or it was fatally wounded. It died. After death the scene closed to normal perception.

Anything after physical death is abstract. Anyone can testify based on his/her intuition, belief, or mystic perception, but proof on the physical side is hard to acquire. In this case we should allow Lord Krishna to explain his perception. We will proceed with the idea that he has mystic perception and can see the unseen psychic events.

The invisibility of what is psychic is an ongoing reality which no limited person can change. We must accept that there are so many events which are invisible to our senses. Even a person's birth and what happens in the development of its fetus is abstract to one's perception. Thus, the alarm about psychic phenomena is unjustified. We continue to be astonished because we are focused on the physical side. We constantly look for and expect to force events to be restricted to the physical plane.

आश्चर्यवत्पश्यति कश्चिदेनम्
आश्चर्यवद्वदति तथैव चान्यः ।
आश्चर्यवच्चैनमन्यः शृणोति
श्रुत्वाप्येनं वेद न चैव कश्चित्
॥२.२९॥

āścaryavatpaśyati kaścidenam
āścaryavadvadati tathaiva cānyaḥ
āścaryavaccainamanyaḥ śṛṇoti
śrutvāpyenaṁ veda na caiva kaścit (2.29)

āścaryavat — wonderful; paśyati — perceives; kaścidenam = kaścid — someone + enam — this; āścaryavad — fantastic; vadati — describes; tathai 'va = tathā — so + eva — indeed; cānyaḥ = ca — and + anyah — another person; āścaryavaccainam = āścaryavat — amazing + ca — and + enam — this; anyaḥ — another; śṛṇoti — hears; śrutvāpyenaṁ = srutva — having heard + api — also + enam — this; veda — knows; na — not; caiva = ca — and + eva — in fact; kaścit — anyone

Someone perceives this embodied soul as being wonderful. Another person describes it as amazing. Another hears of it as being fantastic. And even after hearing this, no one knows this embodied soul in fact. (Bhagavad Gītā 2.29)

Analysis

The embodied soul, the psychic governor of the physical system, is a mysterious something. Some admit it as a psychic reality. Some reject it as nothing. Some feel that it is a biological construction. Some regard it as fantastic.

But they are others who feel that a discussion, will cause no solution about its discovery and proof. The question? Who is the person?

Comprehension of Bhagavad Gītā Verse 2.29

There is an argument regarding the reality of a person which is the core around which character takes place. This argument will continue forever. Since it is based on subjective evidence, one person may never agree to the opinion of another.

If there are varying degrees of subjectivity in each person, the evidence culled will vary, resulting in disagreement. Since to objectify the self to itself, a certain environment and existential conditions are necessary, no limited person can standardize the evidence for all persons.

Thus, Krishna declared that someone perceives this embodied soul as being wonderful. Another person describes it as amazing. Another hears of it as being fantastic. And even after hearing this, no one knows this embodied soul in fact.

Since the conventional person is a construction, that Is no mystery except the factor of it having an everlasting core. How can one discover that? What are the indications of that?

देही नित्यमवध्योऽयं देहे सर्वस्य भारत । तस्मात्सर्वाणि भूतानि न त्वं शोचितुमर्हसि ॥२.३०॥	dehī nityamavadhyo'yaṁ dehe sarvasya bhārata tasmātsarvāṇi bhūtāni na tvaṁ śocitumarhasi (2.30)

dehī — embodied soul; nityam — eternally; avadhyo = avadhyaḥ — non-killable; 'yaṁ = ayam — this; dehe — in the body; sarvasya — of all, in all cases; bhārata — O descendant of Bharata; tasmāt — therefore; sarvāṇi — all; bhūtāni — beings; na — no; tvaṁ — you; śocitumarhasi = śocitum — to mourn + arhasi — should

In the body, in all cases, this embodied soul is always non-killable, O descendant of Bharata. Therefore, you should not mourn for any of these beings. (Bhagavad Gītā 2.30)

Analysis

This would require a reconsideration of one's social interactions. One should value a physical body as a person and also know that such a person is a fabrication which is temporary. It is used as if it is the total value of the self.

The physical body is not the self, but it has value to the self which is the basis upon which the physical system was created by the biological process of nature.

There should be respect for the physical body, but this view of the self as a temporary reality should be evaluated in reference to the core of the self, whereby, it is understood that the psychic part of the personality will persists beyond the life of the physical system.

From one perspective the intangible self which is a psychic reality has all value and from another view, it is irrelevant. The same is true about the physical body as the self. In one environment everything depends on the existence of the physical system. In another it all hinges on the psychic self.

Comprehension of Bhagavad Gītā Verse 2.30

Krishna presented. He expects us to trust his information, that in a physical body, in every case, there is a personSelf who cannot be fatally assaulted. If that is the situation, no one should mourn for someone whose body is dead.

However, mourning for others, for relatives, friends and even strangers, will persist because until one can shift reference from the physical to the psychic, one will feel a lost or displacement whenever a related body perishes.

सर्वकर्माणि मनसा
संन्यस्यास्ते सुखं वशी ।
नवद्वारे पुरे देही
नैव कुर्वन्न कारयन् ॥५.१३॥

sarvakarmāṇi manasā
saṁnyasyāste sukhaṁ vaśī
navadvāre pure dehī
naiva kurvanna kārayan (5.13)

sarvakarmāṇi = sarva — all + karmāṇi — actions; manasā — with the mind; saṁnyasyāste = saṁnyasy (saṁnyasi) — renouncing + āste — he sits; sukhaṁ — happily; vaśī — director; navadvāre = nava — nine + dvāre — in the gate; pure — in the city; dehī — the embodied soul; naiva = na — not + eva — indeed; kurvan — acting; na — nor; kārayan — causing activity

Renouncing all action with the mind, the embodied soul resides happily within as the director in the nine-gated city, not acting nor causing activity. (Bhagavad Gītā 5.13)

Analysis

Of the two declared selves, one is the conventional physical person, the other is the psychic core which is intangible. Just as the physical person is a mockup, so the psychic one is also a composite with a stable core.

Initially when researching, one begins with the physical person. One discovers that it is a combination of psychological energy and physical substance, but presented as one person in the physical world.

Even the bare physical body is combination of various materials, which function as a certain social entity, which is earmarked in society with a name and function. The psychic person is also a combination of various psychic energies with a coreSelf as the primal factor.

The psychological self has one arm which is its willpower. This manifests as mental request which the physical body is expected to execute. Krishna proposed that if the psychic self renounces all action mentally, it will reside in the physical body happily because of not projecting itself into every action and reaction in the physical environment.

Comprehension of Bhagavad Gītā Verse 5.13

The nine-gated city is the physical body which is like a city with nine entrances. For the body, we have these openings.

- two ears
- two eyes
- two nostrils
- one mouth
- one genital
- one anus

The body is enclosed by a skin which acts as a touching surface and which simultaneously protects its cells from invasion. The psychic self resides in that enclosure which is energized by feelings. These form a massive layout of touch sensation. A yogi uses these feelings to map the inner movements within the body.

Assuming that there is a coreSelf, it has an ongoing ever-challenging task to be happy within the physical body. This self is supposed to be the director of what happens in and with the body, but invariable things go to the contrary where the core is directed, supervised and controlled by other factors.

The mere consideration that the core must strive to control its bodily environment and its relationship with what is outside of the physical body, means that declarations stating that it is the absolute or that it is antiseptic, require verification.

If a man is frightened by a rope because sensually his psyche reported the cord to be a snake, the issue is not the mistaken identity of the rope but the fact that the senses of the man caused fright in the first place. The mere act of realizing that the rope is not a reptile does not solve the problem of the mistaken viewpoint. The man should get his sensing device in order so that his vision is correctly interpreted.

Because the coreSelf provides the major energy which runs the body, it is supposed to be the director of the operations. And yet, in most cases of the conventional self, that is not the case. What happens is that an embodied soul resides miserably within as the factor which is directed in the nine-gate city of the body. It feels the trauma just as if it acted and directly caused physical activity.

As something which is connected to another factor, may feel tremors when that other principle operates, so the personSelf feels agitation either as happiness, distress or indifference when the physical body interacts internally or with the physical environment. How can this cease?

न कर्तृत्वं न कर्माणि
लोकस्य सृजति प्रभुः ।
न कर्मफलसंयोगं
स्वभावस्तु प्रवर्तते ॥५.१४॥

na kartṛtvaṁ na karmāṇi
lokasya sṛjati prabhuḥ
na karmaphalasaṁyogaṁ
svabhāvastu pravartate (5.14)

na — not; kartṛtvaṁ — means of action; na — nor; karmāṇi — actions; lokasya — of the creatures; sṛjati — he creates; prabhuḥ — the Lord; na — nor; karmaphalasaṁyogaṁ = karma — action + phala — consequence + saṁyogaṁ — cyclic connection; svabhāvaḥ — inherent nature; tu — but; pravartate — it causes

The Lord does not create the means of action, nor the actions of the creatures, nor the action-consequence cycle. But the inherent nature causes this. (Bhagavad Gītā 5.14)

Analysis

The supreme being, the ultimate person, or his agent, does not gather and mix the ingredients which comprise the physical circumstances which we find ourselves in. Krishna stated that the inherent nature of the materials, does the creative urges and the resulting actions and formations.

This begs the question as to the function and operation of the Lord and the limited personalities. A limited self considers itself to be an agent of operations and an architect and worker in the production of events and products. If it is not that, if indeed the inherent nature of this physical world is the producer of events, how does this history imprint itself on a self, whereby that person considers itself to be the producer and agent.

Comprehension of Bhagavad Gītā Verse 5.14

The Lord, the supreme being, Krishna, is a person. Krishna presented the limited self as a person as well. He stated that neither God nor the limited person creates the means of action, nor the actions done by any physical being. God does not necessarily supervise the action-consequence cycle. These operations transverse the reality because each motive or substance reacts by its inherent nature.

The conventional person is a mockup but even as such it is not the means of action, nor the action itself nor is it magically producing consequences for actions. The physical body as a person is not the creator of what happens but it is involved in the roll of events. Regardless of if it is dead or alive, the physical body remains as part of the physical world. When it is dead, the psychic remnant energy which enlivened it, continues to exist on a psychic plane, but without access to being used for direct operations on the physical level.

The God oversees the situation from a distant place. He is immune to the alterations, but the limited person may be afflicted unless it is situated in a realm which is not part of the involvement. Whenever it can, the inherent nature reacts with and influences the psychic senses of the limited person. Thus, that someone appears to be affected or feels adjusted.

नादत्ते कस्यचित्पापं
न चैव सुकृतं विभुः ।
अज्ञानेनावृतं ज्ञानं
तेन मुह्यन्ति जन्तवः ॥५.१५॥

nādatte kasyacitpāpaṁ
na caiva sukṛtaṁ vibhuḥ
ajñānenāvṛtaṁ jñānaṁ
tena muhyanti jantavaḥ (5.15)

nādatte = na — not + ādatte — perceives; kasyacit — of anyone; pāpaṁ — evil consequence; na — not; caiva = ca — and + eva — indeed; sukṛtaṁ — good reaction; vibhuḥ — the Almighty God; ajñānenāvṛtaṁ = ajñānena — by ignorance + avṛtam — shrouded; jñānaṁ — knowledge; tena — through which; muhyanti — they are deluded; jantavaḥ — the people

The Almighty God does not receive from anyone, an evil consequence nor a good reaction. The knowledge of this is shrouded by ignorance through which the people are deluded. (Bhagavad Gītā 5.15)

Analysis

The Almighty God, Krishna, is so remote from the physical and psychic interactions that he does not absorb part or all of the repercussions which target and pierce the body or mind of a limited self.

This does not mean that the limited self cannot send energy or appeals for assistance to the Almighty God. Such communication happens with the God either responding or ignoring. The God may defer to an agent. Or he may ignore a friendly or hostile communication.

Many human beings feel that they have a right to send appeals for assistance, as well as report resentments for unfavorable conditions. However as stated, such energy may not directly reach the deity. This is because his existence is abstract to the transmissions.

Under the impression of our emotions, we derive confidence that we can petition God. We have beliefs which support the need to commandeer the Almighty. In so far as we are convinced of our mental and emotional methods, we will proceed with convictions, but the information from Krishna is informative and hints at how we can correct those viewpoints.

Comprehension of Bhagavad Gītā Verse 5.15

Each personSelf has priorities and tries to frame history for convenience. As the history of the world rolls out, each person engages in the process of confining or releasing factors which give pleasure to the self.

However, this method is impractical because even the supreme self, even Krishna, must take into account that there are other pressing factors which comprise the sum total existence. The cosmos is more than the Supreme Person. It is not any specific limited self alone. It is a massive mix of personalities with a predominant supreme person, who is Krishna.

Why then is there an infinite array of limited personalities, each with its individual needs and pressing concerns? Why does each person make efforts to be a centralized self which tries to arrange physical and psychic aspects for convenience?

This happens because the expression of a self, comes with a need to be dominant. However, each self should minimize that need. Each self should face reality and willingly give way to providence instead of being frustrated when providence refuses to yield to its demands.

So much is unknown to the limited self. Due to its limited sense perception as well as its inaccurate assessments about circumstances, that self should subsidize its ignorance with information from the Supreme Person. In every way, the limited self should be open for more information, experience and super-normal perception, so as to properly gage where it stands and properly access what facilities it is allowed by providence.

There is no possibility of a limited self being the supreme person. Any plan or action, which intends to establish its supremacy should be discarded. At no point in history will the God act for the elevation of a limited self to Godhead status. That idea whenever it arises in the mind, even with massive confidence, should be ignored.

विद्याविनयसंपन्ने
ब्राह्मणे गवि हस्तिनि ।
शुनि चैव श्वपाके च
पण्डिताः समदर्शिनः ॥५.१८॥

vidyāvinayasaṁpanne
brāhmaṇe gavi hastini
śuni caiva śvapāke ca
paṇḍitāḥ samadarśinaḥ (5.18)

vidyāvinayasaṁpanne = vidyā — learning + vinaya — trained + saṁpanne — accomplished; brāhmaṇe — in a brahmin; gavi — in a cow; hastini — in an elephant; śuni — in a dog; caiva = ca — and + eva — indeed; śvapāke — in a dog-flesh eater; ca — and; paṇḍitāḥ — scripturally-conversant mystic seers; samadarśinaḥ = sama — common factor + darśinaḥ — observing

In a learned, trained, accomplished brahmin, in a cow, an elephant, a dog, or a dog-flesh eater, the scripturally-conversant mystic seers observe a common factor. (Bhagavad Gītā 5.18)

Analysis

The common factor, the unadulterated issue, the ever-radiant reality which serves as the axis around which all other formations occur, is the coreSelf. It is around this reality that the various formats assumed, occur. That common factor does not have to be objectively self-conscious to be the center of attention or the magnetic collector of other attributes.

It does not have to power only a human body. It could serve as the core for a calf or puppy. Two evidences are required for a limited self to know this. He should be spiritually conversant and have psychic perception which he can use to verify spiritual information. Mere acceptance of the information even from Krishna, is insufficient. The yogi should develop supernatural means of perception, and then work to realize valid scriptural statements. He should not be superstitious and should not fanatically accept scripture.

Information about *Sāṁkhya* is the theory of existence having to do specifically with the person and its primal cause. Such a discussion must be checked and rechecked by the yogi so that he can convince himself by direct evidence that *Sāṁkhya* is based on what can be experienced.

Comprehension of Bhagavad Gītā Verse 5.18

Some behavior of the bodies of educated mystic humans, bovine animals, dogs and humans who eat dog flesh, is different. Some is similar. And yet the coreSelf around which these formats occur, is similar in the sense that each can operate the physical body of the other.

Given the opportunity, a coreSelf using an educated human's body, could just as well efficiently use a cow's form. It can adopt a cow's behavior to such an extent that if seen and observed, it would be mistaken as an animal. However, in a cow's body it is unlikely that the personSelf would recall the operation and identification of a human form, or of any other past body.

The lack of memory is the cause of the ignorance. Besides, one cannot imagine, visualize or realize that one can use any other body but the one which a self currently operates. The cow cannot understand that it would operate a dog's body. The dog does not understand that it can use a human body. Most human beings lack the humility and insight to know that a human can become a lesser species. Due to identifying with the human body-format, the coreSelf in the human body displays an unreasonable prejudice about other species.

Becoming convinced that one is a human body, dog's body or an elephant's body, causes a prejudice where one cannot identify as the self which uses the body. One mistakes the self for the body. This creates a rigidity in self-concept which solidifies the ignorance about how the coreSelf becomes the format of the body. Through its spread of consciousness in the formation of an embryo, that core feels its feelings saturated in the body. Through that it identifies with the particular species.

A yogi should retreat his feelings from its spread through the lifeform. These feelings should be gathered into the center of consciousness. Then he/she may realize the self as a radiance which governs the collection of factors which comprise a living physical form.

इहैव तैर्जितः सर्गो
येषां साम्ये स्थितं मनः ।
निर्दोषं हि समं ब्रह्म
तस्माद्ब्रह्मणि ते स्थिताः ॥५.१९॥

ihaiva tairjitaḥ sargo
yeṣāṁ sāmye sthitaṁ manaḥ
nirdoṣaṁ hi samaṁ brahma
tasmādbrahmaṇi te sthitāḥ (5.19)

ihaiva = iha — here in this world + iva (eva) — indeed; tair = taiḥ — by those; jitaḥ — conquered; sargo = sargaḥ — birth; yeṣāṁ — of whom; sāmye — in impartiality; sthitaṁ — established; manaḥ — mind; nirdoṣaṁ — faultless; hi — indeed; samaṁ — equally disposed; brahma — pure spirit; tasmāt — therefore; brahmaṇi — on the pure spiritual plane; te — they; sthitāḥ — established

Here in this world, birth is conquered by those whose minds are established in impartiality. Indeed, pure spirit is faultless and equally disposed. Therefore, they are established on the pure spiritual plane. (Bhagavad Gītā 5.19)

Analysis

When for one reason or the other, under one apparent or real influence or the other, a coreSelf becomes subjective to the lifeform it enlivens, that self loses self-analysis and partitions itself with the particular habits of that form. It is unable to sort itself from the body it uses.

To get differentiation between what it is and the body it psychically energizes, the core must become impartial, where it considers every creature form in any species to be a personSelf using and empowering the particular life form.

For birth, for the formation of a body, a particular core must become the center of attention of many other factors. This begins when the coreSelf is psychically within the influence of parents. These may be human, animal, insect, or even vegetation parents.

When it becomes the center, it gains the idea that it is the development of the embryo concerned. This causes it to abandon its neutrality which results in ignorance of the reality which is that it is in a combination of factors as the central energy.

Comprehension of Bhagavad Gītā Verse 5.19

By developing impartiality when viewing physical circumstances, one breaks the spell of feeling that one is the physical body. Instead of identifying as a physical system, and assigning other bodies as other physical selves, one should view circumstances detachedly.

The reference of being a living physical body of a species, may be changed if one replaces it with the reference of being the psychic energy which uses and services that form.

Krishna announced that the pure spirit, the self, when it does not project its energy into lower elements, is faultless and equally disposed. It is faultless because it does not directly commit good or bad physical or psychic acts. It is equally disposed because it is neither this nor that.

बाह्यस्पर्शेष्वसक्तात्मा
विन्दत्यात्मनि यत्सुखम् ।
स ब्रह्मयोगयुक्तात्मा
सुखमक्षयमश्नुते ॥५.२१॥

bāhyasparśeṣvasaktātmā
vindatyātmani yatsukham
sa brahmayogayuktātmā
sukhamakṣayamaśnute (5.21)

bāhyasparśeṣvasaktātmā = bāhya — external + sparśeṣv (sparśeṣu) — sensation + asakta — not attached + ātmā — soul; vindatyātmani = (vindati) — finds + ātmani — in the spirit; yat — who; sukham — happiness; sa = saḥ — he; brahmayogayuktātmā = brahma — spiritual plane + yoga — yoga process; yukta — linked + ātmā — spirit; sukham — happiness; akṣayam — non-fluctuating; aśnute — makes contact with

The person who is not attached to the external sensations, who finds happiness in the spirit, whose spirit is linked to the spiritual plane through yoga process, makes contact with the non-fluctuating happiness. (Bhagavad Gītā 5.21)

Analysis

From one angle, the quest of personality is continuous access to happiness with no discomfort and dissatisfaction. Many solutions to this need of a personSelf were proposed by various philosophers down the Ages. Nihilistic people suggest varies methods for eliminating the self. Their idea is that if there is no self there would be no need for happiness and no target for discomfort.

If, however, Krishna is correct, if the personSelf is perpetual with or without an objective awareness of itself, it makes sense that it should seek the non-fluctuating happiness as its basis of consciousness. This objective eludes the self because there are inversions occurring continually in physical existence, whereby something presents itself in one way but renders from itself a sensation which is anything but happiness.

First the yogi must practice ceasing the habit of external hunting. One must work introspectively to cause the inner nature to be content with itself, to continually review and focus on itself, to abandon external objects as its reference.

Happiness which was induced previously in the conventional way of making sensual contact externally and then enjoying pleasing feelings which result, should change so that the self finds happiness within itself. If there is no happiness within, the self should strive to find the place within the psyche where such happiness which normally remains in a hidden enclosure, exists. This requires dedicated meditation for hours, for a time.

Comprehension of Bhagavad Gītā Verse 5.21

The conventional person, the living physical body, began as a baby with a quest for air and liquid nutrition. It was equipped only for that. Its very existence relied on that. It had to seek that external assistance in the form of air for breathing and milk for suckling.

From that beginning, the idea of a high value for the external environment to supplement life, was derived. In the infancy stage and then the juvenile years, this value for the external world increases. One after the other, need and necessity arise. Pleasure and displeasure are defined by the attitude of the senses of the physical body to whatever is experienced. These are mostly out-going quest with internal responses which are rated according to the external contact made.

What Krishna proposed is radical to the normal way of estimating sensual responses. He requested an internal focus, using the very senses which are oriented to external gratifications, but which become introverted.

योऽन्तःसुखोऽन्तरारामस्
तथान्तर्ज्योतिरेव यः ।
स योगी ब्रह्मनिर्वाणं
ब्रह्मभूतोऽधिगच्छति ॥५.२४॥

yo'ntaḥsukho'ntarārāmas
tathāntarjyotireva yaḥ
sa yogī brahmanirvāṇaṁ
brahmabhūto'dhigacchati (5.24)

yo = yaḥ — who; 'ntaḥsukho = antahsukhaḥ — he who is happy within; 'ntarārāmas = antarārāmas — he who is spiritually delighted; tathāntarjyotir (tathāntarjyotiḥ) = tathā — as a result + antarjyotiḥ — he who has brilliant consciousness within; eva — indeed; yaḥ — who; sa = saḥ — he; yogī — yogi; brahmanirvāṇaṁ — stoppage of disturbing sensuality and attainment of constant spirituality; brahmabhūto = brahmabhūtaḥ — absorption on the spiritual plane; 'dhigacchati = adhigacchati — he attains

The person who is happy within, who is spiritually delighted and as a result, experiences the brilliant consciousness, he, that yogi, experiences the stoppage of disturbing sensuality and attains constant spirituality in absorption on the spiritual plane. (Bhagavad Gītā 5.24)

Analysis

To discover and use the personSelf which is the core of what is normally considered to be the person, a yogi should imbibe Krishna's information, that deep in the psyche, there is the brilliant consciousness, the radiance of perpetual life. That is the person in fact, not the additives to that, which are cultural tags suitable for the social world in which the physical body functions.

It requires special training in meditation techniques to practice what Krishna suggest about establishing the brilliant consciousness. Even though the corePersonality is established by Krishna's statement, still it takes effort to silence the disturbing sensuality. Even if that is achieved, one may not become spiritually delightful by the resulting state of consciousness.

Comprehension of Bhagavad Gītā Verse 5.24

The switch in meditation from mental chaos to radiant consciousness, which the self can appreciate as spiritual delight, does happen in the meditation of some yogis. It may happen infrequently for others.

What normally occurs, is that there is switch from mental chaos to a blank mental state which is devoid of radiance, and which does not feel delightful. This is why many people shy away from meditation and adopt methods whereby they can enjoy some happiness or induce enjoyment during the meditative state.

A yogi should be prepared to meditate for long periods and to experience a blank or neutral state of mind, whereby after the chaos in the mind ceases, one witnesses nothing occurring, no demands for attention. This condition with no thoughts or images, should be maintained for a time, until the state described by Krishna is experienced.

In time, the yogi being happy in a state of mind in which there is no hankering for indulgence with thoughts, memories or ideas, he/she feels a shift where a clean steady happiness is spread within the mind. The yogi feels the brilliant consciousness, and notes that the disturbing sensuality ceases. A constant spirituality is identified with confidence of being on the enduring spiritual plane.

उद्धरेदात्मनात्मानं
नात्मानमवसादयेत् ।
आत्मैव ह्यात्मनो बन्धुर्
आत्मैव रिपुरात्मनः ॥६.५॥

uddharedātmanātmānaṁ
nātmānamavasādayet
ātmaiva hyātmano bandhur
ātmaiva ripurātmanaḥ (6.5)

uddhared = uddharet — should elevate; ātmanā — by the self; 'tmānaṁ = ātmānam — the self; nātmānam = na — not + ātmānam — the self; avasādayet — should degrade; ātmaiva = ātmā — self + eva — only; hyātmano = hyātmanaḥ = hy (hi) — indeed + ātmanaḥ — of the self; bandhur = bandhuh — friend; ātmaiva = ātmā — self + eva — as well; ripur = ripuḥ — enemy; ātmanaḥ — of the self

One should elevate his being by himself. One should not degrade the self. Indeed, the person should be the friend of himself. Or he could be the enemy as well. (Bhagavad Gītā 6.5)

Analysis

Regardless of if the personSelf is perpetual or not, it is imperative that the yogi seek self-elevation. It is best for someone to elevate himself/herself even for those who only know the person as the physical body. For the social progress of the world, each person should befriend himself/herself and live for the benefit of one and all.

Krishna requested that each person should elevate his/her being by himself/herself. This is preferred, rather than be suicidal or throw the responsibility on someone else.

Comprehension of Bhagavad Gītā Verse 6.5

There is a protracted struggle for survival of the self. One who identities himself/herself as a physical body, is confronted with the specter of death by a lethal means. Such a person naturally does what he/she can, to forestall the termination of the body. Some try to kill the body so as to escape physical or psychic trauma.

All the same some struggle against psychic threats. One person feels that he/she is the mind or all or part of the psychological energy which people target as a self. Again, it is best to be the friend of the self and not act in a way which increases the perils which afflict it.

बन्धुरात्मात्मनस्तस्य
येनात्मैवात्मना जितः ।
अनात्मनस्तु शत्रुत्वे
वर्तेतात्मैव शत्रुवत् ॥६.६॥

bandhur ātmātmanastasya
yenātmaivātmanā jitaḥ
anātmanastu śatrutve
vartetātmaiva śatruvat (6.6)

bandhur = bandhuḥ — friend; ātmā — personal energies; 'tmanas = ātmanas — of the self; tasya — of him; yenātmaivātmanā = yena — by whom + ātmā — self + eva — indeed + ātmanā — by the self; jitaḥ — subdued; anātmanas — of one who is not self-possessed; tu — but; śatrutve — in hostility; vartetātmaiva = varteta — it operates + ātmā - self + eva — indeed; śatruvat — like an enemy

The personal energies are the friend of the person by whom those energies are subdued. But for one whose personality is not self-possessed; the personal energies operate in hostility like an enemy. (Bhagavad Gītā 6.6)

Analysis

In this usage the personal energies do not pertain to the conventional self, which is the cultural target, the physical body. By using the Sanskrit, *ātmā*, Krishna highlights the sourcePerson which survives the physical form, and which is a feature of permanence, the core around which other aspects of the conventional self adhere.

The display of the personSelf shines through adjuncts which are psychological aspects. These particulars of the core, if subdued, serve as friendly compliments, otherwise they function towards the core as enemies. They bring on superimpositions which threaten the very existence of the perpetual core. Even though such assaults are illusory, they still affect the expectations of the self and cause it to consider what is unrealistic.

Comprehension of Bhagavad Gītā Verse 6.6

Even though the conventional self poses as the real identity, if the coreSelf allows the psyche to be guided only for the interest of social connections, that core will be afflicted during the life of the physical body and at the end of it, at its death.

When regarded as a reality unto itself the conventional self is hostile to the core. Hence the core must discipline and pilot itself for its long-ranged interest, otherwise it will be afflicted by traumas which are supportive of having a physical body life after life.

The coreSelf should strike a compromise so that it consents for the maintenance of the physical self but not with intentions that the physical body will last forever, only with the idea that it is best to serve that body for the healthiest condition it can be in during its years of existing.

Ultimately, the focus of interest should be on the coreSelf with limited circumspect concern for the conventional self, the physical body identity. Even if the physical body feels well and gets its fulfillments, that does not mean that this is in the interest of the core. Immediate gratification for the physical body may convert into severe discomfort at the next moment or in some year hence. This is because the physical system does not usually make decisions for its wellbeing in terms of the consequences of its action. The core should calculate this and restrict the physical.

योगी युञ्जीत सततम्
आत्मानं रहसि स्थितः ।
एकाकी यतचित्तात्मा
निराशीरपरिग्रहः ॥६.१०॥

yogī yuñjīta satatam
ātmānaṁ rahasi sthitaḥ
ekākī yatacittātmā
nirāśīraparigrahaḥ (6.10)

yogī — yogi; yuñjīta — should concentrate; satatam — constantly; ātmānam — on the self; rahasi — in isolation; sthitaḥ — situated; ekākī — alone; yatacittātmā = yata - controlling + citta - thinking + ātmā — self; nirāśīr — without desire; aparigrahaḥ — without possessions

In isolation, the yogi should constantly concentrate on the self. Being alone, he should be of controlled thinking and subdued self without desire and without possessions. (Bhagavad Gītā 6.10)

Analysis

This is the struggle in the psyche of a yogi. Instead of indulging mentally in ideas, instead of enjoying mental scenes which are imagined, the yogi is required to be of controlled thinking, having subdued the impulsive psychological aspects of the self.

For this practice, isolation is required because time and again, the yogi will be harassed for social involvements, fulfillment of desires and the endeavors required to produce physical results.

To reduce the pressure of society, a yogi is required to be in isolation. He should not be famous. His interaction with society should be to the minimum. If he raises his profile and is recognized for social usefulness, there will be demands which will consume his time, and force him to be externally occupied. This will put a damper on any attempt at meditation.

Comprehension of Bhagavad Gītā Verse 6.10

Yogic meditation consists of full withdrawal from objects which are external to the physical body. Whatever is usually procured through the physical senses, should be abandoned. External interest should be curtailed. If possible, one should struggle internally with the mind so that it ceases the efforts to grasp at external sense objects by seeing, hearing, tasting, touching and smelling. These actions are both voluntary and involuntary but the coreSelf should make the effort to terminate the interest, and in time cause it to cease during the meditation sessions.

Once the hunting force for external objects is reduced, the self should turn about within the mind and face backwards so that it loses concern with the interest for the security of the physical body. This causes an increase in inner perception, where much of what was not within view of the self internally, becomes visible to it.

The first observation is that many thoughts are illustrated in the mind involuntarily. These have a power over the self whereby the self is compelled to view the development, spread and curtailment of one thought pattern after another. The coreSelf will note that it is unable to control the running events of these thoughts. It will find that for most of these, it cannot command their termination.

Such observation about the weakness of the core, causes it to ponder the reason for the lack of control. A self may then consult an advanced yogi for an explanation of why it is unable to control the dramatic events which are conjured in the mind. The self may ask a teacher for an effective method of squelching the involuntary mental operations.

After making attempts at meditation for a time, a yogi realizes that unless he/she is isolated, the progress will be haphazard. This is due to the fact that there are interruptions which arrive during a meditation session. These disrupt the practice.

As Krishna declared, meditation should be done in isolation. The yogi should be alone. He should be proficient at the control of his thinking motions. His sensual desires should be squelched. He should lack possessions. If these restrictions are not in place, it will be difficult to make progress because of the constant inner and outer interruptions.

शुचौ देशे प्रतिष्ठाप्य
स्थिरमासनमात्मनः ।
नात्युच्छ्रितं नातिनीचं
चैलाजिनकुशोत्तरम् ॥६.११॥

śucau deśe pratiṣṭhāpya
sthiramāsanamātmanaḥ
nātyucchritaṁ nātinīcaṁ
cailājinakuśottaram (6.11)

śucau — in clean; deśe — in place; pratiṣṭhāpya — fixing; sthiram — firm; āsanam — seat; ātmanaḥ — of his self; nātyucchritaṁ = na — not + atyucchritaṁ — too high; nātinīcam = na — not + atinīcam — too low; cailājinakuśottaram = caila - cloth + ajina — antelope skin + kuśa — kusha grass + uttaram — underneath

In a clean place, fixing for himself a firm seat which is not too high, not too low, with a covering layer of cloth, antelope skin and kusha grass underneath, (Bhagavad Gītā 6.11)

Analysis

This yogi who ventures inward to research his/her psyche, does not have a place of pilgrimage. He/She does not have dedicated followers and devotees. This person may advice others on the spiritual path, but he/she does not establish an institution to attract disciples.

He/She should have a simple place, but it should be clean. There should be a firm seat which is not so high that he overlooks others. It should not be so low, that it serves to attract insects or becomes easily flooded. The seat should be firm but not luxurious and extravagant. In the time of Krishna, yogis used a simply covering of cloth, with deer skin and kusha grass. Today that is not as readily available but padding and other inexpensive materials may be used.

Comprehension of Bhagavad Gītā Verse 6.11

Once the decision is made to do inner research in meditation, there comes a time when a yogi realizes that he/she requires isolation. This need may be serviced by providence but for some yogis it will cause a state of depression due to the realization that circumstantially it cannot be done.

When a yogi understands that he/she is not absolute, that conclusion will cause a need for understanding the workings of fate. What/Who controls it? Can a yogi design geographic and social conditions?

Putting aside the urgency, how can a yogi make progress even though circumstances do not yield to his needs? Why is a yogi not facilitated in every instance of a yogic method which if practiced would yield enlightenment about his personSelf?

Due to political and social conditions, a yogi may not afford to be alone. His living conditions may be in an area that is hostile to silent meditation. If he goes to a remote region, he may encounter predatory animals. There may be nuisance insects. A disease may be prevalent. People may be hostile. There may be insufficient food.

This instruction of Krishna for a yogi to be in a clean place, where he fixes for himself a firm seat which is not too high, not too low, with a covering layer of cloth, antelope skin and *kusha* grass underneath, is ideal.

तत्रैकाग्रं मनः कृत्वा
यतचित्तेन्द्रियक्रियः ।
उपविश्यासने युञ्ज्याद्
योगमात्मविशुद्धये ॥६.१२॥

tatraikāgraṁ manaḥ kṛtvā
yatacittendriyakriyaḥ
upaviśyāsane yuñjyād
yogamātmaviśuddhaye (6.12)

tatraikāgraṁ = tatra — there + ekāgram — single-focused; manaḥ — mind; kṛtvā — having made; yatacittendriyakriyaḥ = yata - controlled + citta — thought + indriyakriyaḥ — sense energy; upaviśyāsane = upaviśya — seating himself + āsane — in a posture; yuñjād = yuñjāt — should practice; yogamātmaviśuddhaye = yogam — to yoga discipline + ātma — self + viśuddhaye — to purification

...being there, seated in a posture, having the mind focused, the person who controls his thinking and sensual energy, should practice the yoga discipline for self-purification. (Bhagavad Gītā 6.12)

Analysis

For such focus of the mind, one must be away from sensual attractions and alarms. Both, positive and negative features which attract one's attention from the meditative objective cause failure in meditation practice. The control of the thinking and sensual energy is a must for successful meditation.

The objective is self-purification which means a cataloging of the aspects of psychology and bringing the various adjuncts and energies to order for the discovery of the coreSelf and the drafting of its relationship with its adjuncts.

The sitting posture is important. Even that should be assumed with intention to use the least amount of attention for its maintenance. It should not disturb the yogi. It should not cause cramps or discomfort. It should be a pose which is easy, in which the yogi develops inner sensitivity.

Comprehension of Bhagavad Gītā Verse 6.12

Once a yogi decides to meditate with intentions to research the inner aspects of the personSelf, he/she should sit or recline in an easy pose. The mind should be inspected to be sure that it no longer indulges impulsively in thinking, analysis and visualization which does not concern the object of the practice. Efforts should be made to stop the mind from its attempts to reach the external environment. Even the mind's reach for memories should cease.

After inspecting the area of the mind, and getting everything in order, the yogi/yogini should focus on the objective which is practiced according to the progress in the last session. The journey of withdrawing the senses from their objects, continues to the realization that the mind is resistant to being controlled. There is also the fact that the coreSelf is addicted to the mental operations even some which are detrimental to the core.

Sooner or later, the yogi should advance to confront the core. This is research into the quality of the core and to understand how the adjuncts attract the core and through that, bring the core under spells.

समं कायशिरोग्रीवं
धारयन्नचलं स्थिरः ।
संप्रेक्ष्य नासिकाग्रं स्वं
दिशश्चानवलोकयन् ॥६.१३॥

samaṁ kāyaśirogrīvaṁ
dhārayannacalaṁ sthiraḥ
saṁprekṣya nāsikāgraṁ svaṁ
diśaścānavalokayan (6.13)

samam — balanced; kāyaśirogrīvaṁ = kāya — body + śiro (śiraḥ) — head + grīvam — neck; dhārayan — holding; acalam — without movement; sthiraḥ — steady; saṁprekṣya — gazing at; nāsikāgraṁ = nāsikā — nostril + agram — tip; svam — own; diśaścānavalokayan = diśaḥ — the directions + ca — and + anavalokayan — not looking

Holding the body, head and neck in balance, steady without movement, gaze at the tip of the nose, not looking in any other direction. (Bhagavad Gītā 6.13)

Analysis

The specific posture recommended in the time of Krishna, was the *padmasana* lotus pose. Yogis at that time were accustomed to sitting in that position. If done with ease, it facilitates the practice because the physical system remains upright and balanced, because of having no tension in the legs and thighs, and no vertebra under lateral stress.

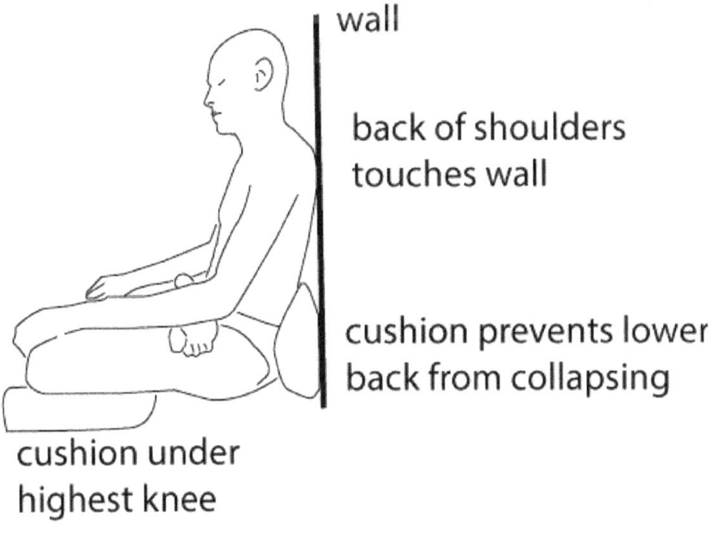
wall
back of shoulders touches wall
cushion prevents lower back from collapsing
cushion under highest knee

Currently many yogis have bodies which are tense, and which are pained and cramped when assuming the lotus posture. A modern yogi may recline or use a cushioned seat in which there is the least stress caused by sitting for fifteen or thirty minutes, or more, without changing the posture.

The physical and psychological focus of gazing between the eyebrows is a preliminary practice which cause the yogi to develop resistance towards and command of the mental operations which are hostile to meditation.

The task of gazing between the eyebrows is physical to some extent. Yet, it disciplines the mind, making it near impossible for the mind to drum up ideas and images for indulgence. Doing this practice, a yogi develops dictatorial power over the intellect.

Comprehension of Bhagavad Gītā Verse 6.13

When sitting to meditate where the spine is erect, the vertebrate should be balanced one on the other with the natural curve of the back and without weight tension due to misalignment.

For those who cannot sit at ease with feet resting on thighs, some other pose may be assumed, even that of a position where the body is reclined. Meditation is not sleep. Postures in which sleep is assumed should be avoided.

The eyes as well as their interest in seeing things outside the physical body, should be suspended during the meditation. The interest of the self should be the discovery of internal events, with the need for external interactions being suspended during the session.

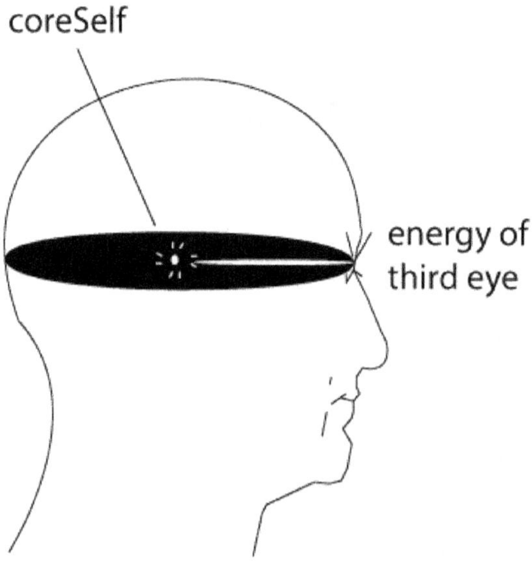

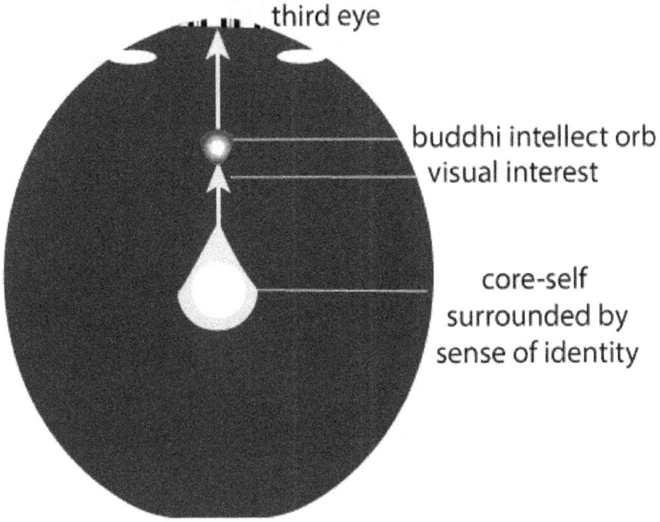
third eye
buddhi intellect orb
visual interest
core-self
surrounded by
sense of identity

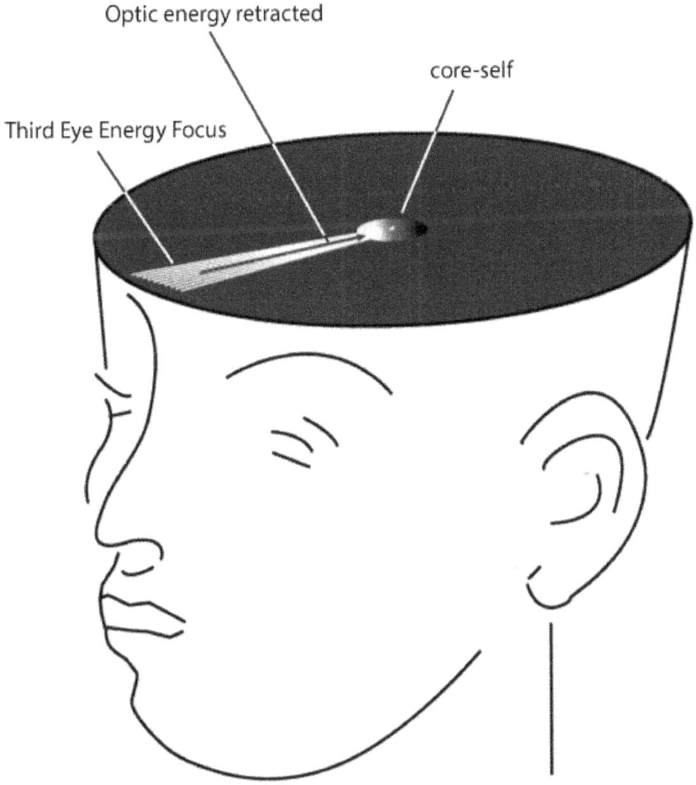
Optic energy retracted
core-self
Third Eye Energy Focus

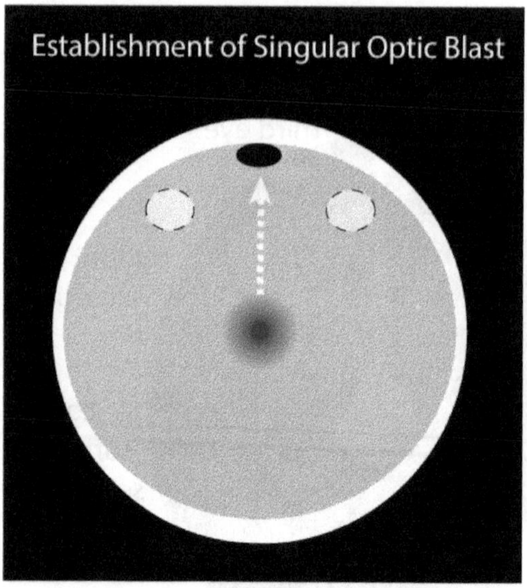

By focusing vision energy to the top of the nose between the eyebrows, the vision sense is tasked with an objective which makes it near to impossible for the mind to generate thoughts. Once the yogi practices this procedure at length, he/she develops confidence that the mind can be subdued.

प्रशान्तात्मा विगतभीर्
ब्रह्मचारिव्रते स्थितः ।
मनः संयम्य मच्चित्तो
युक्त आसीत मत्परः ॥६.१४॥

praśāntātmā vigatabhīr
brahmacārivrate sthitaḥ
manaḥ saṁyamya maccitto
yukta āsīta matparaḥ (6.14)

praśāntātmā = praśānta — pacified + ātmā — self; vigatabhīr (vigatabhīḥ) =vigata - gone away + bhīḥ — fear; brahmacārivrate — in the vow of sexual restraint; sthitaḥ — established; manaḥ — mind; saṁyamya — controlling; maccitto = maccittaḥ — though fixed on Me; yukta — disciplined; āsīta — should sit; matparaḥ — devoted to Me

With a pacified self, free from fears, with a vow of sexual restraint firmly practised, with mind controlled and having Me in his thought with his mind concentrated, he should sit, being devoted to Me as the Supreme Objective. (Bhagavad Gītā 6.14)

Analysis

The search for the coreSelf begins by hearing of it or suspecting that it may exist. There are two exceptions:

- The person who is spiritually realized and knows himself/herself as the core.
- The person who suspects that there is no core but who wants conclusive evidence either for or against its existence.

Some other persons on the spiritual path are unconcerned about the coreSelf. These are interested not in the self but in the supreme being. They neglect the search for the core and pursue information and experience with intentions of meeting the Supreme Person.

In this Chapter six of *Bhagavad Gītā*, Krishna began with an explanation of self-purification (verse 6.12), having to do not with the person whom he presented as the Supreme Person, Himself, but with the limited self who is currently a social function in the physical world. Hence the quest for self-discovery is itself the start of the Krishna recommended path.

Krishna required that the person should elevate himself and not act in a way as if he/she was the enemy of the self. First one must discover the personSelf of the self, then one can better appreciate other selves including the supreme one.

Comprehension of Bhagavad Gītā Verse 6.14

Having this information from Krishna about the durability of the core, a yogi should begin by becoming pacified as instructed by Krishna in some preceding verses. This means being mostly resistant to the thoughts and suggestions which are presented in the mind to the self, energies which usually hypnotize the self and cause it to endorse self-destructive ideas.

Attaining that in meditation by ceasing the mind's involuntary actions, the yogi becomes free from the fears of sensual harassment. In this verse Krishna mentioned a vow of sexual restraint which is firmly practiced. First one must make such a vow to a teacher or deity. Then one must practice it firmly but not fanatically. Because sexual attraction is compelling, the vow to the teacher or deity is required. In resisting lust, one should take help from a teacher. One must know or be advised as to when one should not be celibate.

With the mind controlled in meditation and also in external dealings, and remembering Krishna's instruction in *Bhagavad Gītā*, consulting teachers who are consistent with his advice, a yogi should sit to meditate with the idea that Krishna is the Supreme Objective which begins with research into one's coreSelf.

यत्रोपरमते चित्तं
निरुद्धं योगसेवया ।
यत्र चैवात्मनात्मानं
पश्यन्नात्मनि तुष्यति ॥६.२०॥

yatroparamate cittaṁ
niruddhaṁ yogasevayā
yatra caivātmanātmānaṁ
paśyannātmani tuṣyati (6.20)

yatroparamate = yatra — where + uparamate — it stops; cittaṁ — thinking; niruddhaṁ — restraint; yogasevayā = yoga — yoga discipline + sevayā — by practice; yatra — where; caivātmanā = ca — and + eva — indeed + ātmanā — by the self; 'tmānaṁ = ātmānam — the self; paśyan — seeing; ātmani — in the self; tuṣyati — is satisfied

At the place where being restrained by yoga practice, thinking stops, and at the place where the yogi perceives the self by the self, he is satisfied in the self. (Bhagavad Gītā 6.20)

Analysis

It is important to understand that when resolving the issue of a perpetual person, location is important. Even with abstract reality or with psychic stuffs, there is location. It is not a position in the physical sense but it is referenced and positioned anyway. If one is disinclined to keep tabs on abstract places, it is because of being familiar with physical solidity. Since the nature-given reference which began as a baby, is the physical body, that must be uprooted by the yogi. He must transfer his allegiance to the subtle side. He should uproot his markers from the physical side and implant them in the psychic reality.

It is not sufficient to cease the thinking/imaging displays of the mind. A yogi should define this further by knowing the location of the thinking/imaging displays, as well as the subtle organ which does the ideation. He should know where in the mind space he becomes aware of the core. He should gage the feelings derived.

Comprehension of Bhagavad Gītā Verse 6.20

There will be a struggle in the mind. There will be confusion of objective. There will be misunderstanding of the instructions of Krishna. Due to beginning with incorrect information, which was given freely by nature at the onset of the body, a yogi will inevitably start this mystic research with much misunderstanding.

What Krishna explained is the best information but for the beginner it is only that. It is knowledge. It is not the experience of the student. The student begins with incorrect views, misunderstanding and confidence in concepts which initially one has no experience of. Krishna knows what he described. However, that does not mean that one can know the same factors experientially merely by reading Krishna's statements.

One must work in the mind during the meditation sessions to gain the clarity. One must shock treat the mind to cause it to fragment so that one can see its parts and understand how they are inter-related to each other, and how they keep the self in ignorance of events in the psyche.

During the meditation sessions, after one successfully influences the mind to cease its external interest, one should mark the place where thinking is restrained, where it ceases. This is a mental location only, but it is vital for recognizing the intellect, which is the psychic organ which displays thoughts. The viewer is not the thinking gadget. It must cease identifying itself as if it is its thoughts. The viewer is not the display which the viewer sees. By tagging where the mental displays occur, and then referencing where the viewer coreSelf is located, one will have some idea about the location of intellect and the position of the core.

From this one learns where to be self-aware and where to retract the interest of the coreSelf in the psyche. It is one achievement to retract interest from what is outside of the psyche, outside of the subtle body. It is a deeper more advanced achievement to retract the energy of the coreSelf within the psyche into the core. This also includes retracting the interest of the coreSelf from the intellect, where the core has no interest in the ideas or images the intellect displays.

cross-section of subtle head

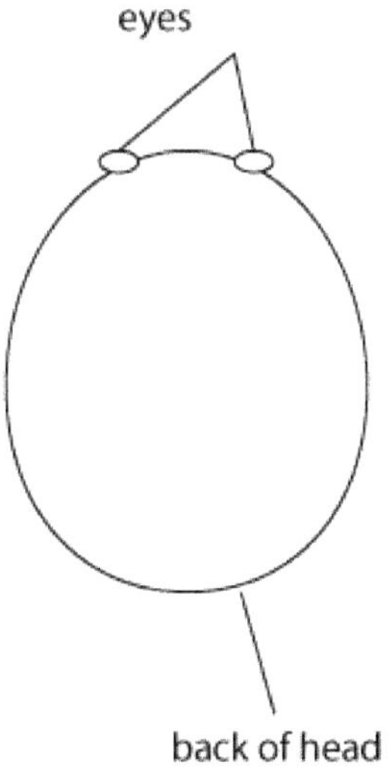

normal human being, entity experiences psyche as self
entity pursues things which are not within its psyche

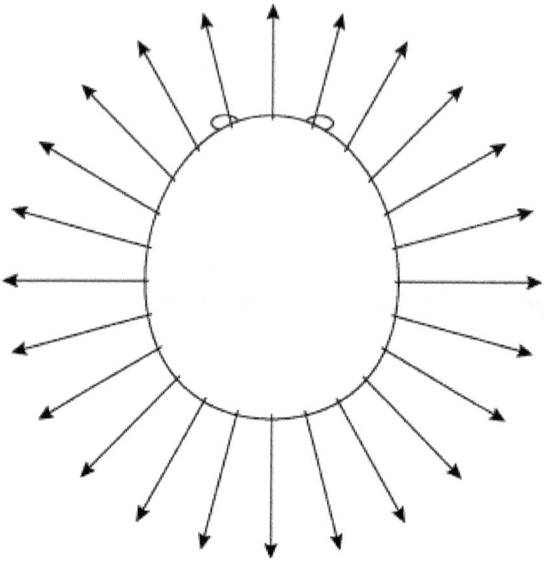

student yogi who experiences psyche as the self,
begins pratyahar sensual energy withdrawal
by pulling in sensual energies into the subtle edge of psyche

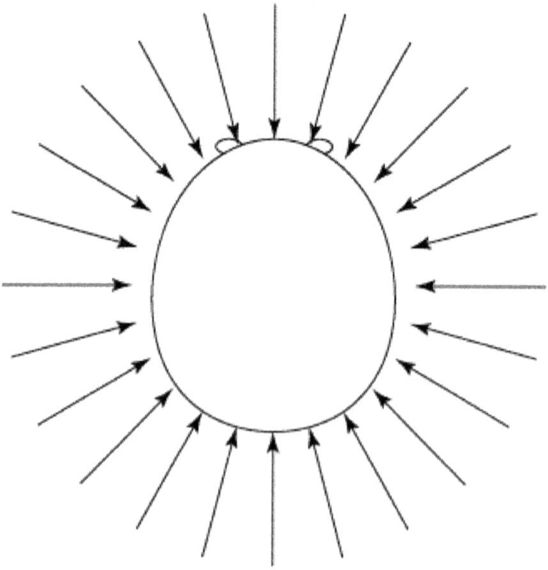

advancing a little the student revises the definiton of the self
to be something which exist in the psyche
and which is only one component of the psyche
this student feels that the self is the core of the psyche

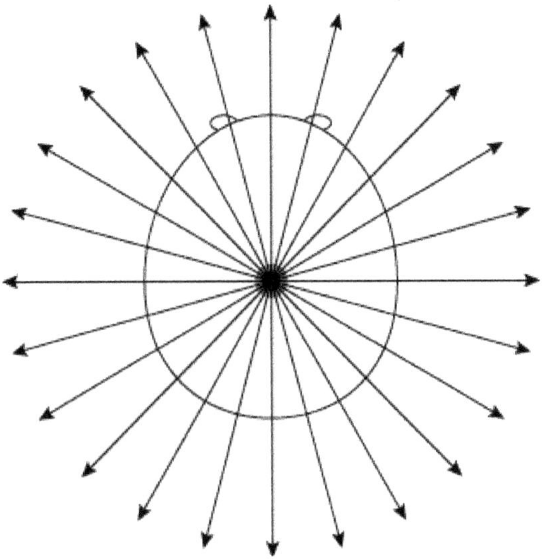

experiencing the self as the core of the psyche
this student practices withdrawal of sensual energy
by pulling all energy which he or she experiences
to be coursing outwards away from the core-self

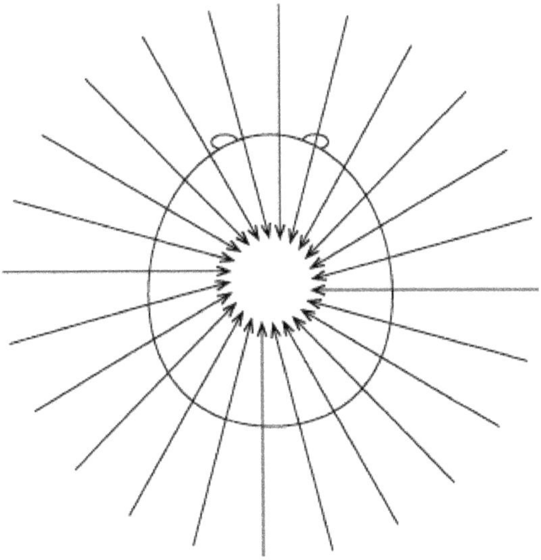

सुखमात्यन्तिकं यत्तद्
बुद्धिग्राह्यमतीन्द्रियम् ।
वेत्ति यत्र न चैवायं
स्थितश्चलति तत्त्वतः ॥६.२१॥

sukhamātyantikaṁ yattad
buddhigrāhyamatīndriyam
vetti yatra na caivāyaṁ
sthitaścalati tattvataḥ (6.21)

sukham — happiness; ātyantikaṁ — continuous; yat = yad — which; tad — this; buddhigrāhyam — grasp by the intellect; atīndriyam — beyond the mundane senses; vetti — he knows; yatra — whereabout; na — not; caivāyam = ca — and + eva — indeed + ayam — this; sthitaścalati = sthitaḥ — established + calati — he shifted; tattvataḥ — the reality

He knows the whereabouts of that continuous happiness, which is grasped by the intellect, and which is beyond the mundane senses. And being established, he does not shift from that reality. (Bhagavad Gītā 6.21)

Analysis

The continuous happiness is a transcendental experience of a higher grade than the normal happiness experienced as a physical body. A yogi may experience it in meditation, but it may happen infrequently which may discourage the yogi from practicing. It is not that during every session, the yogi will experience this and will be encouraged by it.

Since the continuous happiness will not be frequent for many students, there has to be a staying experience which encourages the yogi to practice day after day, even if the experience in the mind is a blank state with no sublime joy.

A yogi must realize that he/she should stick to the practice and remain in the blank state in anticipation of eventually attaining the continuous happiness which is desired.

The switch from a thought impelling mind to that of continuous happiness based on being the coreSelf, has a delay in it, a blank state. A student yogi is apt to be stalled in the blank state instead of switching from a thought ridden mental condition directly with no blank to the continuous happiness condition.

Some persons who read *Bhagavad Gītā* get the idea that the switch from a thought impelling mind to that of the spiritual happiness is instant with no transition state. Some others feel that if they think along the lines of the *Bhagavad Gītā*, even without meditation they will be in that happiness state and trashy thinking will be suspended automatically. Some persons think that if they think about Krishna and remember the scriptural stories about his life, they will have the continuous happiness as the base of consciousness. These views are imaginary.

What happens is that when someone enters the mind and finds thoughts arising, there is a struggle to shut down the thinking system. If one shifts to thinking about and remembering the scriptural stories about Krishna, that becomes only an over-coating in the thinking apparatus. The mundane ideas and memories continue with an overcoating of the Krishna related memories and mental constructions. That does not remove the unwanted thinking of the mind. It only creates an overcoating, like a painted surface being covered by another coat of paint. The undercoat remains, nevertheless.

The meditation which Krishna described is for the removal, not over-coating, of the pesty thinking of the mind. When that is removed and there is nothing in the mind, no thoughts of anything, not even of Krishna stories, that condition is the blank mind. From that if the meditation shifts to the continuous happiness, the yogi is successful. Otherwise, if the mind only remains in the blank condition and does not shift to the continuous happiness, the yogi is partially successful. He should not be discouraged and should not be influenced to think that this blank condition is unwanted.

The yogi should train himself to remain in the blank state and wait for the arrival of the continuous happiness sublime state. Much patience is required for this. Substituting thoughts about Krishna will not help the yogi. It will not cause the transfer to the continuous happiness nor to the spiritual place where Krishna is resident.

For this meditation, thinking of Krishna, violates his instruction. It will further delay the access to the continuous happiness state. It will make it longer before the yogi can access that sublime level. This is due to the fact, that thinking involves the use of the intellect, which should be silenced.

At the place where being restrained by yoga practice, thinking stops, and at the place where the yogi perceives the self by the self, he is satisfied in the self. (Bhagavad Gītā 6.20)

In this respect one should adhere to what Krishna said about the location where thinking ceases. That pertains to all thinking, which includes thinking about Krishna even. The idea or the suggestion that thinking of Krishna will move one to a transcendental level is misleading in this case.

Why?

Because the idea about ceasing the thinking refers not to the thinking but to the use of the intellect. It has to do with curtailing the use of the intellect and unlinking the intellect from the coreSelf, so that the core is free from the hypnotic influence of the intellect. Using the intellect to think about Krishna is still use of the intellect. This gives power to the intellect, so that the effort to disable it, is frustrated by any thinking, even thinking about Krishna.

It is important to follow the instructions of Krishna in the *Bhagavad Gītā*, rather than to comply with the Krishna teachers who are against meditation as it is described in the very *Bhagavad Gītā* which they recommend.

The idea of Krishna, his suggestion about the place where thinking ceases, is mentioned by Patanjali in the Yoga Sutras.

योगश्चित्तवृत्तिनिरोधः ॥२॥
yogaḥcittavṛtti nirodhaḥ

yogaḥ – the skill of yoga; cittavṛtti = citta – mento-emotional energy + vṛtti – vibrational mode; nirodhaḥ – cessation, restraint, non-operation.

The skill of yoga is demonstrated by the conscious non-operation of the vibrational modes of the mento-emotional energy. (Yoga Sutras 1.2)

This never meant that one should operate the vibrational modes of the mento-emotional energy to remember and think of Krishna. Meditation as explained by Krishna and as suggested by Patanjali, is as described. Thinking and considering the scriptural stories of Krishna is a separate practice which does not replace nor make redundant or unnecessary the meditation procedure.

Comprehension of Bhagavad Gītā Verse 6.21

There are various types of happiness experienced by any human being. The one described by Krishna, which should occur if a self abandons physical interests, moves to a blank state of mind devoid of thinking and imaging, and transits to one of continuous happiness, is a specific level of awareness. Krishna earmarked it further, as being grasped by the intellect but being beyond the physical senses.

This means that this happiness cannot be seen by the physical eyes. It cannot be heard by the physical ears. It cannot be touched by the physical skin. It cannot be smelt by the nostrils. It cannot be tasted by the tongue. However, it can be experienced by the intellect, which is the image producing, thought-displaying adjunct of the self.

That sublime happiness is steady, continuous and ongoing on its level of awareness. It is uninterrupted. It pulses continually. The yogi, once he/she makes contact with it, rates its location when becoming aware of its spread.

तं विद्याद्दुःखसंयोग -
वियोगं योगसंज्ञितम् ।
स निश्चयेन योक्तव्यो
योगोऽनिर्विण्णचेतसा ॥६.२३॥

taṁ vidyādduḥkha-saṁyoga -
viyogaṁ yogasaṁjñitam
sa niścayena yoktavyo
yogo'nirviṇṇacetasā (6.23)

tam — this; vidyād = vidyāt — let it be understood; duḥkhasaṁyoga = duḥkha — emotional distress + saṁyoga — emotional identity with; viyogaṁ — separation; yogasaṁjñitam = yoga — mastery of yoga + saṁjñitam — recognized as; sa = saḥ — this; niścayena — with determination; yoktavyo = yoktavyaḥ — to be practiced; yogo = yogah — yoga; 'nirviṇṇacetasā (anirviṇṇacetasā) = anirviṇṇa — not depressed + cetasā — with thought

Let it be understood that this separation from emotional distress is the mastery of yoga. This yoga is to be practiced with determination and without depressing thought. (Bhagavad Gītā 6.23)

Analysis

The reformation of the intellect where it no longer presents ideas and images to the coreSelf during the meditation session, is a highlight for yogis. The struggle for power in the mind happened from the dawn of time. It will continue into the foreseeable future. One or two yogis will be successful at ceasing the involuntary and undesirable harassments of the intellect. Others must keep fighting the adjuncts until their independence is forfeited by the coreSelf.

The emotional distress, the trauma which bleeds from events, should not reach a yogi. If it does, he is not in the advanced stage of practice and must strive more efficiently. He must be detailed to know the parts of the psyche which cause him to indulge uncontrollably.

When a yogi sees his lack of control of the intellect, he may take steps to detach himself from the services of that adjunct. This will cause the development of detachment where he may ignore the intellect, which would result in resistance to it.

Comprehension of Bhagavad Gītā Verse 6.23

Emotional distress is complicated. The origin of any particular emotional feeling is so complex that to figure its origin is a masterful task that would require many types of mystic investigation. We know however that we get happiness and distress from emotional fluctuation.

The startling side of these experiences which is unwanted are the unpleasant emotions. To eliminate these one should practice yogic meditation, where the intellect is confined so that by steady practice, it is no longer free to conjure thoughts, ideas, and memories. There is an objection where someone feels that in meditation it should be possible to render pleasant emotions and to restrict and block the unpleasant venues.

However, the way the psyche is designed if one only blocks the unpleasant mento-emotional experiences, one will find that one lacks the power to end all unpleasant ones. The issue is not the emotions but the rendering act of the intellect. That adjunct must be curtailed in all its actions, not just its unpleasant ones.

As Krishna said, this separation from emotional distress by disabling the intellect during meditation, is the mastery of yoga, which is to be practiced with determination to achieve full control. While practicing one should not give in to any depressing thought or energy. Otherwise, the meditation effort will collapse. One will again be subjugated by the intellect.

यतो यतो निश्चरति मनश्चञ्चलमस्थिरम् । ततस्ततो नियम्यैतद् आत्मन्येव वशं नयेत् ॥६.२६॥	yato yato niścarati manaścañcalamasthiram tatastato niyamyaitad ātmanyeva vaśaṁ nayet (6.26)

yato yato = yataḥ yataḥ — wherever; niścarati — wanders away; manaścañcalam = manas — mind + cañcalam — drifting; asthiram — unsteady; tatastato = tatastataḥ — from there; niyamyaitad = niyamya — restrain + etad — it; ātmany (ātmani) — in the self; eva — indeed; vaśam — control; nayet — should direct

To wherever the unsteady, drifty mind wanders, from there he should restrain it. He should direct the mind to control it in the self. (Bhagavad Gītā 6.26)

Analysis

Initially Krishna gave the instruction for the abrupt cessation of the thoughts and ideas generated by the mind. Then he indicated that it is not that easy to bring the mind under absolute control.

There will be a struggle during meditation. It concerns two factors.

- the thought generating psychic mechanism
- the observing self

Initially it will be the observing self which in the compartment of the mind, will endeavor to seize control from the thought generating mechanism which is the intellect. However, for one who is not accustomed to this practice, there will only be a mind space and a struggle in it for the cessation of ideas.

Most students begin meditation practice with no distinct and clear experience of an observing self which is separate to the thinking produced in the mind. It may take weeks or years of practice to get the clarity where one knows in the mind and sees in it, that the intellect is one factor, an adjunct and the iSelf is another factor as the principle which is in the mind as a viewer as opposed to the principle in the mind which is the displayer of ideas.

A man in a theatre may lose track of himself as an individual apart from the actors in the movie, where when one actor points a weapon at the audience, the man gets cold sweat feeling that he will be killed. In fact, if the gun is fired and an explosive sound is heard, the spectator may jerk as if he was targeted.

Comprehension of Bhagavad Gītā Verse 6.26

Krishna's admittance that during meditation the yogi's mind will drift, indicates that he knew this annoyance will be a problem for student yogis, who may become frustrated when trying to experience the continuous spiritual happiness.

The question is. How long will one make meditation attempts before the unsteady drifting mind ceases its spontaneous behavior? The yogi should restrain the mind but if he cannot do that, if the mind continues shifting and presenting attractive ideas, what should he/she do? How should he/she feel? Where will he/she derive confidence to continue with one failed meditation session after another.

The method of reforming the haphazard conjuring of the mind, is making the attempt to control its displays, and to do so repeatedly in one meditation after another. This causes the yogi to observe how the mind conjures the presentations. A yogi must also study the strength of each display, to understand why each has varying powers of dominance.

Some displays vanish as soon as the yogi makes the decision to suppress them. Other presentations stand their ground and remain operating, even gaining strength. The more the yogi tries to terminate them, the more they exert a viewing power over the self. The self feels pained because it cannot escape their influence.

A yogi should direct the mind to control thinking within the psyche. It does not matter what happens outside the rim of the mind. The yogi should be concerned with the coreSelf, the mind environment, and the thought producing mechanism.

Even if the mind conjures a memory, that is shown by the intellect. Memories have no visibility if they are not entertained by and illustrated by the intellect. Hence it is the relationship in the mind of the coreSelf and the intellect which causes the core to control or to be dominated by the intellect.

प्रशान्तमनसं ह्येनं
योगिनं सुखमुत्तमम् ।
उपैति शान्तरजसं
ब्रह्मभूतमकल्मषम् ॥६.२७॥

praśāntamanasaṁ hyenaṁ
yoginaṁ sukhamuttamam
upaiti śāntarajasaṁ
brahmabhūtamakalmaṣam (6.27)

praśāntamanasaṁ = praśānta — psychologically pacified + manasaṁ — mind; hyenaṁ = hy (hi) — indeed + enam — him; yoginaṁ — yogi; sukham — happiness; uttamam — superior; upaiti — experiences; śāntarajasaṁ = śānta — calmed + rajasam — emotion; brahmabhūtam — spiritual level; akalmaṣam — free from bad tendencies

Indeed, being psychologically pacified, the yogi, whose emotions are calmed, who is on the spiritual plane, who is free from bad tendencies, experiences superior happiness. (Bhagavad Gītā 6.27)

Analysis

The result in meditation of being in the superior happiness, spiritual bliss, does not become consistent until the student becomes psychologically pacified. This is a big issue because it may take years of meditation before a student comes to terms with his mento-emotional energies and their contrary operations.

Sudden rapid success in this practice is unlikely. That is perhaps why some teachers of *bhakti* yoga stated that the only way to control the mind is to think of Krishna and verbally praise, adore, and address Krishna. They abolish these instructions from Krishna about meditation. Instead, they present the path of hearing and chanting of the glories of Krishna as the prime solution to any mental problem.

For this yoga explained by Krishna, these achievements are required.

- emotions calmed
- shift to the spiritual plane
- being free from bad tendencies
- being psychologically pacified

How does one **calm the emotions** during meditation and also have the effects of such calming manifest when one does not meditate?

How does one shift from physical focus and from mental compulsions which are contrary to meditation? How does one do this and **shift to the spiritual plane** where one experiences continuous transcendental happiness?

How does one **become free from bad tendencies**? First of all, what is the list of faults. If these are deep-seated, how can one totally eliminate them?

Since there are so many potential desires and it will take time to fulfil these, since some of these are currently unknown to the yogi, how will he **become psychologically pacified**?

Comprehension of Bhagavad Gītā Verse 6.27

When this practice is successful, the yogi will have no experiences where in the mind, he/she is unable to control the thinking, imaging, illustrating feature of the intellect.

Some presentations of the mind will be persistent. Some will be resistant. Still the yogi can apply a force of control to cease the unwanted operations. The mind will be brought to a standstill in so far as its power over the self is weakened. This happens after the yogi figures the design of the mind, its configuration, its components and their interrelationships.

Because the yogi went to the trouble to painstakingly practice mind control, because the yogi studied the operation of his/her individual mental space and its components, the power over the mind is factual. It works because it is tailored to the individual's mind and is specific for the yogi.

युञ्जन्नेवं सदात्मानं
योगी विगतकल्मषः ।
सुखेन ब्रह्मसंस्पर्शम्
अत्यन्तं सुखमश्नुते ॥६.२८॥

yuñjannevaṁ sadātmānaṁ
yogī vigatakalmaṣaḥ
sukhena brahmasaṁsparśam
atyantaṁ sukhamaśnute (6.28)

yuñjan — applying yoga disciplines; evaṁ — thus; sadā — constantly; 'tmānaṁ = ātmānam — the self; yogī — yogi; vigatakalmaṣaḥ — free from faults; sukhena — easily; brahmasaṁsparśam — constanting the spiritual plane; atyantaṁ — endless; sukham — happiness; aśnute — attains

Applying the yoga disciplines constantly to the self, the yogi being freed from faults, easily contacting the spiritual plane, attains endless happiness. (Bhagavad Gītā 6.28)

Analysis

The yoga practice must be regular and consistent. Over time, there will be success. *Patience! Patience! Patience!* Those who want instant results may or may not get that. One must be determined. One must yield to slow progress. Progression may be in increments with some acceleration occurring.

It is more than a matter of rapidly reaching the spiritual plane to enjoy the endless happiness. Before one can be switched to a supernatural level, one must confront faults in the psyche. One must rid the self of these. It takes time for this. It takes persistence with effective methods which one discovers, or which one is taught by an advanced yogi.

Comprehension of Bhagavad Gītā Verse 6.28

Repeated practice is necessary. One should not expect instant success. Even if one has sublime experiences, it will be that one returns to the normal level of consciousness where previous tendencies arise and command the psyche to operate in a spiritually incompatible way.

The yoga disciplines are for application to the psyche and its contents. The relationship between the coreSelf and its adjuncts must be reconfigured with the core taking command of the intellect and keeping the mind clean of ideas and images during the meditation session and at other times.

It is not what the body does, as to its moral or immoral behavior. It is how the coreSelf acts, what the intellect renders and what the kundalini lifeForce induces. This yoga is a total interior regulation.

सर्वभूतस्थमात्मानं
सर्वभूतानि चात्मनि ।
ईक्षते योगयुक्तात्मा
सर्वत्र समदर्शनः ॥६.२९॥

sarvabhūtasthamātmānaṁ
sarvabhūtāni cātmani
īkṣate yogayuktātmā
sarvatra samadarśanaḥ (6.29)

sarvabhūtastham — existing in all mundane creature forms; ātmānaṁ — spirit; sarvabhūtāni — all creatures; cātmani = ca — see + ātmani — in the self; īkṣate — he sees; yogayuktātmā — one who is proficient in yoga; sarvatra — in all cases; samadarśanaḥ — seeing the same

With a spirit existing in every creature, and with every creature based on a spirit, a person who is proficient in yoga, perceives the same existential arrangement in all cases. (Bhagavad Gītā 6.29)

Analysis

A yogi must on occasion abandon isolation. He/She must socialize from time to time. When this happens, a relationship is activated on the basis of the yogi's social profile in society. Should a yogi revise his idea of people as he advances? Should his self-perception be adjusted?

As a yogi shifts more and more from being a mere body, to being a psyche which is saturated with consciousness on one or the other level, that yogi will adjust his relationship with ordinary people. When he is isolated, it does not matter what his view of sociology is. However, as soon as he encounters others, he must decide on what basis and with what general consideration, he should associate.

To maintain the physical body, for its food, clothing, and residence, he may have to relate to others who may be farmers, cloth manufacturers and property owners. He may have to meet the demands of ordinary people. How should the yogi consider others?

What about animals? Before, they were considered to be inferior creatures. Now that the yogi has insight into the coreSelf which is not the physical body, how would the yogi relate to a dog or cat? Would he give it the same respect which humans deserve?

Comprehension of Bhagavad Gītā Verse 6.29

At present what is obvious to the majority of human beings is that there is a person existing as a living physical body. Some others include animals, to say that there is a person existing in every living animal or human body. Others include vegetation, with each plant, animal, and human as a person.

This is given value by Krishna but with the understanding that it is not the physical body which is the person but there is a psychic factor which is related to the physical system, and which is the person. Krishna pins this person as the enduring factor in the psyche.

Krishna increases our depth perception by stating that there is a spirit existing in every creature and that every such creature is based on a spirit, so that for there to be a living form, there must be an enduring psychic presence.

The existential arrangement is such that it is similar in each case of each living body, in that there is the physical body, which is interspaced with psychic energy which has an enduring person as inner radiance.

An ascetic must develop this vision of the psyches and their similar components. There is the personSelf. There is the intellect, memory, and kundalini lifeForce. Each living body has these psychic factors. Mind control involves realizing this through inner search in meditation.

अर्जुन उवाच योऽयं योगस्त्वया प्रोक्तः साम्येन मधुसूदन । एतस्याहं न पश्यामि चञ्चलत्वात्स्थितिं स्थिराम् ॥६.३३॥	arjuna uvāca yo'yaṁ yogastvayā proktaḥ sāmyena madhusūdana etasyāhaṁ na paśyāmi cañcalatvātsthitiṁ sthirām (6.33)

Arjuna — Arjuna; uvāca — said; yo = yah — who; 'yaṁ = ayaṁ — this; yogas — yoga practices; tvayā — by you; proktaḥ — explained; sāmyena — by comparative similarity; madhusūdana — O slayer of Madhu; etasyāhaṁ = etasyā — of this + aham — I; na — not; paśyāmi — see; cañcalatvāt — due to shiftiness; sthitiṁ — position; sthirām — standard

Arjuna said: O slayer of Madhu, due to a shifty vision, I do not see this standard position of a comparatively similar view which is yielded by this yoga practice, declared by You. (Bhagavad Gītā 6.33)

Analysis

Arjuna honestly declared that whatever Krishna explained about the comparatively similar features of each creature form, was not perceptible. Krishna saw it but others do not have the view. For others each person is his/her body.

It is indicated in this verse that Arjuna did not have the result of the yoga practice Krishna described. However, in the *Mahabharata* literature, before this *Bhagavad Gītā* was spoken, Arjuna acquired some yoga proficiency. He was transferred to the *Swargaloka* angelic world and even defeated criminal sorcerers there.

Some feel that this verse indicates that Arjuna never did yoga but that is incorrect. Arjuna was an advanced yogi but somehow his yoga expertise was focused for gaining mystic weapons and for communicating with supernatural beings, who monitor and influence political history on this planet.

He was an advanced yogi but not in terms of inSelf clarity. When he mastered certain yoga practices, his intention was not to study the personal energies as described in this chapter six of *Bhagavad Gītā*.

It is an important hint, that one's motive in studying yoga will cause one to be restricted in what one gains from the practice.

Comprehension of Bhagavad Gītā Verse 6.33

The aforementioned method declared by Krishna was a special type of mysticism. The details of which were unknown to most warriors on the battlefield.

The *Mahabharata* literature describes that before the battle, Arjuna was instructed by his eldest brother, *Yudhishthira*, who was directed by the great yogi, Vyasa, who composed *Bhagavad Gita*. He gave *Yudhishthira* the yogic method, a mystic process, which *Yudhishthira* explained to Arjuna who went into isolation and mastered the procedure. Arjuna was transferred to a heavenly world where he learned the use of supernatural weapons. He defeated some psychic criminals whose presence empowered the Kauravas, Arjuna's hostile cousins.

What Krishna explained to Arjuna in this chapter was not explained to Arjuna before. He had no coherence about it in that lifetime up to that point. He admitted that it was new information. Without further explanation and supportive perception, he was not of a mind to grasp it.

प्रयत्नाद्यतमानस्तु
योगी संशुद्धकिल्बिषः ।
अनेकजन्मसंसिद्धस्
ततोयाति परां गतिम् ॥६.४५॥

prayatnādyatamānastu
yogī saṁśuddhakilbiṣaḥ
anekajanmasaṁsiddhas
tatoyāti parāṁ gatim (6.45)

prayatnāt — from steady effort; yatamānaḥ — consistently controlled; tu — but; yogī — yogi; saṁśuddha — thoroughly cleansed; kilbiṣaḥ — bad tendencies; anekajanmasaṁsiddhas = aneka — not one + janma — birth + saṁsiddhaḥ — perfected; tato = tataḥ — from then onwards; yāti — reaches; parāṁ — supreme; gatim — goal

From a steady effort and a consistently controlled mind, the yogi who is thoroughly cleansed of bad tendencies, who is perfected in many births, reaches the supreme goal. (Bhagavad Gītā 6.45)

Analysis

This is the dismal truth, that in time, with steady effort, and with a consistently controlled mind in meditation, a yogi who is perfected in many births, reaches the supreme goal which is to transcend this physical existence and its subtle basis and reach the spiritual dimensions.

The proposition for an easier method by another means is not proposed. In some commentaries of *Bhagavad Gītā*, alternate methods are given. For instance, chanting of holy names, especially of Krishna's name, is given as an easy and suitable method which does not entail the mental austerities described above. However, any process which does not give the result of the ascetic becoming perfected, is not useful in this case.

One should stick to the recommendation of Krishna and not follow teachers who present easy methods which gives confidence, but which do not yield the results described. If chanting Krishna's name is the method, the recommendations given to Arjun makes no sense. The proposal that Krishna gave this difficult method but came and shared an easier one in this era, is irrational. The reason is that in the current time, the mind, which is to be controlled, is similar to the mind which was used by Arjuna. The mind did not become easier to control. In fact, it is more difficult to control because it is exposed to more attractions due to the advances made in civilization.

If anything, one needs the same means or even a method that is more powerful, more difficult to master. If someone thinks that an easier method would work now when circumstances are more challenging and more resistant to self-discovery, that person has a perverse mentality and follows an illogical proposition.

One must realize that the Supreme Person, Krishna, was present to personally guide Arjuna. Still Arjuna with God before him did not at first understand and could not even visualize much of what Krishna described regarding the contents and construction of the psyche and its relation to its physical body. How then can someone, merely by calling Krishna's holy name, achieve the perception of the coreSelf who operates the psyche, which is the basis of formation of the physical body?

Comprehension of Bhagavad Gītā Verse 6.45

Many teachers list Krishna Consciousness as the supreme goal. However, in this verse what is described prior in this chapter six of *Bhagavad Gītā*, is listed as the objective. Why is this so?

It is because the basis for the perceptions is the self. One does not perceive because of the way the Supreme Person sees. We just had evidence of that, where Arjuna could not see as Krishna saw and described. Arjuna's sense perception was not the same as Krishna's. Until Arjuna's personal perception changed, he could not understand the Supreme Person. This is because the change must be made in Arjuna's psyche.

The Supreme Person is the ultimate individual. To perceive that an adjustment must be made in the being of a limited self. Unless the limited person's psyche is upgraded, he/she cannot perceive Krishna as the Supreme

One. Krishna established a hard truth, which may be realized after progress over a period of many births. One lifetime is insufficient for the attainment.

Bad tendencies must be ditched. The habits and urges which are counterproductive to elevation are deep-seated. These must be singled out in meditation. Chanting holy names, if that can cause someone during the chanting to focus internally, identify the unwanted traits and take psychological action to remove them, would be a suitable method. However, that is not what happens. Repeatedly we find that those who use the holy names for this cleansing become disappointed when after years of practicing, still the unwanted behaviors assert themselves.

Meditation is the only process of recognizing, identifying, isolating and mentally removing the unwanted spiritually stunting behaviors.

श्रीभगवानुवाच मय्यासक्तमनाः पार्थ योगं युञ्जन्मदाश्रयः । असंशयं समग्रं मां यथा ज्ञास्यसि तच्छृणु ।७.१॥	śrībhagavānuvāca mayyāsaktamanāḥ pārtha yogaṁ yuñjanmadāśrayaḥ asaṁśayaṁ samagraṁ māṁ yathā jñāsyasi tacchṛṇu (7.1)

śrībhagavān — the Blessed Lord; uvāca — said; mayy = mayi — in Me; āsaktamanāḥ — attention absorbed in; pārtha — O son of Pṛthā; yogam — yoga; yuñjan — practicing; madasrayah = mad — on me + āśrayah — being dependent; asaṁśayaṁ — without doubt; samagraṁ — fully; māṁ — Me; yathā — as; jñāsyasi — you will know; tac = tad — this; chṛṇ = śṛṇu — hear

The Blessed Lord said: With attention absorbed in Me, O son of Pṛthā, practicing yoga, being dependent on Me, you will know of Me fully without a doubt. Hear of this. (Bhagavad Gītā 7.1)

Analysis

At some stage, being honest about it, researching deeply into the origins of the factors which comprise the world, a yogi admits to himself/herself that he/she is limited, and is reliant on much, besides what he/she knows himself/herself to be.

Confidence in oneself is limited. Since as an individual person, in any definition of that, one is limited and is reliant on so many factors, one needs to supplement the self with reliance on other reliable factors. Here, there and everywhere, one must depend on other factors. It begins with physical existence. As a physical person, a limited body, one is reliant on an environment for support. As a psychic person, a limited psychic unit, one is reliant on subtle dimensions for support. Any which way one turns, one is confronted with a need for something somewhere, somehow.

Krishna suggested himself as the ultimate reference. Even so he mentioned the need for yoga practice for those who are dependent on him, who know of him, and whose attention is absorbed in him.

What we have of him in the form of *Bhagavad Gītā* is his information.

Comprehension of Bhagavad Gītā Verse 7.1

This verse itemizes what is required to benefit from Krishna.

- attention absorbed in Krishna
- practice of yoga as described in chapter six of *Bhagavad Gītā*
- dependence on Krishna
- knowing Krishna fully as he described
- harboring no doubts about his information

Practically speaking, having one's **attention absorbed in Krishna** may be done by reading *Bhagavad Gītā* and by being inspired by Krishna directly or by an agent.

The **practice of yoga as described in chapter six of *Bhagavad Gītā*** should be learnt from a teacher who agrees that there should be no adjustments. For instance, there should be no deletions where yoga is changed to mean something other than what Krishna described. Another powerful teacher who was present after the time of Krishna should not substitute some other process and delete nor erase the yoga Krishna taught in the *Bhagavad Gītā*.

There should be or it should be developed that one feels **dependence on Krishna**. Getting insight into the construction of the psyche, into its parts, and realizing how the coreSelf is related to the intellect, should cause the yogi to realize that he must take assistance from superior persons, especially from Krishna, the Supreme Lord. One should not be embarrassed to admit that one is a limited being, even one's coreSelf is limited.

Knowing Krishna fully as Krishna described, a yogi should study the Bhagavad Gītā and gain insight into the scope of Krishna's supremacy in relation to the physical world and the subtle dimensions. Much of what Krishna declared of himself cannot be verified immediately. However, there should be faith in Krishna, that what he says of himself is true for all time.

A yogi should **harbor no doubts about Krishna's information**. However, a yogi should not be a fanatic, where he feels that he understands and can explain every bit of Krishna's situations. Much of what Krishna said cannot be verified physically or psychically. Thus, a devotee should not pretend that anyone anywhere may get verifiable proof about the supremacy of Krishna.

ज्ञानं तेऽहं सविज्ञानम् इदं वक्ष्याम्यशेषतः । यज्ज्ञात्वा नेह भूयोऽन्यज् ज्ञातव्यमवशिष्यते ॥७.२.	jñānaṁ te'haṁ savijñānam idaṁ vakṣyāmyaśeṣataḥ yajjñātvā neha bhūyo'nyaj jñātavyamavaśiṣyate (7.2)

jñānam- information; te — to you; 'ham = aham -I; savijñānam — with experience; idam — this; vakṣyāmy(vakṣyāmi)- I will explain; aśeṣataḥ — without deleting anything; yaj = yad — which; jñātvā — having known; neha = na — not + iha — in this world; bhūyo = bhūyaḥ — further; 'nyaj = anyat — other; jñātavyam — to be discovered; avaśiṣyate — is left

I will explain the information and give the experience to you without deleting anything. Having known that, no other experience would be left to be discovered in this world. (Bhagavad Gītā 7.2)

Analysis

This promise about giving the experience, is particular to Arjuna. Others, without the experience being bestowed, may hear the information just as Arjuna did. How the individual mind interprets and utilizes the description, is a different matter. That depends on the level of consciousness, which relies on the psychic perception each person is capable of. It is by yoga practice, that one improves his/her consciousness, where one can follow Krishna's explanations by mystic penetration.

The information, without the experience being bestowed, will not render the experience. Mere confidence in Krishna without the experience of reality as he described, will not render direct perception of the abstract reality which Krishna directly perceives. This verse is particular to Arjuna and anyone who has the mystic experience which Krishna granted to Arjuna.

Comprehension of Bhagavad Gītā Verse 7.2

Krishna did not tell Arjuna, to repeat Krishna's name or say a mantra about Krishna. That may or may not be done. This information was spoken to Arjuna. It can be read by someone else. It may be heard by someone who listens to someone who reads it. However, unless one hears and understands the original Sanskrit, one must be sure that the translator does not distort it nor substitute contrary words and processes.

And even then, without the experience being bestowed, the information itself is not the complete communication. It lacks sensual access to the planes of consciousness in which one may directly access the truths of higher reality.

Much is left to be discovered if one has only the information. Worse yet, are those who get an adjusted version of what Krishna said. In the final analysis one needs the information directly from Krishna or from someone who renders it with no deviation. One must also have the experience, either bestowed by Krishna or by someone who is a divine being with access to the higher planes of consciousness and who could cause one's sensual focus to shift to higher levels.

भूमिरापोऽनलो वायुः
खं मनो बुद्धिरेव च ।
अहंकार इतीयं मे
भिन्ना प्रकृतिरष्टधा ॥७.४॥

bhūmirāpo'nalo vāyuḥ
khaṁ mano buddhireva ca
ahaṁkāra itīyaṁ me
bhinnā prakṛtiraṣṭadhā (7.4)

bhūmir = bhūmiḥ — solid substance; āpo = āpaḥ — liquid substance; 'nalo = analaḥ — flames; vāyuḥ — gas; kham — space; mano = manaḥ — mindal energy; buddhir = buddhiḥ — intelligence; eva — indeed; ca — and; ahaṁkāra — initiative; itīyam = iti — thus + iyam — this; me — My; bhinnā — apportioned; prakṛtir = prakṛtiḥ — mundane energy; aṣṭadhā — eight-sectioned

Solid substance, liquid substance, flame, gas, space, mindal energy, intelligence, and initiative are My apportioned, eight-sectioned mundane energy. (Bhagavad Gītā 7.4)

Analysis

This is a summary about what is not person substance. It includes even the abstract materials and apparatus, which are a necessary part of this situation. The tag of the person is its ability to observe but the observation may take place only under certain conditions. When those circumstances are absent, the observing capacity may become inoperative, which for the time being, means that the person is suspended as an objective being. It remains in existence then as a subjective something only.

The five lower aspects of the eight-sectioned mundane energy are materials which though reactive are not apparatus or adjuncts. The three higher aspects are adjuncts. These three are.

- mindal energy
- intelligence
- initiative

The **mindal energy** is also known as kundalini psychic lifeForce. The **Intelligence** is known as analytical illustrative ability or power of reasoning. The **initiative** is known as the sense of identity, the method of primitive grasping.

The adjuncts are the border between mere materials and personality. The personality can grasp any of the five materials when it uses an adjunct to handle a material. By itself the person cannot indulge in any of the five aspects. Communication between the person and the materials occurs through the medium of the adjuncts.

Comprehension of Bhagavad Gītā Verse 7.4

It is of interest that Krishna defined himself as the Supreme Person, the ultimate individual. Yet, he claims the five lower aspects and the three subtle ones as his apportioned eight-sectioned mundane energy. This is a self-award as the proprietor of everything mundane.

A relevant inquiry concerns the strength of Krishna's possessive hold on this. What is the benefit to the limited individual in knowing this? The limited person, unlike the Supreme Being, does not control the massive mundane energy. If anything, it may control a miniscule portion and may only do so momentarily.

What value is it, to a limited self, to know that Krishna owns these materials and psychic adjuncts? Our experience is that we are dominated by the environment and made to serve it in many experiences. How does that relate to Krishna's management of this?

अपरेयमितस्त्वन्यां
प्रकृतिं विद्धि मे पराम् ।
जीवभूतां महाबाहो
ययेदं धार्यते जगत् ॥७.५॥

apareyamitastvanyāṁ
prakṛtiṁ viddhi me parām
jīvabhūtāṁ mahābāho
yayedaṁ dhāryate jagat (7.5)

apareyam = apara — inferior + iyam — this; tv = tu — but; anyām — another; prakṛtiṁ - energy; viddhi — know; me — of Me; parām — higher; jīvabhūtām — the hosts of individual spirits; mahābāho — O strong man; yayedam = yaya — through which + idam — this; dhāryate — is sustained; jagat — universe

That is inferior. But, O strong man, know of My other higher energy which consists of the hosts of individual spirits, through which this universe is sustained. (Bhagavad Gītā 7.5)

Analysis

The twist between the philosophy of the *Upanishads* and that of Krishna's *Sāṁkhya* is the element of personality. The *Upanishads* dismiss, ignore and indirectly subtract personality. Its idea is that there are three considerations.

- *prakriti or maya*
- *atma or jiva*
- *brahman*

Of the three factors, *prakriti* is dismissed forthwith as *maya* or an illusory recurring aberration. As far as the Upanishads is concerned, *prakriti* is not worth mentioning because it is not enduring. It misleads as in the example of a rope which is mistaken for a snake. The misconception does not add power to the rope. Hence it can never act as a snake. It is no danger to anyone and need not be considered.

Of the three factors, *atma* is rated as a *jiva*, which is a particular entity. However, in the final analysis that specification is dropped because *atma* is part of a vast genus or spiritual species which loses value if it is isolated, especially if the isolation was reinforced by the *prakriti* or illusory factors. For example, if a queue of persons walks through a path, the first one who sees a rope and mistakes it for a snake, will raise an alarm by his action of jumping or running away. Others in the queue who see him, will assume his danger when they get near the place where he saw the rope. Many of them will avoid that place or approach it with caution. Thus, the original person's sense perception, which was faulty, triggered a sense of alarm in the others.

Hence when an individual self, *atma*, acts in a peculiar way, he/she is termed as a *jiva* which is unwanted because it may affect others and bring others away from their independence from misconceptions.

Atma is fine with the *Upanishads* but *jiva* or *jivatma*, a particular *atma,* is not encouraged. As *atma* the self can be relegated to the status of *brahman* which is the ultimate energy, which is infallible. Otherwise, if *atma* is *jiva*, is individualized, it loses its identity with *brahman* and is for the time being parceled alone where it is subjected to misconceptions.

In this respect the *Upanishads* dodge from and disqualifies personality or *purusha*. Conversely, *Sāṁkhya* asserts and qualifies it.

Comprehension of Bhagavad Gītā Verse 7.5

Krishna lists the physical and psychic energies as his lower energy. He segregates the persons as higher energy. He stated that they sustain the universe. What is interesting is that he regards the collective of these persons to be his higher energy, a type of *prakriti*.

In this usage *prakriti* is power, some type of it, some grade of it, with specific capacity. The feature of these persons, the hosts of individual spirits, is that they sustain the universe. Their energies are scattered through it, energizing and monitoring.

एतद्योनीनि भूतानि सर्वाणीत्युपधारय । अहं कृत्स्नस्य जगतः प्रभवः प्रलयस्तथा ॥७.६॥	etadyonīni bhūtāni sarvāṇītyupadhāraya ahaṁ kṛtsnasya jagataḥ prabhavaḥ pralayastathā (7.6)

etadyonīni = etad — this + yonīni — multiple origins; bhūtāni — the creatures; sarvāṇīty = sarvāṇi — all + ity (iti) — thus; upadhāraya — understand; aham — I; kṛtsnasya — of the entire; jagataḥ — of the universe; prabhavaḥ — cause of production; pralayaḥ — cause of the destruction; tathā — as well

This higher energy functions as the multiple origins of all creatures. Understand this. I am the cause of production as well as destruction of the entire universe. (Bhagavad Gītā 7.6)

Analysis

The operation of this reality, this physical situation, is that it is a combination of physical and psychic factors which are based on origins which are abstract factors. The higher energy (of Krishna the supreme being) are innumerable selves whose radiance pervades the creation.

The inexplicable combination of the lower energy and the persons, results in what we experience as the physio-psychic universe. The life forms manifested in this situation are based mainly on the personSelves whose energy radiance in combination with the lower aspects cause the appearance of life forms in this world.

Krishna listed himself as the cause of the production and destruction of the universe, which we may surmise, is based on his involvement in the mix of factors. His direct participation is required before the limited selves and the lower energies could mix to produce living organisms.

This suggests that at some state, the lower energies and the higher ones (the limited selves) are unmixed. At that time, there is no activation of the lower ones, no formation of living organisms, no interplay between one higher or lower energy with any other. The interest of the supreme being, of Krishna, is the trigger which causes the mixture of the energies resulting in the manifestation we are a part of and which we perceive.

Comprehension of Bhagavad Gītā Verse 7.6

The declaration of Krishna is that he is the necessary and ultimate cause of the universe, of this cosmic display which we partially perceive. However, the part played by the limited selves is that once God triggers the formation of this cosmos, those limited persons become the basis for creature forms which are reproduced.

This does not mean that all limited selves are predominant. Merely because they are the basis does not necessarily make each one a controller or supervisor. The selves' radiant energy, which is continuous, functions as a power source, an enduring ignition factor, but some selves discover their consciousness as part of a lifeform which they partially regulate.

It is different with the supreme being. He, Krishna, remains as the supervisor. He does not lose autonomy even though he is the universal power activator.

The lower energies are also power points. These influence formations and their events. The interactions may affect a particular self or several selves.

मत्तः परतरं नान्यत्
किंचिदस्ति धनंजय ।
मयि सर्वमिदं प्रोतं
सूत्रे मणिगणा इव ॥७.७॥

mattaḥ parataraṁ nānyat
kiṁcidasti dhanaṁjaya
mayi sarvamidaṁ protaṁ
sūtre maṇigaṇā iva (7.7)

mattaḥ — than myself; parataram — higher; nānyat = na — not + anyat — other; kiṁcid — anything; asti — is; dhanaṁjaya — O conqueror of rich countries; mayi — on Me; sarvam — all; idam — this; protam — strong; sūtre — on a thread; maṇigaṇā — pearls; iva — like

O conqueror of rich countries, no other reality is higher than Myself. All this existence relies on Me, like pearls strung on a string. (Bhagavad Gītā 7.7)

Analysis

Verification of this by a self, who is other than Krishna, would require a vision experience to see how this existence is dependent on Krishna for its upkeep. It is difficult enough to check local origins. Humanity's scientific sector aggressively pursues solutions about the origin of the universes but how, even with scientific tools, can one prove or disprove that Krishna is or is not what he declares?

Either one takes what Krishna says about himself as a matter of faith, or one rejects it, or one hopes that one may get a revelation which certifies his claims.

Comprehension of Bhagavad Gītā Verse 7.7

It is hardly likely that one can prove that there is no other reality which is higher than Krishna and that he underlines everything that exist. The proof to be had is not a religious factor. It is psychological, where a self within the psyche, has or gets evidence of this declaration of Krishna.

Proving that one is eternal is enough challenge itself. That is a monumental task because a limited self does not have a grasp on the range of time, even the duration of planet earth, what to speak of the cosmos. With a lifespan of one hundred years as a physical body, one cannot possibly reference the duration of the planet what to speak of the universe. To proceed with Krishna's information, one would have to read his statements and accept whatever he declared.

वेदाहं समतीतानि
वर्तमानानि चार्जुन ।
भविष्याणि च भूतानि
मां तु वेद न कश्चन ॥७.२६॥

vedāhaṁ samatītāni
vartamānāni cārjuna
bhaviṣyāṇi ca bhūtāni
māṁ tu veda na kaścana (7.26)

vedāham = veda — know + aham — I; samatītāni — the departed souls; vartamānāni — the living creatures; cārjuna = ca — and + arjuna — Arjuna; bhaviṣyāni — those who are to be born; ca — and; bhūtāni — creatures; mām — Me; tu — but; veda — recognizes; na — not; kaścana — anyone

I know the departed souls and the living creatures, O Arjuna, as well as those beings who are to be born. But no one recognizes Me. (Bhagavad Gītā 7.26)

Analysis

Krishna made this statement because the shifting history of the physical world is underscored by a constant identifiable source of limited persons. Each of whom is tagged with specific tendencies. Each self can be positively identified because each is a core factor which adopts varying features from time to time.

Krishna is specific but he is not recognized because the limited selves do not have the subtle senses which can tag Krishna. To identify him, one must have supernatural sense perception which is refined enough to recognize the supreme being.

In terms of transmigration, the recognition of anyone is a task. This is due to the fact, that the birth of a body, its maturation, its reproduction and death, produces changes in the lifeform. There may be slight variations. Regardless, to tag a body with an identity, one must figure many changes in the form.

When the body dies, one is left with no way to tag the psyche physically. Then the only trace is a psychic register, which is a remnant of the total energy which was the person during its life.

When it is born again, it begins with a new record, because its social value was diminished when its previous form was deceased.

Comprehension of Bhagavad Gītā Verse 7.26

Assuming that Krishna has accurate, precise psychic perception, assuming that he can recognize every individual coreSelf, his statement about knowing the departed souls and the living beings is not far-fetched.

There is a corePerson in the psyche. By introspection the individual can recognize itself. With persistent meditation, with full attention within the psyche, with sorting between the coreSelf and the intellect image producing adjunct, one can know oneself. This however may not give one the ability to perceive another limited self or the supreme self.

Each person learns to recognize someone else who appears as a physical or astral body. Besides that, we normally have no way of recognizing someone else. However, by constantly shifting focus to the subtle plane of consciousness, by better accessing what is psychic and abstract, one can develop enough supernatural perception to recognize those selves whom one relates to frequently. A limited self can know some departed souls, but not all.

श्रीभगवानुवाच
अक्षरं ब्रह्म परमं
स्वभावोऽध्यात्ममुच्यते ।
भूतभावोद्भवकरो
विसर्गः कर्मसंज्ञितः ॥८.३॥

śrībhagavānuvāca
akṣaraṁ brahma paramaṁ
svabhāvo'dhyātmamucyate
bhūtabhāvodbhavakaro
visargaḥ karmasaṁjñitaḥ (8.3)

śrībhagavān — the Blessed Lord; uvāca — said; akṣaram — unaffected; brahma — spiritual reality; paramam — supreme; svabhāvo = svabhāvaḥ — personal nature; 'dhyātmam = adhyātmam — supreme soul; ucyate — it is said; bhūtabhāvodbhavakaro = bhūtabhāva — existence of mundane forms + udbhava — production + karo (karaḥ) — causing; visargah — creative power; karmasaṁjñitaḥ = karma — cultural activity + saṁjñitaḥ — is known

The Blessed Lord said: The spiritual reality is unaffected and supreme. The Supreme Soul is described as a personal existence Who causes the production of the mundane world. Cultural action is known as creative power. (Bhagavad Gītā 8.3)

Analysis

The *Upanishads* advocate the *brahman* supreme situation of infallible power which is the basis of itself and everything else. And yet, the *Upanishads* do not stress the Supreme Soul. It is in Krishna's teaching, his enumeration, his *Sāṁkhya*, that we are alerted to the *param purusha*, Supreme Person.

Upanishads dismiss the limited self (*atma/jivatma*) as being an incidental portion of *brahman*, which it advocates as the supreme reality. It does not admit a Supreme Soul who is a personal existence (*svabhāvaḥ*). Krishna and everyone else, the selves of varying powers and glory, are relegated in the *Upanishads* as being unimportant when contrasted to *brahman*.

However, Krishna declares otherwise, posting himself above *brahman*. In fact, in the Vedic literature the terms *param brahman* are used. This indicates that the limited selves are specks of *brahman,* while the supreme person is *param brahman*, which is the supreme level of *brahman*.

Since the proof is hard to come by, which idea should be accepted? Either Krishna is rejected, and the *Upanishads* are accepted. Or Krishna is accepted, and the *Upanishads* are appreciated but not regarded as the reference.

Comprehension of Bhagavad Gītā Verse 8.3

The supreme reality, *brahman* is declared as being unaffected and supreme. This concerns the topic of what is supreme in reference to the physical world. There is a psychic background which is studied by physicists. Relatively speaking it is more real than the physical manifestation, but its abstractness causes us to dismiss it as being irrelevant. It is the basis of this but its status as a non-manifested appearance makes it difficult to rate it as the origin and support of this.

Putting aside a God of the world, dismissing the idea of a primal deity, we are left with the physical world and the subtle background energy which supports it. With that, there would be the persons whom we interact with socially and who are tagged as physical bodies. Behind this there is a spiritual basis which is unaffected as the supporting structure and which is supreme because when the physical manifestation fizzes, what will be left is that psychic basis. Whatever would be left should be regarded as the unaffected and supreme basis of this.

But Krishna explained that besides the unaffected spiritual basis, there is a Supreme Soul who is a personal existence, which causes the production of this world. While the *Upanishads* end the affair with *brahman* as the background of the *prakriti* material nature and the *atma* selves, Krishna explains further that besides that, He is the ultimate factor.

अव्यक्ताद्व्यक्तयः सर्वाः
प्रभवन्त्यहरागमे ।
रात्र्यागमे प्रलीयन्ते
तत्रैवाव्यक्तसंज्ञके ॥८.१८॥

avyaktādvyaktayaḥ sarvāḥ
prabhavantyaharāgame
rātryāgame pralīyante
tatraivāvyaktasaṁjñake (8.18)

avyaktād = avyaktāt — from the invisible world; vyaktayaḥ — the visible world; sarvāḥ — all; prabhavanty = prabhavanti — they are produced; aharāgame — at the beginning of Brahma's day; rātryāgame — at the beginning of Brahma's night; pralīyante — they are reverted back; tatraivāvyaktasaṁjñake = tatra — at the time + eva — indeed + avyakta — invisible world + saṁjñake — is understood as

When the day of Creator Brahmā begins, all this visible world is produced from the invisible world. When his night comes, the manifested energies are reverted back into the invisible world. (Bhagavad Gītā 8.18)

Analysis

So far Krishna described himself as the Supreme Lord. He explained about the limited selves. He spoke of the physical and psychic environments. Another person is introduced. He is Creator Brahma, a sub-deity who is under the authority of Krishna.

This person is not the supreme being, Krishna. Brahma is not a limited self like most of the entities who are assumed as physical creatures. Apart from day and night having to do with the influence of the physical sun which we see, Krishna presented another type of day and night. This new day and night involves the cosmic expression and grand collapse.

Comprehension of Bhagavad Gītā Verse 8.18

Krishna presented another way of viewing and comprehending this situation. The method is to regard that there is the visible world which we partially see. Then there is, as the basis for that, an invisible world, which is perceived through supernatural perception.

This verse introduces the idea of this manifestation being produced by the mind of a creatorGod, who is a sub-deity under Krishna, someone who is licensed and approved by Krishna for initiating this cosmic manifestation merely by his imaginative powers.

When a rich man thinks of having a palace, it may be constructed. This is because the wealthy individual has the funds for the expenses. When Brahma thinks of the world, it comes into being. Reality supports his ideas. When Brahma's Day begins, this visible world is produced from the invisible situation.

The invisible world is real. It is realer than this physical manifestation. We should cease dismissing or ignoring it. Even though the invisible world is the basis of the physical situation, the invisible energy yields only a minuscule part of itself to render this cosmic situation.

When Brahma's night comes, his sleeping occurs. The manifested energies revert to the invisible world which is its basis.

भूतग्रामः स एवायं भूत्वा भूत्वा प्रलीयते । रात्र्यागमेऽवशः पार्थ प्रभवत्यहरागमे ॥८.१९॥	bhūtagrāmaḥ sa evāyaṁ bhūtvā bhūtvā pralīyate rātryāgame'vaśaḥ pārtha prabhavatyaharāgame (8.19)

bhūtagrāmaḥ — multitude of beings; sa = saḥ — this; evāyam = eva — indeed + ayam — this; bhūtvā bhūtvā — repeatedly manifesting; pralīyate — is shifted out of visibility; rātryāgame — at the arrival of Brahma's night; 'vaśaḥ = avaśaḥ — happening naturally; pārtha — O son of Pṛthā; prabhavaty = prabhavati — it comes into existence; aharāgame — on the onset of Brahma's day

O son of Pṛthā, this multitude of beings which is repeatedly manifested, is naturally shifted out of visibility at the arrival of each of Brahmā's nights. It again comes into existence at the onset of Brahmā's day. (Bhagavad Gītā 8.19)

Analysis

Brahma is a superPerson, such that his consciousness is the basis of objective awareness of the limited selves. In sequence, there is a person behind a person, such that at some point, Brahma is the immediate source of someone. Every self is not sourced directly from Brahma. Only a limited number of selves can trace their origin directly as Brahma. There may be a series of sub-sources.

In summary, the beings in this cosmos come into existence in a grand performance which vanishes after a time. The limited selves continue existence when the performance fizzes, but they do so without objectivity. As leaves on a gigantic tree lose vitality, have color changes and fall during the autumn coolness, and then leaves again emerge from the branches during the spring season, so the coreSelves are indirectly manifested in creature forms and then lose objectivity when the cosmos crashes. it is reliant on Brahma's awakened and sleeping conditions.

Comprehension of Bhagavad Gītā Verse 8.19

Sāṁkhya philosophy of Krishna includes personSources. It is more than a matter of an *atma* being a miniscule part of *brahman*, the absolute energy. In

Sāṁkhya a person, a godPerson, Brahma, is the highlight of objective awareness. His consciousness is primal such that the limited self can be objective if Brahma is objective. The limited ones lose objectivity when Brahma's awareness lapses.

The coreSelf as a continuous radiance has two phases of awareness as either objective or subjective. This means that in the subjective state, a self will lose reference of itself. It will be as if it does not exist even though it remains part of reality.

The realization about Brahma's existence is difficult to experience. It is hardly likely that a yogi could know it. There is a narration of a yogi who experienced this. That was *Markandeya*. The story is told in the *Markandeya Purana* and in the *Mahabharata*. It was explained to King *Yudhishthira*, Arjuna's brother.

Survival when Brahma is in a drowsy condition just before he sleeps, is near impossible because that would mean having some other supportive person whose consciousness transcends Brahma's. For *Markandeya*, Krishna the divine child supported his awareness.

It is not likely that any other yogi would survive objectively through Brahma's drowsy condition or sleep. It is also narrated in the *Puranas* that *Madhu* and *Kaitabha*, two criminal yogis, consciously survived the condition of Brahma's drowsiness. Those were exceptions.

Person has personSource. The source transcends the person. This means that the person cannot research its origin unless it is given special boosts of consciousness by the source. That is hardly likely. Hence, we are dependent on this information from Krishna to understand the secrets of existence.

परस्तस्मात्तु भावोऽन्यो
ऽव्यक्तोऽव्यक्तात्सनातनः ।
यः स सर्वेषु भूतेषु
नश्यत्सु न विनश्यति ॥८.२०॥

parastasmāttu bhāvo'nyo
'vyakto'vyaktātsanātanaḥ
yaḥ sa sarveṣu bhūteṣu
naśyatsu na vinaśyati (8.20)

paraḥ — high; tasmāt — than this; tu — but; bhāvo = bhāvaḥ — existence; 'nyo = anyaḥ — another; 'vyakto = avyaktaḥ — invisible; 'vyaktāt = avyaktāt — than the unmanifest state of the dissolvable creation; sanātanaḥ — primeval; yaḥ = which; sa = saḥ — it; sarveṣu — in all; bhūteṣu — in creation; naśyatsu — in the disintegration; na — not; vinaśyati — is disintegrated

But higher than this, there is another invisible existence, which is higher than the primeval unmanifested states of this dissolvable creation. When all these creatures are disintegrated, that is not affected. (Bhagavad Gītā 8.20)

Analysis

In the *Upanishad* system of thinking and also in the *advaita vedanta* way of considering, there are essentially three factors to consider. These are.

- *prakriti*
- *atma*
- *brahman*

Prakriti is the physical energy with its psychic counterpart. This does not denote personality. It concerns materials and environments at large. This is dismissed as being a temporary manifestation. It is relegated to be illusion at best.

Atma is an individualized observational factor, which outlives the manifested *prakriti*. It is invited and requested to reclaim its absolute status by transferring itself into ***brahman***, which is presented as the absolute underpin of everything else including whatever is temporary.

This way of thinking does not accommodate anything which is another invisible existence which is higher than the primeval unmanifest states of this dissolvable creation. Even though this view accommodates an invisible existence which is beyond this cosmic manifestation, it does not indicate, admit or announce any personSelves existing individually in the invisible existence. No individuality is declared except in this cosmic manifestation which is a compounded physical and psychic reality.

Clarification about this in the *Upanishads* and in *advaita vedanta* may be rendered simply by replacing the word *brahman* with other vocabulary but the custom is to avoid that and stamp the word *brahman* on anything which is inexplicable, and which leaves the student with a puzzle and with fear that he/she should go no further in the research.

No clarity about the abstraction of supernatural energy is listed. As soon as something is out of the sensual range of the physical body, it is posted as being unexplainable and devoid of color or form.

Comprehension of Bhagavad Gītā Verse 8.20

Pushing aside the *Upanishads* and *Advaita Vedanta*, Krishna declared another reality, which is higher than this cosmic manifestation with its people and habited and uninhabited environments. That is another invisible existence. It is beyond even the unmanifest version of this situation. It transcends even the situation which transcends this, and which is the basis for this.

When this situation fizzes, there will be the unmanifest version of this as the only trace. Beyond that there is another situation which is not affected and is not directly linked to this as the source of this.

अव्यक्तोऽक्षर इत्युक्तस्
तमाहुः परमां गतिम् ।
यं प्राप्य न निवर्तन्ते
तद्धाम परमं मम ॥८.२१॥

avyakto'kṣara ityuktas
tamāhuḥ paramāṁ gatim
yaṁ prāpya na nivartante
taddhāma paramaṁ mama (8.21)

avyakto = avyaktaḥ — invisible world; 'kṣara = akṣara — unalterable; ity = iti — thus; uktaḥ — is declared; tam — it; āhuḥ — authorities say; paramām — supreme; gatim — objective; yam — which; prāpya — attaining; na — not; nivartante — return here; tad — that; dhāma — residence; paramam — supreme; mama — My

That invisible world is unalterable, so it is declared. The authorities say that it is the supreme objective. Attaining that, they do not return here. That place is My supreme residence. (Bhagavad Gītā 8.21)

Analysis

Whatever retrogresses or is crunched into being nothing and which is currently an obvious or hidden part of this manifestation, will become as nothing when this history terminates. Then, this situation and its psychic parts will become something unmanifest.

But there is still something else, which is unalterable, and which cannot be seen with any sense perception developed in this creation or in the sourceEnergy of this place.

That other place is declared by Krishna. It is a place that the seers of the *Upanishads* and the expounders of *advaita vedanta* neither described nor declare. That invisible world was rated by other seers who either had insight about it or heard of it from persons with the required vision.

It is not a void region. It is not a blank existence. It is not devoid of personality (*purusha*). It is the residential situation of the Supreme Lord. This is what he declared.

Comprehension of Bhagavad Gītā Verse 8.21

For this event of believing what Krishna said about his supreme residence, one must either experience directly or accept Krishna's word. For those who do not believe it but who are open to the evidence of it, they need to understand that direct evidence is unlikely. This is because Krishna would have to grace someone with the spiritual vision to see as Krishna sees.

Some teachers of the Krishna religion, say that one should believe Krishna and that through this cooperative attitude, one will in time see what Krishna sees. They present a grace-bestowing person, Krishna, who easily reveals his truth to devotees. However, in my opinion, that is unlikely.

What I suggest to the reader is to take Krishna's word as it is and wait for revelations from him.

In the time of Krishna some seers like *Bhishma*, declared Krishna as the Supreme Person. Before the time of Krishna some other seers declared what Krishna said about his supreme residence. They may or may not have stated it about Krishna specifically, but they declared it about God without giving the name Krishna.

The relevant pledge for anyone in this verse, is that if one attains the habitat of Krishna, the spiritual world, one will not surface again in this cosmic situation.

पुरुषः स परः पार्थ
भक्त्या लभ्यस्त्वनन्यया ।
यस्यान्तःस्थानि भूतानि
येन सर्वमिदं ततम् ॥८.२२॥

puruṣaḥ sa paraḥ pārtha
bhaktyā labhyastvananyayā
yasyāntaḥsthāni bhūtāni
yena sarvamidaṁ tatam (8.22)

puruṣaḥ — person; sa = saḥ — this; paraḥ — supreme; pārtha — O son of Pṛthā; bhaktyā — by a devotional relationship; labhyaḥ — attainable; tv = tu — but; ananyayā — not by any other; yasyāntaḥsthāni = yasya — of which + antaḥsthāni — existing within; bhūtāni — beings; yena — by which; sarvam — all; idam — this; tatam — energized

That Supreme Person, O son of Pṛthā, is attainable through a devotional relationship and not by any other means. Within His influence, all beings exist. By Him, all the universe is energized. (Bhagavad Gītā 8.22)

Analysis

For attaining *brahman* as per the *Upanishads* and *advaita vedanta*, no relationship with a deity (*bhaktyā*) is required. In fact, such an affair is never mentioned and is at best, ridiculed. This, however, is different because it is the attainment of a location which is beyond even the invisible existence from which this cosmic display was sourced.

To go to *brahman*, to be *brahman*, the seers of the *Upanishads* and the *advaita vedantists*, require one to segregate from the material energy and everything psychic which pertains to it.

But if one is interested in Krishna's residence as described, one must have a devotional relation with him. That is the central requirement. Krishna said there is no other means for attaining this.

Comprehension of Bhagavad Gītā Verse 8.22

Why would anyone be concerned to have a relationship with Krishna, the Supreme Person?

Krishna suggests some reasons in this verse. A person may realize that by Krishna's power, all beings exist. By that there is objective self-consciousness. For existential security, knowing of and about Krishna may be beneficial to the yogi.

Krishna's influence is all pervasive but that does not mean that every other influence is value-less. Still, Krishna influence is special. Having it, is beneficial.

मया ततमिदं सर्वं
जगदव्यक्तमूर्तिना ।
मत्स्थानि सर्वभूतानि
न चाहं तेष्ववस्थितः ॥९.४॥

mayā tatamidaṁ sarvaṁ
jagadavyaktamūrtinā
matsthāni sarvabhūtāni
na cāhaṁ teṣvavasthitaḥ (9.4)

mayā — by Me; tatam — pervaded; idam — this; sarvam — all; jagad = jagat — world; avyaktamūrtinā = avyakta — invisible + mūrtinā — by form; matsthāni — standing on Me, surviving on Me; sarvabhūtāni — all beings; na — not; cāham = ca — and + aham — I; teṣv = teṣu — in them; avasthitaḥ — standing on, surviving on

This world is pervaded by My invisible form. All beings survive on My energy, but I am not surviving on theirs. (Bhagavad Gītā 9.4)

Analysis

The saturation of Krishna's energy is a mystic event. For proof of it, one requires supernatural perception. Otherwise, it is a matter of trusting that Krishna is indeed the supreme being who relates this information honestly. How the world is pervaded as he stated, is not given in detail. His influence is not obvious and cannot be perceived by physical nor even by lower psychic means.

The relationship between Krishna and the beings who appear and disappear in this cosmos is not reciprocal. One is not interchangeable with the other. One is reliant on the other. There is no feedback where one can influence the other in exactly the same way as the other may influence the prior one.

The supreme being is in a unique position of providing supports for the objective operations of the limited selves, who in turn are in the special relationship as dependents on the Supreme Person.

But this does not mean that the supreme being can terminate his supportive concern and distribution. He is, in a way, compelled to render this assistance. It is however not an undesirable action.

Comprehension of Bhagavad Gītā Verse 9.4

To move from physical existence into the origins of the manifested energy which we partially perceive, one would have to develop subtle perception, mystic sensing, and vision. The under-structure of physical and gaseous matter is being discovered by scientists but not by using the sense perception of their bodies. They do so only by using scientific instruments which indicate the operations of what is the immediate basis of this physical situation.

Currently we are not equipped to see the origins of substances directly. Thus, one should make the effort to understand this theoretically. Take the physical body for example. It is directly apprehended by our senses where we can see its color and feel its touch. But to go further with only the physical senses cannot be performed. Someone somewhere may switch to the senses of the subtle body, but that person cannot provide physical proof of his vision.

The evidence is theoretical for the most part. It has an element of trust which must be added, before someone will accept it. So much of what Krishna declares may be accepted but not by direct evidence only, by having confidence that he is the supreme being.

Science clarified that the under basis of this physical existence is subtle matter, particle energy. If everything is reduced to that, what is the conclusion?

According to Krishna, the particle energy, which is the substrata of this physical manifestation, is pervaded by Krishna's invisible form. He declared that the beings we know, those who were here before and those who will be manifested later, survive on his energy. However, He is not based in them. He does not rely on them. It is a one-way flow.

न च मत्स्थानि भूतानि
पश्य मे योगमैश्वरम् ।
भूतभृन्न च भूतस्थो
ममात्मा भूतभावनः ॥९.५॥

na ca matsthāni bhūtāni
paśya me yogamaiśvaram
bhūtabhṛnna ca bhūtastho
mamātmā bhūtabhāvanaḥ (9.5)

na — not; ca — and; matsthāni — standing on Me, surviving on Me; bhūtāni — beings; paśya — behold; me — My; yogam = yoga — psychological power; aiśvaram — supremacy; bhūtabhṛn = bhūtabhṛt — sustaining beings; na — not; ca — and; bhūtastho = bhūtasthaḥ — existing on the beings; mamātmā = mama — My + ātmā — self; bhūtabhāvanaḥ — causing beings to be

And the created beings are not existing on Me. Behold My psychological supremacy. While sustaining the beings and not existing on them, I Myself cause them to be. (Bhagavad Gītā 9.5)

Analysis

The puzzles of this existence are diverse. Which solutions should one inquire of and pursue?

The first qualification is the successful inquiry into the self. Why? Because whatever one perceives, is based on the situation of the self. Whatever the self is, that determines the correct or incorrect view of reality. And there are degrees of accuracy. It may be that a limited self will never have the perfect view, the deepest vision, and yet, the self should strive for the perception of its origins, as well as know its reliance.

In one declaration Krishna suggested that he is the major influence. It is not reciprocal. In this verse he issues a reverse statement saying that the created beings do not exist on him. How is this reconciled?

The meaning is that even though the limited selves and the environments which they emerge in, are saturated through and through by Krishna's influence, still there is controlled feedback between Krishna and the situations. The afflictions and even the enjoyments which the limited beings endure, do not invade Krishna's personality.

Krishna gave this information so that a limited self can figure how the personalities, limited and absolute, function and interact with any manifested energy which a limited self may be aware of.

In our experience, for instance in the case of vegetation, we experience that a seed expends itself in the process of sprouting. The seed ceases to be reproductive after it manifests a tree.

Comprehension of Bhagavad Gītā Verse 9.5

To understand the concept of personality as Krishna explains, one should begin with a view that there is a Supreme Being who is exceptional, who is entirely different and who is marked with unique aspects which the limited selves lack, did not have and will not acquire.

Can one agree to that? Is there anything in one's nature which makes that sound familiar. Does one feel that it is satisfactory for there to be someone like Krishna?

To get to the gist of what he proposes, one should have a nature which can accommodate such an exceptional Supreme Person. I write this because there are some limited selves who are repulsed by the idea of there being someone who is a supreme self, especially if that means that none of the limited selves ever was, is or will be a Supreme Being. Some are of the view, and they are strongly opinionated of this, that each self has the same potential. Some others feel that there is no Supreme Person. Such views are based on the inner experience of these persons.

I recall a conversation I had with Arthur Beverford who was my first yoga teacher. He shared with me the *Markandeya Samaya* extraction from the *Mahabharata*. This was translated by Rishi Singh Gherwal, Beverford's teacher. That text presents this same Krishna as the unique Supreme Being. Beverford was of the view that there was a Primal Creative Cause, but he did not think that this cause was personal or was a person.

The existence of persons like Beverford is proof enough that some philosophers do not accede to Krishna's self-declarations.

सर्वभूतानि कौन्तेय
प्रकृतिं यान्ति मामिकाम् ।
कल्पक्षये पुनस्तानि
कल्पादौ विसृजाम्यहम् ॥९.७॥

sarvabhūtāni kaunteya
prakṛtiṁ yānti māmikām
kalpakṣaye punastāni
kalpādau visṛjāmyaham (9.7)

sarvabhūtāni — all beings; kaunteya — son of Kuntī; prakṛtim — material nature; yānti — retrogress into; māmikām — my own; kalpakṣaye — at the end of a day of Brahma; punas = punar — again; tāni — they; kalpādau — at the beginning of a day of Brahma; visṛjāmy = visṛjāmi — I produce; aham — I

O son of Kuntī, all beings retrogress into My own material nature at the end of Brahmā's day. I produce them again at the beginning of Brahmā's next day. (Bhagavad Gītā 9.7)

Analysis

The beings in this usage are the personSelves and the subtle energy which adheres to each of them. This combination, as massive psychological force, retrogresses into the supernatural energy which is source of the cosmic manifestation. Everything does not unravel at this time. Some aspects remain in combination without sorting. As that, it folds in so that there is an action of reverse manifestation, with the limited persons still apparently combined with the psychological energy which is the environmental display during the manifested phase of the creation.

Brahma, the sub-God serves as a junction in consciousness, where the relaxation of his mental focus results in the collapse of objectivity for the limited selves who emerged prior from his consciousness.

Comprehension of Bhagavad Gītā Verse 9.7

Krishna declared himself as the origin. Then again, he said that it was not reciprocal. He supports but is not supported. As the origin, he is not the direct source of everything. There is an infinite number of selves in this cosmos, but Krishna is not the direct source of each one. He declared Brahma as a direct source and himself, Krishna, as the source of Brahma, the **source** of the source.

In the details we read that Krishna explained himself as being a remote operator. He presented Brahma as the immediate origin. Brahma exists parallel to the non-reactive material nature in which the selves and their psychologies subside when Brahma falls asleep.

प्रकृतिं स्वामवष्टभ्य
विसृजामि पुनः पुनः ।
भूतग्राममिमं कृत्स्नम्
अवशं प्रकृतेर्वशात् ॥९.८॥

prakṛtiṁ svāmavaṣṭabhya
visṛjāmi punaḥ punaḥ
bhūtagrāmamimaṁ kṛtsnam
avaśaṁ prakṛtervaśāt (9.8)

prakṛtim — material nature; svām — own; avaṣṭabhya — supported on, founded on; visṛjāmi — I produce; punaḥ punaḥ — repeated, again and again; bhūtagrāmam — the multitude of beings; imam — this; kṛtsnam — whole; avaśam — powerless; prakṛter = prakṛteḥ — of material nature; vaśāt — in respect to the potency

On the foundation of material nature, I repeatedly produce this whole multitude of beings, which is powerless in respect to the potency of material nature. (Bhagavad Gītā 9.8)

Analysis

Brahma, the creatorGod, is himself part of the production but with special resistance and powers. The limited selves under Brahma's jurisdiction are powerfulness in respect to the potency of material nature. That potency causes the influence over the limited selves to be near absolute. They engage in escapades which are suggested by and facilitated by the nature in its production of history.

The cosmic manifestation is declared to be a repeated event. Neither Brahma, nor any other self, except for the Supreme Lord Krishna, can terminate this display. And Krishna does not say that he intends to permanently end it. We can infer that since it recurred from time immemorial, it will continue to appear and disappear, and even Krishna despite his being the ultimate origin, cannot cease this process of manifestation and its abstract hidden condition.

Comprehension of Bhagavad Gītā Verse 9.8

It is important to understand that to Krishna's view, we, the limited selves are powerless in respect to the potency of material nature. Yes, he stated earlier that we are perpetual beings of a higher grade of energy than the manifested or unmanifest nature. Still, that is an inherent contradiction which we need to accept.

From one angle we are a superior aspect. From another, from the one of being influenced, we are inferior. This conclusion is rejected by some writers of the *Upanishad* and by some of the exponents of *advaita vedanta*. They segregate the selves as *atmas* which to their view are *brahman*, just as any speck of sand is sand in a collective.

The *Upanishads* insist that one not consider a grain of sand. One should only regard sand as sand, like for instance sand as seen as a beach. The separation of a sand grain, the consideration of its individual properties is outlawed in *advaita vedanta*.

Krishna *Sāṁkhya* declares the individual personSelf. It stresses the person both individually and collectively, with stress on the individual features and its contrast, which is the material nature which influences a self, or a group of selves, with each feeling the influence unto itself.

There is a proposal for the limited self to become free from the influence of material nature. It raises the issue of if by itself such a self can achieve that separation. What does that entail? Why was the self interspaced with nature in the first place? Who caused that to happen? By itself, can the individual free itself?

न मे विदुः सुरगणाः
प्रभवं न महर्षयः .
अहमादिर्हि देवानां
महर्षीणां च सर्वशः ॥१०.२॥

na me viduḥ suragaṇāḥ
prabhavaṁ na maharṣayaḥ
ahamādirhi devānāṁ
maharṣīṇāṁ ca sarvaśaḥ (10.2)

na — not; me — of Me; viduḥ — they know; suragaṇāḥ — the supernatural rulers; prabhavam — the origin; na — nor; mahārṣayaḥ — great yogi sages; aham — I; ādir = ādiḥ — source; hi — in fact; devānām — of the supernatural rulers; mahārṣīnām — of the great yogi sages; ca — and; sarvaśaḥ — in all respects

The supernatural rulers do not know My origin, nor do the great yogi sages. In all respects, I am the source of the supernatural rulers and the great yogi sages. (Bhagavad Gītā 10.2)

Analysis

The supernatural rulers are persons who preside over entry and exit from subtle dimensions. Most of these are limited selves with special powers and skills. A small number of these are unlimited selves like Krishna. They are more than equivalent to a limited self but for the time being they may act in a limited way which may cause someone's underestimation.

The great yogi sages (*mahārṣayaḥ*) are the persons who composed the *Upanishads* and others who did mystic research and discovered the abstract levels of existence.

When Krishna accredits himself as being the source of these persons, it could mean the direct or remote cause. Previously he listed creatorGod Brahma as the source. Brahma is the direct source. As the immediate source of Brahma, Krishna is the remote source. Krishna is the source of the source in the case of those who were produced directly from Brahma.

Some persons were produced from a person, who was produced from a person, who was produced by Brahma. In most cases, Krishna is the remote source. A retrogression into the personSelf, the core, may cause some psychic vision to understand the immediate source of the self but the research into the source of the source would only go so far.

Brahma had mentally produced sons. One is *Bhrigu*. His power of retrogression may go no further than Brahma. With limited retrogression power *Bhrigu* may resort to questioning Brahma about the creatorGod's source. *Bhrigu* would accept or reject the explanation of Brahma.

Because the psyche is not a physical reality, its inner prying into origins penetrates only so much. One can go so far and then one is left with the admittance of the one whom one determines is one's source. The sensual perception ceases more and more, the further one penetrates. This is why some reliance on higher witnesses is required.

Comprehension of Bhagavad Gītā Verse 10.2

Krishna said previously that his residence is beyond even the dissolvable state of this cosmic manifestation. What dimension is that place? In what direction would one go to locate it. Is it a physical reality? Is it contacted by transiting from a location or vibration in one's psyche?

We can assume that it is in a dimension which transcends our situation, even the source level of this physical dimension. Krishna declared that even though he is the source of the creatorGod Brahma and also the supernatural rulers and the great yogi sages, the mystic penetrators, still they do not know Krishna. This is because his centrality is beyond their sensual perception, even beyond their abstract penetrations.

महर्षयः सप्त पूर्वे
चत्वारो मनवस्तथा ।
मद्भावा मानसा जाता
येषां लोक इमाः प्रजाः ॥१०.६॥

maharṣayaḥ sapta pūrve
catvāro manavastathā
madbhāvā mānasā jātā
yeṣāṁ loka imāḥ prajāḥ (10.6)

mahārṣayaḥ — great yogi sages; sapta — seven; pūrve — in ancient times, of old; catvāro = catvāraḥ — four celibate boys; manavaḥ — primal sensually-disciplined pro-creators; tathā — also; madbhāvā — coming from Me; mānasā — mentally; jātā — produced; yeṣāṁ — of whom; loka — universe; imāḥ — these; prajāḥ — creatures

The seven great yogi sages of old, the four celibate boys, and also the primal sexually disciplined procreators come from Me, being produced mentally. From them, the creatures of this universe evolved. (Bhagavad Gītā 10.6)

Analysis

This is a listing of the initial personality spread from the creatorGod Brahma. However, Krishna mentioned himself as their origin. It does not mean that he is the direct source or preLord but rather that they were sourced from him through Brahma who is the immediate psychological parent.

The Vedic literature gave *Marīci, Atri, Angira, Pulastya, Pulaha, Kratu,* and *Vasiṣṭa* as the seven great yogi sages. The four celibate boys are *Sanaka, Sanandan, Sanat-Kumara and Sanātana.* The primal sexually disciplined procreators are fourteen in number.

Comprehension of Bhagavad Gītā Verse 10.6

The idea of dependent origination is relevant in the discussion about personality and its origins. If there was only one direct primal origin for everything, this existence would be linear. However, it is not. There is cause, cause of cause, cause of cause of cause to an infinite penetration. Even the precious feature of existence which is personality may rarely trace itself to one terminal origin. This is due to the fact that a person from a person from a person is in a relatively endless chain of individuals.

We get physical evidence about dependent origination. There is the direct issue of one's physical appearance beginning as an embryo, then as a newborn infant. That formation originated in two parents, who themselves originated in four parents (two mothers, two fathers), who originated in another set of paired parents. This could be traced to an initial two parents in the beginning of this species.

That is the physical trace. What of the psychological origin? In that situation there could be one person or a pair as the immediate obvious origin but with someone else or with multiple persons as the non-obvious or abstract causes, persons who induced the immediate origin to sprout someone else.

अहमात्मा गुडाकेश
सर्वभूताशयस्थितः ।
अहमादिश्च मध्यं च
भूतानामन्त एव च ॥१०.२०॥

ahamātmā guḍākeśa
sarvabhūtāśayasthitaḥ
ahamādiśca madhyaṁ ca
bhūtānāmanta eva ca (10.20)

aham — I; ātmā — self; guḍākeśa — sleep-regulator; sarvabhūtāśayasthitaḥ = sarva — all + bhūta — beings + āśaya — mystic resting place + sthitaḥ — situated in; aham — I; ādiśca = ādiḥ — beginning + ca — and; madhyam — middle; ca — and; bhūtānām — of the beings; anta — end; eva — indeed; ca — and

O sleep regulator, I am the person Who is situated in the mystic resting place of all beings. I am responsible for the beginning, middle, and end of all beings. (Bhagavad Gītā 10.20)

Analysis

As the origin of origins, as the ultimate in the series of dependent originations, Krishna is situated in each person factor which exist anywhere. It is however near impossible to trace one's sourcePerson back to Krishna. Due to the numberless cross references in personality traces and due to the skill energy, which adheres to the selves, even an immediate source is hard to determine.

As Krishna said earlier, the selves do not know him, but he knows every self. The tracing is difficult. It is an impossible quest because of the compounded subtlety as one progresses backward. Even for what is obvious to one's physical senses, which is the physical body, one can trace its ancestry with limited reach.

Comprehension of Bhagavad Gītā Verse 10.20

Krishna declared that he is the ultimate cause of the manifestation of any self and that he is in the mystic resting place of any being. In meditation one may explore one's abstract spread of existential radiance. But there is something deeper and Krishna is the ultimate stop.

Whatever there is, the beginning, middle and end of its features are caused by motivational energies which emerge from causal factors, which in themselves come from other causal factors, endlessly.

यद्यद्विभूतिमत्सत्त्वं
श्रीमदूर्जितमेव वा ।
तत्तदेवावगच्छ त्वं
मम तेजोंशसंभवम् ॥१०.४१॥

yadyadvibhūtimatsattvaṁ
śrīmadūrjitameva vā
tattadevāvagaccha tvaṁ
mama tejoṁśasaṁbhavam (10.41)

yad yad — what, whatever; vibhūtimat — fantastic; sattvam — real object; śrīmad = śrīmat — prosperous; ūrjitam — powerful; eva — indeed; vā — or; tat tad = tad tat — this, that, any case; evāvagaccha = eva — indeed + avagaccha — realize; tvam — you; mama — of Me; tejo = tejaḥ — splendor; 'mśasaṁbhavam (amśasaṁbhavam) = amśa — fraction + saṁbhavam — origin

You should realize that whatever fantastic existence, whatever prosperous or powerful object there is, in any case, it originates from a fraction of My splendor. (Bhagavad Gītā 10.41)

Analysis

In one sense, Krishna directly nurtures each person, but in another view, Krishna is the most remote factor. Except for Brahma, where Krishna directly produced him, someone else is the immediate origin. And yet, through abstract expression and powers, Krishna is the nearest influence.

The existential support of one person, is itself supported by another person, who in turn is supported by someone else. We can assume that this is an infinite regression, where several factors are involved for a dependent origination until there is an ultimate terminal, who is Krishna, as the origin of all origins, the centralized complex root.

Comprehension of Bhagavad Gītā Verse 10.41

Krishna instructed Arjuna to realize that whatever fantastic existence, whatever prosperous or powerful object there is, in any case, it originated from a fraction of Krishna's splendor.

To realize this with evidence in sense perception is hardly likely. One may understand this intellectually but to experience this, even to experience a fragment of this would require special mystic reach.

अथ वा बहुनैतेन
किं ज्ञातेन तवार्जुन ।
विष्टभ्याहमिदं कृत्स्नम्
एकांशेन स्थितो जगत् ॥१०.४२॥

atha vā bahunaitena
kiṁ jñātena tavārjuna
viṣṭabhyāhamidaṁ kṛtsnam
ekāṁśena sthito jagat (10.42)

athavā — but; bahunaitena = bahunā — with extensive + etena — with this; kim — what is the value? jñātena — with information; tavārjuna = tava — of you + arjuna — Arjuna; viṣṭabhyāham = viṣṭabhya — supporting + aham — I; idam —

this; kṛtsnam — entire; ekāṁśena = eka — one + amśena — by a fraction; sthito = sthitaḥ — based, standing; jagat — world

But Arjuna, what is the value of this extensive information? As the foundation, I support this entire universe with a fraction of Myself. (Bhagavad Gītā 10.42)

Analysis

It is a good question, regarding what to do with this information about the details of Krishna's position in reference to whatever exist as this cosmic presentation.

- What is the relevance if Krishna is as he declared?
- Who can track the ultimate?
- Who will be conscious to observe the termination of this cosmos?
- Who can rate the time of this display?
- Why does it matter if Krishna is the ultimate source of the selves?
- What changes for anyone who investigates the sources of personality?

Comprehension of Bhagavad Gītā Verse 10.42

It may be that knowing about the ultimate person has little relevance in the routine of any creature. Here, it is a matter of the eating, sleeping, mating and defending of oneself and one's dependents. The social interplay is fraught with hazards which assail the temporary features of a self.

Despite the fact that the temporary additions and subtractions are not the real self but directly or indirectly adhere to it, still those alterations and skins have influence on the self. The preoccupation with that seems to be the urgency which makes the information and research into the origins to be of little importance.

For Krishna as he presented himself, this situation borders on the irrelevant because with a fraction of himself, he supports this. His vast entity is not required for the maintenance of this, only a tiny portion of his interest supports this.

श्रीभगवानुवाच
पश्य मे पार्थ रूपाणि
शतशोऽथ सहस्रशः ।
नानाविधानि दिव्यानि
नानावर्णाकृतीनि च ॥११.५॥

śrībhagavānuvāca
paśya me pārtha rūpāṇi
śataśo'tha sahasraśaḥ
nānāvidhāni divyāni
nānāvarṇākṛtīni ca (11.5)

śrībhagavān — the Blessed Lord; uvāca — said; paśya — see; me — My; pārtha — son of Pṛthā; rūpāṇi — forms; śataśo = śataśaḥ — hundred; 'tha = atha — or; sahasraśaḥ — thousand; nānāvidhāni — variously manifested; divyāni — supernatural; nānāvarṇākṛtīni = nānā — various + varṇa — color + ākṛtīni — shapes + ca — and

The Blessed Lord said: O son of Pṛthā, see My forms in the hundreds or rather in the thousands, variously manifested, supernatural and of the various colors and shapes. (Bhagavad Gītā 11.5)

Analysis

The clarification we get from Krishna, which is most relevant to our individual selves, is that the core of the person is eternal. Some philosophers, denounce this. They relegate the self to being a temporary mockup. They present hard evidence in the form of showing that the person which is known as the son/daughter of this man and that woman, is a social construction. Krishna presents a coreSelf which endures despite the additions and subtractions. The difference is that some teachers show only the social construction as the person. They deny a core around which the social additives and voids adhere.

Krishna renders new ideas about himself, as being not just one personSelf but as multiple persons existing and functioning simultaneously. He displayed that to Arjuna. Krishna has multiple personality power, where he is here, there and everywhere, functioning as multiple selves with each being himself.

Comprehension of Bhagavad Gītā Verse 11.5

Some forms of Krishna are identical copies of any specific form of his. Each form is unique with minute or obvious variations. The actions of each are not a duplicate but is novel and applicable to its situation. Each Krishna form is not an *atma* or a limited self. It is a *paramatma*, an unlimited self with superpowers.

Besides these duplicates of the Supreme Person, there are semi-absolute selves who are coordinate to Krishna. There are also limited selves who are powered-up by Krishna. These display features of absoluteness as allowed by him.

पश्यादित्यान्वसून्रुद्रान्
अश्विनौ मरुतस्तथा ।
बहून्यदृष्टपूर्वाणि
पश्याश्चर्याणि भारत ॥११.६॥

paśyādityānvasūnrudrān
aśvinau marutastathā
bahūnyadṛṣṭapūrvāṇi
paśyāścaryāṇi bhārata (11.6)

paśyādityān = paśya — look at + ādityān — supernatural rulers; vasūn — Vasus; rudrān — supernatural destroyers; aśvinau — two supernatural doctors; marutaḥ — supernatural stormers; tathā — also; bahūny = bahūni — many; adṛṣṭapūrvāṇi = adṛṣṭa — unseen + pūrvāṇi — before; paśyāścaryāṇi = paśya — view + āścaryāṇi — wonders; bhārata — O relation of the Bharata family

Look at the supernatural rulers, the supernatural destroyers, the two supernatural doctors and the supernatural stormers. View many wonders which were unseen before, O relation of the Bharata family. (Bhagavad Gītā 11.6)

Analysis

Apart from Krishna Himself as multiple varied persons of Himself, there are supernatural beings who are aligned with Krishna. In addition, there are supernatural beings who are in opposition to Krishna. These are personSelves all the same. These have cores which are eternal just the same, and to which temporary personality features adhere or are discarded.

Besides the perpetual personSelves, there are supernatural environments which Krishna is aware of and which his consciousness sustains. A limited self is usually aware of one-, two- or three-dimensional levels. The supreme being is aware of selected dimensions and he is selectively conscious of all dimensions simultaneously.

Comprehension of Bhagavad Gītā Verse 11.6

Arjuna was aware of the physical situation at the place of Kurukshetra where Krishna was present as Arjuna's chariot driver. At the same place, Krishna displayed many other dimensions and the persons inhabiting those realms. Krishna displayed other places, showing the relationship between those existences and what occurred at Kurukshetra.

This apparition revealed what was invisible and what was never seen by the persons who were present with Krishna and Arjuna at that place. The evidence is that unless one has supernatural perception and can sensually apprehend other realities, one cannot thoroughly comprehend the cause of what happens on this earthly domain.

One should not assume that only the physical world exists. It is better to conclude that there are other dimensions which remain invisible because one lacks the sense perception which can picture the other situations.

इहैकस्थं जगत्कृत्स्नं
पश्याद्य सचराचरम् ।
मम देहे गुडाकेश
यच्चान्यद्द्रष्टुमिच्छसि ॥११.७॥

ihaikasthaṁ jagatkṛtsnaṁ
paśyādya sacarācaram
mama dehe guḍākeśa
yaccānyaddraṣṭumicchasi (11.7)

ihaikastham = iha — here + ekastham — situated in one reality; jagat — universe; kṛtsnam — entire; paśyādya = pasya — see + adya — now; sacarācaram — with active and inactive; mama — of Me; dehe — in the body; guḍākeśa — O conqueror of sleep; yac = yad — what; cānyad = cānyat = ca — and + anyat — other; draṣṭum — to see; icchasi — you desire

Here, O conqueror of sleep, you see the entire universe with all active and inactive manifestations, situated as one reality, in My body. And observe any other manifestations which you desire to see. (Bhagavad Gītā 11.7)

Analysis

The one reality is the oneness which some philosophers hanker for, except that they have difficulty figuring individuality, especially considering that the conventional self is a mock-up or fabrication of cultural and environmental features.

The entire cosmos is situated in Krishna's body, or rather in one of his parallel forms. In a discussion about Krishna's supremacy, the yogin *Markandeya*, described an experience, where he entered a divine child Krishna, and experienced a parallel cosmos as being the inner situation in that child's form.

Krishna invited Arjuna to see whatever other reality, Arjuna had a desire to see or was curious about.

Comprehension of Bhagavad Gītā Verse 11.7

This form of Krishna is known as the visvaRupa, the all-format, the living breathing totality of the cosmos as a personal reality which has a primary governor as Krishna.

There are innumerable sub-levels of this universal form, so many that it may be regarded as infinite even though Krishna does relax and suspend the manifestation of this energy and its persons, from time to time.

Even though this has temporary energy and constructed social roles, still the influence of this cannot be resisted in total by a limited entity. When one considers the circumspect power and containment of this form, where whatever is in it, as its composite, cannot become independent at any stage, all discussions about the limited self being the absolute is worthless.

Whatever happened, whatever happens, whatever will occur in time, all of this is within the confines of the universal form. It comprises personalities of varying powers and jurisdictions. It has immobile non-sentient materials. It has life force which causes animation.

न तु मां शक्यसे द्रष्टुम्
अनेनैव स्वचक्षुषा ।
दिव्यं ददामि ते चक्षुः
पश्य मे योगमैश्वरम् ॥११.८॥

na tu māṁ śakyase draṣṭum
anenaiva svacakṣuṣā
divyaṁ dadāmi te cakṣuḥ
paśya me yogamaiśvaram (11.8)

na — not; tu — but; mām — Me; śakyase — you can; draṣṭum — to see; anenaiva = anena — by this + iva (eva) — indeed; svacakṣuṣā — with your vision; divyam — supernatural; dadāmi — I give; te — to you; cakṣuḥ — sight; paśya — look at; me — Me; yogam — mystic power; aiśvaram — majesty

But you cannot see with your vision. I give you supernatural sight to look at My mystic majesty. (Bhagavad Gītā 11.8)

Analysis

For Krishna, the physical perception, the invisible dimensions and the transit zones between the two are ever available and perceptible. For Arjuna as a limited self, it is not. There are three methods for increased access. These are.

- uplift by a deity
- increase in vibration rate by yogic practice of a limited self
- combined mystic actions of a deity and a limited self

The limited self is not limited in terms of his/her duration of existence. In fact, the existence of a self is not reliant on the self nor on the concept the self has of itself, nor on the ability of the self to realize its perpetuation.

The limited self is eternal despite itself, despite its limitation of power radiance. The extent of its powers is limited but it is perpetual all the same. Even though that self has no recall of itself from the hoary past, still it existed way back when. Its inability to remember itself during periods of suspended objectivity, does not in any way delete its existence. Its inability to use itself, assert itself or absorb impacts from others, does not indicate that it is not perpetually radiant.

As a limited self, Arjuna did not have the perpetual sensual perception of the transcendental levels which Krishna exposed on this occasion. Arjuna would need to be refitted with new perceptive senses to perceive what Krishna exposed.

Comprehension of Bhagavad Gītā Verse 11.8

Even though Krishna exposed the universal form with its various parallel levels of action and interaction, still Arjuna as he was sensually outfitted, could not perceive the display. In response, Krishna allowed supernatural sight as a special sensual perception for Arjuna. The physical person whom Arjuna knew as Krishna was more than a limited transcendent self-governing human being. Krishna changed Arjuna's psychic being. Arjuna was outfitted with vision of what occurred in the supernatural levels which related to the scenes which Arjuna was in on the physical plane.

संजय उवाच
एवमुक्त्वा ततो राजन्
महायोगेश्वरो हरिः ।
दर्शयामास पार्थाय
परमं रूपमैश्वरम् ॥११.९॥

saṁjaya uvāca
evamuktvā tato rājan
mahāyogeśvaro hariḥ
darśayāmāsa pārthāya
paramam rūpamaiśvaram (11.9)

saṁjaya — Sanjaya; uvāca — said; evam — thus; uktvā — having said; tato = tataḥ — then; rājan — O King; mahāyogeśvaro = mahāyogeśvaraḥ — the great Master of Yoga; hariḥ — Hari, the God Vishnu; darśayāmāsa — reveals; pārthāya — to the son of Pritha; paramam — supreme; rūpam — form; aiśvaram — supernatural glory

Sanjaya said: O King, having said that, the great Master of Yoga, Hari, the God Vishnu, revealed to the son of Pṛthā, the Supreme Form, the supernatural glory. (Bhagavad Gītā 11.9)

Analysis

Up to this point in the discourse, Arjuna had no hard evidence which he could relate to directly with his senses. When Krishna increased the sensual range, Arjuna suddenly accepted that Krishna was as Krishna described.

The great Master of Yoga, the natural effortless lord of it, known as Hari, the God Vishnu, Krishna, revealed himself and his contents to the fascination of Arjuna, who just a moment before, was stunned by Krishna's self-description, even though Arjuna could not verify Krishna's mystic glory. The supernatural glory of Krishna is his widespread governing power which is directly and indirectly applied to all events in various dimensions simultaneously. This does not mean that everything which occurs in the cosmic manifestation happens because Krishna expressly wants, requests or forces it. He governs even what is not in total harmony with his desire but in a way that keeps the situations within the limits of containment.

Comprehension of Bhagavad Gītā Verse 11.9

After Arjuna wanted to directly perceive the mystic events which Krishna described, the Supreme Lord nonchalantly remarked that the reality which was invisible was now in plain sight. Still, Arjuna viewed as he did before, as a limited self would.

Arjuna then requested to be equipped to see the truths. Then by a direct grace, Krishna energized Arjuna's psyche, giving him the supernatural perception. A limited entity, though a spiritual being, is sensually equipped to a limited degree. It can only see or sense according to its lifeform and its natural mystic reach into higher dimensions. Thus, it is unusual for it to have extended sensual perceptions which can pry the invisible basis of this creation.

अनेकवक्त्रनयनम्
अनेकाद्भुतदर्शनम् ।
अनेकदिव्याभरणं
दिव्यानेकोद्यतायुधम् ॥११.१०॥

anekavaktranayanam
anekādbhutadarśanam
anekadivyābharaṇaṁ
divyānekodyatāyudham (11.10)

anekavaktranayanam = aneka — countless + vaktra — mouth + nayanam — eye; anekādbhutadarśanam = aneka — countless + adbhuta — wonders + darśanam — vision; anekadivyābharaṇaṁ = aneka — countless + divya — supernatural + ābharaṇam — ornament; divyānekodyatāyudham = divya — supernatural + aneka — countless + udyata — uplifted + āyudham — weapon

Countless mouths, eyes, wondrous visions, countless supernatural ornaments, supernatural uplifted weapons, (Bhagavad Gītā 11.10)

Analysis

The issue of a supernatural divine being, the Supreme Lord or some other powerful person, carrying or displaying weapons on a higher plane of existence which is the permitting energy for this physical manifestation, causes a puzzle.

Some wonder why there would be danger on the supernatural plane, where God controls what happens. Why does God need weapons on that level? Are there criminals and opponents there? Do the adversaries of Krishna live in his influence while competing with and challenging his management?

Countless mouths and eyes were seen by Arjuna. These belonged to persons there. It was energy with personalities. Even though from one angle it was one form, still on close observation, Arjuna perceived a composite of persons with massive powers interacting.

Comprehension of Bhagavad Gītā Verse 11.10

The universal form, though the format of one person from one angle, was a composite of countess persons and environments. Everyone had mouths, eyes, ornaments and uplifted weapons. Each governed some dimensional area or domain. Ultimately, Krishna is the central figure in the outlays of energies and personalities.

Due to the hostility and breaches of some persons, there were supernatural uplifted weapons used to suppress encroachments of territories, properties and families.

दिव्यमाल्याम्बरधरं
दिव्यगन्धानुलेपनम् ।
सर्वाश्चर्यमयं देवम्
अनन्तं विश्वतोमुखम् ॥११.११॥

divyamālyāmbaradharaṁ
divyagandhānulepanam
sarvāścaryamayaṁ devam
anantaṁ viśvatomukham (11.11)

divyamālyāmbaradharam = divya — supernatural + mālya — garland + ambara — garment + dharam — wearing; divyagandhānulepanam = divya — supernatural + gandha — perfume + anulepanam — ointment;

sarvāścaryamayam = sarvaścarya — all wonder + mayam — made of; devam — God; anantam — infinite; viśvatomukham — facing all directions

...wearing supernatural garlands and garments, with supernatural perfumes and ointments, appearing all wonderful, the God appeared infinite as He faced all directions. (Bhagavad Gītā 11.11)

Analysis

Besides weapons, there were garlands, garments, perfumes and ointments. The personalities were attired wondrously. The God, Krishna, specifically appeared infinite in range and duplication. One got the intuition that Krishna faced every direction and penetrated every portion and level of reality.

The supervisory reach of the God Krishna was infinite, spreading beyond any other person and manifestation. The Supreme Lord was distinctly himself in contrast to everyone else who in reference had limited spread.

The interlocking of the various dimensions, the extrasensory control by various deities and their agents, cannot be figured by a limited being. However, if permitted and assisted by someone with the power and ability, a limited self can derive some understanding of how it is possible to have extensive supervisory power over multiple events in different dimensions simultaneously.

Comprehension of Bhagavad Gītā Verse 11.11

Subtle planes of existence and higher realms, supernatural or spiritual environments, are beyond our physical sense perception. The profile one has at birth of the body, is one of physical access with psychic senses which do not illustrate psychic forms with clarity. For that matter, the psychic world is vague and indefinite to the sensual perception of a physical body.

This makes it unlikely that any human being will have confidence in psychic people and environments. It is likely that the mind will regard psychic events as illusory or formless, indefinite and uncertain. Due to this the idea of people being attired, even perfumed, appearing outfitted wonderfully, and with precise expressive powers, requires some application of trust in Krishna. Arjuna noticed that there was no acceptable limit to the God Krishna. One could not say that his influence was here, but it was not there, or that his powers were focused somewhere but not everywhere. With supernatural senses, wherever Arjuna scanned, he found no place or person who was outside the disciplinary reach of the Supreme Lord.

दिवि सूर्यसहस्रस्य
भवेद्युगपदुत्थिता ।
यदि भाः सदृशी सा स्याद्
भासस्तस्य महात्मनः ॥११.१२॥

divi sūryasahasrasya
bhavedyugapadutthitā
yadi bhāḥ sadṛśī sā syād
bhāsastasya mahātmanaḥ (11.12)

divi — in the sky; sūryasahasrasya = sūrya — sun + sahasrasya — of one thousand; bhaved = bhavet — should be; yugapad — at once; utthitā — risen; yadi — if; bhāḥ — brilliance; sadṛśi — such; sā — it; syād — it may be; bhāsaḥ — of brightness; tasya — of it; mahātmanaḥ — of the great personality

Imagine in the sky, a thousand suns, being at once risen together. If such a brilliance were to be, it may be compared to that Great Personality. (11.12)

Analysis

The fracturing of this apparition is that from physical perception it does not exist. Yet, on a supernatural level, where Krishna displayed it and installed extrasensory perception for Arjuna, it is so manifested that it overpowers the senses and requirs visual shielding.

It impressed Arjuna as a reality over a reality, into a reality, endlessly. The accounting of it was beyond anything within Arjuna's frame of reference.

Comprehension of Bhagavad Gītā Verse 11.12

For those who do not have access to this supernatural perception, which was inserted into Arjuna's psyche, Sanjaya, the person who first narrated *Bhagavad Gītā*, and who saw the Universal Form just as did Arjuna, shared the experience with King Dhritarashtra. He suggested that to understand the shock experience of this colossal reality, one could imagine in the sky, one thousand suns, being at once risen together.

If such a brilliance were to be, it may be compared with the brilliant radiance of that Great Personality, Krishna. That form of his is ongoing, shining from moment to moment but it is not enforced on each limited being, except on specific psychic planes of existence. Its effects may be blatant or subtle. It limit-setting power, though unseen, is infallible.

तत्रैकस्थं जगत्कृत्स्नं
प्रविभक्तमनेकधा ।
अपश्यद्देवदेवस्य
शरीरे पाण्डवस्तदा ॥११.१३॥

tatraikasthaṁ jagatkṛtsnaṁ
pravibhaktamanekadhā
apaśyaddevadevasya
śarīre pāṇḍavas tadā (11.13)

tatraikastham = tatra — there + ekastham — one position; jagat — universe; kṛtsnam — entire; pravibhaktam — divided; anekadhā — in many ways; apaśyad

= apaśyat — he saw; devadevasya — of the God of gods; śarīre — in the body; pāṇḍavas — Arjuna Pandava; tadā — then

There the entire universe existed as one reality divided in many ways. Arjuna Pandava then saw the God of gods in that body. (Bhagavad Gītā 11.13)

Analysis

Here we get information that the form which Arjuna saw in the apparition of the Universal Form, was a colossal body in which Krishna was the significant factor both as a person, as the supreme being, and as raw influence through radiant power.

Krishna said he would show himself, as to how he controlled everything within a time limit. When Arjuna saw the form, he realized that it was multi-persons with some being Krishna and Krishna's multiples and others being other persons who functioned under Krishna's supervisory influence. It was Krishna, the Supreme Person, plus Krishna multiplied and parallel without reduction of authority, plus agents of Krishna having various specific powers and jurisdictions. There were countless dimensions and environments experienced by Arjuna.

Comprehension of Bhagavad Gītā Verse 11.13

The universe is one reality as a physical and compounded psychic conglomerate. It is a huge layout of environments and persons with innumerable forms in places. Some forms overlap others. Some are superimposed in or on others. The presentation is tremendous. It overpowers a limited entity, who cannot grasp its influence.

As Arjuna peered the form to satisfy his curiosity about its construction and mission. In every instant, he was aware of the central person, Krishna, the Supreme Personality of Godhead.

ततः स विस्मयाविष्टो
हृष्टरोमा धनंजयः ।
प्रणम्य शिरसा देवं
कृताञ्जलिरभाषत ॥११.१४॥

tataḥ sa vismayāviṣṭo
hṛṣṭaromā dhanaṁjayaḥ
praṇamya śirasā devaṁ
kṛtāñjalirabhāṣata (11.14)

tataḥ — then; sa = saḥ — he; vismayāviṣṭo = vismayāviṣṭaḥ — one who is amazed; hṛṣṭaromā — one whose hair is bristled; dhanamjayaḥ — Arjuna, conqueror of rich countries; praṇamya — bowing; śirasā — with the head; devam — God; kṛtāñjalir = kṛtāñjaliḥ — making reverence with palms pressed for prayers; abhāsata — he spoke

Then he, who was amazed, whose hair bristled, Arjuna, the conqueror of rich countries, bowing his head to the God, with palms pressed for prayers, spoke. (Bhagavad Gītā 11.14)

Analysis

Evidence of greatness may render humility in the person who is subjected to it. Arjuna requested the revelation which would support Krishna's claims. When Krishna energized Arjuna so that his psyche rendered supernatural perception of what was unseen, Arjuna was shocked to see the extent of Krishna influence and powers.

The experience was horrendous, whereby Arjuna's hair bristled. It was so compelling, that Arjuna bowed his head to the God. With palms pressed for prayers, Arjuna glorified Krishna.

Comprehension of Bhagavad Gītā Verse 11.14

The outlandish claims of Krishna, the mere human being, friend and chariot driver of Arjuna, were fantastic but Arjuna had no idea of how Krishna could prove himself. Previously, whatever Krishna said about himself, was accepted by Arjuna but the extent of Krishna's powers was not experienced.

When Arjuna saw the apparition, he was shocked. The psychological distance between Arjuna and Krishna became evident. Arjuna, the limited self, got evidence that he was not in the rating of Krishna, the supreme being. This caused a feeling of inadequacy which could only be compensated by humility and formal recognition of Krishna as God Supreme.

अर्जुन उवाच
पश्यामि देवांस्तव देव देहे
सर्वांस्तथा भूतविशेषसंघान् ।
ब्रह्माणमीशं कमलासनस्थम्
ऋषींश्च सर्वानुरगांश्च दिव्यान्
॥११.१५॥

arjuna uvāca
paśyāmi devāṁstava deva dehe
sarvāṁstathā bhūtaviśeṣasaṁghān
brahmāṇamīśaṁ kamalāsanastham
ṛṣīṁśca sarvānuragāṁśca divyān (11.15)

arjuna — Arjuna; uvāca — said; paśyāmi — I see; devāṁs — spiritual rulers; tava — your; deva — O God; dehe — in the body; sarvāṁs — all; tathā — as well as; bhūtaviśeṣasaṁghān = bhūta — being + viśeṣa — variety + saṁghān — assembled; brahmāṇam — Lord Brahmā; īśam — Lord; kamalāsanasthaṁ = kamala — lotus + āsana — seat + stham — situated; ṛṣīṁśca = ṛṣīn — yogi sages + ca — and; sarvān — all; uragāṁśca = uragān — serpents + ca — and; divyān — supernatural

Arjuna said: I see the supernatural rulers in Your body, O God, as well as all varieties of beings assembled there, Lord Brahmā, who is lotus-seated, all the yogi sages and the supernatural serpents. (Bhagavad Gītā 11.15)

Analysis

Of interest is that Arjuna saw the deities of the Vedic pantheon of supernatural controllers who monitor situations and people on various levels of this cosmic manifestation. It is inter-related in abstract ways, which a limited being cannot decipher.

Arjuna was surprised to see that the Krishna who stood beside him and who served him as a chariot driver, was indeed the Supreme Lord with control of persons as great as the creatorGod Brahma. This was unbelievable. How could it be that the personSource of Brahma could be a human being? How could God suppress his glories in that way?

What is achieved for God to reduce himself to being a two-bit human being whose body was temporary like that of anyone else? How was anyone to know that Krishna is God, and that one's behavior was witnessed by him and put to the measure of his standard for righteous conduct.

Comprehension of Bhagavad Gītā Verse 11.15

Arjuna saw supernatural rulers whom he recognized because of their attire, weapons, symbols and looks, as these were described in the Vedic literature of his time. These however did not have absolute autonomy over the realms they presided. Instead, they were within Krishna influence and were being subjected to Krishna's censor.

The creatorGod, a primal deity in the Vedic pantheon, was seen with his first productions, who were people of renown in the Vedic text. But Brahma was under the grip of Krishna, who was the only person of absolute range in the apparition.

अनेकबाहूदरवक्त्रनेत्रं
पश्यामि त्वां सर्वतोऽनन्तरूपम् ।
नान्तं न मध्यं न पुनस्तवादिं
पश्यामि विश्वेश्वर विश्वरूप
॥११.१६॥

anekabāhūdaravaktranetraṁ
paśyāmi tvām sarvato'nantarūpam
nāntaṁ na madhyaṁ na punastavādiṁ
paśyāmi viśveśvara viśvarūpa (11.16)

anekabāhūdaravaktranetram = aneka — countless + bāhu — arm + udara — belly + vaktra — face + netram — eye; paśyāmi — I see; tvām — you; sarvato = sarvataḥ — all directions; 'nantarūpam = anantarūpam = ananta — infinite + rūpam — form; nāntam = na — not + antam — end; na — not; madhyam —

middle; na — no; punas = punar — again even; tavādim = tava — of you + ādim — beginning; paśyāmi — I observe; viśveśvara — O Lord of all; viśvarūpa — form of everything

There are countless arms, bellies, faces, and eyes. I see You in all directions, O person of infinite form. There is no end, no middle, nor even a beginning of You. I observe You, O Lord of all, O Form of everything. (Bhagavad Gītā 11.16)

Analysis

To Arjuna this concerned persons, *purushas*, not just a class of reality which was part of an absolute source in which character and personQuality had no significance. It is not just *atmas* who were reduced ultimately to being part of *brahman*, an overarching collective terminal for reality.

There was no dismissing the persons and their uniqueness, one in reference to the other. There were countless arms, bellies, faces and eyes. Which was Krishna's? Which was that of someone who was an agent of Krishna or merely a limited self in the fray?

Comprehension of Bhagavad Gītā Verse 11.16

The vast display of the persons in the universal form, was to Arjuna, something beyond reconning. It was endless, without a median point. He could not discern a beginning of it. In any way possible, measurement was useless.

The summary of this was that Krishna was in a sense the form of everything, the Lord of all. This was the summary conclusion. Instead of a core existence which has nothing but its existence feature, and which was part of a vast origin known as *brahman* in the *Upanishads*, there were persons who were in liaison with the Supreme Lord, who is a superPerson of infinite powers in contrast.

Instead of the *atmas*, or spirituals potentials, adding up to *brahman* as a vast reality, with the *atma* specks having little meaning unless they are totally immerged into *brahman*, there are distinct individual persons who function in relation to the *param purusha*, the Supreme Person.

किरीटिनं गदिनं चक्रिणं च
तेजोराशिं सर्वतो दीप्तिमन्तम् ।
पश्यामि त्वां दुर्निरीक्ष्यं समन्ताद्
दीप्तानलार्कद्युतिमप्रमेयम्
॥११.१७॥

kirīṭinaṁ gadinaṁ cakriṇaṁ ca
tejorāśiṁ sarvato dīptimantam
paśyāmi tvāṁ durnirīkṣyaṁ samantād
dīptānalārkadyutim aprameyam (11.17)

kirīṭinam — crowned; gadinam — armed with a club; cakriṇam — bearing a disc; ca — and; tejorāśim = tejo — splendor + rāśim — a mass; sarvato = sarvataḥ — on all sides; dīptimantam — shining wondrously; paśyāmi — I see; tvām — you; durnirīkṣyam — difficult to behold; samantād = samantāt — in entirety; dīptānalārkadyutim = dīpta — blazing + anala — fire + arka — sun + dyutim — effulgence; aprameyam — immeasurable

This Form is crowned, armed with a club, bearing a discus, a mass of splendor on all sides, shining wondrously with immeasurable radiance of the sun and blazing fire. I see You in entirety, You Who are difficult to behold. (Bhagavad Gītā 11.17)

Analysis

This is about personality. There is no indication of a speck of identity which lies in a sea of other identities which are exactly similar, and which have no personal content or property. It is proposed however that everything on this side of existence, on the side which opposes the *brahman* supreme reality, is illusory, is maya, is fantasy, and is of no consequence in the final analysis. How is this revelation of Krishna, to be reconciled with this? Why were there weapons even though the form shunned wondrously with immeasurable radiance of the sun and blazing fire? Arjuna's newly adopted eyes barely endured the brilliance.

Can a supernatural body of any person, even the supreme being, be wounded or disciplined? What methods of reform are necessary on the level of existence in which this universal form was displayed?

Comprehension of Bhagavad Gītā Verse 11.17

The special insignia of a crown, club, and discus is that of a Vishnu divine personality, an unlimited self as Krishna or as a parallel person. Arjuna recognized this format as that of Lord Vishnu, as that deity was known at the time of Krishna's declaration of *Bhagavad Gītā*.

The brilliance of the forms, their splendor, the immeasurable radiance was not physical because otherwise Arjuna would have seen that before he was given the special vision which shifted his viewing impulse to a supernatural dimension to which his physical eyes had no access.

Arjuna saw the range of persons, powers, and environments, with Krishna being the governor of those personal and environmental events. The span of it was an entirety which was difficult to gaze upon. Efforts to measure and categorize it, proved to Arjuna that his supernatural sensual grasp was insufficient for the task.

त्वमक्षरं परमं वेदितव्यं
त्वमस्य विश्वस्य परं निधानम् ।
त्वमव्ययः शाश्वतधर्मगोप्ता
सनातनस्त्वं पुरुषो मतो मे
॥११.१८॥

tvamakṣaraṁ paramaṁ veditavyaṁ
tvamasya viśvasya paraṁ nidhānam
tvamavyayaḥ śāśvatadharmagoptā
sanātanastvaṁ puruṣo mato me (11.18)

tvam — you; akṣaram — imperishable; paramam — supreme; veditavyam — to be revealed; tvam — you; asya — of it; viśvasya — of all; param — ultimate; nidhānam — shelter; tvam — you; avyayaḥ — imperishable; śāśvatadharmagoptā = śāśvata — eternal + dharma — law + goptā — guardian; sanātanaḥ — most ancient; tvam — you; puruṣo = puruṣaḥ — person; mato = mataḥ — thought; me — of me

You are the indestructible Supreme Reality, to be realized. You are the ultimate shelter of all. You are the imperishable, eternal guardian of law. It seems to me that You are the most ancient person. (Bhagavad Gītā 11.18)

Analysis

The idea that the *atma* individual self is the *brahman* supreme reality, does not in any way clarify the issue of what or who controls the *atma's* separation from or unification with the *brahman*.

If the *atma* absolutely controls itself and what it is subjected to, then other challenges arise. Why did the *atma* subject itself to depart from the *brahman* supreme reality in the first place?

If it did not separate itself and was separated by another personal or natural agency, who or what was that influence? Will the *atma* be again parceled from *brahman* if that *atma* reunifies itself. How does it know if its re-unification with *brahman* will be permanent, especially if the partition was committed forcibly by another agency?

Comprehension of Bhagavad Gītā Verse 11 18.

Arjuna gave the opinion that Krishna is the indestructible Supreme Reality who should be realized. In summary, whatever is displayed as this creation on any level, is regulated, permitted and terminated by Krishna or by his influence.

What Arjuna saw was that whatever existed on the level of the universal form and on any level which was below it, will repose into Krishna at the end of permitted time. In terms of accountability, Krishna is the one who ultimately defines righteous conduct. His influences enforce the laws of nature but within his time scale and according to his view of what is legal and what is unwanted.

Arjuna said that Krishna is the most ancient person, the father of fathers, mother of mothers, the ultimate parentSource. Krishna's perception supersedes every other person.

अनादिमध्यान्तमनन्तवीर्यम्
अनन्तबाहुं शशिसूर्यनेत्रम्
पश्यामि त्वां दीप्तहुताशवक्त्रं
स्वतेजसा विश्वमिदं तपन्तम् ॥११.१९॥

Anādimadhyāntam anantavīryam
anantabāhuṁ śaśisūryanetram
paśyāmi tvāṁ dīptahutāśavaktraṁ
svatejasā viśvamidaṁ tapantam (11.19)

anādimadhyāntam = an — without + ādi — beginning + madhya — middle + antam — end; anantavīryam = ananta — unlimited + vīryam — manly power; anantabāhuṁ = ananta — unlimited + bāhum — arm; śaśisūryanetram = śaśi — moon + sūrya — sun + netram — eye; paśyāmi — I see; tvām — you; dīptahutāśavaktraṁ = dīpta — blazing + hutāśa — oblation-eating + vaktram — mouth; svatejasā — with Your splendor; viśvam — universe; idam — this; tapantam — heating

You who are without beginning, middle, or ending, Who has infinite manly power, Who has unlimited arms, Who has the sun and moon as Your eyes, I see You, with the blazing oblation-eating mouth, heating this universe with Your Own splendor. (Bhagavad Gītā 11.19)

Analysis

The emphasis for Arjuna was the disciplinary power and glory of the supreme being, Krishna. This involved persons and their clashing actions. Who will best the other? Is every person potentially the same as every other?

We have two events of person force.

- person raw
- person adorned and outfitted with adjuncts

If ultimately every person is identical in power, additions to any person does not change the identicalness of the self of each. If, however when the adjuncts and assistant formats are removed, each self will be found to be non-identical in any respect, then we must figure the situation afresh.

The apparition, once experienced visually and otherwise by Arjuna, got him to think that the supreme being, Krishna, was dissimilar to other selves in many respects. The fact that each is an individual and that each can assume various forms in one or the other dimensions, does not make each to be equal to the other.

The tremendous influence of Krishna when contrasted to that of Arjuna, for instance, shows that person must be considered and that merely assigning the term *atma* only avoids the issue of the disparity between one being and another. Proposing that somehow at some time, a self (*atma*) will merge into the supreme reality of *brahman*, is of little value in the discourse. At every step, the limited selves are confronted to explain their similarity with the supreme being, Krishna, and to relate to their similarity especially when it means that they have little or no control over the events which expose their dependent condition.

Comprehension of Bhagavad Gītā Verse 11.19

Arjuna saw what he saw. He formed conclusions on the basis of the cosmic personal events which he witnessed in the world of the universal form. He declared Krishna as the beginning, middle and end. Krishna, Arjuna felt, had infinite manly power. Krishna possessed unlimited arms. Krishna used the sun and moon as eyes. Krishna's mouth had fire for eating oblations. Krishna heated the world with radiance.

This brings personality into the scene of the origins. It pushes aside the *atma* idea and brings to fore that of the *purusha* personality as the primal force. This is how Krishna *Sāṁkhya* topples the parts of the *Upanishads* which suggest *advaita vedanta* and other energy oneness views.

द्यावापृथिव्योरिदमन्तरं हि
व्याप्तं त्वयैकेन दिशश्च सर्वाः ।
दृष्ट्वाद्भुतं रूपम् उग्रं तवेदं
लोकत्रयं प्रव्यथितं महात्मन्
॥११.२०॥

dyāvāpṛthivyoridam antaraṁ hi
vyāptaṁ tvayaikena diśaścasarvāḥ
dṛṣṭvādbhutaṁ rūpam ugraṁ tavedaṁ
lokatrayaṁ pravyathitaṁ mahātman (11.20)

dyāvāpṛthivyor = dyāvāpṛthivyoḥ — of heaven and earth; idam — this; antaram — space between; hi — indeed; vyāptam - pervaded; tvayaikena = tvaya — by you + ekena - alone; diśaḥ — directions; ca — and; sarvāḥ — all; dṛṣtvā — having seen + adbhutam — marvelous; rūpam — form; ugram — terrible; tavedam = tava — your + idam — this; lokatrayam = loka — world + trayam — three; pravyathitam — trembling; mahātman — O great personality

In all directions, the space between heaven and earth is pervaded by You alone. Seeing Your marvelous Form, of a terrible feature, the three worlds tremble, O great Personality. (Bhagavad Gītā 11.20)

Analysis

Even though the limited selves have influence and pervade some space, that is limited in spread. The supreme being pervades even what is pervaded by anyone, as well as anything unoccupied.

The universal form which Arjuna saw, the phase of it which he focused on, was of a terrible feature. It was fierce, stern. It caused every level to vibrate.

Comprehension of Bhagavad Gītā Verse 11.20

This is not the space we perceive between the higher atmosphere and the earth. This pertains to the supernatural version of the earth and the heavenly world which is above it on a supernatural plane. For the time being, unless one is transferred into the version of the subtle body which has this perception, one should not allow one's mind to note this as one would note physical reality of a planet on which surface we live and a sky above which is space containing planets and stars.

The supernatural situation, which was infinite even to Arjun's supernatural body through which he viewed that reality, was pervaded by Krishna. It was marvelous to behold but terrible and threatening as well. It upset Arjuna's mental equilibrium, causing him to be uncertain about his relationship with Krishna.

Arjuna saw the worlds tremble as they were in contrast to Krishna, as if they could not defy the God's authority.

अमी हि त्वा सुरसंघा विशन्ति
केचिद्भीताः प्राञ्जलयो गृणन्ति ।
स्वस्तीत्युक्त्वा महर्षिसिद्धसंघाः
स्तुवन्ति त्वां स्तुतिभिः
पुष्कलाभिः ॥११.२१॥

amī hi tvā surasaṁghā viśanti
kecidbhītāḥ prāñjalayo gṛṇanti
svastītyuktvā maharṣisiddhasaṁghāḥ
stuvanti tvāṁ stutibhiḥ puṣkalābhiḥ
(11.21)

amī — those; hi — truly; tvām — you; surasaṁghā = sura — supernatural ruler + saṁghā — groups; viśanti — they enter; kecid — some; bhītāḥ — terrified; prāñjalayo = prāñjalayaḥ — bowing with palms pressed together; gṛṇanti — they offer praise; svastīty = svastīti = sv (su) — suitable + asti — there be + iti — thus; uktvā — saying; maharṣisiddhasaṁghāḥ = mahārṣi — great yogi sages + siddha — perfected yogis + saṁghāḥ — groups; stuvanti — they praise; tvām — you; stutibhiḥ — with glorification; puṣkalābhiḥ — with lavish

Those groups of supernatural rulers enter You. Some being terrified, bowing with palms pressed together, offer praise. "May everything be suitable," they say. The groups of great yogi sages and perfected yogis praise You with lavish glorification. (Bhagavad Gītā 11.21)

Analysis

The supernatural rulers entered Krishna to submit their completed assignments. Some who did not finish tasks were terrified. Each one bowed with palms pressed together, offering praise to Krishna for not discarding them because of their failures.

How could a limited being, attain liberation while neglecting the requirements of the universal form? That is a mystery to anyone who is conscious of the presence of this Krishna.

The groups of great yogi sages and the perfected yogis, who are relatively exempt from social duties and governing tasks, praised Krishna, the central person of the universal form. They lavish glorification in the realization that he was it. Krishna, to them, was the root of everything, the saturation influence, the person superior to every other one.

Comprehension of Bhagavad Gītā Verse 11.21

While some were pleased to be aware of the universal form, others were uncertain. Some were terrified and responded to Krishna supremacy as if it was a crisis. They bowed with palms pressed together. They instinctually offered him praise. They appealed that hopefully everything was in order.

Some who are compatible with the *advaita vedanta* philosophy, give no acclaim to the universal form as reported by Arjuna. This presumes that there may be persons who are great yogi sages and perfected yogis who are unaware of the universal form and of Krishna being the central issue and supervisor with absolute powers to express and curtail influence.

If one accepts that there are yogi sages and perfected ascetics who give no credence to the idea of a universal form, it means that Arjuna only saw mystics who were compatible to Krishna, the central person.

If other perfected beings exist, and if such persons are unaware of Krishna, or are aware of him without knowing his cosmic majesty, it makes sense that such persons would not attest as Arjuna did.

It may be that they are unaware of the supernatural planes where the universal form is manifest. Or they are aware of these realms but give them no importance and do not feel that to be liberated, one has to converse with those authorities.

Can an unliberated self, be liberated without being permitted by Krishna in the universal form? So far, we heard that Arjuna saw the universal form as it relates to the physical society of Arjuna's time. Does this mean that one can bypass the form and not have its approval for going beyond its jurisdiction?

In the *Bhagavad Gītā*, Krishna suggested that Arjuna should fulfill his cultural duties and simultaneously cultivate yoga. Arjuna did not like the dual approach for lifestyle. The proposal of Krishna meant that one has no choice but to fulfill righteous duty as it is defined for the individual by the Supreme Lord. Liberation is only possible through the proficient practice of yoga but not by itself, only with the completion of social obligations which Krishna insists that the individual should perform.

रुद्रादित्या वसवो ये च साध्या
विश्वेऽश्विनौ मरुतश्चोष्मपाश्च ।
गन्धर्वयक्षासुरसिद्धसंघा
वीक्षन्ते त्वां विस्मिताश्चैव सर्वे ॥
११.२२ ॥

rudrādityā vasavo ye ca sādhyā
viśve'śvinau marutaścoṣmapāśca
gandharvayakṣā surasiddhasaṁghā
vīkṣante tvām vismitāś caiva sarve
(11.22)

rudrādityā = rudra — supernatural destroyers + ādityāḥ — supernatural rulers; vasavo = vasavaḥ — Vasus, assistants to supernatural rulers; ye — who; ca — and; sādhyā — Sādhya, guardian angels; viśve — Vishvadevas supernatural priests; 'śvinau = aśvinau — two primal supernatural doctors; marutaścoṣmapāś = marutaḥ — supernatural stormers + ca — and + uṣmapāḥ — spirits who take vapor bodies; ca — and; gandharvayakṣāsurasiddhasaṁghā = gandharva — celestial musicians + yakṣa — spirits guarding natural resources + asura — supernatural rebels + siddha — perfected souls + saṁghā — groups; vīkṣante — they behold; tvām — you; vismitāścaiva = vismitāḥ — amazed + ca — and + iva (eva) — indeed; sarve — all

The supernatural destroyers, the supernatural rulers, the assistants to those rulers, these and the Sādhya guardian angels, the Vishvadeva supernatural priests, the two primal supernatural doctors, the supernatural stormers, the spirits who take vapor bodies, the groups of celestial musicians, the spirits guarding natural resources, the supernatural rebels and the perfected souls, behold You. And they are all amazed. (Bhagavad Gītā 11.22)

Analysis

Except for the rebels, each group of the supernaturals mentioned, had positive relationship with the universal form's central person, Krishna. Seeing the extent of his glories and being reliant on him, they were amazed at every moment. They did not sense insecurity. They were blessed by their relationship with him.

These are groups of beings who normally remain imperceptible to humans. One may experience an entire lifetime as a human without having any idea that anyone exist on a supernatural plane. And yet, these persons are involved in our daily affairs as invisible but imposing influences.

Comprehension of Bhagavad Gītā Verse 11.22

In this world there are three classes of philosophical beliefs. Each has particular features. These are.

- theist
- atheist
- agnostic

Bhagavad Gītā is for theistic people of a certain persuasion. Those who are atheistic have little use for it. The other set, the agnostics, also have no use for it. They place no value on the idea that there may be a deity presiding over this.

There are sub-groups in each group of philosophers. The arguments and proposals are endless. The practical thing is to be tolerant of the different persons with their different outlooks. By being friendly to everyone, one can search for a philosophy which suits one's taste. If you read this book, I assume that you are either a theist or you are curious about this particular theistic presentation of someone who had a physical body on earth and who presented himself as the Supreme Personality.

There are many ideas about liberation. Some minimize or attempt to obliterate the idea of a personSelf. This book is for the establishment of a permanent coreSelf as much as that can be done through hearing from someone who is reliable, and through meditation practice for self-verification.

In the course for enlightenment, one should keep the coreSelf in view. One should make a record of its whereabouts. One should not fuse it into an absolute energy, as is done by some philosophers, where *atma*, the self, is voided by stressing *brahman*, the ultimate reality.

The enigma about a coreSelf is that it is unable to remain objectively conscious at all times. This is its singular handicap. In the proof for a continuous existence, a problem always arises when the self has lapses of consciousness.

Thus, to proceed one must define if something with limited conscious duration can exist perpetually. If something can endure despite not knowing that it is present, we cannot dismiss it because it is a temporary display.

There are yet other problems, like for instance, how can the self verify if it is eternal or not. The answer to that is that honestly speaking, it can neither verify its perpetual existence or its temporary stay. But here again in every aspect of a limited something, a person, reliance on someone with superior sense perception becomes relevant.

One does not have to personally verify everything. Some features can be verified. In every sphere of life, we are faced with individual limitations. We rely on the testimony of others. This holds true for the solution to the problem about a self's continuation forever or its demise in a few years.

In this discourse, the person to rely on is Krishna. The idea he presents is that the limited self is perpetual.

रूपं महत्ते बहुवक्त्रनेत्रं
महाबाहो बहुबाहूरुपादम् ।
बहूदरं बहुदंष्ट्राकरालं
दृष्ट्वा लोकाः प्रव्यथितास्तथाहम् ॥
११.२३ ॥

rūpaṁ mahatte bahuvaktranetraṁ
mahābāho bahubāhūrupādam
bahūdaraṁ bahudaṁṣṭrākarālaṁ
dṛṣṭvā lokāḥ pravyathitās tathāham
(11.23)

rūpam — form; mahat — great; te — your; bahuvaktranetram = bahu — many + vaktra — mouth + netram — eye; mahābāho — O mighty-armed Person; bahubāhūrupādam = bahu — many + bāhu — arm + ūru — thigh + pādam — foot; bahūdaram = bahu — many + udaram — belly; bahudaṁṣṭrākarālam = bahu — many + daṁṣṭrā — teeth + karālam — terrible; dṛṣṭvā — having seen; lokāḥ — the world; pravyathitāḥ — trembling; tathā — as well as; 'ham = aham — I

O mighty-armed Person, having seen Your Great Form with many mouths, and many arms, thighs, and feet, many bellies and many terrible teeth, the worlds tremble as well as I. (Bhagavad Gītā 11.23)

Analysis

At this stage of the revelation, Arjuna exhausted his efforts to come to terms with the apparition. There seem to be no way to appease, relate to or converse with the central person. Arjuna while still having supernatural perception, momentarily resumed his ordinary self as a warrior on the battlefield of *Kurukshetra*, a cousin of Krishna in the physical world.

Appealing to Krishna, Arjuna informed the Lord, that the expression of influence on the supernatural plane, caused the world to tremble. Perhaps it was not in the jitters on the physical level, but it was disturbing on that plane of consciousness where people experienced Krishna as the all-pervading cosmic influence.

Comprehension of Bhagavad Gītā Verse 11.23

When Arjuna requested direct perception of Krishna's cosmic majesty, Arjuna had no idea of the reality. When he perceived it, he was frightened. How was he to reconcile that Krishna was a human being with a limited physical body and was simultaneously the God of the world in the personal and energetic assessments.

The God that Krishna is, the one which Arjuna witnessed, is mighty-armed, militarily equipped. He governed politically from a higher plane. He had many mouths, arms, thighs and feet, many bellies and terrible teeth. He was capable of defending his principles.

Krishna is not a remote energy which is helpless to confront humans or other species who misbehave. Despite the presence of impersonal laws of nature, there are opinions and views which can be enforced personally. Krishna is the ultimate judge, the demarcation, the limit and the ultimate reference of any physical, psychic or spiritual society.

नभःस्पृशं दीप्तमनेकवर्णं
व्यात्ताननं दीप्तविशालनेत्रम् ।
दृष्ट्वा हि त्वां प्रव्यथितान्तरात्मा
धृतिं न विन्दामि शमं च विष्णो
॥११.२४॥

nabhaḥspṛśaṁ dīptamanekavarṇaṁ
vyāttānanaṁ dīptaviśālanetram
dṛṣṭvā hi tvāṁ pravyathitāntarātmā
dhṛtiṁ na vindāmi śamaṁ ca viṣṇo
(11.24)

nabhaḥspṛśaṁ = nabhaḥ — sky + spṛśaṁ — touching, extending; dīptam — glowing; aneka — many; varṇam — colors; vyātta — open; ānanam — mouths; dīpta — glowing; viśāla — very great; netram — eyes; dṛṣtvā — seeing; hi — certainly; tvām — You; pravyathita — perturbed; antaḥ — within; ātmā — soul; dhṛtim — steadiness; na — not; vindāmi — I have; śamam — mental tranquillity; ca — also; viṣṇo — O Lord Viṣṇu.

Having seen You, sky extending, blazing, multi-colored, with gaping mouths and blazing vast eyes, there is a shivering in my soul. I find no courage, nor stability, O God Vishnu. (Bhagavad Gītā 11.24)

Analysis

The problem with the universal form of Krishna, the problem for Arjuna or any limited person, is the disciplinary profile. What relationship is possible with such a Krishna. It crippled Arjuna's ability to relate and respond to the Krishna whom he knew as his cousin.

The personality of Krishna as the friend and cousin of Arjuna was not available in the universal form. What happened was the emotional change in Arjuna, such that there was a shivering in his soul. He lost even the courage to act. His sense of security as a prince in the *Kuru* dynasty was uprooted. Krishna's sky extending format, which blazed and was multi-colored, which had gaping mouths and blazing vast eyes, caused Arjuna to lose self-confidence and feel a sense of irrelevancy, as if Arjuna's existence was trivial.

The God Krishna that Arjuna witnessed was sky extending such that this God looked for compliance with his opinions and for non-compliance which he could forcibly adjust. Arjuna could find neither a posture, nor some usefulness, to suit Krishna.

Comprehension of Bhagavad Gītā Verse 11.24

In acquiring the sensual perception of the universal form, Arjuna lost the perception of the human physical person, the same Krishna. Wanting to reestablish the relationship with the human Krishna, Arjuna failed to stabilize it. It was as if he was switched to a different reality where there was no way to regain his human self and that of Krishna.

Arjuna was troubled because he did not forget himself as a human being but all the same, he could not fully switch himself back into the human situation where he had a footing and was a prince in a dynasty.

Arjuna recognized the central person in the universal form, as the God Vishnu. According to the information in the time of Arjuna, this was the Supreme Lord. What he heard of from religious authorities, fit the description of what Krishna displayed in the revelation. This person was sky extending, blazing, multi-colored, with gaping mouths and blazing vast eyes. There was no relating to him on equal terms, no friendship with this critical person. He could not be relied on to agree with anyone's opinion. There was no leeway in relationships with him. Someone became nervous, lost courage and was without stability in the presence of this absolute version of personality.

दंष्ट्राकरालानि च ते मुखानि
दृष्ट्वैव कालानलसंनिभानि ।
दिशो न जाने न लभे च शर्म
प्रसीद देवेश जगन्निवास ॥११.२५॥

daṁṣṭrākarālāni ca te mukhāni
dṛṣṭvaiva kālānalasaṁnibhāni
diśo na jāne na labhe ca śarma
prasīda deveśa jagannivāsa (11.25)

daṁṣṭrā — teeth; karālāni — terrible; ca — also; te — Your; mukhāni — faces; dṛṣtvā — seeing; eva — thus; kāla-anala — the fire of death; sannibhāni — as if; diśaḥ — the directions; na — not; jāne — I know; na — not; labhe — I obtain; ca — and; śarma — grace; prasīda — be pleased; deva-īśa — O Lord of all lords; jagat-nivāsa — O refuge of the worlds

And seeing Your Form with many mouths, having terrible teeth, glowing like the fire of universal destruction, I cannot determine the cardinal points. I do not find any peace of mind. Have mercy, O Lord of the gods, Abode of the universe. (Bhagavad Gītā 11.25)

Analysis

It appears that a limited being can neither embrace nor encompass the cosmic personality. Unless Krishna assumes a reduced diminutive profile and functions only like a human being, there seems to be no room for an agreeable pleasant relationship with his cosmic being.

On that supernatural level, which was displayed as requested by Arjuna, there was nothing pleasant and enjoyable. It brought to mind only the disciplinary and limiting powers of the divine Krishna. Arjuna was so disturbed that he lost sense of direction. Addressing Krishna as Lord of the gods and Abode of the Universe, Arjuna pleaded for mercy.

Comprehension of Bhagavad Gītā Verse 11.25

This revelation, which was astonishing and challenging for Arjuna, was manifested as requested by him. It was fantastic but not in an agreeable way, only to show the strict aspects of the Supreme Person in dealing with clashes of willpower between the supreme being and some limited selves.

On that level, the deviations which were possible on the psychic plane were plainly visible. Control of the worlds was enacted there, such that limits came into effect, on the physical and lower astral planes.

This was to inform Arjuna and everyone else, that despite the capacity to challenge the preferences of Krishna, still Krishna was the governor, the limiter, the terminal of the minute or cosmic events.

श्रीभगवानुवाच
मय्यावेश्य मनो ये मां
नित्ययुक्ता उपासते ।
श्रद्धया परयोपेतास्
ते.मे युक्ततमा मताः ॥१२.२॥

śrībhagavānuvāca
mayyāveśya mano ye māṁ
nityayuktā upāsate
śraddhayā parayopetās
te me yuktatamā matāḥ (12.2)

Śrībhagavān — the Blessed Lord; uvāca — said; mayyāveśya = mayi-on me + āveśya — focusing on: mano = manaḥ — mind; ye — who; māṁ — me; nityayuktā — those who are always disciplined in yoga; upāsate — they worship; śraddhayā — with faith; parayopetās = parayā — with the highest degree; + upetāḥ — endowed; te they; me — to me; yuktatamā — most disciplined; matāḥ — considered

The Blessed Lord said: Those whose minds are focused on Me, who are always disciplined in yoga, who are always involved in worship of Me, who are endowed with the highest degree of faith, they are considered to be the most disciplined. (Bhagavad Gītā 12.2)

Analysis

Person, Person, Person! From Krishna the stress is on person, *purusha*. If one considers that there is no real person, or that there is no coreSelf around which personal attributes temporarily adhere, one has no appreciation for person, neither a Supreme Self nor a limited one.

The word *atma* indicates a neutral speck reality which is featureless and blank. While this featureless real something is displaced into physical nature, it is subjected to projects which utilize its energy. The *advaita vedantists* suggest that the *atma* should free itself from being utilized. To do so, the suggestion is that it should resume its original surrounding, which is the collective absolute energy, *brahman*.

This explanation of existence makes sense to some persons, but it lacks credibility for others, especially those who know or suspect that there is a person self which is not featureless. This real something as a person has unique traits. To this is added other traits when this is displaced into physical nature.

The focus on the person of Krishna is done by other personSelves. But if one does not believe in person as a reality, this method would not serve the purpose. This is for those who are confident that persons are perpetual. However, it does not mean that the skills and traits which one developed in a particular life are permanent features of a self. In either case that of a featureless self (*atma*) and that of a unique self (*purusha*), there could be additives which adhere to the core personSelf, when he/she transmigrates and acquires a social role in varying associations.

The additions which adhere to a self, and which are temporary skills and traits, do not undermine the perpetual value of that self. Its value persists but it may feel undone or expanded according to the effects of the additives.

Comprehension of Bhagavad Gītā Verse 12.2

This involves yoga practice with the interest in Krishna as the Supreme Lord, the ultimate authority from every existential angle. The supreme being does not have to be interested and does not have to apply himself to every and any circumstance. He is selective in who or what he relates to.

When Arjuna got the increased sensual perception, whereby he could view Krishna as the central figure in the universal form, the vision though extensive, was limited to a particular phase of Krishna's focus. Other applications were not seen by Arjuna. Though unlimited to Arjuna, what he saw was a limited phase of Krishna's majestic supervisory glances.

For those who accept that personality is perpetual, even though additives to it are temporary, the ultimate focus should be on Krishna. To do this one must be disciplined in the meditation practice of yoga. Such a person should always be involved in worship of Krishna. He/She should be endowed with the highest degree of faith in the information of Krishna. That person is the most disciplined because he/she relies on Krishna's information and on others who are confident of the Supreme Lord.

ये त्वक्षरमनिर्देश्यम्
अव्यक्तं पर्युपासते ।
सर्वत्रगमचिन्त्यं च
कूटस्थमचलं ध्रुवम् ॥१२.३॥

ye tvakṣaramanirdeśyam
avyaktaṁ paryupāsate
sarvatragamacintyaṁ ca
kūṭasthamacalaṁ dhruvam (12.3)

ye — who; tu — but; akṣaram — imperishable; anirdeśyam — undefinable; avyaktaṁ— invisible; paryupāsate — they cherish; sarvatragam — all-pervading; acintyam — inconceivable; ca — and; kūṭastham — unchanging; acalaṁ —- immovable; dhruvam — constant

But those who cherish the imperishable, undefinable, invisible, all-pervading, inconceivable, unchanging, immovable, constant reality, (Bhagavad Gītā 12.3)

Analysis

Krishna does not ridicule anyone who feels that the conclusion of everything is a void, is an absolute non-person energy, instead he recognizes those ascetics who have a non-person belief. However, some teachers who worship Krishna and advocate his glories, give the opinion that Krishna slighted the impersonalists and other types of no-supreme-person and temporary persons ideas.

The *brahman* spiritual reality is described in this verse, as the imperishable, undefinable, invisible, all-pervading, inconceivable, unchanging, immovable, constant reality.

If one has the view that this reality is the ultimate and that person is an illusory flash only, and if one seeks liberation and deeper insight into reality, one can focus on this supreme energy or environment and try to be situated in it.

Comprehension of Bhagavad Gītā Verse 12.3

If Krishna, a person who declared his GodSelf, admitted to the reality of a set of persons who cherish the abstract reality, then others who deny those people should be ignored. Their clamor and objection about people who are atheistic or agnostic, is useless chatter.

There is nothing untenable about thinking or perceiving what is imperishable as a source of anything which is physically present. If someone's mystic perception only penetrates so far, that is to his/her credit. What is undefinable, or all-pervading or inconceivable on one level may be perceptible to someone from the same or another level, if that person has senses which render a format for that abstract source.

What is unchanging or immovable, and is the constant reality, like on earth, we have the pulling force of gravity, cannot be denied. It may not be proven or disproven through arguments. There is no necessity to make someone an enemy because his ideas run contrary to mine. Not accepting Krishna's declaration of himself as the Supreme Lord, the Cause of all causes, is no fault of anyone. In so far as that person is sensually limited, he does not get direct proof about this and may not accept Krishna's word for it. After all, Krishna is not physically present so that anyone can approach him for evidence as Arjuna did.

संनियम्येन्द्रियग्रामं
सर्वत्र समबुद्धयः ।
ते प्राप्नुवन्ति मामेव
सर्वभूतहिते रताः ॥१२.४॥

saṁniyamyendriyagrāmaṁ
sarvatra samabuddhayaḥ
te prāpnuvanti māmeva
sarvabhūtahite ratāḥ (12.4)

saṁniyamyendriyagrāmaṁ = saṁniyamya — controlling + indriyagrāmaṁ — all sensual energies; sarvatra — in all respects; samabuddhayaḥ — even-minded; te — them; prāpnuvanti — they attain; mām — me; eva — also; sarvabhūtahite = sarvabhūta — all creatures + hite — in the welfare; ratāḥ — rejoicing

...by controlling all sensual energies, being even minded in all respects, rejoicing in the welfare of all creatures, they also attain Me. (Bhagavad Gītā 12.4)

Analysis

This statement is of interest because Krishna accepts the process of source research based on the sensual prowess of the specific yogi or philosopher. Regardless of the theistic, atheistic, or agnostic stance of the person, still Krishna said that such a person would attain, but with a caveat.

The person must control all sensual energies, be even minded in every respect, and rejoice in the welfare of all creatures. The person must not have class or species bias. He/She must rate lifeforms to the extent of seeing that there is a similar core within each creature. His/Her sensual energies should be controlled so that it is not reactionary.

If no person is acknowledged anywhere, or if the person recognized is considered as a temporary somebody, even then the philosopher should equally regard that person. No prejudices and preferences should arise in relationship even with strangers.

Comprehension of Bhagavad Gītā Verse 12.4

A yogi who is an avowed atheist, one who is an agnostic, and another who believes that energy is the origin, current situation, or future resolution of this cosmic situation, will also gain access to Krishna, as he said. But there are requirements. The yogi must restrict his/her sensual involvements. He/She must be even minded in all respects, so that fickle emotional flareups do not arise. He/She must be friendly to one and all and must appreciate the existence of every creature.

ये तु सर्वाणि कर्माणि
मयि संन्यस्य मत्पराः ।
अनन्येनैव योगेन
मां ध्यायन्त उपासते ॥१२.६॥

ye tu sarvāṇi karmāṇi
mayi saṁnyasya matparāḥ
ananyenaiva yogena
māṁ dhyāyanta upāsate (12.6)

ye — who; tu — but; sarvāṇi — all; karmāṇi — actions; mayi — in me; saṁnyasya — deferring: matparāḥ — regarding me as the most important factor; ananyenaiva = ananyena — without another, undistracted + eva — indeed; yogena — with yoga discipline; māṁ — me; dhyayānta — meditating on; upāsate — they worship

But those who defer all actions to Me, regarding Me as the most important factor, who meditate on Me with undistracted yoga discipline, do worship Me. (Bhagavad Gītā 12.6)

Analysis

Krishna sorted the philosophers and yogis into two categories, both being approved and recognized by him, but he gave emphasis to those who are attracted to him positively.

Every lifeform has a sense of identity and calculative capacity. Each may not be equal to another. Still the similarity in the construction of the living creatures is evident.

If a yogi defers actions to Krishna, it will mean that he reserved his physical, mental and emotion power for use in getting the approval of Krishna. If someone somehow regards Krishna as the most important factor, and meditates on Krishna with undistracted yoga discipline, worshipping Krishna, that person would find his/her spiritual progress to be accelerated.

The acceptance of Krishna facilitates and promotes a deeper penetration into the mysteries of existence. Still, it is not the only way to dive into the sources of oneself. Krishna admitted this truth.

Comprehension of Bhagavad Gītā Verse 12.6

No matter what, if one is a theist, atheist or agnostic, one deals with persons. No matter where one goes, one will encounter and will relate to persons. Not just here, but hereafter even, one will find persons. We have hereafter encounters in dream states. There, we repeatedly meet persons. The involvement of persons is one of relational interplay.

The temporary function of a person as a social somebody, the character features of a person as a reliable or unreliable human or animal, involves obligation and service. Krishna suggested that it is best to defer actions to Him, to redirect the action impulse so that it is compatible to his demands.

This means that even though there are pressing concerns, which are defined by others, as per how their needs are configured, one should by all means, be inspired by Krishna so that one satisfies the obligations in a way which is approved by him.

This footnote is important because otherwise, one may feel that one should satisfy every need of everyone and be kind to one and all in a way which is desired by the recipients. It does not mean that. One is required to be equally disposed to others but as defined and governed by Krishna, the supreme being. His view of cordial reciprocation may be different to that of another person, but since Krishna is the reference, it makes for a stable measure when one checks for Krishna's approval when acting.

Meditation on Krishna is a mysterious process. This is because Krishna is not physically present as he was when he explained the *Bhagavad Gītā* to Arjuna. When Krishna revealed the universal form, Arjuna was jerked into the reality of Krishna's extensive powers.

The meditation on Krishna, whose location is hard to detect, is difficult to master. To pinpoint any abstract principle, personal or non-personal, is uncertain. To cultivate undistracted yoga discipline is an achievement that may take years to master. Lip service to Krishna, believing what Krishna said, all of this is praiseworthy, but it is not the achievement of meditating on him with undistracted yoga discipline.

Genuine worship of Krishna is a near-impossible feat. Many take credit for this worship. They do so on the basis of doing rituals to man-made idols which are supposed to be Krishna in fact. However, his worship requires his presence and the worshipper's purity of intent as well as Krishna's acceptance of the relationship and service. How does one know if one is pure enough to worship? How can one determine if Krishna has a relationship as one conceives or believes?

While in *advaita vedanta* one does not have to consider a relationship, in this person-to-person exchange, one has more requirements to fulfill. In the matter of the *atma* and *brahman*, the out-of-touch self and the collective non-involved massive pool of consciousness, there are two methods of relationship. One is the apparent or imaginative separation of the self from the collective security of the non-involved pool of consciousness. The other is the self, either foolishly considering itself as a self which is a reality in its own right, or it is in the collective with full security and no feeling of anything untoward.

तेषामहं समुद्धर्ता
मृत्युसंसारसागरात् ।
भवामि नचिरात्पार्थ
मय्यावेशितचेतसाम् ॥१२.७॥

teṣāmahaṁ samuddhartā
mṛtyusaṁsārasāgarāt
bhavāmi nacirātpārtha
mayyāveśitacetasām (12.7)

teṣām — of those; aham — I; samuddhartā — delivered; mṛtyusaṁsārasāgarāt = mṛtyu — death + saṁsāra — reincarnations + sāgarāt — from the vast existence; bhavāmi — I am; nacirāt — soon; pārtha — son of Pṛthā; mayyāveśitacetasām = mayi — in me + āveśita — intently, invested in + cetasām — of thoughts

I am the deliverer of those devotees, rescuing them from the vast existence of death and reincarnation. O son of Pṛthā, I soon deliver those devotees whose thoughts are intently invested in Me. (Bhagavad Gītā 12.7)

Analysis

Krishna's information, *Bhagavad Gītā*, contains the formula for escaping from the vast existence of death and reincarnation. This is a time exhibit which no limited being can totally exempt himself/herself from. Saying that one is a nothing in essence or that one is endurance personified, does not explain how one became self-aware in this place.

Even if one figures how that happened as to if some personal or energetic agency initiated that, one is still confronted with the specter of removing this or removing oneself from this.

As for those who indicate that there is no self, even those who avoid the ugly truth which is that they must endeavor to break free from the encrustation of physical and psychic energies, the feature of self persists.

Some say that it does not matter how anyone got into this. They relate that the only solution is to face the events and break loose from this. That view is valid only if the method of escape is unrelated to the method of capture.

An understanding of how one got involved could shed clarity on what is possible for escaping from this. If the agency for installing anyone in this, is personal, then a deityPerson may be approached for exit from this. If the embedding factor was a cosmic collective, then smashing the self into that may be the solution.

One may go towards the past event to meet the initiation point, or one may penetrate to the future and meet the freedom event. Krishna declared that he is the deliverer of the devotees whose thoughts are intently invested in him as he presents himself. That accords the person to deityPerson relationship as the method of release. The yielding one is the limited person with the deity providing a tailored method for release.

On the other hand, those who greet an ultimate collective as the origin, can gain release as Krishna described before. That course is more strenuous because it lacks the assistance of the deity.

Comprehension of Bhagavad Gītā Verse 12.7

Krishna can play a part in the deliverance of any limited self. As the Supreme Lord, he is liable for this. However, the limited entity must request of and be favorable to Krishna. The situation of this wavy existence is that it offers death and reincarnation.

Once a body is born, its death is certain. This is a mandatory inversion. Once a body dies, the self which was the body is deprived of the form and is left as a psychic something only. Usually, that psychic self seeks another body which is reborn somewhere somehow as a physical species. The reappearance as a physical lifeform may take years to format but it will happen unless the self is freed from the need for physical participation.

The passage from a living physical form to being a mere psychic self with a sense of insufficiency, is resolved temporarily by the psychic self assuming a new physical form as the son/daughter of a physical being. As soon as the new form is birthed, the body development begins again with that self having no cohesive recall of its former life. This dip into the psychic existence and rise from it as a physical being, is repeatedly enacted by the course of psychic and physical nature.

मय्येव मन आधत्स्व
मयि बुद्धिं निवेशय ।
निवसिष्यसि मय्येव
अत ऊर्ध्वं न संशयः ॥१२.८॥

mayyeva mana ādhatsva
mayi buddhiṁ niveśaya
nivasiṣyasi mayyeva
ata ūrdhvaṁ na saṁśayaḥ (12.8)

mayyeva = mayi — on me + eva — alone; mana — mind; ādhatsva — place; mayi — on me; buddhiṁ — intellect; niveśaya — cause to be absorbed; nivasiṣyasi — you will be focused: mayyeva = mayi — in me + eva — indeed; ata ūrdhvaṁ — from now onwards; na — not; saṁśayaḥ — doubt

Placing your mind on Me alone, causing your intellect to be absorbed in Me alone, you will be focused on Me from now onward. There is no doubt about this. (Bhagavad Gītā 12.8)

Analysis

Here, Krishna suggests that he is the only person who can free someone. In this case it is Arjuna specifically. But the context extends this to everyone. It may be taken in another way, which is that one may take assistance from more than one teacher but in any case, one must also be graced by Krishna.

Previously Krishna explained that those who do not regard him as the primal person and who strive sincerely and are not prejudiced, they can become liberated, even though for them, the means is a difficult and abstract practice. For Arjuna, it was easy to focus on Krishna and to put into practice Krishna's ideas. What is the situation for others? How are they to develop the reliance on Krishna?

Comprehension of Bhagavad Gītā Verse 12.8

Somehow, a yogi should be informed by Krishna. A yogi should know what about Krishna is unpleasant. It is not that the yogi must agree wholeheartedly with each of Krishna's proposals. A devotee should have a sharp degree of self-honesty, so that he knows what about Krishna he does not prefer. With that, he should come to terms with the fact that as a limited being, there is no chance of existing without the help of the Supreme Person.

At some stage one should learn how to place the mind on Krishna alone. That may result in being instructed by or intuitively directed by Krishna to learn from someone else, from an agent of Krishna or from someone who is hostile to Krishna's ideas but who is skilled in a discipline which is required to master yoga.

Kacha was from the side of the supernatural rulers, but he submitted to *Shukracharya* for learning. That teacher had a special skill which no one else knew. *Shukracharya* was hostile to *Kacha's* relatives and still *Kacha* served *Shukracharya* in a formal and submissive way (read *Mahabharata*).

Surrendering to Krishna does not necessarily mean that one will experience a relationship like that enjoyed by Arjuna. For that matter that surrender may result in one learning about Krishna and learning his methods from another person who is skilled sufficiently in a method which one needs for making progress in getting closer to Krishna.

It is important to settle one's differences with Krishna. To do this one has to understand what Krishna is about, regarding what he agrees with and what he opposes. One does not have to agree with him in every respect. One is not the supreme being. One does not have an ongoing full blown mystic perception which can rival Krishna's. Arjuna did not have it.

Person to Supreme Person, one should match to Krishna and get some idea of one's features in comparison to his. This will bring about some genuine admiration for him. It will also cause a healing humility in the psyche of the devotee.

अर्जुन उवाच
प्रकृतिं पुरुषं चैव
क्षेत्रं क्षेत्रज्ञमेव च ।
एतद्वेदितुमिच्छामि
ज्ञानं ज्ञेयं च केशव ॥१३.१॥

arjuna uvāca
prakṛtiṁ puruṣaṁ caiva
kṣetraṁ kṣetrajñameva ca
etadveditumicchāmi
jñānaṁ jñeyaṁ ca keśava (13.1)

arjuna — Arjuna; uvāca — said; prakṛtiṁ — material nature; puruṣaṁ — person; caiva — and indeed; kṣetraṁ — the living space; kṣetrajñam — the experiencer of the living space; eva — indeed; ca — and; etad — this; veditum — to know; icchāmi — I wish; jñānaṁ— conclusion; jñeyaṁ— what is to be experienced; ca — and; keśava — pretty-haired one

Arjuna said: What is material nature? What is the person? What is the living space? Who is the experiencer of the living space? I wish to know this. What is a conclusion? And what is experienced, O Keshava, pretty-haired One? (Bhagavad Gītā 13.1)

Analysis

In general, the rishis who wrote the *Upanishads*, skipped a precise and detailed explanation about the *purusha*, the person. The development in India is that the word used is *atma*. This in turn, developed into a stress term which is *jivatma*. Both *atma* and *jivatma* pale in significance when the word, *brahman* was presented. This is because *brahman* was tagged as the ultimate energy, the supreme stage which is a barrier which cannot be breached.

Lord Krishna presented his *Sāṁkhya* with stress on *purusha*, not on *atma*. Instead of *brahman* ultimate energy, Krishna addressed himself as the Supreme Person, the time limit.

Arjuna is the one who directly perceived the supernatural beings who govern this existence. After being educated in this *Sāṁkhya* enumeration of the factors of reality, he made some inquiries.

Arjuna spoke to the human physical body Krishna but with the understanding that this person was the Supreme Lord, the master of this existence and the ultimate person to regress towards.

When he saw the universal form, Arjuna was frightened. When that terror was muted, he resumed a relaxed state of mind. Recalling the experiences and even seeing it interspaced into physical life, Arjuna felt that he would discuss some related issues with Krishna.

Comprehension of Bhagavad Gītā Verse 13.1.

A barrage of questions. These are relevant because this is the upgraded Arjuna, not the person who did not see the universal form of Krishna. This Arjuna knew the theory of the philosophy as well as its practical application in the form of the Supreme Person, Krishna.

Beginning on the physical plane, Arjuna questioned:

- What is material nature?
- What is the person?
- What is the living space?
- Who is the experiencer of the living space?
- What is a conclusion?
- What is experienced?

A vital question is about the person, as to what it is. Is it real? Is it an illusory formation? Is it temporary so that it last only for the duration of the physical body? Will it exist beyond the physical system which is identified as it, while that physical system lives?

श्रीभगवानुवाच
इदं शरीरं कौन्तेय
क्षेत्रमित्यभिधीयते ।
एतद्यो वेत्ति तं प्राहुः
क्षेत्रज्ञ इति तद्विदः. ॥१३.२॥

śrībhagavānuvāca
idaṁ śarīraṁ kaunteya
kṣetramityabhidhīyate
etadyo vetti taṁ prāhuḥ
kṣetrajña iti tadvidaḥ (13.2)

śrī bhagavān — The Blessed Lord; uvāca — said; idaṁ— this; śarīraṁ— earthly body; kaunteya — O son of Kuntī; kṣetraṁ — the living space; iti — thus; abhidhīyate — it is called; etat — this; yo = yaḥ— who; vetti — knows; taṁ—him; prāhuḥ — they declare; kṣetrajña — experiencer of the living space; iti—thus; tadvidaḥ — of those knowledgeable of that

The Blessed Lord said: This, the earthly body, O son of Kuntī, is called the living space. Those who are knowledgeable of this, declare the person who understands this to be the experiencer of the living space. (Bhagavad Gītā 13.2)

Analysis

As convention would have it, the living space is the environment, consisting of solids, liquids and gases. These we perceive to be in a space. However, that conventional view, even though it has all the value to physical senses, is not the environment in question.

Krishna defined environment in a totally different way. He cited the physical body itself as the living space. From within the body, one accesses the larger environment. The body itself is the reference for perceiving and using the larger space.

Convention gave us the physical body as the experiencer of the living space. That is the collective which is termed as the body, which by convention we assume as one complete self. However, for the yogic profile, the physical body is a living space not a person, not an experiencer. It houses the senses which detects and approximates the format of the bodies of the selves, but the physical body is a composite, which when sorted, renders a psychological experiencer which is the central sensor.

Comprehension of Bhagavad Gītā Verse 13.2

This is a re-definition. First of all, the environment is considered to be exterior to the physical body of the person. One person is assigned as a physical body which has social participation in that exterior world, with other physical bodies, who are considered to be persons involved in the cast of history.

Krishna redefines this, addressing a body itself as an environment, and the experiencer factor which is in the body, as the experiencer or person. Krishna presents a new view of the person and the environment, where the environment is not the situation the physical body is in, but the psychological environment of the body itself. In that psyche there is an experiencer who uses the senses of the body to perceive physical and psychic items.

क्षेत्रज्ञं चापि मां विद्धि
सर्वक्षेत्रेषु भारत ।
क्षेत्रक्षेत्रज्ञयोर्ज्ञानं
यत्तज्ज्ञानं मतं मम ॥१३.३

kṣetrajñaṁ cāpi māṁ viddhi
sarvakṣetreṣu bhārata
kṣetrakṣetrajñayorjñānaṁ
yattajjñānaṁ mataṁ mama (13.3)

kṣetrajñam — the experiencer of the living space; cāpi = ca—and + api—also; māṁ -me, viddhi—know; sarvakṣetreṣu — I all living spaces; bhārata —O man of the Bhārata family; kṣetrakṣetrajñayoḥ — of the living space and the experiencer of it; jñānaṁ — information; yat — which; tat — that; jñānaṁ —knowledge; mataṁ -considered; mama — by me

Know also, that I am the experiencer of all living spaces, O man of the Bharata family. Information of the living space and the experiencer of it, is considered by Me to be knowledge. (Bhagavad Gītā 13.3)

Analysis

The information is that Krishna is the experiencer of every operative body in every species. This highlights the personSource factor and minimizes the energySource origin which is broadcasted in the *Upanishads*. The selves are not rated equally by Krishna as they are suggested in the *Upanishads*. Here, one specific self is the Supreme Lord who is sensually aware of all the living bodies, as contrasted to the limited selves in the trillions, who are sensually aware of their individual bodies.

A segregation is here with there being a supreme person, *mahapurusha* whose supervisory grasp extends through all bodies of all creatures everywhere. That person is different to the *purushas* or limited persons. To accommodate Krishna's declaration, the Sanskrit used is *param brahman*. The *Upanishads* lacks clarity in contrasting *brahman* and *param brahman.* It proposes only one absolute origin which is *brahman*. For that, the term *param* causes an obstruction which requires review. It is the same with the term *purusha*, in that there is also *mahapurusha*. That too is cause for alarm. There is *atma* and *paramatma*.

The Supreme Lord is linked to *param brahman*. The limited selves are categorized as *brahman*, which is similar, but which lacks certain attributes which the supreme being effortlessly exhibits.

While in normal usage, information is the description about the physical environment and its subtle counterpart, for this teaching of Krishna, information (knowledge) has to do with the body as an environment in which the coreSelf lives for the time being, for the duration of the life of that physical form.

By prying into his/her psychological energy, a self may experience the aspects of the subtle body. This sorting may cause the self to discover its core and the adjuncts which supplement its sensual reach.

Comprehension of Bhagavad Gītā Verse 13.3

By this definition of Krishna, the living bodies have a minimum of two personal interests. One is the interest of the limited perpetual self. The other is that of the Supreme Lord who exhibits the ultimate supervisory force. This ultimate person is invisible. In fact, most of the limited selves cannot detect him.

Before getting the revelation, Arjuna could not detect this Supreme Lord. Hence, God's management of the world is subtle and abstract. It happens but it is so transcendent as to have little or no register to a limited self.

By attuning to Krishna, by studying his information, by being upgraded by him, a limited self, Arjuna for instance, may gain direct sensual insight into how the realities interplay. That is knowledge in Krishna's vocabulary.

महाभूतान्यहंकारो बुद्धिरव्यक्तमेव च । इन्द्रियाणि दशैकं च पञ्च चेन्द्रियगोचराः ॥१३.६॥	mahābhūtānyahaṁkāro buddhiravyaktameva ca indriyāṇi daśaikaṁ ca pañca cendriyagocarāḥ (13.6)

mahābhūtāni — major elements; ahaṁkāro = ahaṁkāraḥ- ahaṁ — I, person + kāraḥ — doing, initiative to act; buddhiḥ — intellect; avyaktam — unmanifesled energy; eva — indeed; ca — and; indriyāṇi — senses; daśaikaṁ= dasa — ten + ekam — one; ca — and; pañca — five; cendriyagocarāḥ = ca — and + indriyagocarāḥ — attractive objects

The major categories of the elements, the personal initiative, the intellect, the unmanifested energy, the ten and one senses, the five attractive objects, (Bhagavad Gītā 13.6)

Analysis

This is Krishna's partial list of what comprise the environment. This is not the physical world which one experiences outside of one's physical body. This is the world within the psyche, within the skin of the physical body and within the psychic membrane of the subtle one.

To do this yoga of Krishna, a devotee is required to research within the psyche. This causes the devotee to sort, segregate and recognize the components and energies which comprise the physical and subtle bodies. This frees the devotee from the illusion of knowing himself/herself as either a physical or subtle body.

It is vital because initially the devotee presents himself as a physical body to Krishna. Then he/she presents the self as a subtle body. In each case, the devotee is mistaken because the personSelf is neither the physical nor subtle body but is the coreSelf only. To break the falsity of perceiving the self as a physical body or subtle one, the devotee must do Krishna's yoga, inSelf Yoga™, where in mental research, he/she actually sorts the coreSelf from its adjuncts.

This does not mean that this devotee will reject his/her physical or subtle body. To the contrary, he/she will better utilize the two forms and their contents. With the information from Krishna, the devotee will better understand how to serve Krishna who is the overseer of all social situations.

The bhakti cult, devotional movement, of Krishna Consciousness is well-intended but it misleads the devotees because it does not stress or teach this Krishna yoga. It slides over this with brash explanations. It pretends that there is no necessity to do this yoga where there is inner individual prying into the coreSelf and its adjuncts. The bhakti cult pretends that one can present oneself as a physical body to Krishna. It gives confidence that physical activity in worshiping Krishna and proselyting others to convert them, is all that is needed for establishing a relationship with Krishna. That is a misleading.

The iron grip of the psychological environment on the coreSelf makes it near impossible to upgrade the core which currently is under the influence of the adjuncts in the psyche. Hence there must be a deliberate attempt to sort the psychic equipment which normally is combined with the self.

Comprehension of Bhagavad Gītā Verse 13.6

Here is a partial list of the aspects of the psyche. The rest of the listing is completed in the seventh verse.

- solids
- liquids
- combustives
- gases
- cosmic spaces
- personal initiative
- intellect
- the unmanifest factor

- eye
- ear
- skin
- tongue
- nose
- hand
- foot
- vocal cord
- anus
- genital
- mind
- sound
- surface
- color
- flavor
- color

Krishna graciously listed some aspects of the psyche. He completed the listing in the seventh verse. However, it is not true that reading this or hearing of it, will implant it effectively in the devotee. The idea that the spiritual master will insert this into the mind of the devotee merely by speaking about it and having the devotee submissively hear it, is a fraudulent proposal.

Arjuna had to see the universal form of Krishna with special psychic eyes before Arjuna submitted to Krishna fully and became pliable. To say that a devotee will achieve that by submitting to the teacher who is in succession as a devotional authority, is a disservice to the devotional process and to Krishna.

Reading this information from this writer and making every effort to understand and accept it, is part of the process of becoming Krishna Conscious but one must proceed further and meditate as prescribed in chapter six of *Bhagavad Gītā*. One should not feel that one can present oneself as a physical or subtle body to Krishna for devotional activities, and that Krishna will accept that as a pure act at any stage.

That will not happen. But if one enters the psyche environment as Krishna explained, sorts the coreSelf from its adjuncts, and then expresses control over the adjuncts within the mind space, it will happen over time, that the spiritual aspects will be revealed, and portals of awareness will open so that one gains transit to the spiritual environments.

Solids, liquids, combustives, gases, cosmic spaces are the **major categories of the elements**. These are found inside and outside the psyche. Of special concern in meditation however is their discovery in meditation practice while researching to determine which are the factors that comprise the physical and subtle bodies.

It is not sufficient to know this mentally. A devotee should not bypass this and arrogantly state that because he heard this or read of it from a great devotee, he is in the realization. This presumption is damaging to the potential relationship with Krishna because it suggests that Krishna overloaded on Arjuna by showing him the universal form and giving so much information about mundane things like this knowledge about the contents of the physical and subtle bodies.

It does not matter what another teacher said. What counts is that Krishna did not in the *Bhagavad Gītā,* belittle this meditation research. Hence the good intentions of teachers who are devotees cannot override Krishna. It is also a fact that hiding under the guise of following the instruction of Lord Chaitanya or one of his disciples or grand-disciples, and feeling that their instructions cancel part of the Gītā is absurd. Anyone who does this will be ruined. With no experience of these truths in meditation, one cannot gain the strength over the mind which is required to spiritually approach Krishna.

The **personal initiative** is the one essential tool which a living entity cannot shed or demolish. It does not matter if one is a devotee or not, one cannot rid the self of the personal initiative. The personality, as soon as it is aware in any sense in this creation, is outfitted with a personal initiative. From day one, from the beginning of manifestation of a self in this time medium which we know as the cosmos, that specific self is surrounded by a tool for expressing interest. That is the personal initiative. The Sanskrit is *ahamkara*. It is the one psychic tool which is absolutely necessary for any mental, emotional or physical action.

Because it surrounds the coreSelf, it is difficult to curb. However, it is a neutral equipment. It is not colored except when it is linked to anything other than the core. If the sense of initiative was isolated from the intellect and from the emotions emitted by the kundalini lifeForce, that initiative would be harmless to the core.

This writer released this information, but it must be realized in deep meditation which is described in chapter six of *Bhagavad Gītā,* and which is also divulged in the *Yoga Sutras of Patanjali* and the *Uddhava Gita*. Without this one cannot become a great devotee in fact. Why? Because being an advanced devotee includes knowing the components of the psyche in meditation and gaining direct control of them through meditation.

There is nothing incorrect about doing deity worship and physical practices which involve Krishna-focused behaviors but that is not sufficient. The major practice of Krishna Consciousness is meditation to realize the mystic situation of the self and the superSelf, Krishna. Deity worship and temple activities with association with devotees, is part of the process but it is not all of it. No one should take it upon himself to refute this. One should learn how to meditate and confront the adjuncts. This should be mastered along with the Krishna Conscious lifestyle. One should not blast meditation and kick the yoga process which Krishna described in chapter six of *Bhagavad Gītā*.

The **intellect** is the calculative digital tool in the psyche. There is no way one could function in this cosmic situation without it. The personal initiative travels with the coreSelf wherever it may go in whatever physical or psychic formation, but this initiative always checks with the intellect. This is a problem. Running around, hiding and dodging from the intellect, instead of dealing with it head on, is evidence of the power of that psychic gadget.

The idea that the mind can be stopped in its tracks only by chanting a mantra, even a mantra which stresses Lord Krishna, is admittance that the intellect is so powerful that one must by all means develop the power to directly confront it without a mantra.

Why should it be that a limited self is endowed with an intellect which will only submit itself for control, when God's name is said. This is a ridiculous proposal. It shows that the teachers who said that, were unable to control their minds. But let us look at why that happened, rather than run away telling the whole world that no one can control the intellect. Actually, Krishna in *Bhagavad* Gītā states that the intellect can and must be controlled. Arjuna had some doubts about this.

चञ्चलं हि मनः कृष्ण
प्रमाथि बलवद्दृढम् ।
तस्याहं निग्रहं मन्ये
वायोरिव सुदुष्करम् ॥६.३४॥

cañcalaṁ hi manaḥ kṛṣṇa
pramāthi balavaddṛḍham
tasyāhaṁ nigrahaṁ manye
vāyoriva suduṣkaram (6.34)

cañcalam — unsteady; hi — indeed; manaḥ — the mind; kṛṣṇa — Krishna; pramāthi — troubling; balavat — impulsive; dṛḍham — resistant; tasyāham =

tasya — of it + aham — I; nigraham — controlling; manye — I think; vāyor = vayoḥ — of the wind; iva — compared to; suduṣkaram — very difficult to accomplish

(Arjuna said): Unsteady indeed is my mind, O Krishna. It is troublesome, impulsive and resistant. I think that controlling it is comparable to controlling the wind. It is very difficult to accomplish. (Bhagavad Gītā 6.34)

To say that a divine being or teacher agreed with Arjuna and that now one should chant holy names to achieve this, is bunkum. The chanting of holy names is a sacred practice. It is a valid spiritual means but that has nothing to do with the challenge of intellect, whereby it should be controlled by the self directly with or without sacred mantras. We must get the intellect whittled so that it is obedient to the self. Krishna discussed that:

इन्द्रियाणि पराण्याहुर्
इन्द्रियेभ्यः परं मनः ।
मनसस्तु परा बुद्धिर्
यो बुद्धेः परतस्तु सः ॥३.४२॥

indriyāṇi parāṇyāhur
indriyebhyaḥ paraṁ manaḥ
manasastu parā buddhir
yo buddheḥ paratastu saḥ (3.42)

indriyāṇi — the senses; parāṇyāhur = parāṇi — are energetic; āhur (āhuḥ) — the ancient psychologists say; indriyebhyaḥ — the senses; paraṁ — more energetic; manaḥ — the mind; manasas — in contrast to the mind; tu — but; parā — more sensitive; buddhir = buddhiḥ — the intelligence; yo = yaḥ — which; buddheḥ — in reference to the intelligence; paratas — most sensitive; tu — but; saḥ — he, the spirit

The ancient psychologists say that the senses are energetic, but in comparison to the senses, the mind is more energetic. In contrast to the mind, the intelligence is even more sensitive. But in reference, the spirit is most elevated. (Bhagavad Gītā 3.42)

एवं बुद्धेः परं बुद्ध्वा
संस्तभ्यात्मानमात्मना ।
जहि शत्रुं महाबाहो
कामरूपं दुरासदम् ॥३.४३॥

evaṁ buddheḥ paraṁ buddhvā
saṁstabhyātmānamātmanā
jahi śatruṁ mahābāho
kāmarūpaṁ durāsadam (3.43)

evaṁ — thus; buddheḥ — than the intelligence; paraṁ — higher; buddhvā — having understood; saṁstabhyātmānamātmanā = saṁstabhya — keeping together + ātmānam — the personal energies+ ātmanā — by the spirit; jahi — uproot; śatruṁ — enemy; mahābāho — O powerful man; kāmarūpaṁ — form of passionate desire; durāsadam — difficult to grasp

Thus having understood what is higher than intelligence, keeping the personal energies under control of the spirit, uproot, O powerful man, the enemy, the form of passionate desire which is difficult to grasp. (3.43)

Krishna also said this:

श्रीभगवानुवाच
असंशयं महाबाहो
मनो दुर्निग्रहं चलम्।
अभ्यासेन तु कौन्तेय
वैराग्येण च गृह्यते ॥६.३५॥

śrībhagavānuvāca
asaṁśayaṁ mahābāho
mano durnigrahaṁ calam
abhyāsena tu kaunteya
vairāgyeṇa ca gṛhyate (6.35)

śrībhagavān — the Blessed Lord; uvāca — said; asaṁśayam — undoubtedly; mahābāho — O powerful man; mano = manah — the mind; durnigraham — difficult to control; calam — unsteady; abhyāsena — by practice; tu — however; kaunteya — O son of Kuntī; vairāgyena — by the indifference to response; ca — and; gṛhyate — it is restrained

The Blessed Lord said: Undoubtedly, O powerful man, the mind is difficult to control. It is unsteady. By practice, however, O son of Kuntī, by indifference to its responses, also, it is restrained. (Bhagavad Gītā 6.35)

असंयतात्मना योगो
दुष्प्राप इति मे मतिः ।
वश्यात्मना तु यतता
शक्योऽवाप्तुमुपायतः ॥६.३६॥

asaṁyatātmanā yogo
duṣprāpa iti me matiḥ
vaśyātmanā tu yatatā
śakyo'vāptumupāyataḥ (6.36)

asaṁyatātmanā = asaṁyata —indisciplined + ātmanā — by the self; yogo = yogaḥ — yoga; duṣprāpa — difficult to master; iti — thus; me — my; matiḥ — opinion; vaśyātmanā = vaśya — disciplined + ātmanā — by the self; tu — however; yatatā — by endeavor; śakyo = śakyaḥ — possible; 'vāptum = avāptum — to acquire; upāyataḥ —by effective means

For the undisciplined person, yoga is difficult to master. This is My opinion. For the disciplined one, however, by endeavor, it is possible to acquire the skill by an effective means. (Bhagavad Gītā 6.36)

The idea that chanting a mantra will render complete control of the intellect forever is a hasty conclusion. Why? Because it is simply not true. It is invalid when we observer the mental control of the teachers who speak of it.

It does not matter what a scripture or God or incarnation of God said, what is important is what actually works. If I state that tomorrow the sun will rise in the West, how would you regard me if that does not happen? You give me the benefit of the doubt, that it may happen, but when it does not, what will you say?

If I am given a mantra, and that does not cure my lack of self-control absolutely, then what is the situation? Should I still continue believing something that fails to manifest day after day. The truth is that the intellect must be confronted head on, day after day, so that the self can control it whenever it attempts to rule the psyche by making undue and unrequested suggestions for psychic or physical actions.

The **unmanifested energy** is the foundation of everything physical. Whatever is perceived here, whatever is detected, was produced by stirs in the unmanifested energy. Currently a human being is not sensually equipped to perceive this causal power. It is present inside the psyche. It is also exterior to the psyche. It is encountered in meditation as a blankness, as nothing, as no space or as a containing space.

The **ten and one senses** are the eye, ear, skin, tongue, nose, hand, foot, vocal cord, anus, genital, mind. In this usage, mind is the supervisory ability over the senses and bodily activity. When sorted, this mind consisted of a kundalini lifeForce and the intellect. These are used for procurement and detection of objects.

The **five attractive objects** are sound, surface, color, flavor and fragrance. These doggedly pursue the psyche, which as a whole begs the coreSelf for indulgence. When the sound, surface, color, flavor or fragrance feels unpleasant the self acts to flee from the event.

इच्छा द्वेषः सुखं दुःखं
संघातश्चेतना धृतिः ।
एतत्क्षेत्रं समासेन
सविकारमुदाहृतम् ॥१३.७॥

icchā dveṣaḥ sukhaṁ duḥkhaṁ
saṁghātaścetanā dhṛtiḥ
etatkṣetraṁ samāsena
savikāramudāhṛtam (13.7)

Icchā — desire; dveṣaḥ — hatred; sukhaṁ — pleasure; duḥkhaṁ — pain: saṁghātaścetanā = saṁghātaḥ — the whole body + cetana — consciousness; dhṛtiḥ — conviction: etat = etad — this; kṣetraṁ — living space; samāsena — with brevity, briefly; savikāram — with changes; udāhṛtam — described

...desire, hatred, pleasure, pain, the whole body, consciousness and conviction; this is described with brevity, as the living space with its changes. (Bhagavad Gītā 13.7)

Analysis

This is the rest of the listing of what comprises the living space, or psychological environment which the coreSelf is involved with, and which it is mistaken as.

- desire
- hatred
- pleasure

- pain
- the whole body
- consciousness
- conviction

Desire is a powerful motivational energy. It is near-insurmountable. Like the intellect, it challenges the authority of the observing iSelf. If it can, desire confiscates energy from the coreSelf. It uses that energy at the self's expense so that the liabilities for social or psychic actions are tagged to the self.

A limited self must learn how to dive into the psyche to see the primitive undeveloped forms of desire, which are like seeds yet to sprout. If one confronts a desire after it burst in the mind and is displayed as a pleasurable or unpleasant construction, one will have diminishing power to stop it. The more a desire develops, the more the self loses the authority to squelch it. Thus, the necessity of reaching a desire before it sprouts or just as it is to be displayed legibly in the mind.

Hatred is the frustration energy which arises when something is detested. It is an involuntary reflex which remains hidden and takes control of the psyche for forceful rejection of undesirable events. It requires deep meditation to recognize and control this impulse. A yogi should research it. Its discovery and elimination are vital.

Pleasure is the stir of energy which the psyche interprets to be most desirable. It is an involuntary reflex. To understand its whereabout, arousal, spread and curtailment, a yogi should research it in meditation. One must grip this and sort its aspects to determine how it arises.

Pain is an interpretation of alarming sensations. These are bio-psychic energy movements which force the psyche to abandon other interest and become aware and focused on a particular incidence. It is a composite force. A yogi should dissect it to determine its parts, and to note how certain combinations produce undesirable sensations.

The **whole body** is the composite which is presented to the senses as a personSelf. It is not that but as convention would have it, it is related as that, as if that combination of a coreSelf, adjuncts and energies are a person, in fact.

In the social setting, the whole body consciousness is considered as one person. It is not that, but it is enforced as one body. When the body dies however, the components are reorganized as a dead form and a subtle one which continues to exist with no physical register.

Consciousness is more than the consciousness of the physical body. If for instance a finger is amputated, its physical format will be altered. Its psychological feature, which one cannot see physically, will continue to exist but with no corresponding physical response.

A limited being's consciousness is not universal but all the same it is more than its register through a physical body. One discovers the subtle body in dream states. In some of these, the subtle form is displaced from the physical system and still both bodies remain alive. This shows that consciousness is spread through a physical body but is not limited to it.

Conviction is a determinate force within the psyche. It is similar to any of the involuntary functions. Conviction arises from the collective energy. If each of the parts of the composite self were isolated, the conviction of the form would cease. It arises only because the various parts are in combination.

Comprehension of Bhagavad Gītā Verse 13.7

The focus on the environment as being what is external to the physical body, is the conventional way of regarding the world. This, however, needs to be changed so that one sees the world by Krishna's view. In that perception, the environment is not what is outside the physical body but what is within the physical and subtle bodies.

Instead of the self as the physical body or the self as the subtle form, Krishna considers the self as the coreSelf which is the centralized power in the physical and subtle forms. The reference is not the physical body as it interacts with the environment, which is exterior to it, but rather the coreSelf which is inside the subtle body and is experienced inside the physical one in meditation.

As weather is a concern for the physical body, so moods and inner influences are the concern of the coreSelf.

अमानित्वमदम्भित्वम्
अहिंसा क्षान्तिरार्जवम् ।
आचार्योपासनं शौचं
स्थैर्यमात्मविनिग्रहः ॥१३.८॥

amānitvamadambhitvam
ahiṁsā kṣāntirārjavam
ācāryopāsanaṁ śaucaṁ
sthairyamātmavinigrahaḥ (13.8)

amānitvaṁ — a lack of pride; adambhitvam — freedom from deceit; ahiṁsā — non-violence; kṣāntiḥ — patience; ārjavam — straightforwardness; ācāryopāsanaṁ — sitting near a teacher, attendance to a teacher; śaucaṁ — purity; sthairyam — stability; ātmavinigrahaḥ = ātma — self + vinigrahaḥ — restraint

Lack of pride, freedom from deceit, non-violence, patience, straightforwardness, attendance to a teacher, purity, stability and self-restraint, (Bhagavad Gītā 13.8)

इन्द्रियार्थेषु वैराग्यम्
अनहंकार एव च ।
जन्ममृत्युजराव्याधि-
दुःखदोषानुदर्शनम् ॥१३.९॥

indriyārtheṣu vairāgyam
anahaṁkāra eva ca
janmamṛtyujarāvyādhi-
duḥkhadoṣānudarśanam (13.9)

indriyārtheṣu — towards the attractive objects; vairāgyam — indifference; anahaṁkāra = an — absence of + ahaṁkāra — motivated initiative; eva — indeed; ca — and; janmamṛtyujarāvyādhi =janma — birth + mṛtyu —death + jarā — old age + vyādhi — disease; duḥkhadoṣānudarśanam = duḥkha — suffering + doṣa — danger + anudarśanam — perception

..indifference towards the attractive objects, absence of motivated initiative, the perception of the danger of birth, death, old age, disease, and suffering, (13.9)

असक्तिरनभिष्वङ्गः
पुत्रदारगृहादिषु ।
नित्यं च समचित्तत्वम्
इष्टानिष्टोपपत्तिषु ॥१३.१०॥

asaktiranabhiṣvaṅgaḥ
putradāragṛhādiṣu
nityaṁ ca samacittatvam
iṣṭāniṣṭopapattiṣu (13.10)

asaktiḥ — non-attachment, social detachment: anabhiṣvaṅgaḥ — absence of emotional affection: putradāragṛhādiṣu = putra — child + dāra — wife + gṛha — home + ādiṣu — beginning with, whatever is related to; nityaṁ — always; ca — and: samacittatvam — even-mindedness; iṣṭāniṣṭopapattiṣu = iṣṭa — undesired + aniṣṭa — not wanted + upapattiṣu — in matters

...social and emotional detachment towards child, wife, a home and whatever is related to social life, being always even minded towards what is desired and what is not wanted, (Bhagavad Gītā 13.10)

मयि चानन्ययोगेन
भक्तिरव्यभिचारिणी ।
विविक्तदेशसेवित्वम्
अरतिर्जनसंसदि ॥१३.११॥

mayi cānanyayogena
bhaktiravyabhicāriṇī
viviktadeśasevitvam
aratirjanasaṁsadi (13.11)

mayi — in me; cānanyayogena = ca — and + ananya — no other + yogena — with yoga practice; bhaktiḥ — devotion: avyabhicārinī — not wandering away, unwavering; viviktadeśasevitvam = vivikta — secluded + deśa— place + sevitvam — resorting; aratiḥ — having a dislike; janasaṁsadi — in crowds of human beings

...unswerving devotion to Me, with no other discipline but yoga practice, resorting to a secluded place, having a dislike for crowds of human beings, (Bhagavad Gītā 13.11)

अध्यात्मज्ञाननित्यत्वं तत्त्वज्ञानार्थदर्शनम् । एतज्ज्ञानमिति प्रोक्तम् अज्ञानं यदतोऽन्यथा ॥१३.१२॥	adhyātmajñānanityatvaṁ tattvajñānārthadarśanam etajjñānamiti proktam ajñānaṁ yadato'nyathā (13.12)

adhyātmajñananityatvam = adhyātma — Supreme Spirit + jñana — information + nityatvam -— constantly; tattvajñānārtha darśanam = tattva — reality + jñāna — science + artha — value+ darśanam —perceiving; etat— this; jñānam — knowledge; iti — thus; proktam — declared as; ajñānaṁ — ignorance; yat — whatever; ato = ataḥ — to this; 'nyathā = anyathā — otherwise, contrary

...constantly considering information about the Supreme Spirit, perceiving the value of the science of reality; this is declared as knowledge. Whatever is contrary to this, is ignorance. (Bhagavad Gītā 13.12)

Analysis

Verses 8 through 12 of chapter 13 of *Bhagavad Gītā,* list what Krishna declared as knowledge. This is what one should cull from this manifestation as worth knowing. There are innumerable sources of information, but one should aspire for experiences which highlight what is beneficial to engage with, in terms of discovering and being the coreSelf.

Since a limited being cannot possibly grasp this cosmic manifestation in its entirety. It is beneficial to be schooled by the supreme being, by Krishna. One's education will be the shortest if one can take lessons from the Supreme Lord. As far as that which is infinite, which a limited being cannot access or grasp, he/she may get some understanding after hearing Krishna.

Comprehension of Bhagavad Gītā Verse 13.8-12

The education which is conventional, is one having to do with exploitation of the events and resources. That however is not what Krishna regards as education. Here is his syllabus.

- **lack of pride**.

In one person pride is predominant. In another it rarely asserts itself. There is every reason to undermine pride. A limited being faces dependence at every stage. He/She is reliant on other persons and energies to such an extent as to make pride inappropriate.

In meditation, one should locate the pride emitting part of the psyche. One should monitor its emergence and collapse. One should study its applications and operations.

- **freedom from deceit**

Deceit functions to fool others. This is its ordinary application. However, Krishna is concerned with the interactions between the coreSelf and its psychological environment, the psyche. In the mind and in the lower parts of the subtle body, the yogi should check the intellect and the influence of the kundalini lifeForce. What deceit within the psyche is used by either the intellect or the lifeForce? Is there a war between the coreSelf and its adjuncts or between one adjunct and another? Is the imagination faculty, the memory and the calculative feature of the mind, working in tandem or in opposition to utilize the attention of the core?

- **non-violence**

To curb violent actions, one must sort between the formation of a violent urge, the urge itself and the physical manifestation of the motive. The need for nutrition is itself a violent intention. Thus, violence is integral to this creation. However, in meditation, one may study the operation of the violence energy and find a way to reduce its need. That would be a great reduction in the need for sustaining the body one has. As this creation is designed, one life form eats the other in a predator-to-prey relationship, with nature giving the predator a body which has tools to capture and feed on the prey.

Ultimately the self must exit these parasitic realms, otherwise it would never be out of the realms in which some violence is required. Only in deep meditation can one understand this.

- **patience**

Whatever is achieved as an accomplishment in the environment is sourced in the psyche as desire. Many desires are unknown until the environment allows certain fulfillments. Then those desires explode in the mind. If one is urged by desires, one will do many things which will cause rash reactions. It is best to throttle desires so that they do not commandeer the body and force it to do things which one will regret.

One must go into the psyche in meditation and find the need energies which cause one to be impatient. Every effort should be made to muzzle desire, so that one can avoid frustration and can be patient with providence and not force one's way, whereby one does criminal acts for which one will regret.

- **straightforwardness**

If one is in the habit of being dishonest or of avoiding straightforward dealings, one will find that in the psyche, the coreSelf does not have control of its physical and psychic actions. Instead, it will be motivated by the intellect and kundalini lifeForce to endorse behaviors which are counterproductive to peace of mind, and which will result in many inconvenient involvements.

- **attendance to a teacher**

Every person using a human body took assistance from parents or guardians. There is no exception to this. Just to be a physical being, one is required to be dependent on others. Teachers are a necessary supplement in this existence. For spiritual focus, one must also take help from physical or psychic entities. Internally and on the astral side of life, one must take help from a great yogi who may or may not have a physical body.

- **Purity**

Purity is required for the physical and subtle bodies. The purifying actions for the physical form are mostly conducted by the organs in the body, which remove harmful waste. A yogi is primarily concerned with purity of the subtle body. This is achieved by *pranayama* breath infusion and arrest of the involuntary actions of the intellect.

When the subtle body is purified to a lesser or greater degree one gains access to higher planes. Eventually one transits to those places or perceives them through a transit vision.

- **stability**

Stability is the result of a yogically-facilitating lifestyle. It is not a mental plan. It happens because a yogi is proficient at managing social obligations and conducting spiritual practice daily.

- **self-restraint**

Self-restraint is necessary because the senses are by nature distracting and engaging. If one had little or no self-restraint, one would be lost in many sensual presentations and have no sense of spiritual direction. It is not enough to rely on involuntary self-restraint. When that happens, the self is blessed, but it should study the operation of the involuntary system and learn how the psyche shifts from involvement to disengagement and then from disengagement to involvement. This study would reveal a natural process which the self could use to insulate itself from sensual occupation.

- **indifference towards the attractive objects**

A yogi must study his susceptibility towards animate and inanimate objects. One will not become detached and resistant to sense objects merely by wanting to be transcendental. One must struggle to gain the resistance from the lures and attractions which fascinate the senses.

Step by step as the physical body grows and ages, one is shifted to this or that sense object as the preference. This occurs because of the fancy of the sense organs. A coreSelf should detach itself from the feelings in the psyche, as these sensations drag the attention of the coreSelf here or there to pursue and experience different fragrances, flavors, colors, surfaces and sounds.

A resistance is developed by the yogi, so that the call for sensation is ignored and instead the yogi retracts interest from the various sense objects. This gives one the stress on the coreSelf and one is no longer diffused as sensations which are allied to other sensations inside and outside the body.

- **absence of motivated initiative**

The iSelf when it is not under influences of its adjuncts, has a neutral initiative faculty. This is its single sense in that condition. Since this sense is neutral, it does not have consequences for the self. However as soon as the initiative is linked with the intellect or sensual energies, it exhibits an inclination for being suggested to by the adjuncts.

Due to this, a yogi must cultivate the neutral state of the initiative, so that its relaxed state is one of it being disengaged from the adjuncts. This can only be done in meditation. Patanjali listed meditation as *samyama*, which he said was the three highest stages of yoga as one sequential meditative event.

Dharana or deliberate shifted absorption from mundane psychic concerns is the preparatory stage. *Dhyana* or spontaneous shifted absorption is the median stage. *Samadhi* or continuous and spontaneous shifted absorption is the ultimate stage. These occur in meditation as sudden experiences or as a sequence of achieved states.

- **perception of the danger of birth, death, old age, disease, and suffering**

The danger of birth, death, old age, disease, and suffering is current, but one may be distracted by excitements and stupor states. The distractions mute the alarm which is sounded by the unwanted features of having a physical body.

A yogi, despite the loneliness derived, should keep constant focus on the threat of disease, suffering and old age. One of these or a combination, will in time result in death. Death itself will result in birth. That birth itself will result in death. Death and birth take turns humiliating a living entity.

As soon as a body is born, it is threatened by death. As soon as a body dies, the entity who is the remnant of that event, finds itself to be a psychic being. In that state it hankers for birth because it feels the need to be a participant of physical history.

The scope of it is danger, which lurks from behind and which is portended for the future. What should one do to buffer this trauma?

- **social and emotional detachment towards child, wife, a home and whatever is related to social life**

Full ascetism, an attitude of no social participation is fraught with risks. A yogi cannot be certain that he will not have to be socially involved in the physical and psychic environments ever again. Hence for a preference, he should complete the obligations which confront him. But he should be detached while doing so. One can never be certain that one will not have to enter into the social milieu again. Hence one should commit righteous acts which will yield positive returns in the future. If one is not there to receive these favorable repercussions, someone else will absorb the gracious energy.

The social and emotional detachment towards a home, a wife and child, should be a jovial one, which is free from resentment and negative moods. One should willingly and pleasantly serve obligations but all the same one should sidestep any duty which one can safely bypass for the time being.

- **being always even-minded towards what is desired and what is not wanted**

Regarding personal needs and fulfillments, one should always be even minded towards what is desired and what is not wanted. One should not be over-enthusiastic for what is desired. One should not be hostile to what is unwanted. A yogi should regard his needs as being trivial. He should be eager to serve others whenever he is in a situation where it appears that fate requests his agency.

- **unswerving devotion to Me, with no other discipline but yoga practice**

This gives us the requirements of devotion to Krishna and yoga practice as he defined in chapter six. This does not root out, whitewash, nor lambast yoga. All the same, it does not shadow devotion to Krishna. One should be devoted to Krishna as suggested in *Bhagavad Gītā* and one must practice the yoga disciplines for self-purification.

...being there, seated in a posture, having the mind focused, the person who controls his thinking and sensual energy, should practice the yoga discipline for self-purification. (Bhagavad Gītā 6.12)

- **resorting to a secluded place**

It is necessary for a yogi to resort to a secluded place, but he/she may not do so if certain mandatory obligations prevent that. In that case, the yogi should abscond from society as soon as he/she can. This may be weeks, months, years or even in some other life, where the opportunity arises for his escape.

In war time, one may be conscripted. In a family, one may be obligated as a wage earner. One may be hemmed in by affection which one either gives or receives. Never mind what some philosophers say. The fact is that unless one curtails social involvement, one will have insufficient time to practice meditation. The result will be failure to achieve the objective.

- **having a dislike for crowds of human beings**

An ascetic who greatly appreciates mass gatherings is not a true yogi. At least not by the standard of the *Bhagavad Gītā*. This does not mean that one should avoid every mass religious event. One may participate but if one feels strongly appreciative of that and if one gets a pleasure while being involved with that, it is an indication that one does not desire a high degree of purification.

The cost of purification is isolation where the coreSelf and its adjuncts are discovered, isolated, assessed and confined in the interest of the core. Mass gatherings do not facilitate this. Hence, they are undesirable.

- **constantly considering information about the Supreme Spirit**

Meditation is a major part of the liberation effort. Still, it is only part of the process. The philosophy of Krishna, his information about the layout of this creation, must be studied in detail by a yogi. Krishna's thesis is the map for self-realization. For rapid progress, a yogi should study and put it into practice.

- **perceiving the value of the science of reality**

After becoming an infant body, one is left with the task of sorting the coreSelf from its adjuncts. Each aspect of reality one encounters should be assessed. Without confronting the various aspects of this temporary world, one cannot break away from it to attain transcendence.

- **...this is declared as knowledge. Whatever is contrary to this, is ignorance.**

What was listed above, Krishna declared as valid information. Whatever is contrary, he regarded as misinformation. Even what is directly perceived or intuitively sense, when it is contrary to Krishna's view, should be devalued by the yogi-devotee.

ज्ञेयं यत्तत्प्रवक्ष्यामि
यज्ज्ञात्वामृतमश्नुते ।
अनादिमत्परं ब्रह्म
न सत्तन्नासदुच्यते ॥१३.१३॥

jñeyaṁ yattatpravakṣyāmi
yajjñātvāmṛtamaśnute
anādimatparaṁ brahma
na sattannāsaducyate (13.13)

jṇeyaṁ — to be known, the desired subject; yat — which; tat — that; pravakṣyāmi — I will explain; yat — which; jñātvā — knowing; 'mṛtam = amṛtam — eternal life; aśnute — he gets in touch with; anādimat — beginningless; paraṁ — supreme; brahma — reality; na - not; sat — substantial; tat — this; nāsat = na — not + asat — non-substantial; ucyate — is said

I will explain that which is to be experienced, knowing which one gets in touch with eternal life. The beginningless Supreme Reality is said to be neither substantial nor insubstantial. (Bhagavad Gītā 13.13)

Analysis

There are many aspects of this creation which can be experienced, but much of this does not result in an accurate assessment in terms of which level of reality the specific event or factor is sourced in. A limited being is likely to be victimized because of misidentification and assignment of value to that which is worthless.

Giving value to an item or aspect which is insubstantial, does not increase the status of that object, but the person who assigns the worth will feel that the object has importance. That will eventually produce disillusionment.

Comprehension of Bhagavad Gītā Verse 13.13

Even though there is so much to experience in this manifestation, one should learn from Krishna what experience will cause one to have true assessments of what one encounters. By itself, a limited self cannot measure the events accurately. That self needs to get a vision upgrade so that his/her perception parallels Krishna's.

Krishna declared that what was regarded as the beginningless Supreme Reality was categorized by some as being substantial and by others as being insubstantial. If one reads the *Upanishads*, one will find this ambiguity or the suggestion that the under-basis of this creation is neither here nor there, up nor down, in nor out, of value and having no value, being assertive and being absolutely passive. In consideration, the Supreme Reality was declared as a paradox.

सर्वतःपाणिपादं तत्
सर्वतोक्षिशिरोमुखम् ।
सर्वतःश्रुतिमल्लोके
सर्वमावृत्य तिष्ठति ॥१३.१४॥

sarvataḥpāṇipādaṁ tat
sarvatokṣiśiromukham
sarvataḥśrutimalloke
sarvamāvṛtya tiṣṭhati (13.14)

sarvataḥ — everywhere; pāṇi — hand; pādaṁ — foot; tat = tad — this; sarvato = sarvataḥ — everywhere; 'kṣiśiromukham= akṣiśiromukham= akṣi— eye + śiraḥ — head + mukham — face; sarvasaḥśrutimat - sarvasaḥ — everywhere + śrutimat — having hearing ability; loke — in the world; sarvam — all; āvṛtya — ranging over; tiṣṭhati — stands

Everywhere is Its hands and feet, everywhere Its eyes, head and face, everywhere is Its hearing ability in this world; It stands, ranging over all. (Bhagavad Gītā 13.14)

Analysis

There are three positions granted to the Supreme Reality. One describes it as a person, a special somebody. Another describes it as a reduction energy which is the source of and termination of any manifested energy or thing. And yet another, identifies it as being with a dual format, both person and person-less.

Comprehension of Bhagavad Gītā Verse 13.14

Krishna related the person format of the Supreme Reality which he stated has hands and feet everywhere, with its eyes, head and face placarding everything. Its hearing detects every sound. It stands alive and well, ranging over everything. That description is reminiscent of the universal form which Krishna revealed to Arjuna

सर्वेन्द्रियगुणाभासं
सर्वेन्द्रियविवर्जितम् ।
असक्तं सर्वभृच्चैव
निर्गुणं गुणभोक्तृ च ॥१३.१५॥

sarvendriyaguṇābhāsaṁ
sarvendriyavivarjitam
asaktaṁ sarvabhṛccaiva
nirguṇaṁ guṇabhoktṛ ca (13.15)

sarvendriyaguṇābhāsaṁ = sarva —all + indriyaḥ — sensual + guṇa — mood + ābhāsaṁ — appearance; sarvendriyavivarjitam = sarva — all + indriya — sensuousness + vivarjitam — freedom from; asaktaṁ — unattached; sarvabhṛt — maintaining everything; caiva = ca — and + eva — indeed; nirguṇaṁ — free from the influence of material nature; guṇabhoktṛ experiencer of the modes of material nature; ca — and

It has the appearance of having all sensual moods, and It is freed from sensuousness. Though unattached, It maintains everything. Though free from the influence of material nature, It is the experiencer of that influence nevertheless. (Bhagavad Gītā 13.15)

Analysis

It was denied by some that the Supreme Reality could have sensual moods. Some said that it was devoid of alterations and had no variations. Krishna explained however that even though it has the appearance of having all sensual moods, it was freed from the effects of sensuousness.

Some said that the Supreme Reality was unattached, but Krishna stated that it maintains everything. It is responsible for all. Even though it is free from the influence of material nature, it experiences those operations.

Comprehension of Bhagavad Gītā Verse 13.15

This Supreme Reality as described by Lord Krishna is both personal and impersonal. It lives up to the expectation of the *Upanishadic* rishis who awarded it a quality-less, character-less feature and yet, it experiences the influence which material nature exerts, and it simultaneously remains free of those pressures.

It is sensuous in one sense, but it is free from sensuousness in terms of feedback and contagion. It maintains everything and yet, it is detached as well.

बहिरन्तश्च भूतानाम्
अचरं चरमेव च ।
सूक्ष्मत्वात्तदविज्ञेयं
दूरस्थं चान्तिके च तत् ॥१३.१६॥

bahirantaśca bhūtānām
acaraṁ carameva ca
sūkṣmatvāttadavijñeyaṁ
dūrasthaṁ cāntike ca tat (13.16)

bahiḥ — outside; antaḥ — inside; ca — and; bhūtānām — of the beings; acaraṁ — non-moving; caram — moving; eva — indeed; ca — and; sūkṣmatvāt — from subtlety; tat — this; avijñeyaṁ — not to be comprehended; dūrasthaṁ — situated far off; cāntike = ca — and + antike — in the location; ca — and; tat = tad — this

It is outside and inside the moving and non-moving beings. Because of Its subtlety, this beginningless Supreme Reality is not comprehended. This Reality is situated far away, and it is in the location as well. (Bhagavad Gītā 13.16)

Analysis

There is a feeling that if something is person, it is not capable of full detachment. The idea is that whatever is person is subjected to influences and is a changing feature itself. Thus, it cannot be a reference for anything absolute.

However, Krishna explained that the Supreme Reality is outside and inside the moving and non-moving beings, and yet, because of its subtlety it is not comprehended by most of them. From one view it is remote and transcendent. From another perspective, it is closer than anything which is near.

Comprehension of Bhagavad Gītā Verse 13.16

The Supreme Reality is multi-dimensional in penetration. It cannot be tracked by a limited being. It is so subtle that it is not comprehended. Finding a source for it, is impossible. A limited being cannot emerge on the other side of it in a coherent format. If one goes into one side of it, one may emerge somewhere in it that is not perceptible.

Even though it is here, it cannot be comprehended. If someone senses that it is there in the distance, there is no means for that person to measure it.

अविभक्तं च भूतेषु
विभक्तमिव च स्थितम् ।
भूतभर्तृ च तज्ज्ञेयं
ग्रसिष्णु प्रभविष्णु च ॥१३.१७॥

avibhaktaṁ ca bhūteṣu
vibhaktamiva ca sthitam
bhūtabhartṛ ca tajjñeyaṁ
grasiṣṇu prabhaviṣṇu ca (13.17)

avibhaktam — undivided: ca — and; bhūteṣu — among the beings: vibhaktam — divided; iva — as if; ca — and; sthitam — remaining; bhūtabhartṛ = bhūta — being + bhartṛ — sustainer; ca — and; tat — this; jñeyaṁ — to be known; grasiṣṇu — absorber; prabhaviṣṇu — producer; ca — and

It is undivided among the beings, but It appears as if It is divided in each. It is the sustainer of the beings, and this should be known. It is the absorber and producer. (Bhagavad Gītā 13.17)

Analysis

According to Lord Krishna, the Supreme Reality is personal and impersonal simultaneously. It approaches someone and it is detached from that person simultaneously. It splits itself and is sorted in a relationship to each other self. Yet it is a single reality.

Comprehension of Bhagavad Gītā Verse 13.17

The Supreme Reality produces this, but it absorbs this as well. It sustains the beings and that should be declared. It is to be respected by every other self.

ज्योतिषामपि तज्ज्योतिस्
तमसः परमुच्यते ।
ज्ञानं ज्ञेयं ज्ञानगम्यं
हृदि सर्वस्य विष्ठितम् ॥१३.१८॥

jyotiṣāmapi tajjyotis
tamasaḥ paramucyate
jñānaṁ jñeyaṁ jñānagamyaṁ
hṛdi sarvasya viṣṭhitam (13.18)

jyotiṣām — of luminaries; api — also; tat = tad — this; jyotiḥ — light; tamasaḥ — of gross or subtle darkness; param-beyond; ucyate — declared to be; jñānaṁ — information; jñeyaṁ — education; jñānagamyaṁ = jñāna — education + gamyam — goal; hṛdi — in the psychological core; sarvasya — of all; viṣṭhitam — situated

This is declared as the light of the luminaries, but it is beyond gross or subtle darkness. It is the information, the education and the goal of education. It is situated in the psychological core of all beings. (Bhagavad Gītā 13.18)

Analysis

One can just imagine what that light would be, how it would be so abstract as to be invisible. As the light of lights, how is it to be perceived? It is beyond gross and subtle darkness. It is abstract so that it is imperceptible to normal sense perception. It is the real education and is the ultimate subject for inquiry.

Along with the coreSelf, this Supreme Reality is present in the psychological core of all beings. It transcends even the core which is the spotlight in each psyche.

Comprehension of Bhagavad Gītā Verse 13.18

The realization of the Supreme Reality happens after the yogi researched, discovered and became centralized on his/her coreSelf. In the abstractness of that core, the yogi, over time, develops perception. Like a light seeing itself or another light, the yogi perceives the influence-spread of the Supreme Reality.

That is the information, the education and the goal of being informed about and experiencing the supreme being. When the radiance energy which continually emanates from the coreSelf, becomes visible to a yogi, he/she may meditate deeper and deeper, until the Supreme Reality which transcends even the core, becomes directly visible.

इति क्षेत्रं तथा ज्ञानं
ज्ञेयं चोक्तं समासतः ।
मद्भक्त एतद्विज्ञाय
मद्भावायोपपद्यते ॥१३.१९॥

iti kṣetraṁ tathā jñānaṁ
jñeyaṁ coktaṁ samāsataḥ
madbhakta etadvijñāya
madbhāvāyopapadyate (13.19)

iti — thus; kṣetraṁ— the living space, the psychological environment; tathā — as well as; jñanaṁ — standard knowledge; jñeyaṁ — what is to be known; coktaṁ-ca -and + uktaṁ — described: samāsataḥ — in brief; madbhakta — my devotee; etad — this: vijñāya — experiencing; madbhāvāyopapadyate = madbhāvāya — to my state of being + upapadyate — draws near

Thus, the psychological environment as well as the standard knowledge and what is to be known, was described in brief. Experiencing this, My devotee draws near to My state of being. (13.19)

Analysis

The definitions given by Krishna run contrary to the conventional meanings of the terms. Instead of an environment being the areas surrounding one's physical body, Krishna gave the physical and psychic areas within the physical and subtle bodies. That is a totally different way of regarding a habitat. The self in this is not the physical body as a composite person. Rather the self is within the psychology energies of a physical body, as the observing factor which is conventionally termed as "I".

Comprehension of Bhagavad Gītā Verse 13.19

If one shifts one's perception focus and value assessments to one that is similar to Krishna's, one will move closer to his state of being.

One decision is to be coordinate with Krishna so that one does not act in opposition to him, where one would require being disciplined by the central person in the universal form of personalities. Every person is in the universal form, but each has varying powers. The most powerful one is Krishna, the Supreme Personality of Godhead. His views tip everyone's else. Hence it is conducive to shift one's perception in his direction, rather than to feel that one's opinions are unalterable.

A limited being cannot have an absolute view. Such a being cannot be free from influence. As soon as it is free from one influence, it comes under the sway of another power. The best thing is to select the best of the influences. The idea of not being influenced does not apply to a limited person.

When one submits to the ideas of Krishna, when one practices his recommended disciplines, when one advances into his way of viewing the world, one becomes his devotee. By those adjustments one develops a nature that is similar to his, with spiritual sense perception which allows one to see as Krishna views.

प्रकृतिं पुरुषं चैव
विद्ध्यनादी उभावपि ।
विकारांश्च गुणांश्चैव
विद्धि प्रकृतिसंभवान्॥१३.२०॥

prakṛtiṁ puruṣaṁ caiva
viddhyanādī ubhāvapi
vikārāṁśca guṇāṁścaiva
viddhi prakṛtisaṁbhavān (13.20)

prakṛtiṁ — material nature; puruṣaṁ — spiritual personality; caiva = ca — and + eva — indeed; viddhi — know; anādī — beginningless; ubhau — both; api — also; vikārān — changes of the living space (see 13.4); ca — and; guṇāṁ — moods; caiva = ca— and + eva — indeed; viddhi — know; prakṛtisaṁbhavān = prakṛti — material nature + saṁbhavān — produced

Know that both material nature and the spiritual personality are beginningless and know that the changes of the living space and the moods of material nature are produced from material nature. (Bhagavad Gītā 13.20)

Analysis

No limited being can properly access the duration of nature. Nor can anyone totally dissect the coreSelf. That self is indivisible and part-less but its conventional representation in the forms of either a physical body or a psychic being, can be dissected. The illusion is that the physical body is represented as a person. The illusion is that while being represented as such, one does not take the time to realize the combine of the physical body as a composite. Even more important is the psychic body which in the astral world and in the physical one, functions as a self. It is not a self, but the issue is that there is a self which is the core radiance within the psychic form.

Because of too much focus on the physical body as a person, some philosophers deny the validity of the physical form and say there is no person in fact. There is person. The truth that the physical form is not that, does not deny the existence of a corePerson around which other factors adhere.

Comprehension of Bhagavad Gītā Verse 13.20

The information from Krishna may or may not be accepted as accurate. Some are in disbelief that he declared it. Others become fanatical. They declare it without verification. The fact is however that a limited being cannot verify everything the Supreme Person states.

If there is a Supreme Person, then obviously his/her sense perception would be the most valid viewpoint. But that does not mean that a person with limited spiritual reach can verify everything the Supreme Person declares. For that matter, the way the energies and dimensions exist, no limited person should ever expect to have the complete scope.

Either one accepts what Krishna says and expects some verification of it but not all. Or one may reject what he says because one does not have a way to verify it. Either position is acceptable. Still, this writer suggests that one should accept the information for the time being and make endeavors to verify some of it.

The question of the beginning of time haunts humanity. We think that other animals are not concerned about that, only the humans. When did time begin? When did physical life commence? When did the humans manifest? Who were the first human beings? Was it one person, a few, or many?

What about person? Some feel that only humans are persons, that other lifeforms lack that degree of sentiency.

What about the environment and the elements which comprise it? Where did these originate? How long will these last?

Such inquiry is repeated by some in each generation of human beings. There are many proposals as answers to these questions. Here we review Krishna's.

His view is that the changes of the psychic aspects of anyone and the moods which arise in the psyche of anyone, are produced by the movement of the various aspects of nature, particularly the psychic variations. On all fronts in this situation everything is in flux. It varies from moment to moment. Still, the underlying features are permanent facets.

कार्यकारणकर्तृत्वे
हेतुः प्रकृतिरुच्यते ।
पुरुषः सुखदुःखानां
भोक्तृत्वे हेतुरुच्यते ॥१३.२१॥

kāryakāraṇakartṛtve
hetuḥ prakṛtirucyate
puruṣaḥ sukhaduḥkhānāṁ
bhoktṛtve heturucyate (13.21)

kāryakaraṇakartṛtve = kārya — created work + karaṇa — sensual potency as a cause + kartṛtve — agency; hetuḥ — cause; prakṛtiḥ — material nature; ucyate — is said; puruṣaḥ — the spiritual personality; sukhaduḥkhānāṁ — of pleasure and pain; bhoktṛtve — in terms of experiencing; hetuḥ — cause; ucyate — is said

Material nature is said to be the cause in terms of created work, sensual potency and agency. The spiritual personality is said to be the cause in terms of experiencing pleasure and pain. (Bhagavad Gītā 13.21)

Analysis

In the physical world and in the astral situations, nature is assigned as the cause of created work, sensual potency and agency. This is assigned because of the prevailing responsibility. Incrementally, the personSelf has some liability. This is because it shares itself with nature. That interaction has liabilities.

The spiritual personality, even though it is transcendent to nature, is involved with it and experiences elation and depression in this or that situation which is designed in and by nature.

Comprehension of Bhagavad Gītā Verse 13.21

One must be simultaneously detached and attached to nature, but the attachment should be precise and superficial while the detachment should be prominent and deep. Presently, so long as we are in nature, interlocked with it, there is no possibility of total detachment. In meditation, one must practice detachment, and learn how to separate from the body while being involved and directing it to function with the least discomfort.

In meditation, as a silent witness, one should observe the operations of nature. One should self-critique and take steps to reduce the strength of one's attachment to it. The attachment is an involuntary application. One must note this from within the psyche. One should attempt to redesign this. Gradually over time, one will reduce the involvement and decrease the focus invested in it.

The linking aspect between the spiritual personality and nature, is sensual energy, through which pleasure and pain are experienced. Much of that is psychic electricity but the way the personSelf is connected, causes the self to interpret the flow of current to be pleasure or pain.

पुरुषः प्रकृतिस्थो हि
भुङ्क्ते प्रकृतिजान्गुणान् ।
कारणं गुणसङ्गोऽस्य
सदसद्योनिजन्मसु ॥१३.२२॥

puruṣaḥ prakṛtistho hi
bhuṅkte prakṛtijānguṇān
kāraṇaṁ guṇasaṅgo'sya
sadasadyonijanmasu (13.22)

puruṣaḥ — spirit; prakṛtistho - prakṛtisthaḥ — situated in material nature; hi — indeed: bhuṅkte — experiencing; prakṛtijān — produced on material nature; guṇān — the modes of material nature; kāraṇaṁ — the source; guṇasaṅgo = guṇasaṅgaḥ — attachment to the influence of material nature; 'sya = asya —of it: sadasadyonijanmasu = sad (sat) — reality + asad (asat) — unrealistic + yoni — birth situations + janmasu — birth

The spirit, being situated in material nature, experiences the modes which were produced by that nature. Attachment to the modes is the cause of the

spirit's emergence from realistic and unrealistic situations. (Bhagavad Gītā 13.22)

Analysis

The question of how a self got involved with nature is avoided by some philosophers. Some deny that to the extent of saying that it does not matter how that happened. The urgency they say, is to become totally detached from it.

One human being, a particular person, is said to have attained total detachment in the past. Another is accredited with having attained it during the current history. Still, for oneself, the research into if one can totally detach the self, may depend on retracing one's steps to identify the origins and how one became involved in the first place.

Comprehension of Bhagavad Gītā Verse 13.22

The self is inevitably attracted to the operations of nature, such that it becomes bored if nature ceases her alterations. This is proven by the external behaviors which concern operating a body in the environment, which is external to it, and by the internal maneuvers which are the operations of feelings and thinking.

Our entry into and exit from various events produce trauma but some of it is interpreted as being desirable. Some are rated as being detestable. Due to linking into the circuit of nature, into its psychic and physical events, one experiences its operations either as a helpless victim or as a controller with limited autonomy.

The link of a personSelf to nature, is itself the cause of the feelings of pleasure or pain because the alterations of nature, causes easing or blocking feelings which are interpreted by the mind as positive, neutral or negative pleasure.

उपद्रष्टानुमन्ता च
भर्ता भोक्ता महेश्वरः ।
परमात्मेति चाप्युक्तो
देहेऽस्मिन्पुरुषः परः ॥१३.२३॥

upadraṣṭānumantā ca
bhartā bhoktā maheśvaraḥ
paramātmeti cāpyukto
dehe'sminpuruṣaḥ paraḥ (13.23)

upadraṣṭānumantā = upadraṣṭā —observer + anumantā — permitter; ca — and; bhartā — supporter; bhoktā — experiencer; maheśvaraḥ — Supreme Lord; paramātmeti = paramātmā — Supreme Soul + iti — thus; cāpi — and also; ukto = uktaḥ — is called; dehe — in the body; 'smin = asmin — in this; puruṣaḥ — spirit; paraḥ — highest

The observer, the permitter, the supporter, the experiencer, the Supreme Lord and the Supreme Soul as He is called, He is the highest spirit in the body. (Bhagavad Gītā 13.23)

Analysis

This targets the innate ignorance of the limited self. It does not understand itself. Its query into its dimensions is confusing. How can someone who does not understand itself know the Supreme Soul?

The first self-declaration of the limited self is that it is ignorant regarding itself. It begins in this human life, with a misconception that it is a physical body. It may progress from that to know that it is a psychology. But what else can it truly declare. It can neither define a Supreme Lord nor produce evidence to deny that. The evidence regarding the limited self is abstract even to the very self. Hence how can it posit a supreme somebody?

Comprehension of Bhagavad Gītā Verse 13.23

There was new information from Krishna that the highest spirit is in the physical body. It is obvious that the limited self is in the living physical body. But as for the highest spirit, who can discover that in the same body?

The limited spirit has difficulty sorting itself from its adjuncts and bodily energies, how then can it discern a superPerson who is in the body?

The limited spirit can neither know nor deny the presence of a supreme self, who according to Bhagavad *Gītā*, is present along with the limited person. This is because the sensing capacity for detecting anything which is transcendent to the limited self, is absent in the subtle body. Arjuna could not sense the universal form of Krishna until he was endowed with supernatural sensing capacity.

How the Supreme Lord, permits, supports and experiences what occurs to the limited self is mysterious. For Arjuna, Krishna's physical presence was the evidence. Once Arjuna saw Krishna's mystic reach and how that monitors the physical plane, he resigned himself to Krishna. Others do not have that perception and are left only with the information from Krishna.

य एवं वेत्ति पुरुषं
प्रकृतिं च गुणैः सह ।
सर्वथा वर्तमानोऽपि
न स भूयोऽभिजायते ॥१३.२४॥

ya evaṁ vetti puruṣaṁ
prakṛtiṁ ca guṇaiḥ saha
sarvathā vartamāno'pi
na sa bhūyo'bhijāyate (13.24)

ya = yaḥ — who; evaṁ — thus; vetti — knows; puruṣaṁ — spiritual person; prakṛtiṁ — material nature; ca — and; guṇaiḥ — with the variations of material nature; saha — with; sarvathā — in whatever way; vartamāno = vartamānaḥ —

existing presently, present condition; 'pi = api — also; na — not; sa = saḥ — he; bhūyo = bhūyaḥ — again; 'bhijāyate = abhijāyate — is horn

He who knows the spiritual person and material nature, along with the variations of material nature, is not born again, regardless of his present condition. (Bhagavad Gītā 13.24)

Analysis

Once a limited self transfers its focus to the personSelf in the psyche, once it researches and catalogs nature and its variations, it is no longer subjected to the shocks of birth and death. A yogi of this achievement may still assume embryos and may still pass through the experience of being decommissioned from a physical body, but even so, he will not be jolted from physical focus to psychic reference suddenly at the death of the physical body.

In that sense he is not born again, because his consciousness no longer makes the physical side of existence as the reference. Even if he takes more physical bodies, still he will not be shocked by the change from astral to physical and from physical to astral. A focus on the psychic side of life and a methodical defocus from the physical existence, gives the yogi a continuity because the subtle body is the aspect which persists when the physical body becomes deceased.

Comprehension of Bhagavad Gītā Verse 13.24

How one views events in this world, has everything to do with if one would or would not be liberated. The change in view is an inner occurrence and, on that basis, one will perceive reality in a way that matches the view of the supreme being. This upgrade of one's psyche would cause continual focus on the higher features of existence, the substantial ones, with the insubstantial trivial feelings still occurring but not being convincing.

ध्यानेनात्मनि पश्यन्ति
केचिदात्मानमात्मना ।
अन्ये सांख्येन योगेन
कर्मयोगेन चापरे ॥१३.२५॥

dhyānenātmani paśyanti
kecidātmānamātmanā
anye sāṁkhyena yogena
karmayogena cāpare (13.25)

dhyānenātmani = dhyānena — through meditative perception + ātmani — in the spirit; paśyānti — they perceive; kecit — some; ātmānam — by the spirit; ātmanā — -the spirit; anye — others; sāṁkhyena — by sāṁkhyena philosophical conclusions; yogena — by yoga practice; karmayogena — by yogic disciplined action; cāpare = ca —and + apare — others

Some perceive the spirit by the spirit through meditative perception of the spirit. Others do so with Sāṁkhya philosophical conclusions and others by yogic disciplined action. (Bhagavad Gītā 13.25)

Analysis

Three methods used in the time of Krishna are mentioned by him.

- meditative perception of the spirit
- mystic vision developed through Sāṁkhya philosophical conclusions
- mystic vision developed by yogic disciplined action

Meditative perception of the spirit is for people who have deep mystic perception such that in meditation, even without disciplines, they perceive the self even in its subjective condition, where no reference to anything is known.

Mystic vision developed through Sāṁkhya philosophical conclusions is a process recommended by Krishna, which he elaborated in *Bhagavat Gītā*. This process is abused by some devotees of Krishna who use the initial part of its theory and convince themselves that they have the intended result.

To succeed in this process, one first hears or reads about Krishna's information. Secondly, one must get the experience. An example of this is Arjuna who heard from Krishna and then was graced with the vision of the universal form where he directly perceived some of Krishna's saturation power in the lives of people in this creation.

Some devotees and their teachers (*acharyas*) get this information in its full or incomplete form. After this they form the opinion that reading and hearing of this is sufficient to cause the bestowal of the experience. This is not factual, but many devotees accept this on the basis of self-conviction.

Mystic vision developed by yogic disciplined action is the position of mystic yogis, who just by their yoga practice gain the insight to know what Krishna explained in *Bhagavad Gītā*. These persons gain direct perception about the universal form by entering into higher planes of consciousness where the subtle body has the higher vision, which was bestowed on Arjuna in *Bhagavad Gītā*.

Comprehension of Bhagavad Gītā Verse 13.25

The perception of the spirit by itself with no viewing adjuncts, is the highlight of self-realization. Some feel that it is not important for the limited self to realize itself. Their theistic view is that the limited being should come to terms with the supreme being through service to the supreme and not by indulging itself in studying its abstract format.

However, this idea was not presented by Krishna in *Bhagavad Gītā*. He requested, in fact demanded, that the self should realize itself and also approach and get perception of the supreme spirit. Both features are required. If one cannot perceive the coreSelf, it is not possible to see the Supreme Person. This is because the perception required to view the self is lower than that required to view the supreme being.

One should not feel that if one can see the supreme being or accept his philosophy that will cause one to automatically see the limited self. It does not work like that. Even if one gets the vision of the universal form as Arjuna was awarded it by Krishna, still that does not mean that one will remain anchored in the experience.

Arjuna did not remain in it as was described in the *Anu Gītā* discussion with Krishna in the *Mahabharata*. Arjuna got the vision to see the universal form and to see the divine person, Krishna. Still, he lost that vision because he was not anchored in it. Whatever God bestows at God's convenience may be withdrawn by God. If God gives a mystic perception so as to encourage a devotee to perform a task, as he did with Arjuna, God may revoke that revelation?

Then one will resume ignorance with or without memory of the grace bestowal. But if one cultivated spiritual perception of the self, and if that becomes the reference, one may develop further and have permanent elevation of perception to see the supreme self.

अन्ये त्वेवमजानन्तः
श्रुत्वान्येभ्य उपासते ।
तेऽपि चातितरन्त्येव
मृत्युं श्रुतिपरायणाः ॥१३.२६॥

anye tvevamajānantaḥ
śrutvānyebhya upāsate
te'pi cātitarantyeva
mṛtyuṁ śrutiparāyaṇāḥ (13.26)

anye — others; tu — but; evam — thus; ajānantaḥ — not knowing; śrutvānyebhya = śrutvā — hearing + anyebhya — from others; upāsate — they worship; te — they; 'pi = api — also; catitaranti = ca — and + atitaranti — transcend; eva — indeed; mṛtyuṁ — death: śrutiparāyaṇāḥ = śruti — hearing + parāyaṇāḥ — putting confidence in as the highest

But some, though they are ignorant, hear from others. They worship and by their confidence in what is heard, they also transcend death. (Bhagavad Gītā 13.26)

Analysis

Some persons do not have psychic perception. Some were not graced with supernatural vision by a deity. Some did not practice mystic yoga. But some heard or read about the transcendent self, and somehow, they got the perception in fact. These devotees are a minority.

Most persons who hear of the supreme being from Krishna or from someone else who did or did not have the revelation of the universal form, or who did not experience the self by the self, do not get the supernatural perception.

It is promised to them by some devotional cult teachers, even teachers of *Bhagavad Gītā* but the vast majority do not get the mystic perception by any means. Hence the use of this verse to guarantee the promise of such teachers, is a misuse of the *Bhagavad Gītā*.

Comprehension of Bhagavad Gītā Verse 13.26

Swallowing the statements of Krishna without alteration or gleefully hearing about Krishna from someone who reduces or alters what he presented to humanity in *Bhagavad Gītā*, may not get anyone the required mystic perception. If one believes the alterations, one will have to correct the version of information, before one can make advancement.

Worshiping Krishna through an icon, using standard Vedic mantras during the worship procedure, having confidence that Krishna will free the devotee, any of this could result in the vision of the supernatural and spiritual worlds.

However, it is only a few, a very few, who though ignorant, may hear correctly or incorrectly about Krishna, worship him as directed by a devotional authority, and are confident that Krishna will deliver the devotee, who in the immediate sense will be liberated either by Krishna directly or by his agent.

यावत्संजायते किंचित्
सत्त्वं स्थावरजङ्गमम् ।
क्षेत्रक्षेत्रज्ञसंयोगात्
तद्विद्धि भरतर्षभ ॥१३.२७

yāvatsaṁjāyate kiṁcit
sattvaṁ sthāvarajaṅgamam
kṣetrakṣetrajñasaṁyogāt
tadviddhi bharatarṣabha (13.27)

yāvat — as for; saṁjāyate — is born; kiṁcit = kiṁcid — anything, whatever; sattvaṁ — existence; sthāvarajaṅgamam= sthāvara — stationary + jaṅgamam — moving; kṣetrakṣetrajñasaṁyogāt = kṣetra — living space + kṣetrajña — experiencer + saṁyogāt from the synthesis; tat — that; viddhi — know; bharataṛsabha — strong man of the Bharatas

As for anything that is produced in this existence, be it a stationary or moving object, know, O strong man of the Bharatas, that it is produced from a synthesis of the experiencer and the living space. (Bhagavad Gītā 13.27)

Analysis

This situation is produced from a mixture of the experiencer or personForce and the environment. This applies to physical and psychic phenomena. This situation is a mixture of two basic substances, which are personSelves and environment.

Comprehension of Bhagavad Gītā Verse 13.27

Person and property are the gist of this situation. That is reduced further to coreSelf and atomic matter. Within the social person there is a coreSelf which is indivisible and perpetual. Within the property there are atoms. This creation is a synthesis of person and property. From the physical viewpoint the property is more numerous than the coreSelves.

समं सर्वेषु भूतेषु
तिष्ठन्तं परमेश्वरम् ।
विनश्यत्स्वविनश्यन्तं
यः पश्यति स पश्यति ॥१३.२८॥

samaṁ sarveṣu bhūteṣu
tiṣṭhantaṁ parameśvaram
vinaśyatsvavinaśyantaṁ
yaḥ paśyati sa paśyati (13.28)

Samam — similar; sarveṣu — in all; bhūteṣu — in beings; tiṣṭhantaṁ —situated; parmeśvaram — Supreme Lord; vinaśyatsu — in disintegrations; avinaśyantaṁ — not perishing; yaḥ — who; paśyati—perceive; sa = saḥ — he', paśyati — really sees

The Supreme Lord is similarly situated in all beings without perishing when they disintegrate. He who perceives that, really sees. (13.28)

Analysis

There is disintegration when a body dies. Even if its dead form is preserved for a time, still eventually it will disintegrate. This causes a feeling that everything involved in the formation of the body decays. That is an intuition based on the physicalness.

A yogi should depart from this physical reference. He/She should adapt to psychic reality. Time must be spent cultivating psychic perception and shifting the reference used to the psychic world.

This will allow for direct perception of what continues to exist, intact, after the death of the physical body. The limited spirit continues, with its psychic adjuncts. Certainly, the supreme being remains as is, with no nudging or shocking felt by him.

Comprehension of Bhagavad Gītā Verse 13.28

Even though the Supreme Lord is transcendent to the absolute degree, the limited spirit has only limited immunity. There is feedback between the coreSelf and its adjuncts, where the core's focus on itself is disrupted when an adjunct influences the core.

The primary adjunct, which is involved in shocks to the core, is the sense of identity. It, along with the attention of the core, uses the ever-radiating energy of the core, for supporting the plans of the intellect and the sensual shifts of the kundalini lifeForce.

The ever-fresh non-disturbed reference is the supreme being. He is the ultimate person. He stands above all and serves as the anchor for selfhood. He is situated in all composite beings. He does not perish when they disintegrate. A yogi who develops mystic vision to see this, really sees.

समं पश्यन्हि सर्वत्र
समवस्थितमीश्वरम् ।
न हिनस्त्यात्मनात्मानं
ततो याति परां गतिम् ॥१३.२९॥

samaṁ paśyanhi sarvatra
samavasthitamīśvaram
na hinastyātmanātmānaṁ
tato yāti parāṁ gatim (13.29)

samaṁ — same; paśyan — seeing; hi — indeed; sarvatra — everywhere; samavasthitam — same established; īśvaram — Lord; na — not; hinasti — degrade; ātmānātmānaṁ = ātmanā — by the soul + ātmānaṁ — the soul; tato = tataḥ — subsequently; yāti — goes; parām — supreme; gatim — destination

Seeing the same Lord being situated everywhere, he does not degrade the soul by his own soul. Subsequently, he goes to the supreme destination. (Bhagavad Gītā 13.29)

Analysis

Unless one understands that there is a prevailing deity who monitors events, one will act recklessly. Even if one is not of a criminal bent of mind, still if one does not accept a Supreme Person to whom one is accountable, one will challenge fairness and honor. One will act in a way which supports the idea that life is arbitrary, as a reality which is unsupervised.

The tendency for social interaction and environmental possession, is to exploit the situation. What is here, which is within sensual reach, seems to be here for one's convenience, such that if it does not absorb what one expresses and does not provide what one lacks, one becomes angry.

To avoid this outlook, one must be exposed to evidence that there is a supreme being, to whom one is accountable. Then it is likely that one will not degrade oneself by unreferenced actions which run contrary to God Almighty.

Comprehension of Bhagavad Gītā Verse 13.29

Apart from personal agency, there is the environmental reactions which occur for every action committed by anyone. To either, one is accountable. Even when there is no visible reaction from the personGod there will be a flyback effect from some feature of the environment. Again, if there is no supernatural response as Arjuna saw in the Bhagavad *Gītā*, still one can be sure that in time, there will be a consequence.

There is no escape. A yogi should aspire for increase mystic perception, so that he sees the same Lord being situated everywhere. That vision causes the yogi to not degrade the self. In time, he/she goes to the supreme destination.

प्रकृत्यैव च कर्माणि
क्रियमाणानि सर्वशः ।
यः पश्यति तथात्मानम्
अकर्तारं स पश्यति ॥१३.३०

prakṛtyaiva ca karmāṇi
kriyamāṇāni sarvaśaḥ
yaḥ paśyati tathātmānam
akartāraṁ sa paśyati (13.30)

prakṛtyaiva = prakṛtya — by material nature + eva — indeed: ca — and; karmāṇi — actions; kriyamāṇāni — performed; sarvaśaḥ — in all cases, yaḥ — who; paśyati — he sees; tathātmānam = tathā— as regarding + ātmānam — self; akartāraṁ — non-doer; sa = saḥ— he: paśyati — truly sees

He who sees, that in all cases, the actions are performed by material nature, and who regards himself as a non-doer, truly sees. (Bhagavad Gītā 13.30)

Analysis

It is difficult to accept that every action performed with the physical body is done by material nature and that the self is one of the factors which fund nature's operations. A yogi may question like this:

Why should I be the initiative if nature performs the actions?

Three realities are presented.

- limited but perpetual coreSelf
- supreme being
- environment

The situation is that one has no alternative but to act in one way or the other. The environment is such that even the decision not the act, and the power to refrain from acting, is itself an act. Regardless, a limited being cannot at any stage be the origin of an act, nor can it completely curtain all forces in an event.

Comprehension of Bhagavad Gītā Verse 13.30

A yogi knows that he must participate in the activities of nature but those events are still within the scope of nature and are not the actual strikes of the coreSelf. A certain power from the core endorses the acts of nature but that investment does not give the core the right to claim the positive, neutral or negative reactions.

The coreSelf, by necessity, partially funds the activities of nature but that does not mean that the core should claim the returns. If it attempts to do so, it will be subjected to fluctuations some of which are pleasant, some which are bland and some which are unpleasant.

Surely the coreSelf may use nature to help the self to realize itself in contrast to nature, but otherwise, the self should be detached and should not be drawn into nature's intrigues.

As Krishna said to Arjuna, someone who sees, that in all cases, the actions are performed by nature, and who regards himself as a non-doer, truly estimates the reality of events.

यदा भूतपृथग्भावम्
एकस्थमनुपश्यति ।
तत एव च विस्तारं
ब्रह्म संपद्यते तदा ॥१३.३१॥

yadā bhūtapṛthagbhāvam
ekasthamanupaśyati
tata eva ca vistāraṁ
brahma saṁpadyate tadā (13.31)

yadā — when; bhūtapṛthagbhāvam = bhūta — being + pṛthak — various + bhāvam — existential state: ekastham — based in one foundation; anupaśyati — be sees; tata — from that conclusion; eva — only; ca — and; vistāraṁ — extending, emanating; brahma — spiritual plane; saṁpadyate — he reaches: tadā — then

When a person sees that all the various states of being are based on a single foundation, and only from that everything emanates, then he reaches the spiritual plane. (Bhagavad Gītā 13.31)

Analysis

The glimpse of the universal form with its vast outlay of persons and superPersonalities was experienced by Arjuna. Someone else may have some idea by reading of it in the *Bhagavad Gītā*. Otherwise, one may hear of it. Rarely does anyone have the vision directly as did Arjuna. After hearing of this or reading of it, one should have an open mind and patiently wait for the revelation to be given by Krishna.

Comprehension of Bhagavad Gītā Verse 13.31

The vast spread of the physical universe which we see in the night sky, the display of so many lifeForms on the earth and in the water, all of this is based on a single foundation. From that this situation emanates.

अनादित्वान्निर्गुणत्वात् परमात्मायमव्ययः । शरीरस्थोऽपि कौन्तेय न करोति न लिप्यते ॥१३.३२॥	anāditvānnirguṇatvāt paramātmāyamavyayaḥ śarīrastho'pi kaunteya na karoti na lipyate (13.32)

anāditvāt = due to being without a beginning; nirguṇatvāt — due to being devoid of the influence of material nature; paramātmāyam = paramātmā — Supreme Soul + ayam — this; avyayaḥ — imperishable; śarīrastho = śarīrasthaḥ — situated in the material body; 'pi = api — even though; kaunteya — O son of Kuntī; na — not; karoti — he does; na — not; lipyate — become contaminated

Since this imperishable Supreme Lord is beginningless and devoid of the influence of material nature, even though He is situated in the material body, O son of Kuntī, He does not act nor become contaminated. (Bhagavad Gītā 13.32)

Analysis

The position of being involved as the essential factor and not being affected by everything else but holding one's abstract immunity, is reserved for the imperishable Supreme Lord. While the limited selves remain spiritual no matter what happens, they are superficially affected if they contribute to nature's operation. However, the supreme being is not degraded, not even in a superficial sense.

The limited self does not act physically and yet it attempts to do so. These attempts cause it to feel affected, but the Supreme Lord is not positioned for that.

Comprehension of Bhagavad Gītā Verse 13.32

Even though the energy and some fractional attention of the Deity, is involved in the publication of this cosmos, still the imperishable Supreme Lord does not act nor become contaminated. The same cannot be said for the limited selves who are involved. For immunity, they must perform special austerities which insulate them from the apparent influence of their awareness of nature's operations.

The rush to experience is the gap through which a coreSelf is influenced. As soon as it can reduce interest in whatever the sense of identity touches, the core can synchronize with the supernatural side of existence and from there, it can develop spiritual perception which causes it to be unaware of mundane events and to not give focusing register to those circumstances.

There is an idea that the Supreme Lord and the limited self, resides in the heart of the living being. This is sometimes given as an invitation for the limited self to communicate with the God. The concept is highlighted with a hint that the limited self can directly converse with God. Some feel the limited self can do that in the silence of the mind. Others feel that it can do so by serving the wishes of God.

These proposals are for the most part absurd. Why? Because the limited self and the Supreme Lord are on different planes of existence, where the limited self does not perceive the Supreme Lord. The limited self cannot relate to someone it cannot perceive. The level of the Supreme Lord's spiritual appearance is not perceptible to the average limited self. Arjuna could not see the displayed universal form of Krishna. How then can any other self see any other supernatural or spiritual form of the Lord?

This God, who is Krishna, described himself as beginningless and being devoid of the influence of nature. He is so transcendental, so abstract, so beyond our sense perception, that even though this God is situated in the physical body, still He does not act or become contaminated. And yet, he performs. Arjuna viewed his wondrous impact on physical history.

यथा सर्वगतं सौक्ष्म्याद्
आकाशं नोपलिप्यते ।
सर्वत्रावस्थितो देहे
तथात्मा नोपलिप्यते ॥१३.३३॥

yathā sarvagataṁ saukṣmyād
ākāśaṁ nopalipyate
sarvatrāvasthito dehe
tathātmā nopalipyate (13.33)

yathā — as; sarvagataṁ — all-pervading; saukṣmyāt — as by subtlety; ākāśaṁ — sky. nopalipyate = na — not + upalipyate — is polluted; sarvatrāvasthito = sarvatra — all over +avasthitaḥ — situated; dehe — in the body; tathātmā = tathā — so + ātmā — soul; nopalipyate = na — not + upalipyate — affected

As by subtlety, the all-pervading space is not polluted, so the soul, though situated all over the body, is not affected actually. (Bhagavad Gītā 13.33)

Analysis

The proximity of the limited spirit causes it to experience feelings which are responses to the environment which it is aware of. For all time, the limited self is different to nature but all the same this difference does not protect it from becoming aware of energy movements in nature.

Just as when an armature is stationary, it does not cause current to transmit within a wire, so when nature is quiescent, the limited self does not experience it. When the armature spins, the movements of the magnets are felt by the wire which is in the core of the mechanism. This causes the wire to have feelings and to be affected by the armature.

Some philosophers say that a self which is susceptible to nature's influence imagines that it is affected but this explanation is incomplete. It is an attempt to give the limited self an immunity which it does not have. It is best to admit that the limited self is affected, though the affect is superficial because that self will resume its detachment when it is not in proximity to nature.

The Supreme Lord is different in that he is aware of the movements of nature and still he is not affected. But that ability is not shared with the limited selves. For immunity, a limited self must be out of proximity to nature's fluctuations.

Comprehension of Bhagavad Gītā Verse 13.33

In one instant, the limited self is affected. In another it is unaffected. What are the conditions which warrant either state?

It is the self's concern about the influences which affect it, that may cause the self to research in the psyche to understand when it can or cannot resist nature.

यथा प्रकाशयत्येकः
कृत्स्नं लोकमिमं रविः ।
क्षेत्रं क्षेत्री तथा कृत्स्नं
प्रकाशयति भारत ॥१३.३४॥

yathā prakāśayatyekaḥ
kṛtsnaṁ lokamimaṁ raviḥ
kṣetraṁ kṣetrī tathā kṛtsnaṁ
prakāśayati bhārata (13.34)

yathā — as; prakāśayati — illuminates; ekaḥ — one, alone; kṛtsnaṁ —- whole; lokam — world; imaṁ — this; raviḥ — sun; kṣetraṁ — living space; kṣetrī — the user of the living space; tathā — so; kṛtsnaṁ — entire; prakāśayati — gives feeling; bhārata — O man of the Bhārata family

As the sun alone illuminates the whole world, O man of the Bharata family, so the user of the living space gives feeling to the entire psyche. (Bhagavad Gītā 13.34)

Analysis

The coreSelf must realize itself within its psyche but it cannot do so if it does not understand its adjuncts, their supplementary assistance to it and their influence on it. One should not be arrogant about a degree of self-control which one does not have. It is best to research honestly and figure the degree of dependence one has on the adjuncts. Then one can figure the strength of the coreSelf and exercise a greater degree of detachment, instead of saying that one is immune, while in fact one is influenced.

Even though the sun alone illuminates the world, still there are limits to its influence. We experience that the moon has a dark side. We experience hours of darkness because the sun's rays are limited in penetration through various materials. We experience climatic heat variation because of the varying relationship between the earth and the sun. This indicates a sun which has limitations in its light spread.

The sun gives heat. In fact, it is the major source of heat. If the earth was deprived of solar energy, every other source of heat would be irrelevant because the other grantors are supplementary only. Similarly, the self is the major influence overall, but other factors have significance as well. For instance, in a wintry month, a human being must have some other source of heat to subsidize the sun's influence.

Mentally even though the coreSelf is the major influence, the intellect is required for analysis and idea illustration. The kundalini lifeForce is necessary for sensual access to psychic reality. There is a need for memory to retain information which the coreSelf cannot register.

Comprehension of Bhagavad Gītā Verse 13.34

The user of the living space, the coreSelf in the psyche, gives feelings to the entire subtle body but how it does so and under what authority, that must be realized.

The axial power of the core is rated differently according to which adjunct uses the core's energy. The core itself should realize this. It is insufficient for the core to accept this information without going to the pains of realizing it in the abstract states of meditation.

क्षेत्रक्षेत्रज्ञयोरेवम्
अन्तरं ज्ञानचक्षुषा ।
भूतप्रकृतिमोक्षं च
ये विदुर्यान्ति ते परम् ॥१३.३५॥

kṣetrakṣetrajñayorevam
antaraṁ jñānacakṣuṣā
bhūtaprakṛtimokṣaṁ ca
ye viduryānti te param (13.35)

kṣetrakṣetrajñayoḥ — of the experiencer and the living space; evam — thus; antaraṁ - difference; jñānacakṣuṣā - jñāna — perceptive knowledge + cakṣuṣā — intuitive vision; bhūtaprakṛtimokṣaṁ = bhūta — being + prakṛti—material nature + mokṣaṁ — liberation; ca — and; ye — who: viduḥ — they know; yānti — they go; te — they; param — supreme

Those who by intuitive perception know the difference between the living space and the experiencer, as well as the liberation of the living being from material nature, go to the Supreme. (Bhagavad Gītā 13.35)

Analysis

The sensual observation of the inner workings of the psyche is done through intuitive perception. Physical vision helps but it is insufficient because it finds subtle reality to be abstract. A yogi must develop his intuitive perception so that he can develop confidence in abstract perception and also develop supernatural vision which allows the perception of supernatural form.

As it is, the physical body conditions a self to physical perception only. The self should break from this view of reality. He/She should slip from it, while developing confidence in intuition and subtle sensual viewing.

Comprehension of Bhagavad Gītā Verse 13.35

For success in self-realization, the confidence one has in physical perception must be transferred to psychic objects. At first there are no psychic objects, but this is due to the application of confidence to physical reality. That physical sensual access for the body, began at its birth, when it was evicted from the mother's uterus and had to fend for itself.

Over time, a yogi shifts this confidence so that psychic perception which at first is mere intuition, develops and is confirmed as a real perception in contrast to what is physical which before was rated as the only reality worth accessing.

The coreSelf, the spiritual person which is the central feature in the subtle body or psyche, must be realized as something existing with adjuncts in a subtle enclosure, a psyche. Meditation is the method for developing this perception.

Confidence in physical reality is developed during the infant years. Initially a child does not see clearly. Some of what it sees is in black and white perception. But when the eyes develop fully, color is perceived. Initially a child cannot walk. But after some months it crawls and then gradually it learns how to balance its body while striding. There are other physical actions and methods which a child develops over time. Patience in meditation is required to develop psychic perception.

श्रीभगवानुवाच
परं भूयः प्रवक्ष्यामि
ज्ञानानां ज्ञानमुत्तमम् ।
यज्ज्ञात्वा मुनयः सर्वे
परां सिद्धिमितो गताः ॥१४.१॥

śrībhagavānuvāca
paraṁ bhūyaḥ pravakṣyāmi
jñānānāṁ jñānamuttamam
yajjñātvā munayaḥ sarve
parāṁ siddhimito gatāḥ (14.1)

śrī bhagavān — the Blessed Lord; uvāca — said; paraṁ — highest; bhūyaḥ — further; pravakṣyāmi — I will explain; jñānānāṁ — of the knowledges; jñānam — information; uttamam — the very best; yat — which; jñātvā— having experienced; munayaḥ — yogī philosophers; sarve — all; parāṁ — supreme; siddhim — perfection; ito = itaḥ — from here; gatāḥ — done

The Blessed Lord said: I will explain more, giving the highest information of all knowledges, the very best. Having experienced that, all the yogi philosophers went away from here to the Supreme Perfection. (Bhagavad Gītā 14.1)

Analysis

The highest information is about person, and yet, the *Upanishads* and some other ancient and modern text, either ignore or flatten anything having to do with the question of the value of personality.

Those who oppose the idea of eternal persons, are persons. Those who support that are persons as well. There is no evidence to date that experience can be assessed by anything besides persons.

Comprehension of Bhagavad Gītā Verse 14.1.

The person issue must be settled one way or the other. Avoidance of it does not make it disappear. There is no guarantee that someone will be a non-person hereafter. If someone is person now, how is it that he can be assured that his person will be permanently erased in the future?

The recurrence of person after sleeping, after injury which caused an unconscious state, after application of anesthesia, is proof enough that the individual does not have the power to abolish itself.

Even if the infinity of things, places and energies were to have value and the selves have none, those other factors would be irrelevant if the personSelves were a complete mirage with no portion having permanence.

The ultimate destination given by Krishna was attainment for a person. It was not the abolition of person or erasure of self. Krishna said he would explain more to Arjuna, giving the highest information, the very best. Such that after experiencing, the yogi philosophers went from here to the supreme perfection.

इदं ज्ञानमुपाश्रित्य
मम साधर्म्यमागताः ।
सर्गेऽपि नोपजायन्ते
प्रलये न व्यथन्ति च ॥१४.२॥

idaṁ jñānamupāśritya
mama sādharmyamāgatāḥ
sarge'pi nopajāyante
pralaye na vyathanti ca (14.2)

idaṁ — this; jñānam — experience; upāśritya — resorting to; mama — my; sādharmyam — a nature that is similar; āgatāḥ — transformed into; sarge — at the time of the universal creation; 'pi = api — even; nopajāyante = na — not + upajāyante — they are born; pralaye — at the time of universal dissolution; na — not; vyathanti — disturbed; ca — and

Resorting to this experience, being transformed into a nature that is similar to My own, they are not born even at the time of the universal creation, nor are they disturbed at the time of dissolution. (Bhagavad Gītā 14.2)

Analysis

Shifting from this mundane existence to the supreme environment, a yogi attains a nature which is similar to that of the supreme being. The result of which is that he is not born at the time of universal creation and is not disturbed at the time of dissolution.

The coreSelf shifts to another environment and is supported there by divine energy which maximizes the sublime condition of the self. Due to losing the footing in this physical creation and in the subtle counterpart of this, the yogi gains the transcendental reference such that the display of this world, as well as its shattering, does not affect the coreSelf of the yogi.

Comprehension of Bhagavad Gītā Verse 14.2

When a yogi gets the experience of his/her selfCondition in the divine environment, the insecurities which were experienced as a self prior, no longer occur. Even when such a yogi, resynchronizes to this situation again, it does not have the impact on him as it did prior.

The bruises and other injury which he/she felt before when interspaced with physical and subtle nature, are no longer enforced into the self. Events continue here but with little or no impact to the person of the yogi. Thus, resorting to the transcendental level of consciousness, the yogi is transformed into a nature that is similar to Krishna's. He/She is not born even at the time of the universal creation, nor is he/she disturbed at the time of dissolution.

मम योनिर्महद्ब्रह्म
तस्मिन्गर्भं दधाम्यहम् ।
संभवः सर्वभूतानां
ततो भवति भारत ॥१४.३॥

mama yonirmahadbrahma
tasmingarbhaṁ dadhāmyaham
saṁbhavaḥ sarvabhūtānāṁ
tato bhavati bhārata (14.3)

mama — my; yoniḥ — womb; mahat — extensive; brahma —reality; tasmin — into it; garbhaṁ — essence; dadhāmi — I impregnate; aham — I; saṁbhavaḥ — origin; sarvabhūtānāṁ — of all beings: tato = tataḥ — from that; bhavati — comes into being; bhārata — O man of the Bharata family

The extensive mundane reality is My womb. I impregnate the essence into it. The origin of all beings comes from that reality, O man of the Bharata family. (Bhagavad Gītā 14.3)

Analysis

The personSelves have origin. They are not a perishable principle. They are not dependent on themselves for perpetuation. They lean on the supreme being. That is their perpetual condition. A limited self is not dependent on its ability to be objective, to exist. The way to test the quality and value of the self, is to consult with the supreme being, to know from him the self's potential.

If we begin the investigation from this creation, that would be a practical genesis. From a local view, the limited self appeared here as a physical body which was capable of growth and maturity. The question about that is one of origin, as to if this physical collective which is called a self, was interspaced here but was from another plane. Was it attracted here, inducted by another power in the formation of its body?

Was that power transcendental to the self, subtler than it? Can something which is not physical be inducted to organize and manage something which is perishable but mobile? That should be the inquiry.

Comprehension of Bhagavad Gītā Verse 14.3

As a woman's womb provides an environment for the growth of an embryo, so this extensive mundane reality (*mahat brahma*) serves as a realm for impregnation of limited selves. Position wise, Krishna is situated as the father. Nature serves as the mother.

All beings in this creation, those which are unmanifest to others and those who are perceived by others, are installed in this situation by the Supreme Person. The limited entities are persons. The God is the Supreme Person with unlimited powers.

The elimination of personhood is not in the discussion. The limited people did not derive themselves. They do not have the power to end themselves. *Nirvana* if it means de-existence of the ascetic through meditation, or some other means, is not possible. The power to commit spiritual suicide is absent.

A self may in disgust or in desire, commit an act to eliminate itself from one dimension but that does not mean that it can eliminate itself from all environments. A disappearance here means an appearance somewhere. The removal of objectivity in no way means the elimination of a personality. The subjective face of a self cannot be altered by the same self because the power to act is suspended during a purely subjective condition.

सर्वयोनिषु कौन्तेय
मूर्तयः संभवन्ति याः ।
तासां ब्रह्म महद्योनिर्
अहं बीजप्रदः पिता ॥१४.४॥

sarvayoniṣu kaunteya
mūrtayaḥ saṁbhavanti yāḥ
tāsāṁ brahma mahadyonir
ahaṁ bījapradaḥ pitā (14.4)

sarvayoniṣu — in all wombs; kaunteya — O son of Kuntī; mūrtayaḥ- forms; saṁbhavanti — they are produced; yāḥ— which; tāsāṁ — of them; brahmā — mundane reality; mahat — great; yoniḥ — giving; aham — I; bījapradaḥ —seed-giving; pitā — father

Forms are produced in all types of wombs, O son of Kuntī, I am the seed-giving father. The extensive mundane reality is the great womb. (Bhagavad Gītā 14.4)

Analysis

The life forms occur in various realms. The physical world is one of the situations but there are an infinite number of other levels, psychic planes on which manifestation occurs. The duration of a form is dictated by the endurance of the materials used in the particular realm.

The physical form is not the person. The psychic form is not the person. However, the person is part of the composite of his/her physicalness. To deny the person because the physical form is a composite is to be hasty and to accommodate ignorance.

Even though the God is regarded as the seed-giving father, still that does not mean that he created the limited selves. He has supervisory responsibility for the creation, which is an admixture of personSelves and materials. His magic is the production of the forms as combination of selves, adjuncts and materials.

Comprehension of Bhagavad Gītā Verse 14.4

The person energy is mixed with the other energies which abound in the creation. Some energies take formats as adjuncts which cling to a particular self and help it to format itself as being compatible with a certain creature lifestyle. Ultimately, the God has the supervisory responsibility but all the same he does not involve himself in every format of every creature, nor in every composite attraction of a self, adjuncts and related energy.

The presence of a limited spirit in an environment is itself a cause for the admixture of that self, adjuncts and materials which appear as a specific type of body in a specific species.

God does not create the formats. These arise naturally because of the attraction of a coreSelf to adjuncts and materials.

सत्त्वं रजस्तम इति
गुणाः प्रकृतिसंभवाः ।
निबध्नन्ति महाबाहो
देहे देहिनमव्ययम् ॥१४.५॥

sattvaṁ rajastama iti
guṇāḥ prakṛtisaṁbhavāḥ
nibadhnanti mahābāho
dehe dehinamavyayam (14.5)

sattvaṁ — clarity; rajaḥ — impulsion; tama — retardation; iti — thus; guṇāḥ — influences; prakṛtisaṁbhavāḥ = prakṛti— material nature + saṁbhavāḥ — produced of; nibadhnanti — they captivate; mahābāho — O great-armed hero; dehe — in the body; dehinaṁ — embodied soul; avyayam — imperishable

Clarity, impulsion and retardation are the influences produced of material nature. They captivate the imperishable embodied soul in the body, O strong-armed hero. (Bhagavad Gītā 14.5)

Analysis

Despite a self's endurance and its existential superiority over what is temporary, still it is captivated by energies and adjuncts. Each self has a certain degree of resistance. Some resist more than others. That is the variation of the selves. Ultimately the person with full immunity is the Supreme Lord. The closer any other self can get to the supreme being the more resistant that one will be.

Comprehension of Bhagavad Gītā Verse 14.5

Krishna categorizes nature as having three broad influences. These have three types of effects on the limited selves. The highest influence gives clarity in perception, whereby the self who is assisted by its adjuncts and related energies which inhabit its psyche, gets true information about what is perceived.

The median influence is the impulsive one. This forces the self to endorse actions which when committed by the psyche will result in positive or negative reactions. The impulsive force does not allow the person to see the truth. It shows an aspect which is desirable, but which may cause satisfaction or regret later.

The lowest influence is the retardative one. It suppresses clarity and enthusiasm. It results in regret. It affords miscalculation.

तत्र सत्त्वं निर्मलत्वात्
प्रकाशकमनामयम् ।
सुखसङ्गेन बध्नाति
ज्ञानसङ्गेन चानघ ॥१४.६॥

tatra sattvaṁ nirmalatvāt
prakāśakamanāmayam
sukhasaṅgena badhnāti
jñānasaṅgena cānagha (14.6)

tatra — regarding these; sattvaṁ — clarifying influence; nirmalatvāt — relatively free from perceptive impurities; prakāśakam — illuminating; anāmayam — free from disease; sukhasaṅgena = sukha — happiness + saṅgena — by attachment; badhnāti — it binds; jñānasaṅgena = jñāna— knowledge of expertise + saṅgena — by attachment; cānagha = ca — and + anagha — sinless one

Regarding these influences, the clarifying one is relatively free from perceptive impurities. It is illuminating and free from disease, but by granting an attachment to happiness and to expertise, it captivates a person, O sinless one. (Bhagavad Gītā 14.6)

Analysis

The question which faces a limited self is this.

Why does one need assistance from nature for perceptive faculties? If nature is not on an equal footing, why does it exhibit an influence into the coreSelf, where nature's moods cause variations in the consciousness of the core?

Until these questions are answered, a self cannot understand its needs. It will fail to evaluate its position in relation to everything else. To declare the coreSelf as an absolute something or to publish it as illusion or nothing, does not change the situation of the selves who participate in nature's history.

Comprehension of Bhagavad Gītā Verse 14.6

To understand nature, to understand the impact of the environment on the coreSelf, the self should sort the impact of nature on the self. Krishna gave the hint that the highest influence is relatively free from perceptive impurities. This means that it is not perfect, but it is near perfect in its illustration of the environment. But there are two environments in consideration: the one inside the psyche and the one outside the physical body. Nature affects both environments but the one of concern, is the one within the psyche.

When that inner environment is relatively free from perceptive impurities, the core takes advantage of it and can interpret events properly. However, there is a hazard derived from this highest of the influences of nature. It grants an attachment to happiness and to expertise. That causes one to become attached to this perception energy. Such attachment lowers the psyche to the median influence, which causes the self to miscalculate.

रजो रागात्मकंविद्धि
तृष्णासङ्गसमुद्भवम् ।
तन्निबध्नाति कौन्तेय
कर्मसङ्गेन देहिनम् ॥१४.७॥

rajo rāgātmakaṁviddhi
tṛṣṇāsaṅgasamudbhavam
tannibadhnāti kaunteya
karmasaṅgena dehinam (14.7)

rajo - rajaḥ — impulsive influence; rāgātmakaṁ — characterized by passion; viddhi — know; tṛṣṇāsaṅgasamudbhavam= tṛṣṇā— desire + saṅga — earnest + samudbhavam — produced from; tat — this; nibadhnāti — it captivates; kaunteya — O son of Kuntī; karmasaṅgena — by attachment to activity; dehināṁ — the embodied soul

Know that the impulsive influence is characterized by passion. It is produced from earnest desire and attachment. O son of Kuntī, this mode captivates the embodied soul by an attachment to activity. (Bhagavad Gītā 14.7)

Analysis

Enthusiasm for physical action and psychic dreams, is provided by the median influence of nature. It comes from earnest desire and attachment which a self is infected with at the onset of its appearance in a nature environment.

There are two aspects.

- coreSelf using the impulsive energy
- impulsive energy using a coreSelf

The convention is that the radiance of the coreSelf is used by nature for producing responses and actions, alternately. The mastery of yoga is denoted, shown, when a yogi develops resistance to nature, when he/she loses the need to have nature provide enthusiasm and excitement.

Comprehension of Bhagavad Gītā Verse 14.7

Earnest desire and attachment are donated by nature for use by the coreSelf, but another desire/attachment energy is in the core itself. When these two energies connect, there is a current flow through the core, such that it is subjected to a variety of feelings which cause it to make prejudiced decisions.

Without the clarity of the highest mode, the coreSelf makes choices in terms of excitement. Such decisions are faulty and carry unwanted returns.

तमस्त्वज्ञानजं विद्धि
मोहनं सर्वदेहिनाम् ।
प्रमादालस्यनिद्राभिस्
तन्निबध्नाति भारत ॥१४.८॥

tamastvajñānajaṁ viddhi
mohanaṁ sarvadehinām
pramādālasyanidrābhis
tannibadhnāti bhārata (14.8)

tamaḥ — depressing mode; tu — but; ajñānajaṁ — produced of insensibility; viddhi — know; mohanam — confusion; sarvadehināṁ — of all embodied beings; pramādālasyanidrābhiḥ = pramāda — inattentiveness + ālasya — laziness + nidrābhiḥ - sleep; tat — this; nibadhnāti — captivates; bhārata — O man of the Bharata family

But know that the depressing mode is produced of insensibility which is the confusion of all embodied beings. This captivates by inattentiveness, laziness and sleep, O man of the Bharata family. (Bhagavad Gītā 14.8)

Analysis

The depressing energy attenuates the energy which reaches the senses. This influence causes the senses to give false information about the external and internal environments. With that the self is misinformed. It makes faulty decisions.

For the senses of the physical or psychic body, to operate accurately, there must be unobstructed nerves in the physical system and high-quality psychic energy in the subtle form. Otherwise, there will be obstructions which will result in the coreSelf having access to insufficient or incorrect information.

When the energy which powers the adjuncts and feelings in the physical and subtle body, is attenuated, obstructed or polluted, that will result in sensual inattentiveness, laziness or sleep. These conditions provide false information which the coreSelf is forced to use because of having no other experience.

Comprehension of Bhagavad Gītā Verse 14.8

A living body is a physio-biological complex of materials and volition. This makes for a sentient someone in the physical world. The denial of this physical person is a way of avoiding the fact that the physical body conventional person is a composite. The best approach is to sort the parts, render their relative value and find the most essential and enduring aspect.

When the effort is made to itemize the parts and their functions, a yogi discovers that there are psychic energies which are in the combine which is the physical body. These psychic energies may survive the death of the physical system. Since the observing power in the body is psychic, one should research the possibility of its survival beyond physical death.

List each of the psychic aspects which are part of the physical body. Then do meditation research to know if any part will survive the physical form. If any portion would survive, what is its condition hereafter? Can it cause the production of a new embryo with physical and psychic apparatus?

श्रीभगवानुवाच
ऊर्ध्वमूलमधःशाखम्
अश्वत्थं प्राहुरव्ययम् ।
छन्दांसि यस्य पर्णानि
यस्तं वेद स वेदवित् ॥१५.१॥

śrībhagavānuvāca
ūrdhvamūlamadhaḥśākham
aśvatthaṁ prāhuravyayam
chandāṁsi yasya parṇāni
yastaṁ veda sa vedavit (15.1)

śrī bhagavān — The Blessed Lord; uvāca — said; ūrdhvamūtam = urdhva — upward + mūlam — root; adhaḥśākham = adhaḥ — below + śākham — branch; aśvatthaṁ — ashvattha tree; prāhuḥ — the yogī sages say; avyayam — imperishable; chandāṁsi -Vedic hymns; yasya — or what which; parṇāni — leaves; yaḥ — who; taṁ — this; veda — knows; sa = saḥ— he; vedavit —knower of the Vedas

The Blessed Lord said: The yogi sages say that there is an imperishable Ashvattha tree which has a root going upwards and a trunk downwards, the leaves of which are the Vedic hymns. He who knows this is a knower of the Vedas. (Bhagavad Gītā 15.1)

Analysis

The dismissal of the mundane energy in any, or all of its flares, is an attempt to give the coreSelf some special status. However, the reality is that the core is affected by nature. The core is not affected in its endurance, but it is in other aspects. Thus, the effort to deny the strength of the mundane energy is only a way to ease the pride of a self when faced with its reliance on anything other than itself.

On one side of the self is the reliance on the Supreme Being. On another side is the self's tendency to relate and respond to the mundane energy. Neither of these relationships can be abolished.

Krishna cited some yogi-sages who said that there is an imperishable Ashvattha tree which has a root going upwards and a trunk downwards. This is a description of nature which is an extensive growth which existed through time in various states. It is eternal but as it finds nourishment to consume, it alters.

Comprehension of Bhagavad Gītā Verse 15.1

Ancient yogi sages, by mystic means, determined that the physical situation and its psychic support is a reverse reality, which grew upside down, with roots going upwards and the trunk downwards. Due to its sentiency, information about the use of nature appears just as leaves appear on a tree.

A yogi must understand that the natural situation yields experiences which give hints and displays for understanding the complexity. However, not all beings in this manifestation have access to the information. Some people remain with no understanding about the appearance, disappearance and value of nature. Its worth is that it provides information which can be verified, and which can induce any self to research its corePersonality.

अधश्चोर्ध्वं प्रसृतास्तस्य शाखा
गुणप्रवृद्धा विषयप्रवालाः ।
अधश्च मूलान्यनुसंततानि
कर्मानुबन्धीनि मनुष्यलोके
॥१५.२॥

adhaścordhvaṁ prasṛtāstasya śākhā
guṇapravṛddhā viṣayapravālāḥ
adhaśca mūlānyanusaṁtatāni
karmānubandhīni manuṣyaloke (15.2)

Adhaścordhvaṁ = adhaḥ — downward + ca — and + urdhvam — upward; prasṛtāh — widely spreading; tasya — of it; śākhā — branches; guṇa — mundane influence; pravrddhā — nourished; viṣayapravālāḥ = viṣaya — attractive objects + pravālāḥ — sprouts; adhaśca = adhaḥ — below + ca — and; mūlāni — roots; anusaṁtatāni— stretched out; karmānubandhīni = karmā — action + anubandhīni — promoting; manuṣyaloke = manuṣya — of human being + loke — in the world

Branches spread from it, upwards and downwards. It is nourished by the mundane influences and the attractive objects are its sprouts. The roots are spread below, promoting action in the world of human beings. (Bhagavad Gītā 15.2)

Analysis

The nature and its psychic underbelly is a nourishment-seeking organism. It is alive. It feeds on the coreSelves as a matter of course. In the process, a self becomes bewildered to where it cannot determine where it begins and where the natural energies end.

Its seems that nature is superimposed on the coreSelf, but it also seems that the radiance of the core penetrates nature. This mutually parasitic relationship is regarded as desirable on one occasion and detestable on another.

Comprehension of Bhagavad Gītā Verse 15.2

The material nature is an inside operating living structure, but its inner movements are converted into motivation for outer activity with intention of expressing itself in any open space.

Yoga is for withdrawing the personEnergy from the expressiveness of nature. As it is designed, nature attracts the interest of the coreSelf, which pursues sensations which are derived from the interactions of the various features of nature. A yogi should study nature's design, make alterations and bring the interest of the self away from it.

न रूपमस्येह तथोपलभ्यते
नान्तो न चादिर्न च संप्रतिष्ठा ।
अश्वत्थमेनं सुविरूढमूलम्
असङ्गशस्त्रेण दृढेन छित्त्वा
॥१५.३

na rūpamasyeha tathopalabhyate
nānto na cādirna ca saṁpratiṣṭhā
aśvatthamenaṁ suvirūḍhamūlam
asaṅgaśastreṇa dṛḍhena chittvā (15.3)

na — not; rūpam — form; asyeha - asya — of it + iha — in this dimension; tathopalabhyate = tathā — thus + upalabhyate — it is perceived; nānto = nāntah = na —- not + antaḥ — end; na — nor; cādiḥ = ca — and + ādiḥ — end; na — nor; ca — and; saṁpratiṣṭhā — foundation; aśvatthaṁ — ashvattha tree; enam — this; suvirūḍhamūtam = suvirūḍha — well-developed + mūlam — root; asaṅgaśastreṇa = asaṅga — non-attachment + śastreṇa — with the axe; dṛḍhena — with the strong; chittvā — cutting down

Its form is not perceived in this dimension, nor its end, nor beginning nor foundation. With the strong ax of non-attachment, cut down this Ashvattha tree with its well-developed roots. (Bhagavad Gītā 15.3)

Analysis

In this dimension, the pursuit of the origins is impractical. The secret urge for this does not exist in this environment. The senses one is outfitted with, cannot detect the sources. The same approach applies to the beginning, duration and demolition of this. None of it can be integrated objectively from this side of existence.

Hence, there is a necessity for a yogi to part his self away from this situation. One by one, each yogi should sever the connection with this mundane reality. It cannot be done collectively because a limited self is positioned to release itself only.

Comprehension of Bhagavad Gītā Verse 15.3

The search for the secret origin of this creation, the one for the source of the self, the one for the key to the relationship between the core and its adjuncts, begins by discovering links to physical objects. When a yogi does that for many births, he realizes that his efforts lead to one conclusion, which is that the origins are in abstract territory.

This causes frustration because at that stage one is equipped with only an abstract sense which is the interestEnergy. It is a sense which neither smells, tastes, sees, touches or hears in the conventional way. With only one sense, that of interest, how is the self to determine anything which is abstract?

The solution to this problem is given by Krishna and by advanced yogis who gain access to the *chit akash* spiritual dimension through portals in the psyche or through teleportation into transcendental dimensions. They suggest that there be partial and then complete detachment from the ordinary sense perception. That leads to development of interest in nothing, and then development of an intuition which is not afraid of blankness, which in turn leads to spiritual sense perception.

ततः पदं तत्परिमार्गितव्यं
यस्मिन्गता न निवर्तन्ति भूयः ।
तमेव चाद्यं पुरुषं प्रपद्ये
यतः प्रवृत्तिः प्रसृता पुराणी. ॥१५.४॥

tataḥ padaṁ tatparimārgitavyaṁ
yasmingatā na nivartanti bhūyaḥ
tameva cādyaṁ puruṣaṁ prapadye
yataḥ pravṛttiḥ prasṛtā purāṇī (15.4)

tataḥ — then; padaṁ— please; tat— that; parimārgitavyaṁ — to be sought; yasmin — to which; gatā — some; na — not; nivartanti — they return; bhūyaḥ — again; tam — that; eva — indeed; cādyaṁ = ca — and + ādyaṁ — primal; puruṣaṁ — person; prapadye — I take shelter; yataḥ — from whom; pravrttiḥ — creation; prasṛtā — emerged; purāṇī — in primeval limes

Then that place is to be sought, to which having gone, the spirits do not return to this world again. One should think: I take shelter with that Primal Person, from Whom the creation emerged in primeval times. (Bhagavad Gītā 15.4)

Analysis

When all is said and done, the individual self should locate the place, to which having transferred, one does not return to this situation. This is when that spirit is satisfied with knowing through experience, that this situation, though challenging does not match its needs for stable support.

One should take shelter with that Primal Person, the one self from whom the creation emerged in primeval times. Person to supreme person, self to supreme self, the yogi should turn to face the ultimate.

Comprehension of Bhagavad Gītā Verse 15.4

A question is there. Can a self be freed from this challenging but dissatisfying existence before that self becomes exhausted with the experiences which occur here?

Must a self experience this to the fullest before it will turn away and discover the Primal Person and his super-environment?

The answer is that if by the grace of the Supreme Lord, any self is translated enough, it could leave this situation and never feel the need for what is here. Even though in the final analysis, this place is worthless, it has value to a limited self because it provides contained experiences which cause that self to realize its power limits, its susceptibility to influences and its needs for internal and external supports.

So long as a limited self feels the need for material existence or for the subtle parallel to it, he/she cannot become liberated and will not have a desperate interest in the absolute environment. A method for removing that need for what is mundane, should be applied. If the Supreme Lord does something to remove that need from any particular self, that divine action would result in that soul's elevation even without exhausting the interest in this situation.

निर्मानमोहा जितसङ्गदोषा
अध्यात्मनित्या विनिवृत्तकामाः ।
द्वंद्वैर्विमुक्ताः सुखदुःखसंज्ञैर्
गच्छन्त्यमूढाः पदमव्ययं तत् ॥१५.५

nirmānamohā jitasaṅgadoṣā
adhyātmanityā vinivṛttakāmāḥ
dvaṁdvairvimuktāḥ sukhaduḥkha-saṁjñair
gacchantyamūḍhāḥ padamavyayaṁ tat (15.5)

nirmāna — devoid of pride; mohā — confusion; jita — conquered; saṅga — attachment; doṣā — faults; adhyātmanityā = adhyātma — Supreme Spirit + nityā — constantly; vinivṛtta — ceased; kāmāḥ — cravings; dvandvaiḥ — by dualities; vimuktāḥ — freed; sukhaduḥkha — pleasure-pain; saṁjñaiḥ — known as; gacchanti — they go; amūḍhāḥ — the undeluded souls; padam — place; avyayam — imperishable; tat = tad — that

Those who are devoid of pride and confusion, who have conquered the faults of attachment, who constantly stay with the Supreme Spirit, whose cravings have ceased, who are freed from the dualities known as pleasure and pain, these undeluded souls go to that imperishable place. (Bhagavad Gītā 15.5)

Analysis

This is a guarantee for those persons who are destined to transit to the primal location of the supreme being. One person may exert himself/herself and still not reach the supreme habitat. Another person may be favored to have one or more fleeting experiences of the supreme place, and still not be permanently transferred there.

Comprehension of Bhagavad Gītā Verse 15.5

One should inspect the requirements for being a person who is so favored by fate, that he/she is already selected for translation to the spiritual environment. It is listed.

- devoid of pride and confusion
- having conquered the faults of attachment
- constantly staying with the Supreme Spirit
- having cravings ceased
- being freed from reacting to pleasure and pain

The mastership of the fifth stage of yoga, that of *pratyahar* sensual energy withdrawal results in **termination of cravings**. This is in reference to objects outside the body and to psychic impressions within the psyche. This requires steady practice in meditation.

The retreat from experience of the material world, even from its psychic counterpart, will over time, gradually, cause one's psyche to be more and more **unresponsive to pleasure and pain**, where these are perceived as energy movements and not as precious feelings.

The pleasure or pain may or may not be present but the way it is interpreted is the part played by the self in causing a profound or superficial impact on the self. Understanding that the physical body and the subtle one are a formulation, helps considerably in bringing one to the stage of toning down the impact of pleasure or pain.

Attachment is a blind force which adheres to anything which it can fuse with. In fact, the operation of linking to anything is an ongoing pursuit of the self. Eventually one understands that it is an expensive habit, which should be curtailed. One who is immature thinks that once an attachment is formed it is justified as a matter of concern. This is irrational. A devotee should understand that attachment which is exhibited and applied without Krishna's permission is a liability for one and on. Hence **attachment is a faulty basis for relationship.**

Attachment lubricates social liability but that does not mean that its application is always in the interest of all concerned.

Somehow, somewhere, a yogi should **constantly stay with the supreme spirit.** That is the way to have an ongoing reference from attachment. That frees the self from accepting influences which though justified, are not in the interest of the persons concerned. If possible, every act should be certified by the supreme spirit.

न तद्भासयते सूर्यो
न शशाङ्को न पावकः ।
यद्गत्वा न निवर्तन्ते
तद्धाम परमं मम ॥१५.६॥

na tadbhāsayate sūryo
na śaśāṅko na pāvakaḥ
yadgatvā na nivartante
taddhāma paramaṁ mama (15.6)

na — not; tat — that; bhāsayate — illuminates; sūryo = sūryaḥ — the sun; na — nor; sasaḥko = śaśāṅkaḥ — moon; na — nor; pāvakaḥ — fire; yat — which; gatvā — having gone; na — never; nivartante — they return; tat — that; dhāmā — residence; paramaṁ — supreme; mama — my

The sun does not illuminate that place, nor the moon, nor the fire. Having gone to that location, they never return. That is My supreme residence. (Bhagavad Gītā 15.6)

Analysis

The contention about an enduring spiritual environment where persons live and relate, is that there is no such place because the primal creative cause is a void energy, which produced this cosmic manifestation, which is a temporary phenomenon.

Who should one believe?

Krishna?

Another philosopher?

Krishna specifically described a supreme location where he has residence, a place which is not lit by a sun, moon nor firelight. Where is that place? What is the evidence for it?

Comprehension of Bhagavad Gītā Verse 15.6

The place one should crave, discover and invade is such that having transferred there, one would not return to this world, due to being completely satisfied once going there. The Primal Person, from Whom the creation emerged in primeval times, resides there with a spread of relationships. It is a person to supreme person accommodation.

ममैवांशो जीवलोके जीवभूतः सनातनः । मनःषष्ठानीन्द्रियाणि प्रकृतिस्थानि कर्षति ॥१५.७॥	mamaivāṁśo jīvaloke jīvabhūtaḥ sanātanaḥ manaḥṣaṣṭhānīndriyāṇi prakṛtisthāni karṣati (15.7)

mamaivāṁśaḥ = mama — my + eva — indeed + aṁśaḥ — partner; jīvaloke = jīva — individualized conditioned being + loke — in the world; jīvabhūtaḥ individual soul; sanātanaḥ — eternal; manaḥ — mind; ṣaṣṭhānindriyāṇi = saṣṭhāni — sixth + indriyāṇi — sense, detection device; prakṛtisthāni — mundane; karṣati — draws

My partner is in this world of individualized conditioned beings. He is an eternal individual soul but he draws to himself the mundane senses of which the mind is the sixth detection device. (Bhagavad Gītā 15.7)

Analysis

Krishna's *Sāṁkhya* information is about person, about *purusha*. It is not about *atma* as an energy radiance. Definitely, the *atma* is a speck of spiritual radiance but the perspective of it as a person is the information of *Sāṁkhya*. The *jivaloka* is the world of individualized limited selves who fend for themselves in a contest of influence in the natural world and in its psychic version.

The relationship between the limited self and the supreme person is hampered when the limited self is involved with the natural world and its psychic installments. To remove the influence of the natural world, a specific self must do whatever is necessary to realize the relationship with the Supreme Lord.

How to achieve this?

Dissect the parts of the psyche. Take mystic actions to segregate the coreSelf from its adjuncts.

Comprehension of Bhagavad Gītā Verse 15.7

The secret of inSelf Yoga™ is given in this verse. Here is the formula for the liberation of the limited self with consideration of the need for personal relationship wherever that self may be. Underneath its discomfort is the need for personal relationship which reinforces its person feature and does not attempt to abolish it.

A self will always try to establish person relationship because that is the nature of person. However, the idea of abolishing its person arises. That causes the self to think that the abolishment of itself could be the solution to the problem of the afflictions it is subjected to.

Krishna, lovingly and caringly, addressed the limited self as his partner but as an individualized conditioned being, who somehow, collected a set of senses which include a supervisory adjunct for detection of natural features in this environment.

शरीरं यदवाप्नोति
यच्चाप्युत्क्रामतीश्वरः ।
गृहीत्वैतानि संयाति
वायुर्गन्धानिवाशयात् ॥१५.८॥

śarīraṁ yadavāpnoti
yaccāpyutkrāmatīśvaraḥ
gṛhītvaitāni saṁyāti
vāyurgandhānivāśayāt (15.8)

śarīraṁ — by body; yad — which; avāpnoti — he acquires; yat — which; cāpi — and also; utkrāmatīśvaraḥ = utkrāmati — departs from + īśvaraḥ — master; gṛhītvaitāni = gṛhītvā — taking + etāni — these; saṁyāti — he goes; vāyuḥ — wind; gandhān — perfumes; ivāśayāt = ivā — just as + āśayāt — from source

Regardless of whichever body that master acquires, or whichever one he departs from, he goes taking these senses along, just as the wind goes with the perfumes from their source. (Bhagavad Gītā 15.8)

Analysis

A machine has parts. The bio-psychic machine which is the physical body also has parts. The so-called person who is one of the human species is a psycho-biological machine, with a coreSelf spiritual unit as its central awareness power. This machine has many physical parts. It is a biological operation. It has a psychological spread. In the psychology there is an observing self, an iSelf. That is the central power supply.

Krishna described it as being the master of the physical form. When that master departs from the living physical machine, certain other aspects, psychological features also depart because these are linked more to the coreSelf than they are to any other feature.

A rope which attaches a boat to a dock, will snap at the weakest point. When the subtle body is stressed to depart from the physical one, the connecting strand which held the subtle form to its physical system will break from the physical system, with the subtle form retaining the larger more essential part of the senses.

That movement is unseen to physical eyes but can be viewed with psychic perception. This means that the physical person becomes inactive, dead. Some of its psychological aspects are disconnected or displaced from it. These continue to live in a psychic dimension which physical perception cannot access.

Comprehension of Bhagavad Gītā Verse 15.8

From the dying physical body, physical person, the lifeForce and its psychic accessories leave. These are in a combination with the coreSelf. The same occurs when the subtle body acquires an embryo in any species, where the coreSelf and its adjuncts are fused into the bio-psychic energy of the parent and is birthed as an embryo, a child of that person(s). The convention is that the living physical body is a person. This way of relating though routine is not the complete view.

We must also realize that the physical person is a composite of various factors, some being unseen or psychic. Some psychic aspects will outlive the body, such that this physical person will die but the corePerson which is part of its composition, as well as some psychological aspects, will persist on the psychic side and will be reborn somewhere somehow.

The subtle body will persist beyond the physical person. That subtle body is a person in its own right. Within that subtle form, there is a coreSelf which is the real person and is so substantial that it persists forever with or without adjuncts and psychic or physical format.

श्रोत्रं चक्षुः स्पर्शनं च
रसनं घ्राणमेव च ।
अधिष्ठाय मनश्चायं
विषयानुपसेवते ॥१५.९॥

śrotraṁ cakṣuḥ sparśanaṁ ca
rasanaṁ ghrāṇameva ca
adhiṣṭhāya manaścāyaṁ
viṣayānupasevate (15.9)

śrotraṁ — hearing; cakṣuḥ — vision; sparśanaṁ — sense of touch; ca — and; rasanaṁ — taste; ghrāṇaṁ — smell; eva — indeed; ca — and; adhiṣṭhāya — governing; manaścāyaṁ = manaḥ — mind; ca — and + ayaṁ — this; viṣayān — attractive objects; upasevate — becomes addicted

While governing the sense of hearing, the vision, the sense of touch, the sense of taste, the sense of smell and the mind, My partner becomes addicted to the attractive objects. (Bhagavad Gītā 15.9)

Analysis

While being involved in the drama of the composite person who is a social being in this situation, the coreSelf which is the invisible part of the physical machine, becomes addicted to the events which occur outside and inside the physical body. This flow of attention is spiced with curiosity. That in turn, ties the coreSelf to its senses and psychological tooling. This tooling is the sense of identity, intellect, kundalini sensations and memory.

Comprehension of Bhagavad Gītā Verse 15.9

The coreSelf should govern the sense of hearing, the vision, the sense of touch, the sense of taste, the sense of smell and the mind, but in most cases the energy it continually expresses is used as a governing force by the adjuncts, such that instead of governing, the core's contribution of energy is itself governed by its adjuncts. This shows by the development of being addicted to the attractive objects which are pursued and consumed by the adjuncts.

यतन्तो योगिनश्चैनं
पश्यन्त्यात्मन्यवस्थितम् ।
यतन्तोऽप्यकृतात्मानो
नैनं पश्यन्त्यचेतसः ॥१५.११॥

yatanto yoginaścainaṁ
paśyantyātmanyavasthitam
yatanto'pyakṛtātmāno
nainaṁ paśyantyacetasaḥ (15.11)

yatanto = yatantaḥ — endeavoring; yoginaścainaṁ = yoginaḥ — yogis + ca — and + enam — this (spirit); paśyānti — they sec; ātmani — in the self; avasthitam — situated; yatanto = yatantaḥ — exertion; 'pi = api — even; akṛtātmāno — akṛtātmānaḥ = akṛta — not in order, imperfect + ātmānaḥ — self; nainaṁ= na — not + enam — this (spirit); paśyanti — they see; acetasaḥ — thoughtless ones

The endeavoring yogis see the spirit as being situated in itself; but even with exertion, the imperfected souls, the thoughtless ones, do not perceive it. (Bhagavad Gītā 15.11)

Analysis

Though it may be victimized by nature or by its adjuncts or by some other person, still the coreSelf is situated in itself and is immovable. However, with physical perception and with primitive psychic intuition, the core cannot be perceived even by itself.

Comprehension of Bhagavad Gītā Verse 15.11

The coreSelf can access other selves and locations from its unique position in the person landscape. The God is the central immovable self with each other self radiating around that central person. Self-perception of a self by itself is not an easy achievement for a limited self.

सर्वस्य चाहं हृदि संनिविष्टो
मत्तः स्मृतिर्ज्ञानमपोहनं च ।
वेदैश्च सर्वैरहमेव वेद्यो
वेदान्तकृद्वेदविदेव चाहम्
॥१५.१५॥

sarvasya cāhaṁ hṛdi saṁniviṣṭo
mattaḥ smṛtirjñānam apohanaṁ ca
vedaiśca sarvairahameva vedyo
vedāntakṛdvedavideva cāham (15.15)

sarvasya — of all; cāhaṁ = ca — and + aham — I; hṛdi — in the central psyche; saṁniviṣṭo - saṁniviṣṭaḥ — entered; mattaḥ — from me; smṛtiḥ — memoiy; jñānam — knowledge; apohanaṁ — reasoning; ca — and; vedaiśca = vedaiḥ — by the Vedas + ca — and; sarvaiḥ — by all; aham — I; eva — indeed; vedyo = vedyaḥ— to be known; vedāntakṛt = vedānta — Vedānta + kṛt — maker, author; vedavit — knower of the Vcdas; eva — indeed; cāham = ca — and + aham — I

And I entered the central psyche of all beings. From Me comes memory, knowledge and reasoning. By all the Vedas, I am to be known. I am the author of Vedānta and the knower of the Vedas. (Bhagavad Gītā 15.15)

Analysis

Vedānta is the end of the acquirement of knowledge. It happens through numerous experiences which are granted because of being allied to nature and being subjected to its innumerable equations. These situations are personal and mathematical.

The last education is that of realizing the features of the personEnergy. It culminates in knowing that there is a Supreme Someone who is the sentient axisSupreme. That person is Krishna. It is not that everyone is directly related to him, but everyone is related to someone else, who in turn may be related or sub-related, until the ultimate source is Krishna.

By the Vedas, by this information too, Krishna is to be known. He is the author and teacher of this information which is disseminated by various persons who serve as his teaching staff.

Comprehension of Bhagavad Gītā Verse 15.15

Ultimately, the control of objectivity is done by the Supreme Lord. It is according to the use and value of the limited persons. The subjective aspect of a self is not monitored because it is permanent and steady. Only the objective part is regulated by its relationship distance from the supreme self.

When the psyches appeared, they had the supreme person and the limited self with adjuncts. These were installed. However, the supreme person was positioned centrally as the ultimate factor for the cohesion of each psyche.

From the God presence in the psyche, there comes memory, information acquired from experience and reasoning. The perception of the supreme person, however, is not possible under ordinary circumstances. The God transcends the limited selves, such that usually they cannot discern his presence. He is not involved on the planes of existence where the limited selves operate. A limited self has difficulty sorting itself from its adjuncts as well as knowing itself by itself. Hence, there is lack of perception when it attempts to identify anyone who is higher than itself.

द्वाविमौ पुरुषौ लोके
क्षरश्चाक्षर एव च ।
क्षरः सर्वाणि भूतानि
कूटस्थोऽक्षर उच्यते ॥१५.१६॥

dvāvimau puruṣau loke
kṣaraścākṣara eva ca
kṣaraḥ sarvāṇi bhūtāni
kūṭastho'kṣara ucyate (15.16)

dvau — two; imau — these two; puruṣau — two spirits; loke — in the world; kṣaraścākṣara = kṣaraḥ — affected + ca — and + akṣara — unaffected; eva — indeed; ca — and; kṣaraḥ — affected; sarvāṇi — all; bhūtāni — mundane creatures; kūṭastho = kūṭasthaḥ — stable soul; 'kṣara = akṣara — unaffected; ucyate — is said to be

These two types of spirits are in this world, namely the affected ones and the unaffected ones. All mundane creatures are affected. The stable soul is said to be unaffected. (Bhagavad Gītā 15.16)

Analysis

There is a proposal that the self is never affected by anything, that it is substantial to the extent that its susceptibility is an illusion only and not a factual event. However, Krishna's proclamation in this verse contradicts that.

He declared that in principle every mundane creature is affected. Only those selves which are stable in relation to nature are rated as unaffected. These persons act from a zero position, such that their favorable and unfavorable acts are not reinforced by gashing impulsions which cause them to flee from or rigidly embrace the acts and reactions.

Comprehension of Bhagavad Gītā Verse 15.16

A yogi should assume that he is an affected person, where his relationship with the adjuncts is one of partial control only. There is constant feedback between the coreSelf and the adjuncts, in a give and take, push and pull operation, such that the core controls the psyche part of the time, and is controlled or exploited by it some of the time.

As an affected person, the yogi's confidence is shaken. To smash that feeling of inadequacy some ascetics adopt the belief that their susceptibility to nature is an illusion. This is untrue because the fact is that the coreSelf, though a spiritual radiance in its own right, cannot control all events of nature. A yogi should train himself to live with the fact that even though he is perpetual, he always exists in an environment.

Hence, he should migrate from the physical existence and its subtle counterpart. He should shift or translate to an environment which will give to him/her rather than take from him/her. That place is Krishna's residence.

In the meantime, until that is attained, one should shift to being neutral or as neutral as possible while one is in contact with this physical manifestation. One must learn how to be in the range of the influence of nature and yet be stable because of simultaneously being unresponsive to it.

Nature will do what it will do. It will commandeer the physical and subtle body as it may. And yet, a yogi should be aware of nature's influences and be neutral to them. The reaction force for positive events swings in one direction. The flyback from negative events swings in the other direction. There is a central position. A yogi/yogini should practice to remain anchored in the central energy while nature operates.

Dismissing nature mentally by telling oneself and others, that because it is temporarily manifested, nature is an illusion, will result in hypocritical acts and criminal behavior. Honestly recognizing what nature does, and teaching the self to be an indifferent witness to her behavior, is the method.

उत्तमः पुरुषस्त्वन्यः
परमात्मेत्युदाहृतः ।
यो लोकत्रयमाविश्य
बिभर्त्यव्यय ईश्वरः ॥१५.१७॥

uttamaḥ puruṣastvanyaḥ
paramātmetyudāhṛtaḥ
yo lokatrayamāviśya
bibhartyavyaya īśvaraḥ (15.17)

uttamaḥ — higher: puruṣaḥ — spirit; tu — but; anyaḥ — another; paramātmeti = paramātmā — Supreme Spirit + iti — tims; udāhṛtaḥ — is called; yo = yaḥ — who; lokatrayam — three worlds; āviśya — entering; bibharti — supports; avyaya — eternal; īśvaraḥ — Lord

But the highest spirit is in another category. He is called the Supreme Spirit, Who having entered the three worlds as the eternal Lord, supports it. (Bhagavad Gītā 15.17)

Analysis

The segregation between the Supreme Spirit and the ordinary spiritual individuals is abolished by some philosophers. Krishna declarations are not acknowledged by everyone.

Some feel that there is no difference between the individual limited being and the individual supreme being. Their idea is that the individual can be the supreme and the supreme can be shifted into being limited. The conclusion from this is that all the individuals are one colossal power and nothing else. In other words, the individual person is not to be recognized as anything.

This runs contrary to what Krishna declared. He partitioned the Supreme Spirit as the supporter of every other person

Comprehension of Bhagavad Gītā Verse 15.17

God is unlimited. He supports every other person. This subsidy is perpetual but seasonal. From one perspective he supports the subjective existence of the coreSelf. From another view, he alternately supports and withdraws installments from the objective face of a limited being.

यस्मात्क्षरमतीतोऽहम्
अक्षरादपि चोत्तमः ।
अतोऽस्मि लोके वेदे च
प्रथितः पुरुषोत्तमः ॥१५.१८॥

yasmātkṣaramatīto'ham
akṣarādapi cottamaḥ
ato'smi loke vede ca
prathitaḥ puruṣottamaḥ (15.18)

yasmāt — since; kṣaram — effected; atīto = atītaḥ — beyond; 'ham = aham — I; akṣarāt — than the unaffected spirits; api — even; cottamaḥ = ca — and + uttamaḥ — higher; ato = ataḥ — hence; 'smi = asmi — I am; loke — in the world; vede — in the Veda; ca — and; prathitaḥ — known as; puruṣottamaḥ — Supreme Person

Since I am beyond the affected spirits and I am even higher than the unaffected ones, I am known in the world and in the Vedas as the Supreme Person. (Bhagavad Gītā 15.18)

Analysis

Krishna is known by some as the Supreme Person. The majority of humans who have this information, have no visual evidence of Krishna's supremacy. They accepted his self-declarations as they read or heard of it.

Krishna gave three categories of personality.

- those who are affected due to contact with nature

- those who are unaffected even when in contact with nature
- the supreme being who has the maximum resistance to influence

Comprehension of Bhagavad Gītā Verse 15.18

In India at the time of the war of the *Kauravas*, Krishna was known as the Supreme Person. Krishna gave Arjuna the reference of the Vedas which are an aural history and catalog of religious rites.

Whatever Arjuna knew about the Supreme Person which was explained in the ancient myths and history, could be attributed to Krishna and used to identify his glory.

सत्त्वानुरूपा सर्वस्य
श्रद्धा भवति भारत ।
श्रद्धामयोऽयं पुरुषो
यो यच्छ्रद्धः स एव सः ॥१७.३॥

sattvānurūpā sarvasya
śraddhā bhavati bhārata
śraddhāmayo'yaṁ puruṣo
yo yacchraddhaḥ sa eva saḥ (17.3)

sattvānurūpā = sattva — essential nature + anurūpā — according to; sarvasya — of every person; śraddhā — confidence; bhavati — becomes manifest; bhārata — O man of the Bharata family; śraddhāmayaḥ — made of faith, trend of confidence; 'yaṁ = ayaṁ — this; puruṣo = puruṣaḥ — human being; yo = yaḥ — who; yacchraddhah = yac (yad) — which + chraddhah (śraddhaḥ) —faith; sa = saḥ — he; eva — only: saḥ — he

Confidence becomes manifest according to the essential nature of the person, O man of the Bharata family. A human being follows his trend of confidence. Whatever type of faith he has, that he expresses only. (Bhagavad Gītā 17.3)

Analysis

The effort to banish personality, to rid the world of the idea of unique character, is a failed assault on reality. And yet, year after year there are fresh assaults which many human beings begin. Their valid critique is that the personality, which is a physical body, is a farce.

However, on dissecting the physical person, one finds psychological energy. If the psyche has a coreSelf which is not physical and which endures after the death of the body, the critique should be revised. The physical body as a person is temporary. When that temporary formation ceases, only some of the parts will be eliminated. Whatever is left should be accounted.

The physical parts of a physical person will be demolished. That we know. But we should not assume that the psychological parts will be eliminated or dismantled altogether. Meditation is the research into the value of the psychological remnants of the physical presence.

Comprehension of Bhagavad Gītā Verse 17.3

One feature which continues beyond the physical body is the confidence energy of the person. Someone can be recognized by his exhibition of a particular type and degree of confidence in his next birth or in his abstract presence hereafter. The confidence feature remains with the coreSelf after the death of the body. It is specific and unique in each person.

As every creature has a specific odor, so every person endures with a specific degree of confidence which is expressed in a specific manner.

यजन्ते सात्त्विका देवान् यक्षरक्षांसि राजसाः । प्रेतान्भूतगणांश्चान्ये यजन्ते तामसा जनाः ॥१७.४॥	yajante sāttvikā devān yakṣarakṣāṁsi rājasāḥ pretānbhūtagaṇāṁścānye yajante tāmasā janāḥ (17.4)

yajante — they worship; sāttvikā — clear-minded people; devān — supernatural riders; yakṣarakṣāṁsi = yakṣa — passionate sorcerers + rakṣāṁsi — to cannibalistic powerful humans; rājasāḥ — impulsive people; pretān — the departed spirits; bhūtagaṇāṁścānye — bhūtagaṇān — hordes of ghosts + ca — and + anye — others; yajante — they petition; tāmasā = retarded; janāḥ — people

The clear-minded people worship the supernatural rulers. The impulsive ones worship the passionate sorcerers and the cannibalistic humans. The others, the retarded people, petition the departed spirits and the hordes of ghosts. (Bhagavad Gītā 17.4)

Analysis

There is another set of individuals who honor no person, except as required to survived in a society. Some of these are of the opinion that there is no one who is better than any other person. Some feel that personality is an illusion, and thus worship of any person is absurd.

The denial of personality is based mainly on the fact that the formed social identity is a fabrication which began with the birth of a body and ends with its death.

Comprehension of Bhagavad Gītā Verse 17.4

Worship of person is natural for some human beings. It is unnatural for others. Of those who worship a deity or energy, those who acknowledge supernatural rulers of the environment are the highest. The median group worship sorcerers and cannibalistic humans. The lowest group are retarded people who petition departed spirits and ghosts.

The majority of humans who worship someone as a deity, do so with the motive to benefit by acquiring commodities and power in the physical existence. However, there is another set of worshippers who do so to be inspired with higher sense perception to access forms in the supernatural world.

What is imperceptible appears as formless and substanceless but if one develops supernatural perception one can perceive what seems to be invisible and intangible.

अशास्त्रविहितं घोरं तप्यन्ते ये तपो जनाः । दम्भाहंकारसंयुक्ताः कामरागबलान्विताः ॥१७.५॥	aśāstravihitaṁ ghoraṁ tapyante ye tapo janāḥ dambhāhaṁkāra-saṁyuktāḥ kāmarāgabalānvitāḥ (17.5)

aśāstravihitaṁ = aśāstra — not of scripture + vihitaṁ — recommended; ghoraṁ — terrible; tapyante — tbey endure; ye — who; tapo — tapaḥ — austerity; janāḥ — people; dambhāhaṁkārasaṁyuktāḥ — dambha — deceit + ahaṁkāra — misplaced identity + saṁyuktāḥ — enthused with; kāmarāgabalānvitāḥ = kāma — craving + rāga — rage + bala — brute force + anvitāḥ — possessed with

People who endure terrible austerities which are not recommended in the scripture, people who are enthused with deceit and misplaced identity, who are possessed with craving, rage and brute force, (Bhagavad Gītā 17.5)

Analysis

This is a partial list of the markers of the persons with wicked intentions. If personality is meaningless, if it is mere illusion, why would Krishna itemize this.

Comprehension of Bhagavad Gītā Verse 17.5

Enlightenment must include a regard for the person selves. It must take into account the interaction of persons with an environment and with other persons. At the advanced levels of this practice, the quest changes into an internal one to sort the aspects of the psyche so that the corePerson is isolated and its adjuncts are identified and controlled.

कर्शयन्तः शरीरस्थं भूतग्राममचेतसः । मां चैवान्तःशरीरस्थं तान्विद्ध्यासुरनिश्चयान् ॥१७.६॥	karśayantaḥ śarīrasthaṁ bhūtagrāmamacetasaḥ māṁ caivāntaḥśarīrasthaṁ tānviddhyāsuraniścayān (17.6)

karśayantaḥ — torturing, troubling; śarīrastham — within the body; bhūtagrāmam — collection of elements; acetasaḥ — senseless; māṁ — me; caivantaḥ = ca — and + eva — indeed + antaḥ — within; śarīrasthaṁ — within the body; tān — them; viddhi — know; — āsura — wicked + niścayān — intentions

...those who torture the collection of the elements which comprise the body, who also trouble Me within the body, know that they have wicked intentions. (Bhagavad Gītā 17.6)

Analysis

An obnoxious lifestyle, one in which there are self-destructive habits and addictions, causes pain to the self and the supreme self. But Krishna declared prior that he was unaffected and has superior stability. Thus, his relationship to the limited being's behavior is distant. He is aware of the trauma which a limited self is subjected to but that does not condemn him to being afflicted as a limited self is.

Comprehension of Bhagavad Gītā Verse 17.6

The physical body is a collection of elements which include non-physical components like for instance, the mind space, the analytical mental operator, the memory, the sense of identity and the sensual energy.

The collection of elements works efficiently under certain conditions. One who subjects the body to adverse internal or external conditions, hurts himself/herself and the Supreme Lord. The injury to the self is greater. That is due to the proximity of the limited self and the adjuncts in its psyche.

अर्जुन उवाच संन्यासस्य महाबाहो तत्त्वमिच्छामि वेदितुम् । त्यागस्य च हृषीकेश पृथक्केशिनिषूदन ॥१८.१॥	arjuna uvāca saṁnyāsasya mahābāho tattvamicchāmi veditum tyāgasya ca hṛṣīkeśa pṛthakkeśiniṣūdana (18.1)

arjuna — Arjuna; uvāca — said; saṁnyāsasya — of the rejection of opportunity; mahābāho — O strong-armed hero; tattvam — fact; icchāmi — I want; veditum — to know; tyāgasya — of the rejection of consequences; ca — and; hṛṣīkesa — O Hṛṣīkeśa; pṛthak — distinguish; keśiniṣūdāna — slayer of Keshi

Arjuna said: Regarding the rejection of opportunity, O strong-armed hero, I want to know the fact. And regarding the rejection of consequences, O Hṛṣīkeśa, distinguish these, O slayer of Keshi. (Bhagavad Gītā 18.1)

Analysis

If ultimately there is no person, all efforts at enlightenment, liberation or transcendence, are a waste of endeavor. The fact that the social identity, the bodily self, is a composite which will soon be dismantled, is no reason to dismiss the idea of an enduring person. What a yogi should do, is reduce his interest to the bare factors which remain as the residual instances after death.

Once these are discovered and identified, it is a matter of rendering their respective values to find the ones with the most endurance. This research will take the yogi to the realities which underlie energy and person.

The difficulty in this research is that whatever cannot be apprehended by the physical senses, registers as being abstract, as being invisible and formless. Hence, there is an urgency to develop subtle, supernatural, and spiritual senses to see into other dimensions.

One should not expect that nature should equip the physical body with the necessary sensual perception for transcendence viewing. It is acquired through meditation. It is earned, through meditation.

Portals to the transcendental worlds are opened from within the psyche of the yogi, within the mind. Through these the perception of the supernatural and spiritual environments and their inhabitants is experienced.

Comprehension of Bhagavad Gītā Verse 18.1

The scope of material existence is that an environment is exploited by persons who are present in that situation and who are equipped with a body which can access and sensually consume the place. That is the summary situation.

It is about opportunity and consequences. In opportunity, the individual acts correctly or incorrectly. In consequences, the individual is victimized by conditions, either pleasant, neutral or unpleasant influences.

If a limited self has insufficient information, he/she cannot properly rate a situation. He may act in a way which produces a favorable outcome. He may act to the contrary and be inconvenienced. He may also desist from action, but that neutrality may bring consequences just the same.

As for the consequences which are levied by nature, the limited self may dodge some of what he dislikes but all the same, he may be unable to avoid every reaction.

The mere idea that an act or consequence could be tied to someone, is proof enough about the validity of personSelf. Person is the target of nature. That makes it real enough.

श्रीभगवानुवाच
काम्यानां कर्मणां न्यासं
संन्यासं कवयो विदुः ।
सर्वकर्मफलत्यागं
प्राहुस्त्यागं विचक्षणाः ॥१८.२॥

śrībhagavānuvāca
kāmyānāṁ karmaṇāṁ nyāsaṁ
saṁnyāsaṁ kavayo viduḥ
sarvakarmaphalatyāgaṁ
prāhustyāgaṁ vicakṣaṇāḥ (18.2)

śrī bhagavān — The Blessed Lord; uvāca — said; śrī kāmyānāṁ — prompted by craving; karmaṇāṁ — of actions; nyāsaṁ— renunciation; saṁnyāsaṁ — rejection of opportunity; kavayo — kavayaḥ — authoritative speakers; viduḥ — know; sarvakarmaphalatyāgaṁ= sarva — all + karma — action + phala — benefit + tyāgaṁ — abandonment; prāhuḥ — they declare; tyāgaṁ — rejection of consequences; vicakṣaṇāḥ — the clear-sighted person

The Blessed Lord said: The authoritative speakers know the rejection of opportunity as renunciation of actions which are prompted by craving. The clear-sighted seers declare the abandonment of the results of benefit-motivated action as the rejection of consequences. (Bhagavad Gītā 18.2)

Analysis

The operation of personality is a social display of relationships and the resultant interactions. One should learn how to relate both to the environment and to the persons who are displayed in it. The fact that the social somebody is a composite, part of which will be demolished when the physical body is deceased, is insufficient reason to ignore or trivialize it.

A self should understand the additions to its core. It should properly evaluate the components. Then it can decide whether to accept or reject what is presented to it

Comprehension of Bhagavad Gītā Verse 18.2

Because the person is targeted it should neither ignore itself nor the environment in which it functions. The reassessment is not about the existence of the personSelf but how much of the physical entity is enduring. But even so, even with the information or experience of the bare core, there should be actions and avoidance of actions which the psyche should enact.

Krishna quoted the authoritative speakers of his time, who classified the rejection of opportunity as the renunciation of actions which are prompted by craving. They declared the abandonment of the results of benefit-motivated actions as the rejection of consequences.

The incidental or deliberate target of action or consequences is personSelf, either one or many, but with each feeling the situation personally. If someone has an opportunity to act and does not do so for whatever reason, that is rated as the rejection of the opportunity and its potential history. In another way, if someone takes an opportunity and then leaves aside the results of that benefit-motivated action which he performed, that is classified as the rejection of the consequences of his action. It involves personality and scenery.

त्याज्यं दोषवदित्येके
कर्म प्राहुर्मनीषिणः ।
यज्ञदानतपःकर्म
न त्याज्यमिति चापरे ॥१८.३॥

tyājyaṁ doṣavadityeke
karma prāhurmanīṣiṇaḥ
yajñadānatapaḥkarma
na tyājyamiti cāpare (18.3)

tyājyaṁ — to be abandoned; doṣāvat — full of fault; iti — thus; eke — some; karma — action; prāhur= prāhuḥ — they declare; manīṣaṇaḥ — philosophers; yajñadānatapaḥkarma = yajña — sacrifice + dāna — charity + tapaḥ — austerity + karma — action; na — not; tyājyam — be abandoned; iti — thus; cāpare = ca — and + apare — others

Some philosophers declare that action is to be abandoned, since it is full of faults. Some others say that acts of sacrifice, charity and austerity are not to be abandoned. (Bhagavad Gītā 18.3)

Analysis

There is this tug-of-war between one group of philosophers who adore cultural activities and another group which shun such acts. Those who are in love with physical existence think that for the good of the world and for the upkeep of the personality, everyone should be busy in mundane affairs. The others who think that the world is an unreliable footing, feel that any action done will in the end be futile, because the creation will crash into a final chaos, and no one will survive that ruin.

Comprehension of Bhagavad Gītā Verse 18.3

Actions are full of faults but that is not sufficient justification for a total lack of participation in social affairs. If there is interaction with anyone, new activities are set into motion. These require involvement. Despite the faults of life, one person dies and another lives. Those who live support or degrade society.

For such support concern, donations and self-discipline are required. What would it be if in a future life, one had parents who were so detached from action, that they did nothing for the upkeep of one's infant body? Suppose those who are well situated felt no compassion towards those who were in dire need? What of those who were in an advantageous position who never felt the need to restrain themselves?

The issue of person is crucial. It was not abolished for ancient yogis. It cannot be abolished for modern ascetics. It must be solved by giving it value and discussing its remnant portion which will survive the physical body.

निश्चयं शृणु मे तत्र
त्यागे भरतसत्तम ।
त्यागो हि पुरुषव्याघ्र
त्रिविधः संप्रकीर्तितः ॥१८.४॥

niścayaṁ śṛṇu me tatra
tyāge bharatasattama
tyāgo hi puruṣavyāghra
trividhaḥ saṁprakīrtitaḥ (18.4)

niścayaṁ — view; śṛṇu — hear; me — my; tatra — here, on this matter; tyāge — in the abandonment of consequences; bharatasattama — best of the Bharatas; — tyāgo (tyāgaḥ) — abandonment of consequences; hi — indeed; puruṣavyāghra — tiger among men; trividhaḥ — three-fold; saṁprakīrtitaḥ — designated

Hear my view on this matter of abandonment of the consequences of action, O best of the Bharatas. The abandonment of consequences, O tiger among men, is designated as being threefold. (Bhagavad Gītā 18.4)

Analysis

Krishna will elaborate about the abandonment of consequences, where someone acts and makes efforts successfully or unsuccessfully to sidestep the repercussions. These may be pleasant or unpleasant returns but regardless the person tries to disown the reactions which fate serves him by putting him in specific circumstances where he recalls or does not recall his initial actions.

Most human beings attempt to sidestep unfavorable repercussions. Most desire to have the favorable returns. Sorting a situation is difficult. Nature serves a mix of new opportunities and result-situations which have old actions in the mix. The problem with being a limited self is that one does not have the insight to sort circumstances, to know which parts are repercussions and which are new presentations of fate.

Comprehension of Bhagavad Gītā Verse 18.4

In every aspect of this creation the flow of feelings abounds. There are three major influences. These come about as a result of the combination forces. The exact calculation of a circumstance regarding the percentages of each type of feeling involved, is beyond the scope of a limited self.

Only the supreme self can accurately tally the fragments of each circumstance. The limited self's only way of knowing is to consult with the Supreme Person, with Krishna or with an informed agent of his.

At the moment of the incidence the agent must be immediately informed. Otherwise, his/her information will be incorrect. The contact with the Supreme Lord is not always continuous hence an agent who knows in one circumstance may not be informed of some other event and may have faulty intuition.

Abandonment of consequences, especially of negative undesirable ones is risky. Unless there is assistance from a higher self, such renunciation could lead to heavier penalties being inflicted on the self. All the same passionately claiming desired returns may cause the formation of addictions to the enjoyment which may dull a person's sense of fairness.

यज्ञदानतपःकर्म
न त्याज्यं कार्यमेव तत् ।
यज्ञो दानं तपश्चैव
पावनानि मनीषिणाम् ॥१८.५॥

yajñadānatapaḥkarma
na tyājyaṁ kāryameva tat
yajño dānaṁ tapaścaiva
pāvanāni manīṣiṇām (18.5)

yajñadānatapaḥkrama = yajña — sacrifice + dāna — charity + tapaḥ — austerity + karma — action; na — not; tyājyaṁ — to be abandoned; kāryam — to be performed; eva — indeed; tat — tad — this; yajño — yajñaḥ — sacrifice; dānaṁ — charily; tapaścaiva = tapaḥ — austerity + caiva — and indeed; pāvanāni — purificatory acts; manīṣiṇāṁ — for the wise men

Acts of sacrifice, charity, and austerity are not to be abandoned but should be performed. Sacrifice, charity and austerity are purificatory acts even for the wise men. (Bhagavad Gītā 18.5)

Analysis

Krishna did not agree that anyone should neglect acts of sacrifice, charity and austerity. His opinion is that such acts are necessary even for the masters of renunciation, the wise men. One way to view this is that if such acts are mandatory for the Supreme Person, it follows that everyone else should comply. The incidence is not abandonment of such acts but the curtailment of them so that in the social hazards, the yogi participates to the minimum.

The mundane energy is an enticement for the limited self, who should carefully indulge, otherwise a self will be inflicted with unfavorable repercussions and with favorable ones which result in lack of insight leading to more faulty actions.

Comprehension of Bhagavad Gītā Verse 18.5

One is forewarned by Lord Krishna, that one should not abandon opportunities for performing acts of sacrifice, charity, and austerity. Instead, one should analyze these and in consultation with Krishna made a decision as to which part of any involvement one should take.

The vortex of this is the consultation with Krishna. Who has that? Arjuna had it but which other person has that access?

There were examples in the past, of teachers of the Krishna Conscious way of life, being consulted. These authorities were accepted as pure devotees who had continuous twenty-four-hour contact with Krishna. But then they gave advice which ruined others.

This means that even a person was an agent, is an agent or will be an agent of Krishna, and even if that can be proven beyond a doubt, still that does not guarantee that the agent has continuous consultation. Arjuna did not have it. One should be extra cautious in claiming to be an agent of Krishna with continuous contact.

एतान्यपि तु कर्माणि
सङ्गं त्यक्त्वा फलानि च ।
कर्तव्यानीति मे पार्थ
निश्चितं मतमुत्तमम् ॥१८.६॥

etānyapi tu karmāṇi
saṅgaṁ tyaktvā phalāni ca
kartavyānīti me pārtha
niścitaṁ matamuttamam (18.6)

etāni — these; api — also; tu — but; karmāṇi — actions; saṅgaṁ — attachment; tyaktvā — giving up; phalāni — results; ca — and; kartvyānīti = kartvyāni — to be done + iti — thus; me — my; pārtha — O son of Pṛthā; niścitaṁ — definitely; matam — opinion; uttamam — highest

But these actions are to be performed by giving up attachment to results, O son of Pṛthā. This is definitely My highest opinion. (Bhagavad Gītā 18.6)

Analysis

Anyone who says that he is the continuous agent of Krishna, should be regarded cautiously. Krishna did not direct anyone to go to someone else to get a reading of Krishna opinion about a current circumstance.

The secret to acting in a Krishna Conscious manner, is pronounced clearly. It is not that one should run to a teacher of the Krishna Conscious way of life, nor that one should pray to Krishna for a divine advisory. The method given is this.

Shed attachment to results which are deep-seated in the nature of the individual self. This one act may free one so that one can switch to a plane of consciousness where the advice of Krishna will be evident.

Krishna listed this as his highest opinion. He did not point a finger at himself. He did not say to approach a pure devotee. Opportunities for acts of sacrifice, charity and austerity should be performed but the mental and emotional profile one should have while doing so is that one should be disinclined for the results of the motions.

As soon as a limited entity steps away from result-oriented posture, he/she may harmonize with Krishna. The energy for clarity of perception to make the right decisions, is present everywhere. Access to it, is had by a non-profit attitude towards the returns of the recommended social activities and the isolated austerities.

Comprehension of Bhagavad Gītā Verse 18.6

Definitely one should get rid of the idea that one should be an actionless person. Wherever one may turn in this dimension or elsewhere, one is likely to find other persons. There will be interplay. It cannot be avoided because there is no evidence in this world of one person anywhere. Yes, there is a sun. There is a moon. But one person? No. We do not experience a sole individual. This means that regardless of if personality is a composite, parts of which are non-enduring, still for the time being, so long as we function as or through a physical body, we must deal with persons.

The time may come when one will not be part of the composite physical self, where the remnant psychological factors no longer are in combination with physical aspects as a living physical body. Even so, for the time being one should perform actions but with no attachment to results. One should have a nonchalant attitude so that providence is free to utilize results. One should not function as a claimant.

नियतस्य तु संन्यासः
कर्मणो नोपपद्यते ।
मोहात्तस्य परित्यागस्
तामसः परिकीर्तितः ॥१८.७॥

niyatasya tu saṁnyāsaḥ
karmaṇo nopapadyate
mohāttasya parityāgas
tāmasaḥ parikīrtitaḥ (18.7)

niyatasya — of obligation; tu — but; saṁnyāsaḥ — renunciation; karmaṇo (karmaṇaḥ) — of action; nopapadyate = na — not + upapadyate — it is proper; mohāt — from delusion; tasya — of it; parityāgaḥ — rejection; tāmasaḥ — influence of depression; parikīrtitaḥ — is said to be

But renunciation of obligatory actions is not proper. The rejection of it on the basis of delusion, is said to occur by the influence of depression. (Bhagavad Gītā 18.7)

Analysis

Who is to say what is praiseworthy and what is a dishonorable? The Supreme Person gave his opinion. One who renounces obligatory actions may do so on the premise that the obligation is invalid or that it can be successfully waivered. But if a limited self makes that decision, how are we to know if there will be unfavorable repercussions?

Of the three influences under which one sets priorities, the lowest is the state of depression, when one's mental faculties and emotional energy are dulled. Then, a limited self gets the view that he/she knows what should be done. In fact, this certainty of opinion is misleading.

The mere idea that there is obligation means that inaction is inappropriate but if one is under the depressive influence, one thinks that there is no reaction for non-compliance.

Comprehension of Bhagavad Gītā Verse 18.7

Unless one is a great yogi, who mastered the *ashtanga* eight-step yoga process, and unless one is in continuous transcendental contact with the universal form of Krishna, one cannot be certain that any activity nor any neglect of an activity, is proper. One should always be doubtful of one's capacity to read the mind of the Supreme Lord. And yet, one should act even if one doubts that the action is proper.

Better to act cautiously than to avoid liabilities which fate presents as obligations to be fulfilled promptly. That is better than to be a pretend renunciant and avoid all social interactions while benefiting from society. One should not under any circumstance become a pretend pure devotee teacher of Krishna Consciousness, where one poses as a guide, telling others what they should or should not do.

Renouncing one's reproductive duty to ancestors and adopting the life of a renunciant, where one forms an institution and governs the social and financial life of others in the name of Krishna, is unhealthy and will convey one to hell.

दुःखमित्येव यत्कर्म
कायक्लेशभयात्त्यजेत् ।
स कृत्वा राजसं त्यागं
नैव त्यागफलं लभेत् ॥१८.८॥

duḥkhamityeva yatkarma
kāyakleśabhayāttyajet
sa kṛtvā rājasaṁ tyāgaṁ
naiva tyāgaphalaṁ labhet (18.8)

duḥkham — difficult: ityeva = iti — thus + eva — indeed; yat = yad — which; karma — action; kāyakleśabhayāt = kāya — body + kleśa — suffering + bhayāt — from fear; tyajet — should abandon; sa — saḥ — he; kṛtvā — having performed: rājasaṁ — impulsive influence; tyāgaṁ — renunciation; naiva — na — not + eva — indeed; tyāgaphalam — result of renunciation; labhet — should obtain

He who abandons action because of difficulty or because of a fear of bodily suffering, performs impulsive renunciation. He would not obtain the desired result of that renunciation. (Bhagavad Gītā 18.8)

Analysis

The action of someone is not the end of an event. The refusal to act may only postpone an event. This creation is ongoing. Its end is the beginning of another colossal event.

A yogi should know what to do and what not to do but the idea that action concludes an event or that inaction terminates a scene should be discarded.

The challenge of participation may be muffled by the difficulty presented or because of fear of suffering but that should not promote renunciation. A view about the long-ranged repercussions for inaction should be considered. The key factor which causes action or inaction is the motivation for action. A yogi should do what is necessary so that his/her action or inaction is promoted by the correct impulse.

Comprehension of Bhagavad Gītā Verse 18.8

Impulsive renunciation has justification which satisfies the person who is disinclined to act. After being hedged in by one or more reasons, that person sidesteps an obligation and assumes a cynical frame of mind. This does not free the person from the consequences of not completing a duty. And yet, that individual feels that he/she did what was in his/her interest.

Instead of absolving the circumstances, the renunciation of the opportunity causes more obligations. Eventually this is experienced as regret.

कार्यमित्येव यत्कर्म
नियतं क्रियतेऽर्जुन ।
सङ्गं त्यक्त्वा फलं चैव
स त्यागः सात्त्विको मतः ॥१८.९॥

kāryamityeva yatkarma
niyataṁ kriyate'rjuna
saṅgaṁ tyaktvā phalaṁ caiva
sa tyāgaḥ sāttviko mataḥ (18.9)

káryam — to be done; ityeva — iti — thus + eva — indeed; yat — which; karma — action; niyataṁ — disciplinary manner; kriyate — is performed; 'rjuna= arjuna — Arjuna: saṅgaṁ — attachment; tyaktvā — abandoning; phalaṁ — result;

caiva — and indeed; sa = saḥ — it; tyāgaḥ — renunciation; sāttviko = sāttvikaḥ — of the clarifying mode; mataḥ — is considered

O Arjuna, when an action is done in a disciplinary manner, because it is to be performed, and with renunciation of the attachment to the results, it is considered to be in the clarifying mode. (Bhagavad Gītā 18.9)

Analysis

It is best to act for the pleasure of the universal form of Krishna and to forego the motivation to act for personal benefit. One should understand that there is nothing which was initiated by a limited being without the supreme being and the cosmic mundane energy assisting every step of the way. It cannot be truthfully said that the limited self is responsible for this creation or even for its presence in this situation.

A limited self is so miniscule as to be insignificant. It neither caused, supported, nor will it terminate this. Hence the idea that it is the source of anything is ludicrous. And yet, it should participate, if for no other reason, than to make its existence here as pleasant as possible.

The balance of power in this cosmos, must be settled. There are deities who should be satisfied. Both the person agency and the environment situation must be balanced. If one fails to appease those two powers, one may be inconvenienced.

Comprehension of Bhagavad Gītā Verse 18.9

The attachment to results is the program in the psyche which degrades the actor and makes him/her careless. This attachment may cause unfavorable or desirable returns.

The self-centeredness is present, but it should be ignored because the limited self is not the center of anything besides its individual psyche. It may feel otherwise but such feelings are mere radial energy which exudes from the self. It does not make the self the center at any time.

After detecting an obligation, looking to see if an opportunity for absolving it is present, a yogi should with a self-disciplinary posture, perform it without hankering for favorable events. The fulfillment from the performance, should be transferred to the deity and to the nature which is the scene of the activity.

न द्वेष्ट्यकुशलं कर्म
कुशले नानुषज्जते ।
त्यागी सत्त्वसमाविष्टो
मेधावी छिन्नसंशयः ॥१८.१०॥

na dveṣṭyakuśalaṁ karma
kuśale nānuṣajjate
tyāgī sattvasamāviṣṭo
medhāvī chinnasaṁśayaḥ (18.10)

na — not; dveṣṭi — hates; akuśalaṁ — disagreeable; karma — action; kuśale — is agreeable; nānuṣajjate = na — not + anuśajjate — is attached; tyāgī — renouncer; sattvasamāviṣṭo = sattva — clarity + samāviṣṭo (samāviṣṭah) — filled with; medhāvi — wise man; chinnasaṁśayaḥ = chinna — removed+ saṁśayaḥ — doubt

The renouncer who is filled with clarity, the wise man whose doubts are removed, does not hate disagreeable action, nor is he attached to agreeable performance. (Bhagavad Gītā 18.10)

Analysis

The key feature of proper action is the clarity in consciousness which has as a part of it, the situation of neutrality in terms of the favorable or unfavorable returns which will target the performer. It is not how the yogi will enjoy the desirable aspects of life, nor how he will avoid what is detestable but how he will remain neutral even while completing obligations to the satisfaction of providence.

Comprehension of Bhagavad Gītā Verse 18.10

A yogi must come to understand that he is not the supreme consciousness. He is not the Supreme Lord. His agency is not the axis of actions and movements. There are some other personal and energetic factors which control this. The presence or absence of a limited self is such that it is not essential to this.

And yet, the yogi is required to act. Even though he is non-essential, that does not mean that he is not required to coordinate with the preferences of the Supreme Lord, of Krishna.

When Krishna suggests no action, that is the action of restraint. When Krishna directs for an action, that is the introduction, adjustment, or conclusion of events.

न हि देहभृता शक्यं
त्यक्तुं कर्माण्यशेषतः ।
यस्तु कर्मफलत्यागी
स त्यागीत्यभिधीयते ॥१८.११॥

na hi dehabhṛtā śakyaṁ
tyaktuṁ karmāṇyaśeṣataḥ
yastu karmaphalatyāgī
sa tyāgītyabhidhīyate (18.11)

na — not; hi — indeed; dehabhṛtā — by the body-supported; śakyaṁ — possible; tyaktuṁ — to abandon; karmāṇi — actions; aśeṣataḥ — completely; yaḥ — who;

tu — but; karmaphalatyāgī — karma — action + phala — result + tyāgi — remover; sa = saḥ — he; tyāgīti = tyāgī — renunciate + iti — thus; abhidhīyate — is called

Indeed, it is not possible for the body-supported beings to abandon actions completely. But whosoever is the renouncer of the results of actions is called a renunciate. (Bhagavad Gītā 18.11)

Analysis

After being kicked by nature for centuries, being used by it, being abused by it, being told what to do by it, being held accountable unreasonably by it, a coreSelf derives an insane condition. It draws irrational conclusions about its autonomy in a place where that is not possible.

It develops theories which border on insanity, where it publishes that it is absolute and is not reliant on anything or anyone. Of course, this is illogical. The limited self is reliant on every side. It does not stand on its own. It is not the origin of anything.

It must be influenced. It may select one of many influences, but it cannot be without influence because it is not a reality to itself. If it can position itself in honesty, it would admit its relativity.

Comprehension of Bhagavad Gītā Verse 18.11

A limited self is not in a position to cease acting permanently. The tendency to strike out, to be curious about something, is a permanent function of the sense of identity. It may be disabled from time to time. It may be suppressed here or there. However, a limited self cannot permanently remove it.

Philosophical theories about the complete eradication of actions are invalid. These ideas are based on the assumption that a limited being is not limited and can be an absolute something or can be de-existed.

Krishna declared that it is not possible for the body-supported being to abandon actions completely. It will not happen. There may be temporary cessation of action but permanent abolishment is fantasy.

What a self can do is to renounce the results of action. If anything, one should willingly commit actions to satisfy obligations and if when the returns arrive, one has a feeling to leave that aside, one may do so. Some will be successful, but some will have to indulge in the after-effects of the actions.

अनिष्टमिष्टं मिश्रं च
त्रिविधं कर्मणः फलम् ।
भवत्यत्यागिनां प्रेत्य
न तु संन्यासिनां क्वचित् ॥१८.१२॥

aniṣṭamiṣṭaṁ miśraṁ ca
trividhaṁ karmaṇaḥ phalam
bhavatyatyāgināṁ pretya
na tu saṁnyāsināṁ kvacit (18.12)

aniṣṭam — undesired; iṣṭaṁ — desired: miśraṁ — mixed; ca — and; trividham — three types; karmaṇaḥ — of action; phalam — result; bhavati — it is; atyāgināṁ — of those who do not renounce results; pretya — departing; na — not; tu — but: saṁnyāsināṁ — of the renouncers; kvacit — any at all

Undesired, desired and mixed are the three types of results of actions that occur for the departing souls who do not renounce results. But for the renouncers of opportunity, there is no result at all. (Bhagavad Gītā 18.12)

Analysis

In terms of what carries over to the next life, the results of actions which were not served to the person during the life of a body, will be with him/her and will seek opportunities to manifest. This is irrespective of if the person can remember his/her actions committed in the previous body.

Nature files the accounting so that the manifestation of the undesired, desired or mixed returns happens as soon as there are opportunities, and in a way, whereby the person may or may not be positioned to leave them aside and will be served with the positive, negative or neutral conditions of the resultant energy.

Comprehension of Bhagavad Gītā Verse 18.12

Those persons who while performing actions complete them efficiently and without pride, may be in a detached mood when the returns are served by fate. This is because when the actions were committed, a neutral energy was stored with them. This energy travels with the energy-content hereafter and when again that person assumes a physical body and is formatted in a suitable opportunity, he/she will experience the returns, but the energy will be packed with a restraining force which does not permit him/her to be afflicted.

अधिष्ठानं तथा कर्ता
करणं च पृथग्विधम् ।
विविधाश्च पृथक्चेष्टा
दैवं चैवात्र पञ्चमम् ॥१८.१४॥

adhiṣṭhānaṁ tathā kartā
karaṇaṁ ca pṛthagvidham
vividhāśca pṛthakceṣṭā
daivaṁ caivātra pañcama (18.14)

adhiṣṭhānaṁ — location; tathā — as well as; kartā — the agent; karaṇaṁ — the instrument; ca — and; prthagvidham — various kinds; vividhāśca = vividhāḥ —

various + ca — and; pṛthakceṣṭa — movements; daivam — destiny; caivatra — ca — and + eva — indeed + atra — here in this case; pañcamam — the fifth

The location, the agent, the various instruments, the various movements, and destiny, the fifth factor. (Bhagavad Gītā 18.14)

Analysis

The agent in any action may or may not be of relevance. For that matter the agent can be under an influence. Most agents are. The footing of the agent is likely to control what the agent can or cannot do. Krishna declared five factors for execution. Unless these are in place, the moments of the events can neither start, continue or be terminated.

There must be a location, an independent or influenced agent, instruments wielded for the action, movements of energy and destiny in the form of forces from the past which together prompt the person(s) and environment.

Comprehension of Bhagavad Gītā Verse 18.14

As an agent, the limited self has some autonomy, but it is not sufficient to declare that it is absolute. Even when the agent is major, close accounting may prove that there is an influence which prevails to empower the agent. Hence in most cases, the agent is a factor only.

A location or site for the activity, must be there. Otherwise, nothing can happen. If the four other aspects are present, still unless there is a location nothing will occur. For that matter fertile seeds which lie in soil in a dry place cannot sprout unless water is added. Thus, the environment must be suitable for the location to participate in the action.

Instruments for action must be present because invariable, a limited agent by itself cannot complete an action. This means that at the moment of the event, the instruments must be in place for spontaneous activation. Merely wanting to commit an action is not enough energy to make an event.

Destiny comes from the psychic plane. Usually, the agent has no say in that. Destiny is a combination power which involves a presiding deity and combination forces from previous actions which are residual energy which are attracted to a need force. Rarely does the agent have control over destiny. Regularly, the agent is handled by destiny which operates from a supernatural plane.

ज्ञानं ज्ञेयं परिज्ञाता
त्रिविधा कर्मचोदना ।
करणं कर्म कर्तेति
त्रिविधः कर्मसंग्रहः ॥१८.१८॥

jñānaṁ jñeyaṁ parijñātā
trividhā karmacodanā
karaṇaṁ karma karteti
trividhaḥ karmasaṁgrahaḥ (18.18)

jñānaṁ — experience; jñeyaṁ — the item of research; parijñātā— the experience; trividhā — three aspects; karmacodanā= karma — action + codanā — impetus for; karaṇaṁ — instrument; karma — action; karteti — kartā — agent + iti — thus; trividhaḥ — three; karmasaṁgrahaḥ = karma — action + saṁgrahaḥ — parts

Experience, the item of research, and the experiencer are the three aspects which serve as the impetus for action. The instruction, the action itself, and the agent are three parts of an action. (Bhagavad Gītā 18.18)

Analysis

The past is the basis for the present, which in turn is the basis for the future. At every moment new events are constructed. These play out as events which are a combination of past energy on display. Whatever is new is an interlocking vortex of past factors, but the viewer is positioned to regard it as a new display. The past lives on and recombines to present new events which cause wonder to those selves who do not have the psychic reach to diagram the remnant energy from the past which manipulates what is presented as the event.

The action itself is a composite but to a victim it seems to be one factor. It is a combination of instruction, action and the agent. The instruction is a combination force which forms as motivation or impulsion.

The impetus for action surfaces as motivation from the agent's viewpoint but that is a misrepresentation because the impetus is a crush combination force. It consists of remnant activity energy from the past. This is forced together to create potency as a new driving force

Comprehension of Bhagavad Gītā Verse 18.18

A yogi should integrate into his/her personality that as the experiencer, one is only part of an action. One experiences but the circumstance is more than the person itself. There must also be a target which shifts or changes as time goes by. Much of this is not controlled by the experiencer. Attempts may be made to command an event but unless the event is lubricated favorably, things will happen which will subject the experiencer to trauma.

ज्ञानं कर्म च कर्ता च
त्रिधैव गुणभेदतः ।
प्रोच्यते गुणसंख्याने
यथावच्छृणु तान्यपि ॥१८.१९॥

jñānaṁ karma ca karta ca
tridhaiva guṇabhedataḥ
procyate guṇasaṁkhyāne
yathāvacchṛṇu tānyapi (18.19)

jñānaṁ — experience; karma — action; ca — and; kartā — agent; ca — and; tridhaiva = tridha — three types + eva — indeed; guṇabhedataḥ — categorized by the influences of material nature; procyate — is stated; guṇasaṁkhyāne — in the Sāṁkhya analysis of the influences of material nature; yathāvat — correctly; śṛṇu — hear; tāni — these; api — as well

In the Sāṁkhya analysis of the influence of material nature, it is stated that experience, action, and the agent are of three types as categorized by the influence of material nature. Hear correctly of these as well. (Bhagavad Gītā 18.19)

Analysis

This situation is compounded in various ways and at various stages, such that a limited self cannot get the best of this. Once a yogi integrates this information, his/her troubles are over. His anxiety about gaining control fizzes. He/She realizes that the self is an insignificant part of this.

Comprehension of Bhagavad Gītā Verse 18.19

The *Upanishads* for all it is, do not address in detail the person factor. For that one must study and integrate Krishna's *Sāṁkhya*. One must learn from a superior being because one cannot know the origins directly. In retrogressing into the origins of the components of the psyche, one will reach into abstract territory where one cannot discern anything because one enters into what is transcendent to oneself.

Instead of drawing a blank as the philosophers of the *Upanishads* did, one should take information from a superior being to whom the abstract reality can be perceived sensually. That person is Krishna. Otherwise, one will think that everything ends in the abstraction and that there can be no ultimate format of anything.

The advent of Krishna ended those conclusions about the origins which transcend the limited self.

There is complexity on either side, either on this side of where the self is objective or on the other side beyond the self where the self is subjective. Even here on this objective side there is complexity, as Krishna explained about three types of experience, three of action and three types of agents. That is more than three because there are subdivisions of each of the three versions. Then there are combinations with each.

सर्वभूतेषु येनैकं
भावमव्ययमीक्षते ।
अविभक्तं विभक्तेषु
तज्ज्ञानं विद्धि सात्त्विकम् ॥१८.२०॥

sarvabhūteṣu yenaikaṁ
bhāvamavyayamīkṣate
avibhaktaṁ vibhakteṣu
tajjñānaṁ viddhi sāttvikam (18.20)

sarvabhūteṣu — in all beings; yenaikaṁ = yena — by which + ekam — one; bhāvam — being; avyayam — imperishable; īksate — one perceives; avibhaktaṁ — undivided; vibhakteṣu — in the divided; tat — that; jñānaṁ — experience; viddhi — know; sāttvikaṁ — clarifying

That experience by which one perceives one imperishable being in all beings, undivided in the divided, know it to be an experience in clarity. (Bhagavad Gītā 18.20)

Analysis

The imperishable being in all beings is not the limited self (*atma*). It is the unlimited self, *paramatma*. That is Krishna. All the same there is a limited self in each being or psyche, but each is unique. Each requires ongoing extensive existential and environment support.

The cosmic situation is under control of the supreme being but that does not mean that it must be ordered by the definition of a limited self. Whatever is here is here and is ordered as is.

Comprehension of Bhagavad Gītā Verse 18.20

Experience in clarity, as defined by Lord Krishna, is unnatural for most of the limited beings who use forms in this physical existence. To adopt Krishna's vision, a limited self would have to exert self-discipline in mystic practice, to see that there is another person who inhabits these lifeforms. This other person is the same one within all the forms. He is different to the limited individuals who inhabit each form and who is unique.

To retain this vision from moment to moment would require persistent mystic practice to retrain the self and its adjuncts. This is no ordinary achievement. In the meantime, a limited self can use the information from *Bhagavad Gītā* and try his/her best to put this knowledge into practice.

पृथक्त्वेन तु यज्ज्ञानं
नानाभावान्पृथग्विधान् ।
वेत्ति सर्वेषु भूतेषु
तज्ज्ञानं विद्धि राजसम् ॥१८.२१॥

pṛthaktvena tu yajjñānaṁ
nānābhāvānpṛthagvidhān
vetti sarveṣu bhūteṣu
tajjñānaṁ viddhi rājasam (18.21)

pṛthaktvena — with difference; tu — but; yat — which; jñānaṁ — experience; nānābhāvān = nānā — different + bhāvān — beings; pṛthagvidhān — of different kinds: vetti — realises; sarveṣu — in all; bhūteṣu — in beings; tat — that; jñānaṁ — experience; viddhi — know; rājasam — of the impulsive mode

But that experience by which one realizes different beings of different kinds with differences in all beings, should be known as experience in the impulsive mode. (Bhagavad Gītā 18.21)

Analysis

There is a misinterpretation of this information, where some think that there is only one self and nothing else. They say there is no different unique group of limited selves and that the idea of different selves in different bodies and places is fallacious. However, that way of viewing this is perverted. This verse does not support that opinion.

To understand this verse according to Krishna *Sāṁkhya*, one must remember that there is the universal form of Krishna which is governed by Krishna as the central supervisory self, with other unique selves functioning but only by the allowance granted by Krishna.

Comprehension of Bhagavad Gītā Verse 18.21

This verse does not mean that there are no limited selves. It does not mean that there are no different beings of different kinds with differences in all beings. It means that whenever one becomes aware of these limited beings of different kinds, one's perception occurs with supports from the impulsive mode of material nature.

The fault in this is that usually when this happens one loses grasp on the vision of the central person in the universal form, of Krishna. Then one makes decisions which may run contrary to Krishna's.

There are different limited selves but knowing this, one should shift the focus to the Supreme Self and use his view and indications as the standard for one's behavior.

यत्तु कृत्स्नवदेकस्मिन्
कार्ये सक्तमहैतुकम् ।
अतत्त्वार्थवदल्पं च
तत्तामसमुदाहृतम् ॥१८.२२॥

yattu kṛtsnavadekasmin
kārye saktamahaitukam
atattvārthavadalpaṁ ca
tattāmasamudāhṛtam (18.22)

yat — yad — which; tu — but; kṛtsnavat — appears as the whole; ekasmin — in one; kārye — in order of action; saktam — attached; ahaitukam — without due cause; atattvārthavat — without a valid purpose; alpaṁ — petty; ca — and; tat = tad — that; tāmasam — of the depressive influence; udāhṛtam — is said to be

But that experience which appears to be the whole vision, being attached to one procedure without due cause, without a valid purpose, being petty, that is said to be of the depressive influence. (Bhagavad Gītā 18.22)

Analysis

Realization can be of the depressive influence, such that the conclusion is made on the basis of this creation being one simple deduction which ends with one concept simplified as a unity, a wholeness.

That satisfies someone who has no reach into objective transcendence. That person is satisfied with a simplistic view with no consideration about the parts of this reality, as to its complexity, as to the innumerable factors involved.

Comprehension of Bhagavad Gītā Verse 18.22

When one rushes to a vision of everything, and becomes attached to one procedure without due cause, without a valid purpose, willy nilly, calculated with much simplicity, as if this creation lacks an infinite range of probability, then one is with experience which is in the depressive phase. But even that experience is valid in so far as it is what is afforded from that plane of awareness.

सिद्धिं प्राप्तो यथा ब्रह्म
तथाप्नोति निबोध मे ।
समासेनैव कौन्तेय
निष्ठा ज्ञानस्य या परा ॥१८.५०॥

siddhiṁ prāpto yathā brahma
tathāpnoti nibodha me
samāsenaiva kaunteya
niṣṭhā jñānasya yā parā (18.50)

siddhiṁ — perfection; prāpto = prāptaḥ — attained; yathā — as; brahma — spirituality; tathāpnoti = tathā — thus + āpnoti — attains; nibodha — learn; me — from me; samāsenaiva = samāsena — in brief + eva — indeed; kaunteya — son of Kuntī; niṣṭhā — state; jñānasya — of experience; yā — which; parā — highest

Learn from Me briefly, O son of Kuntī, how a person who attained perfection, also reaches a spirituality which is the highest. (Bhagavad Gītā 18.50)

Analysis

The mapping of the passage or transit from this physical plane to a spiritual level of existence is not possible for a limited being who is combined as a physical person self.

The mystic ability of a limited self is curtailed by its involvement with the mundane energies. That means that it is unlikely that such a self could forge its passage from here to higher planes, especially to a level where its objectivity would not surface and only its subjective quality will be on display.

Comprehension of Bhagavad Gītā Verse 18.50

This concerns inner elevation by isolation of the coreSelf and outer elevation by transit into a spiritual environment. The self may use its power to upgrade itself. That is the action it should take. For a shift to a higher environment, it cannot dictate that. That happens due to its self-elevation where its level of awareness is similar to that of a higher place.

बुद्ध्या विशुद्धया युक्तो
धृत्यात्मानं नियम्य च ।
शब्दादीन्विषयांस्त्यक्त्वा
रागद्वेषौ व्युदस्य च ॥१८.५१॥

buddhyā viśuddhayā yukto
dhṛtyātmānaṁ niyamya ca
śabdādīnviṣayāṁstyaktvā
rāgadveṣau vyudasya ca (18.51)

buddhayā — with intellect; viśuddhyā — with purified; yukto = yuktaḥ — yogically disciplined; dhṛtyātmānaṁ = dhṛtyā — with firmness + ātmānaṁ— self; niyamya — controlling; ca — and; śabdādīn — śabda — sound + ādīn— beginning with, and others; viṣayān — attractive sensations; tyaktvā — abandoning; rāgadveṣau= rāga — craving + dveṣau — hatred; vyudasya — rejecting; ca — and

Being yogically disciplined with purified intelligence and controlling the soul, firmly abandoning sound and other attractive sensations, rejecting craving and hatred, (Bhagavad Gītā 18.51)

Analysis

This is a partial listing of the qualities of a person who is suited to the spiritual level of existence. This person honed qualities of character which make it compatible to the spiritual environment. This is an alert about the requirements necessary for transit to the spiritual plane.

The list is.

- Being yogically disciplined with purified intelligence
- controlling the soul

- firmly abandoning sound and other attractive sensations
- rejecting craving and hatred

Comprehension of Bhagavad Gītā Verse 18.51

Purification of the intelligence is not an intellectual action. In fact, it is the act of disabling the intellect so that it cannot arrest the attention of the self for involuntary operations. This is achieved by the yoga process in the aspect of *pratyahar* sensual energy withdrawal. That is mastered in meditation by retracting and putting at rest, the outward-bound inquiry energy of the coreSelf.

Controlling the soul is the act of tightly regulating the relationship between the coreSelf and its adjuncts. This is a meditation procedure where the core is segregated from the intellect. When that happens, the core becomes more familiar with itself. No longer does it mistake itself as the combination of the core and its adjuncts.

This segregation gives the core the ability to recognize itself and to be itself. It weights its dependence on the adjuncts and makes decisions to increase or reduce the reliance on the other factors.

There is attachment to sensual objects, either a single object or combined ones. These offer complex mixes on occasion. That bewilders and fascinates the core. **Smelling, tasting, seeing, touching and hearing** are the actions of the senses. Some of these are done in subtle ways.

A yogi should realize that the five senses hunt for sound, surface, colors, liquids and solids. The mind constantly pursues these. It is relentless in acquiring the subtle aspect of what it confiscates. One becomes trapped by what one smells, tastes, sees, touches and hears.

Craving and hatred are natural impulses emitted from the suppressive dull energy of nature. This is cast throughout the creation. It enters into any psyche or environmental space which is available to it. When someone is victimized by this parasitic influence, that person is tagged for the activities committed or neglected while under the influence.

Eventually when a self is properly informed and it realizes the possession in meditation, it can remove itself from the suppressive dulling energy and situate itself on a higher psychological plane.

A mere belief in what Krishna says is insufficient for freeing any limited self from the lower tendencies and impulses. The devotee should learn meditation so that he/she can qualify with the qualities listed by Krishna. A direct confrontation of the coreSelf and its adjuncts, is required. The idea that one does not have to do mystic meditation for the control of the adjuncts is not supported by Krishna in the *Bhagavad Gītā*. The teachers who vouch for that cannot validate their promises. That is an injustice to the Krishna Conscious method.

विविक्तसेवी लघ्वाशी
यतवाक्कायमानसः ।
ध्यानयोगपरो नित्यं
वैराग्यं समुपाश्रितः ॥१८.५२॥

viviktasevī laghvāśī
yatavākkāyamānasaḥ
dhyānayogaparo nityaṁ
vairāgyaṁ samupāśritaḥ (18.52)

viviktasevī = vivikta — is isolated + sevī — living at; laghvasi = laghv (laghu) — lightly + āsī — eating; yatavākkāyamānasaḥ = yata — controlled + vāk (vāc) — speech + kāya — body + mānasaḥ — mind; dhyānayogaparo — dhyāna — meditation + yoga — yoga + paro (paraḥ) — devoted to; nityam — always; vairāgyam — dispassion; samupāśritaḥ — resorting to

...living in isolation, eating lightly, controlling speech, body and mind, always being devoted to yogic meditation, resorting to dispassion, (Bhagavad Gītā 18.52)

Analysis

These are more qualities of a person who is suited to the spiritual level of existence.

- living in isolation
- eating lightly
- controlling speech, body and mind
- always being devoted to yogic meditation
- resorting to dispassion

One should neither fool oneself nor any other person that these qualities can be develop merely by chanting holy names of Krishna, or by serving a teacher of the Krishna Conscious lifestyle, or by doing deity worship of Krishna, or by eating sanctified foods or by any other easy method.

These activities of the Krishna Conscious lifestyle do compliment the development of the required purity but when they are published as easy methods for attaining mystic purification, that belief causes false confidence which destroys a devotee's enthusiasm to work in meditation to reach the standards which were declared by Krishna.

Comprehension of Bhagavad Gītā Verse 18.52

Living in isolation means just that. It does not mean that one should build temples, have services for the general population, and mix with others because one has a mission to preach *Bhagavad Gītā* or any other book which extols Krishna.

Ideally a yogi should live in isolation. If, however he is inspired by Krishna, or by an agent of Krishna, to abandon isolation and to be in association with many people to teach about Krishna from *Bhagavad Gītā* or *Srimad Bhagavatam*, he may do that with the understanding that he breaches this rule which requires isolation for deep meditation so as to invade the psyche and get it in order for transfer to a higher level of existence.

Eventually however, one who had a mission to preach the Krishna Conscious lifestyle and to explain Krishna's information, should later in his life, resume isolation so that he can put himself in order in preparation for being deprived of the physical body.

A devotee, a great devotee, should not give a system of belief to his disciples, that he will go back to Godhead or go to a spiritual dimension for sure when he is deprived of the body. For that matter he should not impress the belief on others, that he is so special, that for sure he will quit his body without being deprived of it. Such ideas are undesirable and form a farce for the gullible devotees.

Eating lightly is another quality which should be developed by a devotee. That cannot be done properly if there is no isolation. This is because if one prepares food for deities and serves that food to lay devotees who come to a temple for programs, one will invariably experience increase in appetite. This is due to the association one has with others.

In isolation, one can focus internally in meditation, and by doing that slowly but surely, reduce the food needs and bring the appetite under control. If, however after restricting diet, one again resumes association with many persons at a temple, then again one will find that the diet is increased. Thus, in that case, one should go into isolation near the end of life, so as to establish mystic proficiency.

The idea that one can eat any amount of food, provided that it is ritually offered to the deity of Krishna using the authorized prayers, and that such consumption will not affect one negatively but will instead enhance one's spirituality, is a false view. That will cause a devotee to be degraded. His physical body will suffer. His subtle body will be lowered in vibration. His show of devotion to Krishna will not save him from being lowered.

Controlling speech, body and mind is more than speaking only about Krishna. Control of the body is more than using the body only for doing services which directly relate to the temple of Krishna. Control of the mind is more than chanting, thinking and expressing oneself only in relation to Krishna.

A yogi-devotee cannot settle for a shallow seemingly easy lifestyle where he preaches to the public, lives under the shelter of a religious establishment, and does individual disciplines like chanting a certain count of holy names on beads, eating only at the temple and serving devotees who reside at or visit the temple.

The mystic control of the speech, body and mind should be developed by deep meditation, to get the basis of what comprises the psyche and how the factors in it, interact with each other. This has little, if anything, to do with any other devotee or non-devotee. It is a struggle for control of the coreSelf against the adjuncts which normally utilize energy from the core, with little or no benefit to it.

The mystic practices taught by Krishna in *Bhagavad Gītā* and elsewhere like in the *Srimad Bhagavatam* should not be glossed over by a devotee. One should seriously study about those disciplines and institute them into one psychology.

There is a time for helping others, for spreading the Krishna Conscious way of life. There is also a time for desisting from focusing on the development of others where one focuses within the self to elevate the self so that its qualities become compatible with what is listed in the *Bhagavad Gītā* as requirements for one to transfer to the spiritual environment. Helping others is not the whole path of Krishna Consciousness. It certainly does not replace the work which must be done on the psychic plane to elevate the self.

Nityam means **always being devoted to yogic meditation.** Recently some teachers adjusted this to delete yogic meditation and substitute instead thinking and speaking about Krishna. That change does not delete this requirement for those devotees who want to adhere to Krishna's instructions in *Bhagavad Gītā*.

Whosoever changes the methods and guarantees of *Bhagavad Gītā* should issue proclamations while stating that what is in the Gītā is invalid. However, that level of honesty is missing whereby a teacher rewrites what Krishna said or proclaims that Krishna returned and changed what he required in *Bhagavad Gītā*. One line of reasoning is that in this era, since people are disinclined to meditation and cannot do it, Krishna lowered the requirements such that one can avoid difficult meditation and still attain the spiritual realms by easy methods such as singing holy names and eating sanctified food. These substitute adjustments are insufficient and will result in failure.

A yogi should **resort to dispassion**. In line after line in *Bhagavad Gītā*, dispassion is required. It is the method given for shifting to a level of perception which is compatible to that of the central figure in the universal form, Krishna.

If one is not in isolation, one will find that one can hardly be dispassionate. When mixing with others, even in the name of Krishna, one will invariably become diluted because energy from disinterested people to whom one preaches, will enter the psyche and cause a lowering of the consciousness.

This will result in feelings of concern for others. That will cause one to interfere with the destiny of persons to whom one has no obligation, but to which one develops an interest because of close physical or psychic association.

अहंकारं बलं दर्पं
कामं क्रोधं परिग्रहम् ।
विमुच्य निर्ममः शान्तो
ब्रह्मभूयाय कल्पते ॥१८.५३॥

ahaṁkāraṁ balaṁ darpaṁ
kāmaṁ krodhaṁ parigraham
vimucya nirmamaḥ śānto
brahmabhūyāya kalpate (18.53)

ahaṁkāraṁ — without a misplaced initiative, without a false assertion; balaṁ — brute force; darpaṁ — arrogance; kāmaṁ — cravings; krodhaṁ — anger; parigraham — possessions; vimucya — freeing oneself; nirmamaḥ — unselfish; śānto = śāntaḥ — peaceful; brahmabhūyāya = brahma — spirit + bhūyāyā — to that level, existential; kalpate — is suited

...freeing oneself from a false assertion, from the application of brute force, from arrogance, from craving and from possessiveness, being unselfish and peaceful, one is suited to the spiritual level. (Bhagavad Gītā 18.53)

Analysis

These are the remaining qualities of a person who is suited to the spiritual level of existence.

- freeing oneself from false assertion
- freeing oneself from the application of brute force
- freeing oneself from arrogance
- freeing oneself from craving
- freeing oneself from possessiveness
- being unselfish
- being peaceful

Comprehension of Bhagavad Gītā Verse 18.53

A devotee **should not** under any circumstance **make false assertions**. There is a tendency to cushion untruths by declaring that Krishna said it or that it is said for the benefit of Krishna or for an authority of Krishna. Such tendencies should be removed from the psyche.

A change in the rulings and methods of spirituality which is issued by someone other than Krishna or by someone who is rated to be Krishna's incarnation, should be given in the name of that person, not in the name of Krishna. For Krishna's direct proclamations, *Bhagavad Gītā* and *Srimad Bhagavatam* is enough.

There is no need to bolster, support and reinforce any other person's guarantees by twisting what Krishna said or adjusting the meanings of what he declared. Devotees of persons other than Krishna or someone who said that he was an incarnation of Krishna, may make declarations for those persons and should not substitute Krishna's name and certainly should not whitewash nor erase the requirements Krishna made.

Freeing oneself from the application of brute force happens when one succeeds at adopting a gentle nature. One began with a physical body which requires survival. That involves the application of brute force. The body itself is a crude apparatus that requires physical food. Over time in meditation, one should shift to the subtle form. One should study what is required for its upkeep which is psychic and not physical. One should determine if one can live on psychic nourishment only.

A yogi should **free himself/herself from arrogance**. This is done by careful observation of one behavior when associating with others. It consists of self-criticism and the realization that the coreSelf is subjected to self-destructive psychic acts which can be curbed if the core can deprive the intellect of the power to compel the psyche. Only in meditation can this be achieved.

Saying holy names of Krishna, attending Krishna worship ceremonies and even studying the stories about Krishna in the *Srimad Bhagavatam* may not inspire a person to recognize and to eliminate arrogance. This is because the arrogance is so innate and subtle that it may utilize the energy generated in Krishna-related acts. One must use meditation as explained by Krishna in *Bhagavad Gītā* to get behind arrogance and to uproot it.

A yogi should **free the self from craving**. This too is a meditative procedure for the most part. It is supplemented with physical sense control, especially control of diet and visual consumption. Unless one completes the meditation for this, reforms will have no lasting effect. The undesirable behaviors will reassert soon after one commits to a diet or to sensual restriction.

A yogi should **free himself/herself from possessiveness**. This is more than a matter of taking vows and associating with persons who exhibit great resistance to the territorial instinct. There must be deep meditation to understand the urge for possessiveness. Once it is isolated and studied in meditation, a yogi should check for a way to remove it from the psyche.

This effort will end in failure with the yogi understanding that he/she may disable it even though it will be spontaneously activated from time to time and will have to be disabled repeatedly.

The total possessive energy belongs to the supreme being, but he, Krishna, is disinterested in it. Due to the lack of claim by the Supreme Lord, the limited selves have this idea that the gross and subtle materials are for the taking. This causes fights between the limited beings. A yogi should study this and make the effort to be removed from any environment where the struggle for survival is pending.

A **yogi should be unselfish**. One has to understand that this place is under the supervision of the Supreme Person, the central figure in the universal form. Regardless of if this God is visible or not, his energy is spread through this creation. It has within it, a registering and monitoring capability. That does not allow any incidence to be unobserved. There will be accounting, hence one should act as if there is God. There is agency which measures one's performance.

A **yogi should be peaceful**. Being that the limited self is insignificant, there is all reason for it be peaceful. Why should it flare with arrogance when in truth it is not prominent?

ब्रह्मभूतः प्रसन्नात्मा
न शोचति न काङ्क्षति ।
समः सर्वेषु भूतेषु
मद्भक्तिं लभते पराम् ॥१८.५४॥

brahmabhūtaḥ prasannātmā
na śocati na kāṅkṣati
samaḥ sarveṣu bhūteṣu
madbhaktiṁ labhate parām (18.54)

brabmabhūtaḥ — being absorbed in spiritual existence; prasannātmā = prasanna — peaceful + ātmā — self, spirit: na — not; śocati — laments; na — no; kāṅkṣati — hankers for something; samaḥ — impartial; sarveṣu — in all; bhūteṣu — in the beings; madbhaktiṁ — devotion to me; labhate — attains; parām — supreme

One who is absorbed in the spiritual existence, who has a peaceful spirit, who does not lament nor hanker for anything, who is impartial to all beings, attains the supreme devotion to Me. (Bhagavad Gītā 18.54)

Analysis

This is all about person. Definitely, the physical somebody is a composite. Some of which will be eradicated with the death of the physical form. Yet, the coreSelf will persists with some of its assistors, its adjuncts.

Devotion is from person to person. Is it phony? Can it be used to attract followers and cause spiritual degression?

The supreme devotion to Krishna, the Supreme Person, is a special energy exchange between a limited self and the Supreme Lord. One must be in a special state of mind to link it.

Comprehension of Bhagavad Gītā Verse 18.54

The qualification for linking in supreme devotion to Krishna is outlined in this verse. No one should add or subtract from it. One should not say that another divine being changed this list or made it easier by another process. If we speak about Krishna, we should adhere to his profile and our relationship with him on his terms.

A devotee should be absorbed in spiritual existence. He should have a peaceful spirit. He should neither lament nor hanker for anything. He should be impartial to all beings. Being qualified with these qualities he should meditate on Krishna. He should be impartial to all beings so that his preference towards them does not conflict with the views of the Krishna.

भक्त्या मामभिजानाति यावान्यश्चास्मि तत्त्वतः । ततो मां तत्त्वतो ज्ञात्वा विशते तदनन्तरम् ॥१८.५५॥	bhaktyā māmabhijānāti yāvānyaścāsmi tattvataḥ tato māṁ tattvato jñātvā viśate tadanantaram (18.55)

bhaktyā — by devotion; mām — to me; abhijānāti — he realizes; yāvān — how great: yaścāsmi = yaḥ — who + ca — and + asmi — I am; tattvataḥ — in reality; tato = tataḥ — then; mām — me; tattvato = tattvataḥ — in truth; jñātvā — having known; viśate — enters; tadanantaram — immediately

By devotion to Me, he realizes how great I am and who I am in reality. Then having known Me in truth, he enters My association immediately. (Bhagavad Gītā 18.55)

Analysis

This devotion to Krishna is not a mundane sentiment. It is not a relationship which is composed of enthusiasm and dulling energy. It has to be an affection based on being informed about Krishna as he explained in *Bhagavad Gītā* and on mastering meditation techniques that allows the devotee to see by insight consciousness the role Krishna plays in this cosmic manifestation.

Comprehension of Bhagavad Gītā Verse 18.55

This is not a person-less formula. This concerns character. This stresses person to person relationship with the limited self on one side and God on the other, with the limited person cleared of unwanted tendencies.

By high quality devotion to Krishna, which is based on strict adherence to the disciplines mentioned in *Bhagavad Gītā*, a yogi realizes how great Krishna is, and whom He is in reality. Maintaining the insight consciousness where one sees the realities which Krishna described, one will enter Krishna's association on a transcendental plane.

सर्वकर्माण्यपि सदा
कुर्वाणो मद्व्यपाश्रयः ।
मत्प्रसादादवाप्नोति
शाश्वतं पदमव्ययम् ॥१८.५६॥

sarvakarmāṇyapi sadā
kurvāṇo madvyapāśrayaḥ
matprasādādavāpnoti
śāśvataṁ padamavyayam (18.56)

sarvakarmāṇi — in all actions; api — furthermore; sadā — always; kurvāṇo = kurvāṇaḥ — performing; madvyapāśrayaḥ — taking reliance in me; matprasādāt — from my grace; avāpnoti — gets; śāśvataṁ — eternal; padam — abode; avyayam — imperishable

Furthermore, know that while performing all actions, he whose reliance is always on Me, gets by My grace, the eternal imperishable abode. (Bhagavad Gītā 18.56)

Analysis

The attainment of a spiritual environment is achieved by two factors.

- *suitability of a limited self*

For the yogi devotee, his/her problem is to change, to be compatible with the deity of choice. Once the devotee attains a nature which is similar to that of the deity, it is only a matter of time, when the deity will facilitate a portal for the devotee to travel to the realm of his cherished lord/lady.

- *extraction by the deity of the transcendental realm*

Unless a yogi devotee is extracted by the deity of the transcendental place where the devotee hankers to go, there is no chance for the devotee to attain that realm. All the same if the devotee does not have a compatible format in his subtle body, the deity will rarely provide a portal.

Comprehension of Bhagavad Gītā Verse 18.56

There is this guarantee by Krishna, that if a devotee performs his duty which is approved by the universal form, and who also is reliant always on the views of Krishna, then by Krishna's grace that devotee will attain the eternal imperishable abode.

This declaration is a challenge to the idea that one must be action-less if one is to be liberated. This sets at odds statements which do not include a deity for the liberation of a limited entity.

This statement means that it is not necessarily the case for anyone, that he would have to cease acting to be transferred to the spiritual environment. A devotee of Krishna may continue acting through the life of his/her physical body and yet, because of being Krishna conscious, and because of maintaining the self with detachment while acting and still completing duties to Krishna's satisfaction, that devotee by Krishna's grace, may attain the eternal imperishable abode.

चेतसा सर्वकर्माणि मयि संन्यस्य मत्परः । बुद्धियोगमुपाश्रित्य मच्चित्तः सततं भव ॥१८.५७॥	cetasā sarvakarmāṇi mayi saṁnyasya matparaḥ buddhiyogamupāśritya maccittaḥ satataṁ bhava (18.57)

cetasā — by thought; sarvakarmāṇi — all actions; mayi — on Me; saṁnyasya — devoted to me; matparaḥ — devoted to Me; buddhiyogam — disciplining the intellect by yoga practice; upāśritya — relying on; maccittaḥ — thinking of Me; satataṁ — constantly; bhava — be

Renouncing by thought, all actions to Me, being devoted to Me, relying on the process of disciplining the intellect by yoga, be constantly thinking of Me. (Bhagavad Gītā 18.57)

Analysis

Even though a function of the self is to act, the actions are mystic notions as executed attempts to act. The limited self can neither act physically or directly cause a physical act. It relies on adjuncts, sensory control points and sentient machinery.

We know the sentient machinery is a living physical body in one or the other species. The self cannot drum up activities by itself. It acts as influenced by one agency or the other. Ultimately, it may act after considering Krishna's preference.

The self must resign itself to the supreme being, be devoted to him, rely on the process of disciplining and confining the intellect by the yoga meditation process. It should constantly think of instituting Krishna's process.

Comprehension of Bhagavad Gītā Verse 18.57

One who habitually fails to isolate the intellect may or may not be a devotee of Krishna. However, if the intellect is not segregated from the coreSelf, if the intellect continues influencing the core, it will not be possible for the self to absorb the influence of Krishna, on a fulltime basis.

मच्चित्तः सर्वदुर्गाणि	maccittaḥ sarvadurgāṇi
मत्प्रसादात्तरिष्यसि ।	matprasādāttariṣyasi
अथ चेत्त्वमहंकारान्	atha cettvamahaṁkārān
न श्रोष्यसि विनङ्क्ष्यसि ॥१८.५८॥	na śroṣyasi vinaṅkṣyasi (18.58)

maccittaḥ — thinking of Me: sarvadurgāṇi — all difficulties; matprasādāt — from my grace; tariṣyasi — you will surpass; atha — but; cet = ced — if; tvam — you; ahaṁkārān — false assertion; na — not; śroṣyasi — you will listen; vinaṅkṣyasi — you will be lost

Thinking of Me, you will, by My grace, surpass all difficulties. But if by false assertion, you do not listen, you will be lost. (Bhagavad Gītā 18.58)

Analysis

A devotee can constantly think of Krishna and also not comply with him. Or he/she may think of Krishna as a matter of course and still ignore what Krishna said because of believing false assertions about how to discipline the self, and about methods of Krishna consciousness which were introduced after the time of Krishna by others, even by persons who were pure devotees or were rated as avatar personSelves of Krishna.

A false sense of confidence in being endowed with the grace of Krishna, makes it certain that a devotee will be unsuccessful in the Krishna conscious way of life. It is imperative that if one is to get the grace of the Lord, one should think of Krishna exactly as he diagrammed in the *Bhagavad Gītā*. The proper methods given in that text must be used, not another system which is designed to replace the difficult disciplines which Krishna explained in detail.

If Krishna gave a discipline for a sensual restraint accomplishment, that should be practiced. One cannot get the result by following an easy replacement merely because a pure devotee or an incarnation of Krishna said otherwise.

If anything, easy proposals are not substitute methods but are for the time being introductory process for those who find it difficult to train themselves as Krishna suggested. Later, persons who accept compromises will have to do as Krishna stipulated.

Comprehension of Bhagavad Gītā Verse 18.58

Think of Krishna in the way Krishna described in the *Bhagavad Gītā*, not otherwise. Do not substitute another method and expect to get the result which Krishna promised. The full grace of Krishna will claim a devotee who accepts the disciplines drafted by Krishna. Otherwise, the grace will be partial only and will not serve the full purpose intended. A devotee may also push aside the disciplines of the *Gītā*, as being difficult. But then he/she should go to the authority who gave a substitute easier process and get from that individual, other methods with their guarantees.

If, however, those systems of easy performance do not yield the results promised by the authority who issued them, the devotee will be lost in the sense that he/she will not get the achievements. Then, if he/she realizes this, that person can review the *Bhagavad Gītā* to cull from it the original advisories of Krishna. He/She can learn that and complete those practices. By the grace of Krishna, the devotee will surpass the difficulties in sense control and will not be lost or misled.

यदहंकारमाश्रित्य
न योत्स्य इति मन्यसे ।
मिथ्यैष व्यवसायस्ते
प्रकृतिस्त्वां नियोक्ष्यति ॥१८.५९॥

yadahaṁkāramāśritya
na yotsya iti manyase
mithyaiṣa vyavasāyaste
prakṛtistvāṁ niyokṣyati (18.59)

yat — which; ahaṁkāram — false assertive attitude; āśritya — relying on; na — not; yotsya — I will fight; iti — thus; manyase — you thing; mithyaiṣa = mithya — mistaken + eṣa — this; vyavasāyaḥ — determination; te — your; prakṛtiḥ — material nature; tvāṁ — you; niyokṣyāti — you will be forced

While relying on a false assertive attitude, you may think, "I will not fight." But that determination is mistaken. Your material nature will force you. (Bhagavad Gītā 18.59)

Analysis

There were many authorities who propagated the idea that one does not have to complete social tasks in family life. These persons stated that a devotee only needs to serve Krishna and the devotee of Krishna who preaches Krishna consciousness. However, this idea is condemned in this verse.

Arjuna wanted to leave aside his social duties which were family related. Before the battle of Kurukshetra, Arjuna lived with ascetics, roaming here and there in India. He knew of this free lifestyle. When confronted with the incidence of a civil war in the Kuru dynasty, Arjuna's will to fight collapsed. He did not think that it was something he should do but felt the need to turn away, to adopt the easy life of a wandering yogi.

However, Krishna rejected this opinion of Arjuna. Krishna stated that Arjuna's perspective, which was to abandon his social responsibilities as a member of the Kuru dynasty, was mistaken. Krishna stated that Arjuna's nature would itself force Arjuna to fight. Arjuna was boxed in on one side with social responsibilities in the family of his birth and on the other side with God who had no intention of supporting Arjuna in neglect of social duty.

It is an injustice to devotees, when an authority in the Krishna conscious movement encourages someone who has family obligation to abandon that way of life and join the Krishna conscious movement, leaving aside those obligations.

For one thing, Krishna has no intention of compensating for the neglected act of a devotee. The authority who recommends family neglect, has no intentions of doing so either. Hence if the devotee does not complete the duties, who will perform the services?

What will happen is that the devotee will amass some debits of liability which will plague him in the present or in a future life, or even hereafter. God will not compensate for it because such an act of God would only encourage the devotee in being irresponsible and that is not in God's interest ultimately, because God has the total concern for every living entity.

An authority should advice a devotee in how to efficiently serve the family responsibilities so that more time is used for practicing the spiritual methods described in *Bhagavad Gītā*. Skipping and avoiding the duties is not acceptable.

Comprehension of Bhagavad Gītā Verse 18.59

When God himself did not give Arjuna a waiver from cultural obligations, how is it that someone else, a devotee of God or an incarnation, can do so?

Arjuna has some unpalatable obligations to perform. God did not cancel these so that Arjuna could act in a holy way or in a kind way, or in a way for the propagation of Krishna consciousness by becoming a preacher of the Krishna conscious way of life. Krishna did not instruct Arjuna to gather worship articles and perform a worship ceremony then and there. Krishna did not tell Arjuna to go to holy places and chant the name of Krishna many times per day.

A devotee must be sure that he is not mistaken when he substitutes some other method given by a devotional authority or by someone who claims to be or is rated as an incarnation of Godhead.

Getting into a mood of, "I will not comply with the austerities recommended In *Bhagavad Gītā* for my upgrade," may only postpone the austerities for later in this life or in some other. Why? Because the devotee will not attain Krishna and will have to comply with the Gītā at some other time in the future.

स्वभावजेन कौन्तेय
निबद्धः स्वेन कर्मणा ।
कर्तुं नेच्छसि यन्मोहात्
करिष्यस्यवशोऽपि तत् ॥१८.६०॥

svabhāvajena kaunteya
nibaddhaḥ svena karmaṇā
kartuṁ necchasi yanmohāt
kariṣyasyavaśo'pi tat (18.60)

svabhāvajena — of your own natural tendencies; kaunteya — son of Kuntī; nibaddhaḥ — bound; svena — by your own; karmāṇa — obligation; kartuṁ — to perform; necchasi — na — not + icchasi — you want; yan = yad — which; mohāt — from delusion; kariṣyasi — you will do; avaśo — avaśaḥ — against your own will; 'pi = api — also, even; tat — tad — that

By your natural tendencies, being bound by obligations, O son of Kuntī, that which you do not want to perform due to delusion, you will do even if it is against your will. (Bhagavad Gītā 18.60)

Analysis

Sooner or later, in this life or in some other, one will be forced circumstantially to complete social obligations. Hence it is best to complete duties efficiently and to perform mystic austerities just the same. There is no easy method for control of the psyche. Why? Because the methods for self-control must match the deeply ingrained habits which support habitual rebirth.

Easy methods do not go deep enough. They provide some happiness at the moment, but they do not remove ingrained negative traits which are in the psyche of a living being.

By natural tendencies from many previous lives, being bound by cultural obligations due to taking many physical bodies, one develops ideas about how easy this should be, and that should be, and how God should grace one so that one does not have to strenuously endeavor for anything that is wholesome.

But when all is said and done, one will have to submit to the methods Krishna gave as methods in the *Bhagavad Gītā*. No authority, no incarnation of God, nobody, can adjust the methods recommended by Krishna. Therefore, the sooner one accepts this, the better.

Comprehension of Bhagavad Gītā Verse 18.60

Action is such a technical feat that it requires reference to the Supreme Lord for one to be certain if one should complete, curtail, or avoid it. The solutions offered to rid the self of the liabilities, such a chanting holy names, eating sanctified food, assisting devotees, giving donations to temple of Krishna and so many other recommendations, just do not serve the purpose. These proposals are absurd. They do not free the devotee from social obligations. Instead, they compound the obligations so that the devotee is confronted with them later either in this or a future life.

One should not be foolish enough to think that one can defer or project social obligations away from oneself merely by chanting a name of Krishna or some other absolute person. God is no one's stooge. What happens is that one develops confidence in a method, practices it, fools oneself into thinking that the liabilities will disappear from one's consequential account, when in fact no such deductions occur, and one is logged with more duties as a result.

Social obligations are mandatory. If one avoids these, there will be occasions to complete them again. This is because the energy for them is not exhausted merely by refusal to service them. Serving God or a religious authority and thinking that such service absolves obligation, is fantasy.

ईश्वरः सर्वभूतानां
हृद्देशेऽर्जुन तिष्ठति ।
भ्रामयन्सर्वभूतानि
यन्त्रारूढानि मायया ॥१८.६१॥

īśvaraḥ sarvabhūtānāṁ
hṛddeśe'rjuna tiṣṭhati
bhrāmayansarvabhūtāni
yantrārūḍhāni māyayā (18.61)

īśvaraḥ — Lord; sarvabhūtānām — of all beings; hṛddeśe = hṛd — central psyche + deśe — in the place; 'rjuna — arjuna — Arjuna; tiṣṭhati — is situated; bhrāmayan — cause to transmigrate; sarvabhūtāni — all beings; yantrārūḍhāni = yantra — machine + ārūḍhāni — fixed to; māyayā — by mystic power

The Lord of all beings is situated in the central psyche, O Arjuna, causing all beings to transmigrate by His mystic power, just as if they were fixed to a spinning machine. (Bhagavad Gītā 18.61)

Analysis

Even though God, the Lord of all beings, is in the central psyche of each individual entity, still that does not mean that this God is there for anyone's convenience.

As stated, the Lord is in all beings, side by side with the limited self. This Lord, by his mystic power, causes the limited ones to transmigrate on the basis of their activities. They do this in clockwork, just as if they were part of a timed rotor.

The God is not present to make circumstances easy for anyone, and yet he issues advisories, as he did in speaking *Bhagavad Gītā*. If someone adheres to that, and does not attempt even to change that, that person's profile may be upgraded to that of a divine being.

Comprehension of Bhagavad Gītā Verse 18.61

It is important to understand, to accept, that the Lord of all beings is not present for a limited self's convenience. He is in the psyche in a remote place such that the actions of a limited self may run contrary to that self's immediate or remote interest.

The more mystic distance there is between a self and the God, the more likely it is for that self to commit self-destructive acts for which it will be held responsible. At any time, in any place, the God may come closer to the limited person. When this happens, it is the good luck of the limited being.

To cause the distance between the Lord and a self to be reduced, that self should adhere to the stipulations given by Krishna in *Bhagavad Gītā*. The God is not present to design easy methods of salvation for the limited selves. The mission of God is to clarify the true methods of release, no matter how difficult those processes may be.

तमेव शरणं गच्छ
सर्वभावेन भारत ।
तत्प्रसादात्परां शान्तिं
स्थानं प्राप्स्यसि शाश्वतम् ॥१८.६२॥

tameva śaraṇaṁ gaccha
sarvabhāvena bhārata
tatprasādātparāṁ śāntiṁ
sthānaṁ prāpsyasi śāśvatam (18.62)

tam — to him; eva — only; śaraṇaṁ — shelter; gaccha — go; sarvabhāvena — with all your being; bhārata — O descendant of Bharata: tatprasādāt — from that grace; parāṁ — supreme; śāntiṁ — security; sthānaṁ — place; prāpyasi — you will attain: śāśvatam — eternal

With your whole being, go only to Him for shelter, O descendant of Bharata. You will attain the supreme security and the eternal place by His grace. (Bhagavad Gītā 18.62)

Analysis

Krishna does not state that he will simplify the method of release nor that he would make it easier. The reason is that regardless of the time or place, the nature of the living being remains the same. The complexities in the design of the psyche remain as it is. These factors do not change from time to time. Whatever energy is required in the past, in the time of Krishna, for release from physical existence, is the same that is required at this moment.

Easier processes only serve as introductory approaches. It is left to each devotee to become honest with himself/herself and break away from the fantasy of thinking that an easy method will suffice.

Comprehension of Bhagavad Gītā Verse 18.62

This verse is the ultimate declaration. It cancels and scrubs the easy process which was presented in the name of Krishna or as systems of release divulged by his incarnations or devotee.

With one's whole being,
one should go only to this Krishna of Bhagavad Gītā for shelter.
If one does so, one will attain the supreme security
and the eternal place by His grace.

Chapter 3

Sāṁkhya Theory of Creation*

Terri Stokes-Pineda Art

* Śrīmad Bhāgavatam Canto 11, Chapter 24

*Uddhava Gītā Chapter 19

श्री-भगवान् उवाच
अथ ते सम्प्रवक्ष्यामि
साङ्‌ख्यं पूर्वैर् विनिश्चितम् ।
यद् विज्ञाय पुमान् सद्यो
जह्याद् वैकल्पिक भ्रमम् ॥१९.१॥

śrī-bhagavān uvāca
atha te sampravakṣyāmi
sāṅkhyaṁ pūrvair viniścitam
yad vijñāya pumān sadyo
jahyād vaikalpikaṁ bhramam (19.1)

śrī-bhagavān – the blessed lord; uvāca — said; atha — now; te — to you; sampravakṣyāmi — I will explain; sāṅkhyam — Sāṅkhyaṁ theory of creation; pūrvair = pūrvaiḥ — by ancient sages; viniścitam — figured out; yad = yat — that; vijñāya — knowing; pumān — any person; sadyo = sadyah — immediately; jahyād = jahyāt — can give up; vaikalpikam — that which is based on multiplicity seen in this creation; bhramam — misconception.

The Blessed Lord said: Now I will explain to you, the Sāṅkhya theory of creation, which was figured by the ancient sages. By knowing that, any person may immediately give up the misconception, which is based on the multiplicity seen in this creation. (Uddhava Gītā 19.1)

Consideration:

The *Sāṁkhya* theory of creation contrasts with the philosophy of the *Upanishads*. There is similarity but there are differences, nevertheless. To make both systems seem to be compatible, some commentators use texts from one part of the *Upanishads* which seem to match some part of Krishna *Sāṁkhya* philosophy. This approach simply causes confusion. Krishna *Sāṁkhya* is different to the *Upanishads* and should be regarded as an independent philosophy which neither competes with nor is referenced to the *Upanishads*.

We should appreciate the *rishis* of the *Upanishads*. Whatever they presented was based on their research. It does not have to be the absolute truth to have value. Their contribution stands as it is, regardless of if it was in error or was incomplete.

The confusion in this world is a sensory one. It is due to limited sense perception. When anyone experience sensual limitation, guessing becomes a necessity and that is fraught with error.

The senses however, when they report on anything, may miscalculate. Thus, in every respect, one should cautiously use his/her senses. Invariably there will be miscalculations in the reports given to the coreSelf by the senses. Hence this vast complex manifestation may be misunderstood. Its fragments may not be assessed rightly in relation to the whole scope.

Elucidation:

Lord Krishna explained the *Sāṁkhya* theory of creation, which he approved, and which was known in his time. There are other theories of creation but this one is specific in highlighting the personSelf. *Sāṁkhya* means enumeration of person, time, place or event. Prior to Krishna some ancient sages did mystic research and realized opinions which were in harmony with what Krishna declared. By knowing what Krishna enumerated, any person may give up the misconception of the self as being a hub or center of this creation. He/She would understand that this is a colossal power which contains a controlled multiplicity which is part of a vastness.

आसीज् ज्ञानम् अथो अर्थ
एकम् एवाविकल्पितम् ।
यदा विवेक-निपुणा
आदौ कृत-युगे ऽयुगे ॥१९.२॥

āsīj jñānam atho artha
ekam evāvikalpitam
yadā viveka-nipuṇā
ādau kṛta-yuge 'yuge (19.2)

āsīj = āsīt — there existed; jñānam — knowledge; atho = athau — thus; artha = arthaḥ — object known; ekam — one consistency; evāvikalpitam = eva — only + avikalpitam — without distortion; yadā — when; viveka — discrimination, perception; nipuṇā — people with accurate; ādau — at the beginning; kṛta-yuga — in the age of Easy Realization; 'yuge = ayuge — during the time prior to this manifestation.

Once, the knowledge gained and the object known were of one consistency only, without distortion. That was when there were people with accurate perception at the beginning of the Age of Easy Realization, and during the time prior to this manifestation. (Uddhava Gītā 19.2)

Consideration:

This information is a matter of confidence in Krishna, because there is no way a limited being can verify this. One can neither provide proof for a prior Era of Easy Realization, nor can one prove that there was no such period.

There is reservation, where someone can be neutral for the time being, neither accepting this statement nor rejecting it outright. Then someone can read this and ponder the possibility.

Elucidation:

Prior to the time of Krishna, there was a society of persons who had keen psychic perception. These people did not use the physical world as the reference for vocabulary. They were focused on subtle reality and related to the physical world in a superficial way.

Because the astral existence is the basis for this physical place, when someone uses the physical reality as the reference many errors are made. Decisions which are based only on physical perception fail to take into account the psychic basis. This produces frustration and disappointment, which in turn causes neglect or rash reactions.

Even though born with a need for physical definition, a self should endeavor to shift the interest to the psychic side. This will make one become aware of the opinion of the Supreme Lord. It will render an intuition which coordinates with Krishna.

तन् माया-फल-रूपेण
केवलं निर्विकल्पितम् ।
वाङ्-मनो-ऽगोचरं सत्य
द्विधा समभवद् बृहत् ॥१९.३॥

tan māyā-phala-rūpeṇa
kevalaṁ nirvikalpitam
vāṅ-mano-'gocaraṁ satyaṁ
dvidhā samabhavad bṛhat (19.3)

tan = tat — that primal reality; māyā — productive enterprise; phala — product; rūpena — by the form of; kevalam — unified existence; nirvikalpitam — what is without ambiguity; vān = vāk — description; mano = manaḥ — mind; 'gocaraṁ = agocaram — beyond the capacity; satyam — reality; dvidhā — twofold; samabhavad = samabhavat — that became; bṛhat — the extensive primat existence.

That unified existence, which was without ambiguity, which is beyond the capacity of description and the mind, the Reality, that extensive Primal Existence, did by taking the form of productive enterprise and product, become twofold. (Uddhava Gītā 19.3)

Consideration:

A yogi should always be aware of the fact, that this is a unified existence from one view and a complex multi-layered reality from another perception. Collectively, it is one occurrence like a symphony of musical notes. And yet as in a symphony, it has micro-constituents which challenge or compliment the energies.

A limited self is not the whole existence. It is not the unity of everything. It cannot afford to be in ignorance of the reality which is greater than itself. A self should play its part and be ready to be insignificant at any moment.

Elucidation:

The extensive Primal Existence which is responsible for this physical manifestation, and its subtle source, is a reality unto itself. It is a living mechanism, which in the *Bhagavad Gītā,* is compared to an aggressively growing banyan tree.

In the proximity of the Supreme Lord and the limited selves, the Primal Existence assumes the form of a productive enterprise. From itself it produces products in the form of elements and species.

Even though the supreme self and the limited ones are an independent reality, they are ever in relationship with the Primal Existence. Hence any valid idea of this should take into account the flow of influence from the selves to the active energy. *Purusha*, personality, must be recognized.

तयोर् एकतरो ह्य् अर्थः
प्रकृतिः सोभयात्मिका ।
ज्ञानं त्व् अन्यतमो भावः
पुरुषः सो ऽभिधीयते ॥१९.४॥

tayor ekataro hy arthaḥ
prakṛtiḥ sobhayātmikā
jñānaṁ tv anyatamo bhāvaḥ
puruṣaḥ so 'bhidhīyate (19.4)

tayor = tayoh — of the two; ekataro = ekataraḥ — one; hy = hi — definitely; arthah — aspect; prakṛtiḥ — material nature; sobhayātmikā = sā — that (submissive factor) + ubhaya – two-fold + ātmikā — of the nature of; jñānam — knowledge, awareness; tv = tu — but; anyatamo = anyatamah — the other; bhāvah — conscious aspect; puruṣaḥ — personality; so = sah — that (predominating factor); 'bhidhīyate = abhidhīyate — is called.

Of the two, one aspect is material nature, which has a two-fold nature. But the other conscious aspect is awareness. That predominating factor is called the personality. (Uddhava Gītā 19.4)

Consideration:

The isolation of the personality substance from the mundane energy can be achieved only through psychic detachment and not forever, only for limited periods of time in meditation or by transiting to all-spiritual realms which are environments in which the mundane energy has no foothold.

The concept of the personality substance as being only material nature or conversely as being only itself with no relationship to material nature, is a dogma only. In reality, the contact of the two principles is perpetual with the personality substance making contact with nature on occasion or being presence in the spiritual nature otherwise.

The existence of the personality substance with no contact to any environment is imaginary only. A limited self cannot isolate itself as though it was supreme. Even the supreme being must by any means be in contact with whatever else there is.

Elucidation:

Awareness does not mean objectivity alone. Awareness means subjectivity and objectivity. The selves exist! A limited self does not have to be objective to exist. It can exist subjectivity such that it is unaware of itself in the sense of not contrasting itself to anything else.

It so happens that the objectivity of a limited self is reliant on the type of environment it is related to. When it is in an environment which does not support its objectivity, it becomes unaware of itself. It continues to exist but does not know its presence.

As soon as it is in an environment which supports its objectivity, it resumes awareness of itself with or without memory of prior events. It should not be assumed that existence is reliant on objectivity. The personCore should not be rated as being insubstantial merely because it is not continuously objective to itself.

तमो रजः सत्त्वम् इति
प्रकृतेर् अभवन् गुणाः ।
मया प्रक्षोभ्यमाणायाः
पुरुषानुमतेन च ॥१९.५॥

tamo rajaḥ sattvam iti
prakṛter abhavan guṇāḥ
mayā prakṣobhyamāṇāyāḥ
puruṣānumatena ca (19.5)

tamo = tamah — the retardative energy; rajaḥ — the impulsive force; sattvam — the perceptive ability; iti — thus, namely; prakṛter = prakṛteḥ — from material nature; abhavan — were produced; guṇāḥ — the modes; mayā — by me; prakṣobhyamāṇāyāḥ — was agitated; puruṣānumatena = puruṣa — the collective personality + anumatena — with approving urge; ca — and.

The mundane influences were produced from material nature, namely the retardative energy, the impulsive force and the

perceptive ability. And with the approval urge of the collective personality, it was agitated by Me. (Uddhava Gītā 19.5)

Consideration:

The combination of selves and environments is an ongoing feat, happening in many dimensions simultaneously, and being fused through to some other places. The clock of time keeps ticking whereby the noon hour of one system flashes at the time of the midnight of some other. Some complexities are incoordinate to others whereby the observations appear chaotic. It is orderly but it may be perceived as disorder from a certain perspective. Surely a limited self cannot in every case make sense of the occurrence. It should not expect to tally every circumstance correctly.

The conjunction of a self and material nature, results in an influence on that self which is retardative, impulsive or perceptive. The self in question may or may not resist. A self could be dominated by the influence of nature. That happens.

The end of research is the realization of how this creation was formulated before it was expressed visually. This cannot be known from this side of existence because the formulation was in another plane which fully transcends this display. One must access the original level through a transcendental portal. But if one does so, one will no longer be on this side to report the incidence of what is on the other side.

Mystic penetration is the only method available to a yogi. One example is Markandeya who crossed into source of the sourcePerson's environment.

Whatever is here regardless of if it is limited or infinite, is sourced in its origin. The impressive variety of things which one can sensually apprehend has little or no significance when compared to the source point.

There are two factors to consider.

- *person*
- *environment*

Besides these, there is nothing else which has importance. Is the self a person? If the self is a person, is that self, sourced from a superPerson?

Is the environment enduring? If the environment is not enduring, is there an enduring habitat in some other place. Can that paradise be accessed?

Elucidation:

There is the individual self, the unit limited person. There are combinations of several selves, collective person. Several selves together can act in unison when the environmental energies absorb their combined energy and commit an action, seemingly on their behalf. The fact is however that when this happens, the selves may volunteer their power but do so involuntarily or under the influence of a natural expression.

In that case, the Supreme Lord may not interfere with the transaction. That appears to be the God's granting of permission, while in fact that is not the case. His non-interference is permission, only because he did not apply a cessation of influence to the situation. It is not due to his wish.

Children who play together may do so based on their desire. The parent may not interfere, but that parent may not have a desire for the child to be self-engaged. Ultimately, regardless of permitting, allowing, sanctioning, desiring or preventing, the Supreme Lord has the liability for every incidence.

तेभ्यः समभवत् सूत्रं
महान् सूत्रेण संयुतः ।
ततो विकुर्वतो जातो
यो ऽहङ्कारो विमोहनः ॥१९.६॥

tebhyaḥ samabhavat sūtraṁ
mahān sūtreṇa saṁyutaḥ
tato vikurvato jāto
yo 'haṅkāro vimohanaḥ (19.6)

tebhyah — from those; samabhavat — developed; sūtram — sexually-charge cosmic energy; mahān — the mahat-tattva, primal cosmic energy; sūtreṇa — with the sexual-charge cosmic energy; samyūtaḥ — was mixed; tato = tataḥ — from that; vikurvato = vikurvataḥ — transformation; jāto = jātaḥ — was generated; yo = yah — which; 'haṅkāro = ahaṅkāraḥ — the cosmic assertive sense; vimohanaḥ — that which bewilders.

From those mundane potencies, the sexually-charged cosmic energy developed. The primal cosmic energy and that sexually-charged cosmic force, were mixed. From the admixture, the cosmic assertive sense which bewilders, emerged. (Uddhava Gītā 19.6)

Consideration:

The mundane potencies are in themselves a power. The personForces are also a power. The mix is another type of potency. That is experienced as an assertive sense (*ahaṅkāraḥ*). Because of natural adhesion, these energies and persons in combination are difficult to segregate. The estimation of their individual isolated qualities has value as ideas but factually their isolated powers hardly have application.

Elucidation:

The personForces have assertive power but that is awarded to them naturally as the situation evolves and after the production of the sexually charged cosmic force. For there to be a claim, there must be a claimant and a property. When the personForces are endowed with a sense of identity, they use this psychic limb to grasp objects of interest. That is the way of experience in this psychic and physical reality.

वैकारिकस् तैजसश् च
तामसश् चेत्य् अहं त्रि-वृत् ।
तन्-मात्रेन्द्रिय-मनसां
कारणं चिद्-अचिन्-मयः ॥१९.७॥

vaikārikas taijasaś ca
tāmasaś cety ahaṁ tri-vṛt
tan-mātrendriya-manasāṁ
kāraṇaṁ cid-acin-mayaḥ (19.7)

vaikārikas = vaikārikaḥ — pertaining to the perception-forming energy; taijasaś = taijasaḥ — pertaining to the motivating energy; ca — and; tāmasaś = tāmasaḥ — pertaining to the inertia energy; cety = ca — and + iti — as declared; aham — the sense of assertion; tri-vṛt — threefold; tan-mātrendriya-manasāṁ = tat-mātra — subtle sense objects + indriya — sensual energy + manasam — of mindal energy; kāraṇam — cause; cid = cit – self-awareness; acin = acit — that which has no self-awareness; mayah — comprising.

As declared, the sense of assertion is threefold; as pertaining to the perception-forming energy, the motivational force and the inertial energy. These in turn serve as the subtle sense objects, the sensual power and the mind compartment. Part of it comprise a self-awareness and part has no self-consciousness. (Uddhava Gītā 19.7)

Consideration:

The personFace is there but its objectivity is in question because it needs environmental support to break from its subjective eternal state. In combination with the assertive sense, the person either acts on the basis of sensual information, enthusiastic motivation, or sluggish energy. Due to this combination some philosophers declare the person as a farce, as not being significant and of being subjected to additions and deletions. They present this as evidence that the person is an illusion.

The composite, which is the conventional person, consist of sensual power, a mind compartment and the personSelf either as an objective observer or as a subjective reality without register. In combination or by itself, there is a corePerson to which adjuncts adhere. That core is perpetual regardless of its objective feature. The lack of objectivity does not disqualify that personSelf from being a reality in its own right. It is real and permanent in its subjective state, but its objectivity is out of commission if it is not supported by a registering environment.

In the physical existence, if it does not have support from the perception-forming energy, its objectivity is lost to a lesser or greater degree.

Elucidation:

The sense of assertion is threefold. It is rendered as the perception-forming energy, the motivational force, and the inertial energy. When the personSelf is supported by the perception-forming energy, it has clarity and can make decisions which in the long term are in its interest. Then, it has accurate information and makes decisions which are approved by the supreme being.

When the personSelf is supported by the motivational force, it acts hastily and with enthusiasm, but it is deprived of clarity and are shown justifications which prop it for the occasion but do not protect it from the liabilities. When it is supported by the inertial energy, the personSelf procrastinates or it acts rashly with no assessment of repercussions.

The clarifying energy gives the most support to the objective feature of the self. The motivational force gives some support, but it abandons the self in the long term. It utilizes the subjective energy that is the self, but it does so without informing the self. The inertial energy displaces the spread of objectivity. It does not affect the subjectivity of the self, but it squelches any objectivity bit by bit.

When an entity becomes the child of parents, that infant is challenged to realize what it is as a coreSelf and adjuncts. It must face the fact that it requires support to activate and use its objectivity, but its subjectivity is involuntary and continuous, except that the self has no method for externalizing its subjectivity.

अर्थस् तन्-मात्रिकाज् जज्ञे
तामसाद् इन्द्रियाणि च ।
तैजसाद् देवता आसन्न्
एकादश च वैकृतात् ॥१९.८॥

arthas tan-mātrikāj jajñe
tāmasād indriyāṇi ca
taijasād devatā āsann
ekādaśa ca vaikṛtāt (19.8)

arthas — gross matter; tan-mātrikāj = tan-mātrikāt — from the subtle objects; jajñe — developed; tāmasād = tāmasāt — from the non-energetic assertive force; indriyāṇi — the sensual energies; ca — and; taijasād = taijasāt — from the energetic assertive potency; devatā — the supernatural rulers; āsann = āsan — emerged; ekādaśa — eleven; ca — and; vaikṛtāt — from the perception-oriented assertive potency.

Gross matter developed from the subtle objects, which developed from the non-energetic assertive force. The senses developed from the energetic assertive potency. The eleven supernatural rulers emerged from the perception-oriented potency. (Uddhava Gītā 19.8)

Consideration:

This describes the cosmic sense of identity, which is a vast power from which the individual assertive tendency is derived. The first entities in this creation appear with supervisory powers. Their control is derived from the perceptive powers of the sense of identity. Other limited selves appear in the creation with partial powers, all being derived from the cosmic sense of identity, which releases infinitesimal portions of itself to each personSelf.

Elucidation:

The physical world developed from the subtle objects, which today are known as atoms and subparticles. That subtle domain remains as is. Only a miniscule part converts into substantive forms which we handle as physical objects.

The subtle objects are part of the astral environment which is the psychic underbasis. It developed from the non-energetic random energy. This is invisible to normal sense perception. A yogi may see it if he develops pranaVision.

The senses developed from the energetic assertive potency. This happens initially when a command is given by the cosmic sense of identity, whereby any self in the vicinity is fused to a speck sense of identity. That causes instant creation of senses which are suitable for a species of life, which is created then or in the future.

मया सञ्चोदिता भावाः
सर्वे सहत्य-कारिणः ।
अण्डम् उत्पादयाम् आसुर्
ममायतनम् उत्तमम् ॥१९.९॥

mayā sañcoditā bhāvāḥ
sarve saṁhatya-kāriṇaḥ
aṇḍam utpādayām āsur
mamāyatanam uttamam (19.9)

mayā — by me; sañcoditā = sañcoditāḥ — as motivated; bhāvāh — the factors; sarve — all; saṁhatya — combining together; kārinaḥ — reacting; aṇḍam — cosmic egg-shaped enclosure; utpādayām āsur = utpādayām āsuḥ — produced; mamāyatanam = mama — of mind + āyatanam — habitat; uttamam — most suitable.

As motivated by Me, all the factors by combining together and reacting accordingly, produced a cosmic egg-shaped enclosure, which is a most suitable habitat of Mine. (Uddhava Gītā 19.9)

Consideration:

The factor of location and that of person is important. Philosophic approaches to existence which reduce or eliminate location or person, are flawed and inadequate. Location is experienced experientially as environment. When a limited self discovers itself in a non-environment, that occurs because of a lack of available means for suitable sense perception. There is an inclination to brand blank locations as nowhere-places or as value-nothingness. That however is due to the lack of higher sense perception which would undermine the abstraction.

Elucidation:

The motivation of the supreme being may or may not be deliberate but in either case, it has impact. It can terminate, obliterate, activate or reverse the course of any development. It is not accountable to anyone or anything. It is not within the range of rejection. It cannot be checked by some other power. It is not to be approved or censored by anyone.

For the combination of the various factors which form into being this cosmos, there must be permission from the Supreme Lord but the act of granting a continuation energy is done instinctively by the Lord, as a mere whim of his. It does not require effort on his part.

The energies of this cosmos may be perceived as formless or as abstract and imperceptible but from the view of the Supreme Lord, this cosmic situation is a combine as an egg-shaped enclosure. It has color. It has spape. It is limited.

तस्मिन्न् अहं समभवम्
अण्डे सलिल-सस्थितौ ।
मम नाभ्याम् अभूत् पद्मं
विश्वाख्यं तत्र चात्म-भूः ॥१९.१०॥

tasminn ahaṁ samabhavam
aṇḍe salila-saṁsthitau
mama nābhyām abhūt padmaṁ
viśvākhyaṁ tatra cātma-bhūḥ
(19.10)

tasmin — in that; aham — I; samabhavam — manifested form; aṇḍe — in the cosmic enclosure; salila — water; saṁsthitau — situated within, floating; mama — my; nābhyām — from the navel; abhūt — developed; padmam — lotus; viśvākhyam — known as the universal; tatra — from there; cātma-bhuh = ca — and + ātma-bhūḥ — self-produced person.

In that cosmic enclosure, which floated in water, I manifested a form. From My navel, a lotus developed, which is called the universe. And from there, the self-produced one emerged. (Uddhava Gītā 19.10)

Consideration:

The issue of perception or the lack of it, is ongoing in this creation, where because of the lack of perception, many philosophers regard non-perception to be evidence that there is nothing to be perceived. Instead of stating that there may be subtle or super-subtle formations, some ascetics declare that there is no form. Those persons have no sensual comprehension on the higher levels which they experience as void places.

A lack of sensual clarity is no evidence of the absence of form. The statement is that if there is a lack of sensual perception, the observer has no means to analysis whatever reality he/she encounters.

An ant crawling around a large planet, may well declare that there is no boundary. A blind person feeling the heat of the morning sun may state that it is a hot colorless source. These are incorrect statements based on the inadequacy of the viewer.

Krishna described a cosmic enclosure, which floats in water. He claimed that the self-produced one manifested from a lotus which sprung from his navel.

From within the creation, a limited being cannot measure the cosmos. He/She has no chance of seeing it objectivity. He cannot go outside to view it from a distance.

Elucidation:

The cosmic space is in an egg-shaped enclosure which floats in psychic water. Initially, within it, Krishna manifested a duplicate form. From the navel of the duplicate, a lotus developed. That is the universe. From that supernatural plant, the self-produced one emerged. This person is *Brahma*.

सो ऽसृजत् तपसा युक्तो
रजसा मद्-अनुग्रहात् ।
लोकान् स-पालान् विश्वात्मा
भूर् भुवः स्वर् इति त्रिधा ॥१९.११॥

so 'sṛjat tapasā yukto
rajasā mad-anugrahāt
lokān sa-pālān viśvātmā
bhūr bhuvaḥ svar iti tridhā (19.11)

so = sah — he; 'sṛjat = asrjat — created; tapasā — by rigid sensual restraint; yukto = yuktaḥ — endowed; rajasā — with the impulsive potency; mad-anugrahāt = mat-anugrahāt — due to my grace; lokān — the world; sa-pālān — with the supernatural rulers; viśvātmā — universal soul; bhur – Bhur lower zone; svar – Svar higher zone; iti — namely; tridhā — three regions.

Due to My grace, by his rigid sensual restraint, and by being endowed with the impulsive potency, he, the soul of the universe, created the worlds, in three regions, namely the Bhūr lower zone, the Bhuva middle area and the Svar higher region. (Uddhava Gītā 19.11)

Consideration:

The person factor was, is and will be the instance of concern. Whatever we do, whatever we say, whatever we perceive, is relational to person. This writer is a person. So is the reader.

The addition of adjuncts in the form of psychic or physical compliments, is no reason to negate and deny person. One may strip away the additions. Then, one will find the core essential self. One should not assume that since there are adjuncts, there is no enduring core or that because this core has a subjective phase which only is enduring, it is not perpetual.

Elucidation:

Brahma is more than his coreSelf. He is that core, plus his rigid sensual restraint, plus the impulsive potency of nature, plus the grace of Krishna. That combination as the creatorGod, functions spontaneously to create the world in three regions of Bhur lower zone, Bhuva middle area and Svar highest realm. Brahma is transcendental to those zones. Someone with lower sense perception, cannot perceive this demigod. For that observer, this lord is invisible.

देवानाम् ओक आसीत् स्वर्
भूतानां च भुवः पदम् ।
मर्त्यादीनां च भूर् लोकः
सिद्धानां त्रितयात् परम् ॥१९.१२॥

devānām oka āsīt svar
bhūtānāṁ ca bhuvaḥ padam
martyādīnāṁ ca bhūr lokaḥ
siddhānāṁ tritayāt param (19.12)

devānām — of the supernatural rulers; oka = okah — zone; āsīt — became; svar — Svar higher region; bhūtānām — of the spirits; ca — and; bhuvah — Bhuva middle zone; padam — habitation; martyādīnām — of humans and other species using short-term bodies; ca — and; bhūr – Bhūr lower zone; lokaḥ — region; siddhānām — of the perfected beings; tritayāt — in reference to the three; param — beyond.

The Svar higher region became the zone of the supernatural rulers. The Bhuva middle zone is the habitation of the spirits. And the Bhūr lower zone is that of the humans and other species using short-term bodies. Beyond the three, is the zone of the perfected beings. (Uddhava Gītā 19.12)

Consideration:

The factors of the most interest are the locations and persons. Even those who deride and deny the substance of person, are themselves persons. No non-person is in a discussion about whether person is a substance or not. Persons and environments, these are the issues of prime concern.

According to the quality of the combination of what is a person, that is where that person will be located. The person matches the environment in which that person emerges.

The lowest combination of corePerson and adjuncts, discovers itself in the Bhur lowest zone. The median combination of corePerson and adjuncts, realizes itself in the median zone, the habitation of spirits. The highest combination of corePerson and adjuncts, knows itself in the Svar higher region as a supernatural ruler of lower psychic realms and the physical situations they control.

There is yet another higher zone which are the places of the perfected beings who no longer require the supports which are afforded by the environments below.

Elucidation:

The dimensional situations are such that a person whose body is in a certain zone is likely to be aware of no other level. However, those in a lower zone should assume that people in a higher zone will be invisible to the lower sense perception. It is likely as well that those in a higher zone will be unaware of someone in a lower realm. Outside of the *Bhūr, Bhuva* and *Svar* system, there is yet another higher place which is where the perfected beings reside. They feel no need to benefit from the experiences of lower places.

अधो ऽसुराणां नागानां
भूमेर् ओको ऽसृजत् प्रभुः ।
त्रि-लोक्यां गतयः सर्वाः
कर्मणां त्रि-गुणात्मनाम् ॥१९.१३॥

adho 'surāṇāṁ nāgānāṁ
bhūmer oko 'sṛjat prabhuḥ
tri-lokyāṁ gatayaḥ sarvāḥ
karmaṇāṁ tri-guṇātmanām (19.13)

adho = adhah — below; 'surāṇāṁ = asurānām — of the powerful wicked spirits; nāgānām — of the subtle snakes; bhūmer = bhūmeh — from the earth; oko = okah — habitat; 'sṛjat = asṛjat — created; prabhuḥ — Procreator Brahmā; tri-lokyām — three dimensions; gatayah — destination, environment; sarvāh — all; karmanām — of cultural activities; tri-guṇātmanām = tri-guṇa – three influences of material nature + ātmanām — comprising.

Procreator Brahmā created the habitats of the powerful wicked spirits and the subtle snakes below the earth. All environments in the three dimensions are based on the three influences of material nature which comprise cultural activities. (Uddhava Gītā 19.13)

Consideration:

Here again the stress is on person substance and environment. This must be considered for a philosophy of life to have bearing. The removal of the personality or the environment from the conversation about liberation is really meaningless.

For one thing the person, if it is a limited self, cannot guarantee for itself any preset environment or any preset non-environment. As it emerged and became aware of itself in this circumstance, so it may arrive in some other place hereafter, either with memory of this situation or with no idea of this place.

One may strip from the social self, all that was awarded to it after it appeared as an embryo, but then there would be left a subtle body with its instincts from the past life. That core should not be denied merely because it required adjuncts for having a relationship with objects in the environment.

Elucidation:

According to Krishna, the Procreator *Brahmā* created the habitats. The environments however were derived through the three influences of nature. Their usage produces cultural activities which are events utilized by the entities. In that sense this situation can be reduced to person substance and influences which are the medium for interaction.

योगस्य तपसश् चैव
न्यासस्य गतयो ऽमलाः ।
महर् जनस् तपः सत्यं
भक्ति-योगस्य मद्-गतिः ॥१९.१४॥

yogasya tapasaś caiva
nyāsasya gatayo 'malāḥ
mahar janas tapaḥ satyaṁ
bhaktī-yogasya mad-gatiḥ (19.14)

yogasya — by yoga practice; tapasaś = tapasaḥ — by austerity; caiva = ca — and + eva — indeed; nyāsasya — of the renunciation of cultural oppurtunities; gatayo = gatayah — that which leads to; 'malāḥ = amalāh — pure; mahar — Mahar; janas — Jana; tapah — Tapa; satyam — Satya; bhaktī-yogasya — by devotion as it is applied with the yoga discipline; mad-gatiḥ = mat-gatiḥ — My region.

The practice of yoga, austerity and the renunciation of cultural opportunities, causes one to achieve the pure worlds, namely Mahar, Jana, Tapa and Satya zones. The practice of devotion as it is applied with yoga disciplines leads to My region. (Uddhava Gītā 19.14)

Consideration:

The practice of yoga along with devotion to a deity, may result in transfer to the realm of that personality. All the same the practice of devotion without doing yoga may also result in such transfer. If, however devotion is stripped away, if the person has no interest in the idea of a deity, then yoga along with austerities of various kinds and with renunciation of cultural opportunities, may result in transfer to the pure worlds of *Mahar, Jana, Tapa,* and *Satya* zones.

There however, the ascetic even though he/she doubted that personality is reality, will find that there must be association. That ascetic may reach his spiritual teacher in a higher realm. This means that the facet of personality, which the person spent his last life ridiculing and avoiding, will again become a challenge.

Elucidation:

Yoga, various types of self-discipline, and escaping from cultural participation, if done precisely, may cause someone to reach the supernatural locations, which are known as *Mahar, Jana, Tapa,* and *Satya* zones. Relatively speaking, these places are devoid of traumatic incidences even though there is a residual energy which if the ascetic is not careful, will cause him/her to again descend to the lower zones where the trauma will be reimposed.

There are many types of ascetics. Some are attached to Krishna in a devotional way. If any such person practices yoga and can affirm the devotion to Krishna, that person is likely to go to Krishna's region on a full-time basis, or he/she may transit to a supernatural location, and continue the yoga practice to fine-tune the devotion, and then transfer to Krishna's transcendental place.

Devotion is stressed by Krishna. It is through devotion mainly that one may transit to a divine place. One cannot access a deity's place if one has no developed relationship with that supernatural or divine personality.

मया कालात्मना धात्रा
कर्म-युक्तम् इद जगत् ।
गुण-प्रवाह एतस्मिन्न्
उन्मज्जति निमज्जति ॥१९.१५॥

mayā kālātmanā dhātrā
karma-yuktam idaṁ jagat
guṇa-pravāha etasminn
unmajjati nimajjati (19.15)

mayā — by me; kālātmanā = kāla – time + ātmanā — by the self, by itself; dhātrā — origin of the world; karma – cultural activities; yuktam — devoted to; idam — this; jagat — universe; guṇa – mundane energies; pravāha = pravāhe — in the flow; etasminn = etasmin — in this; unmajjati — develops; nimajjati — subsides.

By Me, who is time itself, who is the originator of the world, this universe which is devoted to cultural activity, develops and subsides in this flow of mundane energies. (Uddhava Gītā 19.15)

Consideration:

The universe is denoted by cultural activity which is based on person substance and environment. Having an existential discussion and devaluing the personality ingredient is senseless. There must be a consideration and calculation about the personSelf.

The Supreme Lord is a person. So is everyone else. The additions and deletions from the social unit person does not remove the core to which the additions adhere or are deleted.

The baffling factor is time which originated, hatched and demolishes this cosmos. When each segment of time operates overly or covertly, the personSelf remains in its core feature, the power around which events are displayed.

Elucidation:

The personSelf operates on two wavelengths. One is the supreme control. The other is the relative control. The supreme person is himself/herself the supreme control, where effortlessly he/she remains as the ultimate limit or barrier. The limited self is part of a vast wash, with each particle of personality, having some limited or some seemingly vast powers.

The limited selves are under the control of the supreme being but that expression of Godpower is not always asserted. Hence a limited self may on occasion have the feeling that it is supreme. When one is not conscious of limits, one may assume oneself as being all-pervasive.

Krishna informed that he is time itself, the originator of the world. He is the factor in which the universe is outlaid. The world by its very nature is devoted to cultural activity. It develops and subsides in the flow of nature forces which are subjected to ripples which ebb and flow.

अणुर् बृहत् कृशः स्थूलो
यो यो भावः प्रसिध्यति ।
सर्वो ऽप्य् उभय-सयुक्तः
प्रकृत्या पुरुषेण च ॥१९.१६॥

aṇur bṛhat kṛśaḥ sthūlo
yo yo bhāvaḥ prasidhyati
sarvo 'py ubhaya-saṁyuktaḥ
prakṛtyā puruṣeṇa ca (19.16)

aṇur = aṇuḥ — tiny; bṛhat — large; kṛśaḥ — thin; sthūlo = sthūlaḥ — thick; yo yo = yaḥ yaḥ — whatever; bhāvaḥ — object; prasidhyati — is manifested; sarvo = sarvah — all; 'py = api — surely; ubhaya — both; saṁyuktah — is mixed; prakṛtyā — with material nature; puruṣeṇa — with the person; ca — and.

Whatever there is in a tiny, large, thick or thin object, which is manifested, all of it surely, is mixed with both the material nature and person. (Uddhava Gītā 19.16)

Consideration:

The deletion of the personality, the *purusha*, is unacceptable in any discussion about transcendence. The fact that the personality which surfaces as a physical body is a temporary composite, does not remove the importance and permanence of the coreSelf.

This information is the Krishna *Sāṁkhya*, the enumeration of existence as experienced by Krishna, who is the Supreme Lord. It gives a map of the realms of existence and the person forces which abound in these environments.

Instead of deleting and devaluing the person substance because in this existence, it does not stand alone but by necessity uses adjuncts, one should parcel the composite parts of the conventional self to find its constituent parts and give each sectors its relative value.

Strip away the adjuncts used by the coreSelf. Identify the parts of the composite cultural identity. Give each its value. Inspect to see if the core to which the adjuncts adhere can ever stand on its own or if it can be transferred to an environment which is supportive or reinforcive of its value.

Elucidation:

Krishna *Sāṁkhya* is about personality and environment. It involves giving credence to these factors. Those whose tendency is to deny personality and to negate environment, will find this discourse to be untenable. Each person is limited to his or her mind, as to how to regard this existence and the persons. If one feels that person, that one's persons and everyone else's, is an illusion and has no ultimate value, one will be attracted to philosophies which advocate no self nor location.

The mere idea that there is opinion, suggest, that there may be different views based on sense perception or the lack of it. As such the arguments will continue. The agreement is between each person who may go left or right according to sensual experience and intuitive instinct. Krishna *Sāṁkhya* is for those who want to research person substance and environmental space.

The person should be stripped to its basic parts. This should be done until a core only remains. Each part which was an addition should be identified. The core should not be assigned a zero value. The core is the value. The adjuncts should not be assigned a nil either. Those who wished for nothing as the absolute should discard the idea. Beginning with a unit value, they should assign that to the core.

Krishna established that whatever there is in a tiny, large, thick or thin object, each part is mixed with the material nature and the personality.

यस् तु यस्यादिर् अन्तश् च
स वै मध्यं च तस्य सन् ।
विकारो व्यवहारार्थो
यथा तैजस-पार्थिवाः ॥१९.१७॥

yas tu yasyādir antaś ca
sa vai madhyaṁ ca tasya san
vikāro vyavahārārtho
yathā taijasa-pārthivāḥ (19.17)

yas = yah — whatever; tu — but; yasyādir = yasya — of which + ādiḥ — beginning; antaś = antaḥ — end; ca — and; sa = sah — that; vai — indeed; madhyam — middle state; ca — as well as; tasya — concerning that; san — reality of the thing; vikāro = vikāraḥ — changed form; vyavahārārtho = vyavahāra – that which is practical, customary + arthah — value; yathā — as; taijasa — that which is produced by ore, metallic objects; pārthivaḥ — that which is produced from clay, ceramic objects.

That which is present as the beginning and ending, and which is the same in the middle stage, alone is the reality of the thing. The

changed forms are a utility only as in the case of metallic or ceramic objects. (Uddhava Gītā 19.17)

Consideration:

In his analogy about the snake, the philosopher *Adi Shankara* give zero value to the rope which was mistaken as the reptile. Actually, the rope has value. The snake which was an idea only also had value. Everything has value. The rope is not a snake and yet as cording the rope is useful. The snake as a mobile creature has so much value and is so feared that if a rope is shaped like the snake, someone becomes alarmed. Value! Everything has value.

Elucidation:

Even though everything has value, each aspect or factor is not of the same worth. One aspect has central value, while another is peripheral. If one adds something of relative value to something of primal value, the prime factor still has importance as a reference. The added factor may or may not increase in value.

It is required that when inSearching, a yogi should use deduction to locate the essential factor(s). Whatever was present before a dependent development, and what was still there after the production and whatever will yet be in existence after the development is demolished, that is the core to which the additions adhered. That alone has prime value. Everything else which manifested was relative in worth.

यद् उपादाय पूर्वस् तु
भावो विकुरुते ऽपरम् ।
आदिर् अन्तो यदा यस्य
तत् सत्यम् अभिधीयते ॥१९.१८॥

yad upādāya pūrvas tu
bhāvo vikurute 'param
ādir anto yadā yasya
tat satyam abhidhīyate (19.18)

yad = yat — that which; upādāya — obvious cause, raw material; pūrvas = pūrvaḥ — previous cause, primal element; tu — but; bhāvo = bhāvaḥ — object; vikurute — created thing occurring due to changes made in an original; 'param = aparam — the effect or changed appearance of an original element; ādir = ādih — beginning; anto = antaḥ — ending; yadā — when; yasya — of which; tat — that cause; satyam — real; abhidhīyate — is identified.

That which is the raw material, which is the primal element, but which produces an object, is the real thing. That cause is identified

as real which is there in the beginning and end of an object, which survived the changes. (Uddhava Gītā 19.18)

Consideration:

Even if it is unseen, unknown or untraceable, a cause is still the real factor. Anything produced by a cause where the cause remains as it was, is the reference for the subsequent productions.

The productions have value in as much as they are qualified on the existence of the enduring cause. The absence of a primal element is no reason to deny its production value. The value is present as the manifested form(s), because as a production, its worth is given according to its source, even if that source is invisible.

Elucidation:

The matter which we find to be tangible as solid materials, liquids, combustives, gases and rarified spaces has temporary duration but the cause of this, the underlying material is perpetual and primal. Though unseen and rated as formless and lacking solidification, still it is primal and real, nevertheless.

प्रकृतिर् यस्योपादानम्
आधारः पुरुषः परः ।
सतो ऽभिव्यञ्जकः कालो
ब्रह्म तत् त्रितयं त्व् अहम् ॥१९.१९॥

prakṛtir yasyopādānam
ādhāraḥ puruṣaḥ paraḥ
sato 'bhivyañjakaḥ kālo
brahma tat tritayaṁ tv aham
(19.19)

prakṛtir = prakṛtiḥ — primal material nature; yasyopādānam = yasya — of which, of this world + upādānam — the substance used, raw material; ādhāraḥ — the person who sustains; puruṣaḥ — person; paraḥ — supreme; sato = satah — of what is real; 'bhivyañjakaḥ = abhivyañjakah — that which causes a manifestation; kālo = kālah — time; brahma — spiritual reality; tat — that specifically; tritayam — the three aspects; tv = tu — but; aham — I am.

Primal Material Nature, which is the raw material of this world, the Supreme Person Who is the one who sustains it, Time which causes the manifestations, and which is real, these three aspects are the spiritual reality. But I am all of this. (Uddhava Gītā 19.19)

Consideration:

Primal Material Nature is an environmental concern which is a habitat which is saturated with influences. It is ever in relationship with the Supreme Person. It is always in his proximity. His power is reflected in and saturated through it. When it is activated as an environment for living species, time is observed in it. Time is ever-present but the mechanics of it, shows when the Supreme Person activates it.

Elucidation:

In one respect the Supreme Lord is in contrast to the primal material nature and its spread of manifestation but from a causal plane, the God is identical to it. In mathematical terms, the Supreme Lord equals the primal material nature, the God himself and the time factor. He is spread through this creation in every dimension and energy. From another perspective, he is not connected to it.

सर्गः प्रवर्तते तावत्
पौर्वापर्येण नित्यशः ।
महान् गुण-विसर्गार्थः
स्थित्य्-अन्तो यावद् ईक्षणम्
॥१९.२०॥

sargaḥ pravartate tāvat
paurvāparyeṇa nityaśaḥ
mahān guṇa-visargārthaḥ
sthity-anto yāvad īkṣaṇam (19.20)

sargaḥ — mundane creation; pravartate — persists; tāvat — so long as; paurvāparyeṇa = paurva –causes + aparyeṇa — through the effects; nityaśaḥ — continuation; mahān — vast, bountiful; guṇa – influences of material nature; visargārthaḥ = visarga — the created object in the mundane creation + arthah — for the purpose; sthity = sthiti – manifested existence; anto = antah — end; yāvad = yāvat — till; īkṣaṇam — glance, mystic interest, developing interest.

The mundane creation persists as long as there is a continuation through effects and causes. The vast world, which is for the purpose of producing created mundane objects, exists till the end of this manifested existence, which is reliant on the developing interest. (Uddhava Gītā 19.20)

Consideration:

There is never a shortage of developing interest but when the creation fizzes, the developing interest disappears as a fire does when there is no fuel. So long as there are personSelves with a sense of identity, there will be developing interest. When the sense of identity is no more, the selves will be deactivated.

Their faces which are turned to this creation, will turn away from it. Then this creation will be as if it never existed.

Elucidation:

The running-start for this creation is the cause which produces an effect, which in turn becomes a cause for a sub-effect. Eventually however, this chain of events reaches its end. Then the original cause ceases expression. It sends no motivation forward.

It is then that the personSelf loses interest in the productions. It turns to view the original cause, which is imperceptible.

विराण् मयासाद्यमानो
लोक-कल्प-विकल्पकः ।
पञ्चत्वाय विशेषाय
कल्पते भुवनैः सह ॥१९.२१॥

virāṇ mayāsādyamāno
loka-kalpa-vikalpakaḥ
pañcatvāya viśeṣāya
kalpate bhuvanaiḥ saha (19.21)

virān = virāt — contained universe; mayāsādyamāno = mayāsādyamānh = mayā — by me + āsādyamānaḥ — held in check (Sanskrit root words: asad – to attack; asedhah – are arrested, hold in custody; asadanam – attacking); loka — world; kalpa — comprising creative duration; vikalpakah — phase of dissolution; pañcatvāya — of the five material elements; viśeṣāya — types; kalpate — is brought to the stage; bhuvanaiḥ — with the planetary zones; saha — along with.

As held in check by Me, the contained universe which comprise the creative durations and phases of dissolution of the world, is brought along with its planetary zones, to the stage of becoming merely the five types of material elements. (Uddhava Gītā 19.21)

Consideration:

Over time, at the end of its potential duration, this situation reverts into origins, one by one, until this is no more a displayed creation. At the time, its ultimate form will continue to exist but with no development. It will be as if it was non-existent.

There is an ingredient which comes from the Supreme Lord and which if he withdraws causes rapid retrogression. That is the time element, the energy for the duration.

Elucidation:

At first, when the interest of the supreme being is disabled, the display of this situation, reverts. Even the dissolving and dismantling phases cease. Hence, contrary to what these did before, they no longer trigger new productions. The five types of material elements no longer interact. Having lost reactive impulses, each remains silent.

अन्ने प्रलीयते मर्त्यम्
अन्नं धानासु लीयते ।
धाना भूमौ प्रलीयन्ते
भूमिर् गन्धे प्रलीयते ॥१९.२२॥

anne pralīyate martyam
annaṁ dhānāsu līyate
dhānā bhūmau pralīyante
bhūmir gandhe pralīyate (19.22)

anne — in food; pralīyate — is converted; martyam — the short-term bodily existence; annam — food; dhānāsu — in the seeds; līyate — is converted; dhānā = dhānāḥ — seeds; bhūmau — in the soil; pralīyante — are turned into; bhūmir = bhūmiḥ — the soil; gandhe — into gas; pralīyate — is turned into.

The short-term bodily existence is converted into food. The food is converted into seeds. The seeds are turned into soil which is turned into gas. (Uddhava Gītā 19.22)

Consideration:

We should accept that sooner or later, this display of physical reality will be no more. Even if one were to live for five hundred years, even so, the body one identifies as, will be terminated. The access it affords one will cease.

If the world dissolves and retrogresses into its invisible source, or if the body one identifies as becomes a non-living form, one will have to face a disconnection with what is taken for granted as an environment for living.

Elucidation:

In the break-down of this situation, the body will deteriorate. It will become food for vegetation. That in turn will produce seed, which will convert into soil if it is not permitted to grow. That soil will ultimately be converted into gas.

The retrogression occurs during the life of the creation, but it does not reach a terminal state until the time when the Supreme Lord withdraws his interest.

अप्सु प्रलीयते गन्ध
आपश् च स्व-गुणे रसे ।
लीयते ज्योतिषि रसो
ज्योती रूपे प्रलीयते ॥१९.२३॥

apsu pralīyate gandha
āpaś ca sva-guṇe rase
līyate jyotiṣi raso
jyotī rūpe pralīyate (19.23)

apsu — in liquid; pralīyate — is converted; gandha — odor, gas; āpaś = āpaḥ — liquid; ca — and; sva-guṇe — its own characteristic; rase — in flavor; līyate — is converted; jyotiṣi — in fire; raso = rasaḥ — flavor; jyotī = jyotiḥ — fire; rūpe — in shape; pralīyate — turns into.

Gas is converted into liquid. Liquid is turned into its own characteristic flavor, which is converted into fire, which turns into shape. (Uddhava Gītā 19.23)

Consideration:

Heating a liquid will eventually cause it to evaporate. It assumes a gaseous state. That in turn will revert to being a liquid again. This converts into flavor, which as subtle gas is converted into a combustible gas. When that gas ignites a shape is assumed.

Elucidation:

In as much that whatever occurs does so on the chalkboard of time, whatever is the conclusion terminates under the schedule of time. The unfolding of this creation occurs within the medium and under the supervision of time. The Supreme Person is the personal agency which supervises time's roar.

रूपं वायौ स च स्पर्शे
लीयते सो ऽपि चाम्बरे ।
अम्बरं शब्द-तन्-मात्र
इन्द्रियाणि स्व-योनिषु ॥१९.२४॥

rūpaṁ vāyau sa ca sparśe
līyate so 'pi cāmbare
ambaraṁ śabda-tan-mātra
indriyāṇi sva-yoniṣu (19.24)

rūpam — shape; vāyau — into air; sa = sah — it; ca — and; sparśe — in contact; līyate — turns into; so = sah — it; 'pi = api — also; cāmbare = ca — and + ambare — in space; ambaram — space; śabda — sound; tan-mātra = tan-mātre — in its subtle aspect; indriyāni — sensual energies; sva-yoniṣu — their own sources.

Shape is converted into air, which turns into contact, which converts into space. This space is converted into the subtle aspect of sound. The sensual energies revert to their own sources. (Uddhava Gītā 19.24)

Consideration:

Each sensual energy which includes sub-parts and parts of sub-parts, unfolding in an orderly manner, either with haste or in slow motion. When the time essence is exhausted, the scene is retracted such that one sensual energy or some other, folds to itself and to its source. Thus, ending the display.

Elucidation:

In deep meditation, a yogi may see how the sensual energies revert to their sources. From that he/she may perceive how the creation spread from the origins in the primal mundane energy which was stimulated by the presence and interest of the Supreme Lord. Personality is involved and so is environment.

The limited selves are objectively aware for a limited time only. The Supreme Person is fully aware for all time. This causes a limited self to be unaware of much of the creative phases.

Visible air is smoke. When rarefied that becomes invisible air, which is experienced through contact. It shares or fills space. As space it is realized when it transmits sound. Each sense and corresponding sense object may revert to its source and be as if it is nothing.

योनिर् वैकारिके सौम्य
लीयते मनसीश्वरे ।
शब्दो भूतादिम् अप्येति
भूतादिर् महति प्रभुः ॥१९.२५॥

yonir vaikārike saumya
līyate manasīśvare
śabdo bhūtādim apyeti
bhūtādir mahati prabhuḥ (19.25)

yonir = yoniḥ — the sensual sources; vaikārike — in the perceptive assertive sense; saumya — my friend; līyate — is converted; manasīśvare = manasi — in the mind + īśvare — in the regulator; śabdo = śabdaḥ — sound; bhūtādim = bhuta – mundane sensation + ādim — to the first; apyeti — reverted; bhūtādir = bhūtādiḥ = bhuta – mundane sensitivity + ādiḥ — the first; mahati — in the Primal Mundane Potency; prabhuḥ — director.

Into the perceptive assertive sense, the sensual sources are reverted as these enter into their regulator, the mind. Sound is reverted into the first mundane sensitivity. That is reverted into the directive primal mundane potency. (Uddhava Gītā 19.25)

Consideration:

The senses we currently use were produced not from the coreSelf but rather from the sense of identity which adhere to the coreSelf, and which the self's primary adjunct.

Because the fusion of the sense of identity to the core, is such a complete bond, the core feels that whatever the identity sense does, is done by the core. That however is not a fact. It is the interest of the core which is the one sense of the core in this situation. Any other sense develops in and by an adjunct with the interest of the self as the innermost pulse for the operation of that other sense.

Elucidation:

The senses are powered mostly by the kundalini lifeForce, but the blueprint for the manufacturing of any sense comes from the sense of identity initially. Within the mind as the head of the subtle body, and within the psyche as the entire subtle form, the sense of identity, the analytical function, the kundalini and the memories reside. A skip above them in frequency is the coreSelf which is usually housed in the head of the subtle body, where it operates its interest through the sense of identity and the analytical function, the intellect.

A yogi must research this in meditation. That is the self-duty. The folding back into origins happens when this cosmic situation is disempowered but a yogi can have a view of it in deep meditation. The subject of this research is to know what is the best possible environment for a personSelf.

As the senses fold in, a coreSelf is left with the perceptive assertive sense, which is the highest operation level of the sense of identity. In that condition, the yogi may perceive general cosmic sound and that may revert into the first mundane sensitivity, which could revert into the directive primal mundane potency. Here the yogi arrives at an existential place which on one hand is interesting, and which on the other is blank and empty. What should he/she do there?

Wait! Wait! Wait! for divine access through a portal which may open for transit.

स लीयते महान् स्वेषु
गुणेसु गुण-वत्तमः ।
ते ऽव्यक्ते सम्प्रलीयन्ते
तत् काले लीयते ऽव्यये ॥१९.२६॥

sa līyate mahān sveṣu
guṇesu guṇa-vattamaḥ
te 'vyakte sampralīyante
tat kāle līyate 'vyaye (19.26)

sa = sah — that; līyate — reverted; mahān — primal mundane potency; sveṣu — in its own; guṇeṣu — in the mundane potencies; guṇa – characteristic; vattamaḥ — endowed with the best; te — these; 'vyakte = avyakte — in the unmanifested mundane energy; sampralīyante — are reverted; tat — that, which; kāle — in the time energy; līyate — reverts; 'vyaye = avyaye — in the unchangeable energy.

That total mundane potency reverts into its own best characteristic, which in turn, reverts into the mundane influence, which reverts into the unmanifested mundane potency, which reverts into the time energy, which converts into the unchangeable energy. (Uddhava Gītā 19.26)

Consideration:

The remnant of what is left of this creation when it subsides, is an abstract energy which only the supreme being can discern. This means that the evidence about what happens cannot be divined by a limited self. Only the testimony of the Supreme Lord can give some idea about the collapse at the end of time. Then the arguments for or against the subsistence of this creation, end for all limited beings with limited sense perception.

In so far as one can perceive, that is how much one can know directly. Otherwise, one is left with no sensual information and with confidence or doubts about Krishna's information.

Elucidation:

When this cosmos regresses, it reverts into its own best characteristic which is the last foothold of a mystic yogi. That state is super-abstract. It is imperceptible and invisible except to the supreme being. But even that state reverts into just being an influence which lingers. That in turn reverts into a potency, which is absorbed into the absolute form of the time energy. This reverts into the unchangeable energy which is the last foothold.

A yogi can experience these states if the objective portion of his self is supported and boosted by the Supreme Lord, who may allow that for the yogi's education about how this cosmos digresses eventually.

कालो माया-मये जीवे
जीव आत्मनि मय्य् अजे ।
आत्मा केवल आत्म-स्थो
विकल्पापाय-लक्षणः ॥१९.२७॥

kālo māyā-maye jīve
jīva ātmani mayy aje
ātmā kevala ātma-stho
vikalpāpāya-lakṣaṇaḥ (19.27)

kālo = kālaḥ — time energy; māyā – bewildering mundane potency; maye — in he who motivates potency; jīve — in the specific spirit; jīva — specific spirit; ātmani — in that spirit, in itself; mayy = mayi — in me; aje — in the birthless person; ātmā — self, itself; kevala = kevalaḥ — one who is not influenced by sensing mechanisms; ātma-stho = ātma-sthaḥ — situated in itself; vikalpāpāya = vikalpa — varied creation; apāya — dissolution; lakṣaṇaḥ — one who is indicated.

Time reverts into the Specific Spirit, who motivates the bewildering potency. That Specific Spirit into his own Self. And He into Me, the birthless person. That Specific Spirit who is not influenced by sensing mechanisms and is self-situated, is the one who is indicated by the varied creation and its dissolution. (Uddhava Gītā 19.27)

Consideration:

Time is a split force in its origins, where it happens because of a potency in the primal mundane energy and due to the glance interest of the Supreme Lord. The situation is such that the removal of the interest of the God, even a slight withdrawal of his concern, causes colossal collapse. If he expresses even the slightest concern, everything is revived, however. The engine of this is realized by a limited being as time emergence and time restraint.

Elucidation:

The GodPerson is multi-existing with one supreme being here and another there, with no clash of wills. One is sequenced to another up or down with each being a Personality of Godhead, and the foremost being the Supreme Personality of Godhead

After this seemingly infinite manifestation is reverted into the time energy, there is a communication between it and the specific self who is the creatorGod. Then time is frozen or is swallowed by the creatorGod. Once swallowed, the GodPerson is recalled to a parallel divinity, who is regarded as the birthless person, the one with no origin because of his foothold outside the contact with the Primal Mundane Energy in any of its phases. Great mystic yogis consider this birthless person to be the Supreme Personality of Godhead, the personInfinite, the Krishna.

एवम् अन्वीक्षमाणस्य
कथं वैकल्पिको भ्रमः ।
मनसो हृदि तिष्ठेत
व्योम्नीवार्कोदये तमः ॥१९.२८॥

evam anvīkṣamāṇasya
kathaṁ vaikalpiko bhramaḥ
manaso hṛdi tiṣṭheta
vyomnīvārkodaye tamaḥ (19.28)

evam — in this way; anvīkṣamānasya — of one who mystically researches the matter; katham — how; vaikalpiko = vaikalpikah — the mundane diversity; bhramaḥ — misconception; manaso = manasaḥ — from the mind; hṛdi — in the center of feelings; tiṣṭheta — can stay; vyomnīvārkodaye = vyomni — in the sky + iva — just as + arka — sun + udaye — of the rising; tamah — darkness.

How can the misconception which is mundane diversity come from the mind or remain in the seat of a person's feelings if he mystically researches the matter in this way, just as darkness would not remain at the rising of the sun? (Uddhava Gītā 19.28)

Consideration:

The realization by mystic penetration is that this creation is a composite. However, each part should be traced as to its origin. The source of this is not seen through physical sense perception, nor even with psychic sense perception of the subtle body.

In researching the origin of this creation, a yogi finally gets to the understanding that this is a combination of personSubstance and environment. The final value is the Supreme Lord and the Primal Material Nature. Each other aspect is relative and has value according to its source.

Elucidation:

The misconception about this diversity, is the instance of accepting the physical and psychic objects as independent causeless real things. In normal sense perception one has no choice but to view the world in that incorrect way. When one cannot realize the sources of the objects, one should remember this *Sāṁkhya* information and use it to adjust the opinions.

एष साङ्‌ख्य-विधिः प्रोक्तः
सशय-ग्रन्थि-भेदनः ।
प्रतिलोमानुलोमाभ्यां
परावर-दृश मया ॥१९.२९॥

eṣa sāṅkhya-vidhiḥ proktaḥ
saṁśaya-granthi-bhedanaḥ
pratilomānulomābhyāṁ
parāvara-dṛśa mayā (19.29)

eṣa = eṣaḥ — this; sāṅkhya – Saṅkhya mystic analysis; vidhiḥ — method; proktaḥ — method described; saṁśaya — doubt; granthi — tangle; bhedanaḥ — that which dismantles; pratilomānulomābhyāṁ = pratiloma – regression + anulomābhyām — and in progression; parāvara = para — supreme + avara — relative; dṛśā — one who perceives; mayā — by me.

This method of Sāṁkhya mystic analysis which dismantles the tangle of doubt, was described by Me, the one who perceives it, in terms of its regression and progression. (Uddhava Gītā 19.29)

Consideration:

The reliance is on Krishna, the Supreme Lord. A limited being should subsidize his lack of sense perception with the information from Krishna.

Elucidation:

As the Supreme Personality, Krishna has unlimited sense perception. His information either in the form of a revelation or as mere information should be used to offset the ignorance.

Back Cover:

It is a wonder that in the annals of philosophy, there were ideas which entertain the elimination of value for personality. How is it that it took personality to strive and arrive at a conclusion that personality itself may be or just is, illusory?

When the objective self kicks the self into oblivion, that action is brought to question because the subjective part of the self may survive that injury, saving us a fatality.

This thesis summarized the self as having two phases, an objective and a subjective being, with the subjective feature being perpetual, such that the objective part does not have the right to define what the subjective part is. The objective self which is uncertain of itself cannot abolish the subjective consciousness. The decommissioning of the objective part in no way tells the condition of the subjective feature.

Krishna *Saṁkhyā* is concerned with *purusha* or corePerson and with environments which either reinforce or diminish but do not eliminate the person. The traditional self is a composite of a corePerson with psychic adjuncts. These adjuncts go through alteration and may even be disconnected from the core. But the core is perpetual. It is not abolished by anyone, not even by itself or by the GodSelf.

The *Upanishads* stress *brahman* as the ultimate energy, with *atma* as a mere fragment of *brahman* which incidentally was projected with an illusory idea of self. This view is left aside by Krishna in his discussion with Uddhava on the Samkhya philosophy. *Bhagavad Gita* is based on that *Saṁkhyā*, more so than it is on the *Upanishads*. This book shows that way.

Index

A

abscond, 164
absolute version, 134
accountability, 125
action,
  explained, 183
  Lord, 46
  performed, 221
additions, 217, 220
additives to self, 136
Adi Shankara, 273
adjunct,
  border, 86
  govern, 207
  primary, 181
  war, 160
Advaita Vedanta, 7, 97, 105, 127
advanced devotee, 152
affected spirit, 209
Age of Easy Realization, 255
agent, 229
ahamkara, 151
all-format, 113
Almighty God, 47
anchor, 181
Angira, 107
ant, 265
Anu Gita, 178
argument, 7
Arjuna, 25, 145
arm of self, 44
armature, 186
arrogance, 241
Arthur Beverford, 103
Ashvattha tree, 197
assertive potency, 263
assertive power, 261
association, 242
atma,
  brahman unity, 141
  definition, 97
  neutral speck, 136
  sand, 25
  Upanishads, 88
Atri, 107
attendance to teacher, 161
awareness
  aspect, 257
  limited, 32
  objectivity, 258
axisSupreme, 208

B

beginning of time, 172
beginningless, 165
Beverford, 103
bhakti cult,149
Bhrigu, 106
Bhur, 266
Bhuva, 266
blank locations, 264
blank self, 11
blank state, 70
blankness, 200
blink, 16
blinking witness, 14,15
body, defined, 196
boundary, 265
Brahma,
  appearance, 265
  junction, 104
  sub-deity, 94
brahman,
  atma, 17, 18
  atma unified, 141
  atma union, 88
  conclusion, 19
  definition, 97

brahman, continued,
sand, 25
surrounding, 136
ultimate, 7
breath infusion, 161

C

cannibals, 213
cause of cause of, 107
celibate boys, 107
central energy, 210
central power supply, 205
central psyche, 250
central sensor, 146
ceramic object, 273
chalkboard, 278
chanting, 82, 152, 237, 250
character, 123
city, nine entrances, 44
clock of time, 259
clockwork, 250
club, 124
coat of paint, 71
collection of elements, 215
collective origin, 142
collective person, 260
composite, 261
confidence, energy, 213
consciousness, 157
conscripted, 164
consequence, Lord, 46
consequences, 216, 219
continuous happiness, 70
control of objectivity, 208
conventional person, 44, 261
conviction, 157
core value, 272
core / coreSelf
absolute? 45
additions, 28, 217
adjuncts control, 209
affected, 184
common factor, 49
different, 186
differentiation, 50
core / coreSelf continued,
environment, 21
essential, 266
feedback, 181
imperceptible, 207
partless, 171
perception, 177
perpetual, 25
persist, 243
phases, 96
radiant, 19
reliance, 197
retraction, 20
scarred, 21
subjective, 21, 50
transcended, 169
use nature, 183
war, 160
weakness, 57
corePerson, 9
cosmic sense of identity, 263
cosmic water, 265
craving, 241
creation, 190
creatorGod, 94
criminal yogis, 95
crowds, 164
crown, 124
cult teachers, 179
cultural obligations, 248
cultural tags, 53
current, 186

D

dangers, 162
day, 94
death,
birth, 163
confrontation, 54
process, 176
reincarnation, 142
transcended, 178
deceit, 160

deity/deityPerson,
prevailing, 181
relationship, 99, 142
violence, 9
worship, 237
demarcation, 134
departed spirits, 213
dependent origination, 107
depressing energy, 196
desire, 156, 160
destiny, 229
detachment, 162-163
developing interest, 275
devotee, advanced, 152
devotion,
necessary,163
supreme, 243
transit, 270
yoga application, 269
devotional cult teachers, 179
devotional movement, 149
dharana, 162
dhyana, 162
diet increase, 238
differences with Krishna, 144
disciplinary power, 126
discus, 124
disease, 162
dislike for crowds, 164
dispassion, 240
dissolution, 190
divine child, 96
donations, 250
dream format, 28
duplicates, Krishna, 111

E

easy methods, 249
Easy Realization, 255
eating, 237-238
eating sanctified food, 250
education, 169
egg-shaped enclosure, 264
electricity, 173
end of research, 259
enemy, self, 54
enjoyment, additions, 220
enterprise, 256
enthusiasm, 195
environment,
deity regulated, 9
essential, 180
medium, 8
necessary, 21
eternal abode, 244
eternal life, 165
even-minded, 163
events, adjustment, 226
excitement, 195
existential support, 109
experience, marking, 21
experiencer, 146, 230
expertise, 195
exploitation, 181
Extensive Primal Existence, 256

F

faceless someone, 11
factors, five, 229
family life, 247
father, 191
father of fathers, 126
feedback, 102
final value, 283
five factors, 229
friend, self, 54
function of person, 140

G

garlands, 118
garments, 118
Gherwal, 103
ghosts, 213
glory of Krishna, 126
God power, 271
God, antiseptic, 47
God, defined, 21
Godhead status, 48
GodPerson, 282
governor, 135
grain of sand, 105

H

habitat, 170
happiness, 195
Hari, 116
hatred, 156
healing humility, 144
hear from others, 178
hereafter encounter, 140
holy names, 241, 250
honor no person, 213
humility, 121, 144

I

icon, 179
ignorance, 165
impulsive energy, 195
inattentiveness, 196
incarnation of Godhead, 248
indifference, 162
individual self, 204
individuality, declared? 98
inertia, 261
infant body, 164
infinity, 21
influences, 157, 194, 268
information, Supreme Spirit, 164
inherent nature, 46
initiative faculty, 162
initiative, 151, 162
injury to self, 215
inSearching, 273
insensibility, 196
instruments, 229
intellect,
  control, 154
  defined, 152
  location, 67
  silenced, 7174
  war, 160
interest, 275
interest in nothing, 200
interest, recalled, 12
interestEnergy, 200
invisible existence, 98
iSelf, 17, 205
isolation, 56, 238

J

Jana, 269
jiva, 88
jivaloka, 204
judge, 134
junction in consciousness, 104

K

Kacha, 142
Kaitabha, 18, 96
knower of Vedas, 197
knowledge, 165
Kratu, 107
Krishna,
  apparition to writer, 25
  body, 113
  complex root, 109
  differences with, 144
  duplicates, 111
  experiencer, 147
  father, 191
  interest, 89
  meditation, 140
  multiple selves, 111
  originator, 270
  paramatma, 111
  time, 270
  trigger, 89
  unaffected, 215
  war, 160
  womb, 191
  worship, 140
  yoga, 149
Krishna Consciousness, 82, 149, 237

L

laziness, 196
lifeform, sorting, 50
limit, 134
limit of containment, 116
limited person, 260
limited self, 186, 232
limiter, 135
location, 229, 264, 272

Lord of all beings, 250
lotus, cosmic, 265
lures, 162

M

Madhu, 18, 96
magnets, 186
Mahabharata, 96
mahapurusha, 25, 147
Mahar, 269
mahat brahma, 191
mantra, 152
map, 164
Marici, 107
Markandeya, 96, 259
Markandeya Samasya, 103
markers, 66, 214
markings, 21
master, 205
material nature, beginningless, 171
matter, 263
maya, 88
median influence, 194
meditation,
    details, 59
    effective, 83
    Krishna, 140
    necessary, 187, 241-242
    research, 213
    switch, 53
meditative perception, 177
memorabilia, 21
memory,
    eternal, 22
    marking, 21
    necessary, 187
metallic objects, 273
method of capture, 142
mind, meditation, 59
misconception, 254
mission, 238
mixture of experiencer, 180
moods, 157
moon light, 187
mother, 191
mother of mothers, 126
motivational force, 261
movements, 229
multiple selves, 111
multiplicity, 254

N

nature,
    mother, 191
    organism, 198
    primal, 274
    similar to Krishna, 190
night, 94
nine-gated city, 44
nirvana, 192
no self, 51, 272
non-attachment, 199
non-interference, 260
non-person energy, 137
non-violence, 160
nothingness, 20
nowhere places, 264
nutrition, violence, 160

O

object, mix. 271
objective awareness, 96, 258
objectivity, control, 208
objectivity, suspended, 18
oblations, 127
obligation, 140
observing self, 205
ointments, 118
old age, 162
one being, 232
one reality, 119
oneness, 21, 125, 127
opportunity, 216
origin, abstract, 200
origin, psychological, 108
origin of act, 183
origin of origins, 108

P

pain, 156
paint, 71

pantheon, 122
paradox, 166
param brahman, 18, 147
param purusha, 93
paramatma, 7, 111, 147, 232
parasitic relationship, 199
parent, 107
parentSource, 126
partner, 204
path of Krishna Consciousness, 239
patience, 160
perception, requirements, 8
perception-forming energy, 261
perfected beings, 267
perfumes, 118, 205
permission, 260
person,
  abolish, 205
  adorned, 126
  all-pervasive, 140
  beginningless, 171
  format, 166
  function, 140
  higher energy, 88
  illusion, 213, 261
  time, 23
  issue of, 219
  none, 272
  powerful one, 170
  psycho-biological machine, 205
  raw, 126
  substance, 271
  superior, 129
  tag, 86
  target, 217-218
  to supreme person, 201
  types, 13
  value, 189
personal energy, 54
personal initiative, 151
Personality of Godhead, 282
personality, absolute, 134
personality, banish, 212
personality, factor, 257
personCore, 258
personEnergy, 199
personFace, 10, 261
personForce, 180, 261
personhood, 192
personInfinite, 282
personQuality, 123
personSelf,
  details, 23
  discovery, 53
  itemized, 261
  origin, 191
  support, 7
  universal, 112, 270
  whole body, 156
personSource, 22, 96
personSubstance, 283
physio-biological complex, 196
pleasure, 156, 174
portals, 151, 216
possessiveness, 242
power to act, 192
prakriti, 88
prakriti, definition, 97
pranaVision, 263
pranayama, 161
pratyahar, 202
predator, 160
preLord, 23, 107
prePerson, 22
prevailing deity, 181
Primal Creative Cause, 103
Primal Existence, 256
Primal Material Nature, 274
primal value, 273
problem, 134
procrastinate, 262
productive enterprise, 256
property, 180
psychic electricity, 173
psychic limb, 261
psychic perception, 188
psychic person, 44
psychic self, 35
psychological origin, 108
psychological parent, 107

Pulaha, 107
Pulastya, 107
purification, 164
purity, 161
purusha,
- explained, 147
- minimized, 25
- samkhya, 88
- Upanishads, 88

Q,R

radiance of life, 53
radiant core, 19
raw material, 273
reality, 256
rebirth, magic, 38
recycling, 40
reference, 133, 181
reform, 124
regret, 224
relationship with deity, 99
relative value, 273
release method, 142
renunciate, 227
renunciation, 223
reproductive duty, 223
research, 259
residential situation, 98
residual instances, 216
retarded people, 213
retrogression, 277, 281
Rishi Singh Gherwal, 103
rishis, 254
root of everything, 129
rope, 88, 273
rotor, 250

S

samadhi, 162
Samkhya theory, 254
Sanandan, 107
Sanatana, 107
sanctified food, 237, 250
sand, 25, 105
Sanjaya, 119
saturation, influence, 129
Satya, 269
science of reality, 164
secluded place, 164
seed, 102
segregation, 211
self,
- abstract, 175
- additives, 136
- affected, 184
- body, 170
- deactivated, 275
- dependent, 83
- different, 186
- elevate, 54
- elimination, 192
- freedom, 105
- insignificant, 242
- limited 175
- none, 52
- partless, 171
- perception, 177
- persists, 141
- powerless, 105
- radiance, 50
- reliance, 197
- research, 9
- stable, 210
- to supreme self, 201
- types, 209

selfCondition, 190
self-produced one, 265
self-restraint, 161
semi-absolute selves, 111
sense of assertion, 262
sense of identity, 17, 181
sense of identity, cosmic, 263
senses, origin, 280
sentient machinery, 245
serve others, 163
service, 140
service to the Supreme, 178
Shankara, 273
shock experience, 119
Shukracharya, 142
skin, 45

sleep, 196
snake, 88, 273
somethingness, 20
sorcerers, 213
source of the source, 106
source of sourcePerson, 259
sourcePerson, 23
species, 245
specific spirit, 282
speck, atma, 136
speck sense of identity, 263
specter of death, 54
speech control, 239
spirit perceive spirit, 177
spirit, types, 209
spiritual personality, 171
spiritual sense perception, 200
stability, 161
stable self, 210
stories of Krishna, 72
straight forwardness, 161
struggle, meditation, 71
sub-God, 104
subjective consciousness, 21
subjective existence, 211
subjective reality, 261
subjective self, 12
subjective viewing, 20
sub-sources, 95
suffering, 162
suicide, 192
sun, heat, 187
supernatural body, 124
superPerson, 95, 259
supreme devotion, 243
Supreme Person, 211
Supreme Personality of Godhead, 282
supreme reality, 165
Supreme Self, 25
Supreme Spirit, 210
Svar, 266
symphony, 256
synthesis, 180

T

tag of person, 86
Tapa, 269
target, person, 217-218
teachers, 161, 221
terminal of events, 135
thesis, 164
think of Krishna, 247
thinking stops, 66
thoughts, involuntary, 57
time,
  activated, 275
  baffling, 270
  beginning, 172,
  chalkboard, 278
  element, 276
  emergence, 282
  restraint, 282
tooling, 207
traditional person, composite, 13, 19
transcendence viewing, 216
transit zones, 115
transit, spiritual place, 235
tree, 102, 197
tremors, 45
truth, demand, 12
tug-of-war, 218

U

unaffected self, 215
unaffected spirit, 209
undercoat, 71
undivided in the divided, 232
union, 125
unit, 260
unity, 234
universal form, 242
universe, 265
universe, Krishna's body, 113
unmanifest energy, 154
unselfish, 242

About the Author

Michael Beloved (Yogi *Madhvāchārya)* took his current body in 1951 in Guyana. In 1965, while living in Trinidad, he instinctively began doing yoga postures and tried to make sense of the supernatural side of life.

Later in 1970, in the Philippines, he approached a Martial Arts Master named Arthur Beverford. He explained to the teacher that he was seeking a yoga instructor. Mr. Beverford identified himself as an advanced disciple of Rishi Singh Gherwal, an Ashtanga Yoga master.

Beverford taught the traditional Ashtanga Yoga with stress on postures, attentive breathing and brow chakra centering meditation. In 1972, Michael entered the Denver Colorado Ashram of *kundalini* yoga Master Harbhajan Singh. There he took instruction in *bhastrika pranayama* and its application to yoga postures.

In 1979 Michael formally entered the disciplic succession of the Brahmā-Madhava-Gaudiya Sampradaya through *Swāmī* Kirtanananda, who was a prominent sannyasi disciple of the great Vaishnava authority *Swāmī* Bhaktivedanta Prabhupada, the exponent of devotion to Krishna.

However, yoga has a mystic side to it, thus Michael took training and teaching empowerment from several spiritual masters of different aspects of spiritual development. This is consistent with Krishna's advice to Arjuna in the *Bhagavad Gītā*:

Most of the instructions Michael received were given in the astral world. On that side of existence, his most prominent teachers were *Swāmī* Shivananda of Rishikesh, Yogiraj *Swāmī* Vishnudevananda, *Bābāji Mahasaya* - the master of the masters of *Kriyā* Yoga, Yogeshwarananda of Gangotri - the master of the masters of *Raja* Yoga (spiritual clarity), and Siddha *Swāmī* Nityananda, the Brahmā Yoga authority.

The course for kundalini yoga using *pranayama* breath infusion was detailed by Michael in the book *Kundalini Hatha Yoga Pradipika*.

Michael's preliminary books relating to meditation are *Meditation Pictorial, Meditation Expertise*, and *Meditation ~ Sense Faculty* (co-author). Every technique (*kriya*) mentioned was tested by him during *pranayama* breath infusion and *samyama* deep meditation practice.

This is a result of over forty years of meditation practice with astute subtle observations intending to share the methods and experiences. The information is published freely with no intention of forming an institution or hogtying anyone as a disciple.

It is a wonder that in the annals of philosophy, there were ideas which entertain the elimination of value for personality. How is it that it took personality, to strive and arrive at a conclusion that personality itself may be or just is, illusory?

When the objective self kicks the self into oblivion, that action is brought to question because the subjective part of the self may survive that injury, saving us a fatality.

This thesis summarized the self as having two phases, an objective and a subjective being, with the subjective feature being perpetual, such that the objective part does not have the right to define what the subjective part is. The objective self which is uncertain of itself cannot abolish the subjective consciousness. The decommissioning of the objective part in no way tells the condition of the subjective feature.

Krishna *Saṁkhyā* is concerned with *purusha* or corePerson and also with environments which either reinforce or diminish but not eliminate the person. The traditional self is a composite of a corePerson with psychic adjuncts. These adjuncts go through alteration and may even be disconnected from the core. But the core is perpetual. It is not abolished by anyone, not even by itself or by the GodSelf.

The *Upanishads* stress *brahman* as the ultimate energy, with *atma* as a mere fragment of *brahman* which incidentally was projected with an illusory idea of self. This view is left aside by Krishna in his discussion with Uddhava. *Bhagavad Gita* is based on that *Saṁkhyā*, more so than it is on the Upanishads. This book shows that way.

Publications

English Series

Bhagavad Gītā English
Anu Gītā English
Markandeya Samasya English
Yoga Sutras English
Hatha Yoga Pradipika English
Uddhava Gītā English

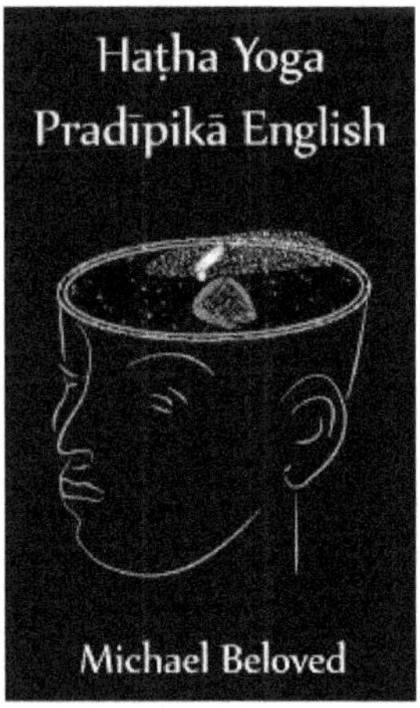

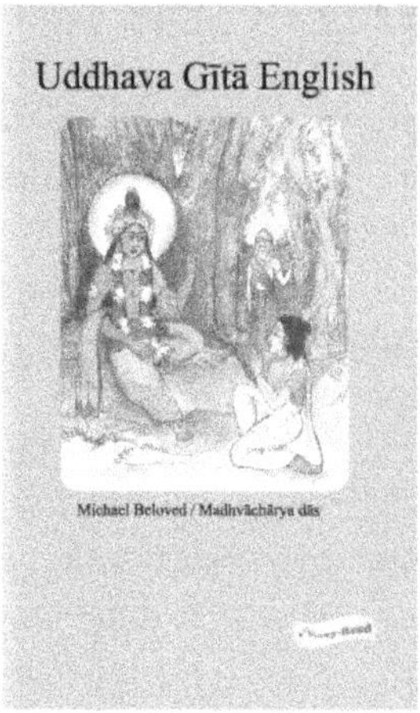

These are in 21st Century English, very precise and exacting. Many Sanskrit words which were considered untranslatable into a Western language are rendered in precise, expressive and modern English.

Three of these books are instructions from Krishna. **In *Bhagavad Gītā* English** and **Anu Gītā English**, the instructions were for Arjuna. In the **Uddhava Gītā English,** it was for Uddhava. *Bhagavad Gītā* and Anu Gītā are extracted from the *Mahabharata*. Uddhava Gītā was extracted from the 11th Canto of the Srimad Bhagavatam (Bhagavata Purana). One of these books, the **Markandeya Samasya English** is about Krishna, as described by Yogi Markandeya, who survived the cosmic collapse and reached a divine child in whose transcendental body, the collapsed world was existing.

Two of this series are the syllabus about yoga practice. The *Yoga Sutras* of Patañjali is elaboration about ashtanga yoga. Hatha Yoga Pradipika English, is the detailed information about *asana* postures, *pranayama* breath- infusion, energy compression, naad sound resonance and advanced meditation. The Sanskrit author is Swatmarama Mahayogin.

My suggestion is that you read ***Bhagavad Gītā* English**, the **Anu Gītā English, the Markandeya Samasya English,** the *Yoga Sutras* English, the Hatha Yoga Pradipika and lastly the **Uddhava Gītā English**, which is complicated and detailed.

For each of these books we have at least one commentary, which is published separately. Thus, one's particular interest can be researched further in the commentaries.

The smallest of these commentaries and perhaps the simplest is the one for the Anu *Gītā*. We published its commentary as the Anu Gītā Explained. The *Bhagavad Gītā* explanations were published in three distinct targeted commentaries. The first is *Bhagavad Gītā* Explained, which sheds lights on how people in the time of Krishna and Arjuna regarded the information and applied it. *Bhagavad Gītā* is an exposition of the application of yoga practice to cultural activities, which is known in the Sanskrit language as karma yoga.

Interestingly, *Bhagavad Gītā* was spoken on a battlefield just before one of the greatest battles in the ancient world. A warrior, Arjuna, lost his wits and had no idea that he could apply his training in yoga to political dealings. Krishna, his charioteer, lectured on the spur of the moment to give Arjuna the skill of using yoga proficiency in cultural dealings including how to deal with corrupt officials on a battlefield.

The second Gītā commentary is the Kriya Yoga *Bhagavad Gītā*. This clears the air about Krishna's information on the science of kriya yoga, showing that its techniques are clearly described for anyone who takes the time to read *Bhagavad Gītā*. Kriya yoga concerns the battlefield which is the psyche of the living being. The internal war and the mental and emotional forces which are hostile to self-realization are dealt with in the kriya yoga practice.

The third commentary is the Brahma Yoga *Bhagavad Gītā*. This shows what Krishna had to say outright and what he hinted about which concerns the brahma yoga practice, a mystic process for those who mastered kriya yoga.

There is one commentary for the **Markandeya Samasya English**. The title of that publication is Krishna Cosmic Body.

There are two commentaries to the *Yoga Sutras*. One is the Yoga Sutras of Patañjali and the other is the Meditation Expertise. These give detailed explanations of ashtanga Yoga.

The commentary of Hatha Yoga Pradipika is titled Kundalini Hatha Yoga Pradipika.

For the Uddhava *Gītā*, we published the Uddhava Gītā Explained. This is a large book and requires concentration and study for integration of the information. Of the books which deal with transcendental topics, my opinion is that the discourse between Krishna and Uddhava has the complete information about the realities in existence. This book is the one which removes massive existential ignorance.

Meditation Series

Meditation Pictorial
Meditation Expertise
CoreSelf Discovery
Meditation Sense Faculty

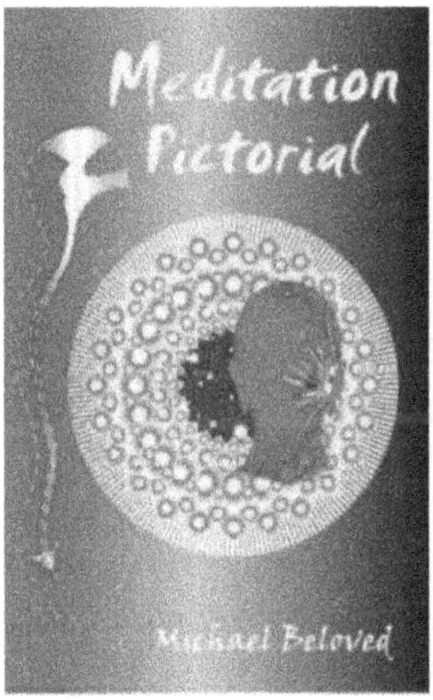

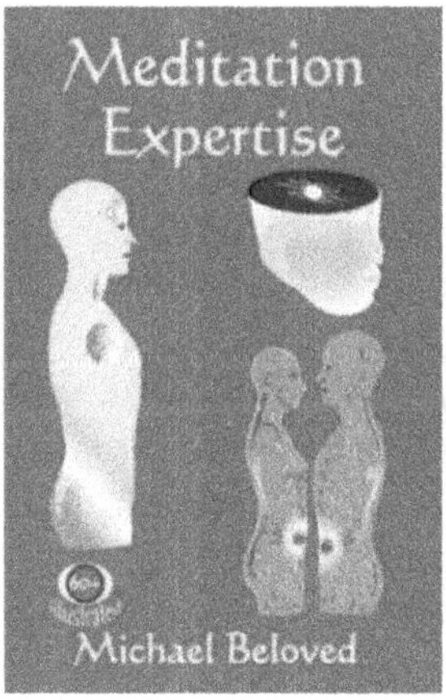

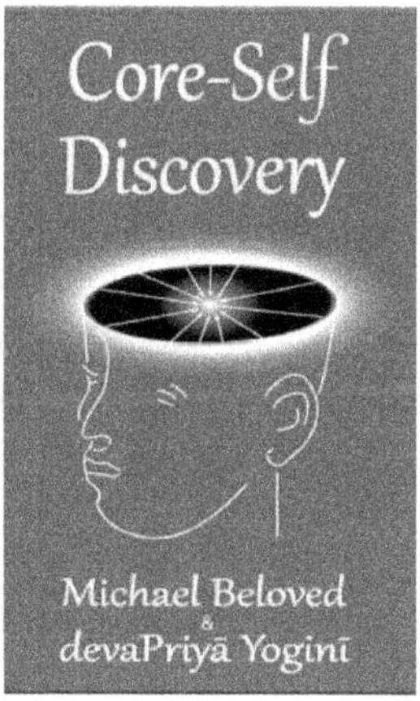

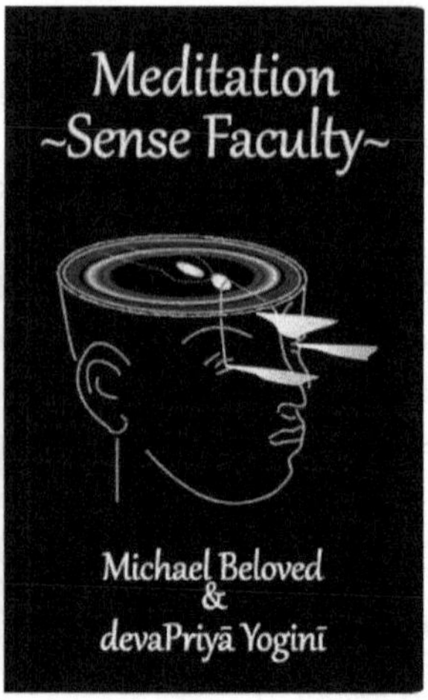

The specialty of these books is the mind diagrams which profusely illustrate what is written. This shows exactly what one has to do mentally to develop and then sustain a meditation practice.

In the **Meditation Pictorial**, one is shown how to develop psychic insight, a feature without which meditation is imagination and visualization, without any mystic experience per se.

In the **Meditation Expertise**, one is shown how to corral one's practice to bring it in line with the classic syllabus of yoga which Patañjali lays out as the ashtanga yoga eight-staged practice.

In **CoreSelf Discovery**, (co-authored with *devaPriya Yogini*) one is taken though the course of *pratyahar* sensual energy withdrawal which is the 5th stage of yoga in the Patañjali ashtanga eight-process complete system of yoga practice. These events lead to the discovery of a coreSelf which is surrounded by psychic organs in the head of the subtle body. This product has a DVD component.

Meditation ~ Sense Faculty (co-authored with *devaPriya Yogini*) is a detailed tutorial with profuse diagrams showing what actions to take in the subtle body to investigate the senses faculties. The meditator must first establish the location and function of the observing self. That self must be screened from the thoughts and ideas which usually hypnotize it.

These books are profusely illustrated with mind diagrams showing the components of psychic consciousness and the inner design of the subtle body.

Explained Series

Bhagavad Gītā Explained
Uddhava Gītā Explained
Anu Gītā Explained

The specialty of these books is that they are free of missionary intentions, cult tactics and philosophical distortion. Instead of using these books to add credence to a philosophy, meditation process, belief or plea for followers, I spread the information out so that a reader can look through this literature and freely take or leave anything as desired.

When Krishna stressed himself as God, I stated that. When Krishna laid no claims for supremacy, I showed that. The reader is left to form an independent opinion about the validity of the information and the credibility of Krishna.

There is a difference in the discourse with Arjuna in the *Bhagavad Gītā* and the one with Uddhava in the Uddhava *Gītā*. In fact, these two books may appear to contradict each other. In the *Bhagavad Gītā*, Krishna pressured Arjuna to complete social duties. In the Uddhava *Gītā*, Krishna insisted that Uddhava should abandon the same.

The Anu Gītā is not as popular as the *Bhagavad Gītā* but it is the conclusion of that text. Anu means what is to follow, what proceeds. In this discourse, an anxious Arjuna request that Krishna should repeat the *Bhagavad Gītā* and again show His supernatural and divine forms.

However, Krishna refuses to do so and chastises Arjuna for being a disappointment in forgetting what was revealed. Krishna then cited a celestial yogi, a near-perfected being, who explained the process of transmigration in vivid detail.

Commentaries

Yoga Sutras of Patañjali
Meditation Expertise
Krishna Cosmic Body
Anu Gītā Explained
Bhagavad Gītā Explained
Kriya Yoga Bhagavad Gītā
Brahma Yoga Bhagavad Gītā
Uddhava Gītā Explained
Kundalini Hatha Yoga Pradipika

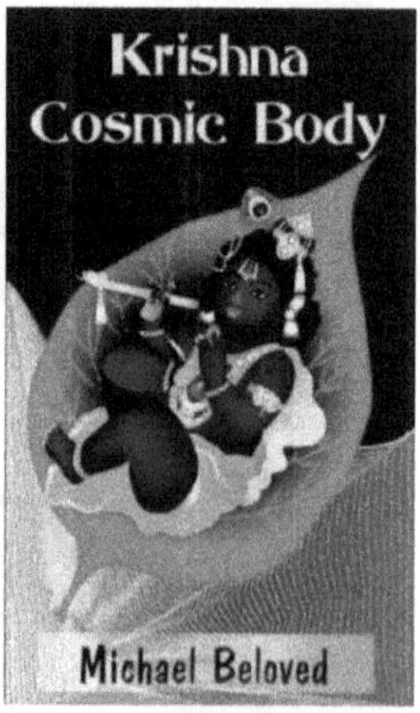

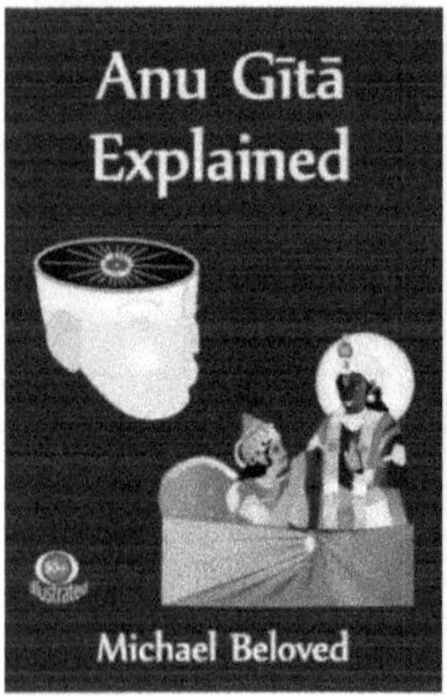

***Yoga Sutras* of Patañjali is** the globally acclaimed textbook of yoga. This has detailed expositions of yoga techniques. Many kriya techniques are vividly described in the commentary.

Meditation Expertise is an analysis and application of the *Yoga Sutras*. This book is loaded with illustrations and has detailed explanations of secretive advanced meditation techniques which are called kriyas in the Sanskrit language.

Krishna Cosmic Body is a narrative commentary on the *Markandeya Samasya* portion of the Aranyaka Parva of the *Mahabharata*. This is the detailed description of the dissolution of the world, as experienced by the great yogin Markandeya who transcended the cosmic deity, Brahma, and reached Brahma's source who is the divine infant, Krishna.

Anu Gītā Explained is a detailed explanation of how we endure many material bodies in the course of transmigrating through various life-forms. This is a discourse between Krishna and Arjuna. Arjuna requested of Krishna a display of the Universal Form and a repeat narration of the *Bhagavad Gītā* but Krishna declined and explained what a siddha perfected being told the Yadu family about the sequence of existences one endures and the systematic flow of those lives at the convenience of material nature.

***Bhagavad Gītā* Explained** shows what was said in the Gītā without religious overtones and sectarian biases.

Kriya Yoga *Bhagavad Gītā* shows the instructions for those who are doing kriya yoga.

Brahma Yoga *Bhagavad Gītā* shows the instructions for those who are doing brahma yoga.

Uddhava Gītā Explained shows the instructions to Uddhava which are more advanced than the ones given to Arjuna.

Bhagavad Gītā is an instruction for applying the expertise of yoga in the cultural field. This is why the process taught to Arjuna is called karma yoga which means karma + yoga or cultural activities done with yogic insight.

Uddhava Gītā is an instruction for apply the expertise of yoga to attaining spiritual status. This is why it explains jnana yoga and *bhakti* yoga in detail. Jnana yoga is using mystic skill for knowing the spiritual part of existence. *Bhakti* yoga is for developing affectionate relationships with divine beings.

Karma yoga is for negotiating the social concerns in the material world. It is inferior to *bhakti* yoga which concerns negotiating the social concerns in the spiritual world.

This world has a social environment. The spiritual world has one too.

Currently, Uddhava Gītā is the most advanced and informative spiritual book on the planet. There is nothing anywhere which is superior to it or which goes into so much detail as it. It verified that historically Krishna is the most advanced human being to ever have left literary instructions on this planet. Even Patañjali *Yoga Sutras* which I translated and gave an application for in my book, **Meditation Expertise**, does not go as far as the Uddhava *Gītā*.

Some of the information of these two books is identical but while the *Yoga Sutras* are concerned with the personal spiritual emancipation (kaivalyam) of the individual spirits, the Uddhava Gītā explains that and also explains the situations in the spiritual universes.

Bhagavad Gītā is from the *Mahabharata* which is the history of the Pandavas. Arjuna, the student of the *Gītā*, is one of the Pandavas brothers. He was in a social hassle and did not know how to apply yoga expertise to solve it. On the battlefield, Krishna gave him a crash-course on yogic social interactions.

Uddhava Gītā is from the *Srimad Bhagavatam (Bhagavata Purana),* which is a history of the incarnations of Krishna. Uddhava was a relative of Krishna. He was concerned about the situation of the deaths of many relatives, but Krishna diverted Uddhava to the practice of yoga for the purpose of successfully migrating to the spiritual environment.

Kundalini Hatha Yoga Pradipika is the commentary for the Hatha Yoga Pradipika of Swatmarama Mahayogin. This is the detailed process about *asana* posture, *pranayama* breath-infusion, complex compressions of energy, naad sound resonance intonement and advanced meditation practice.

This is the singular book with all the techniques of how to reform and redesign the subtle body so that it does not have the tendency for physical life forms and for it to attain the status of a siddha.

These books are based on the author's experiences in meditation, yoga practice and participation in spiritual groups:

Specialty

Spiritual Master
sex you!
Sleep Paralysis
Astral Projection
Masturbation Psychic Details

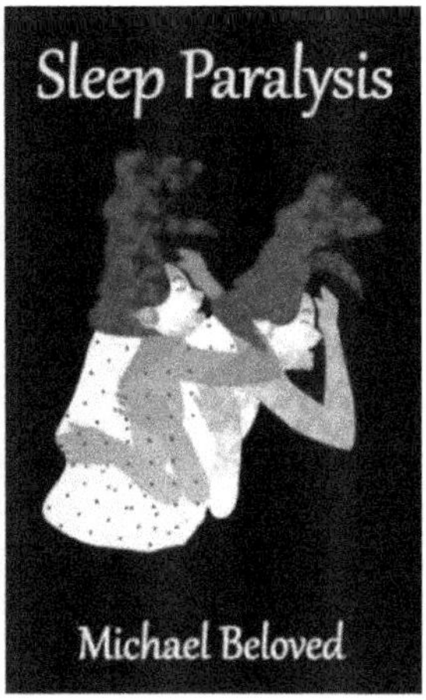

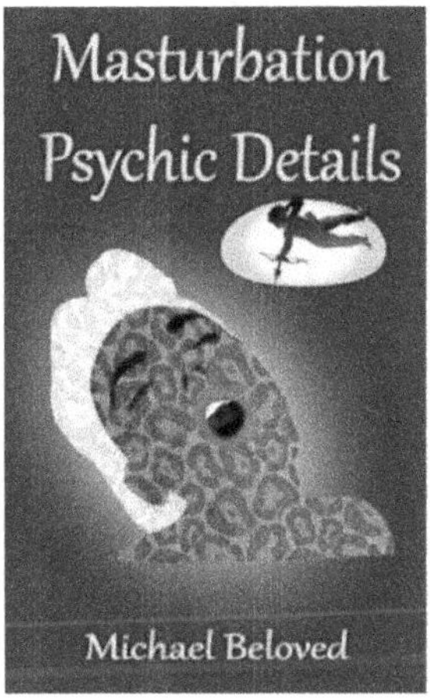

In **Spiritual Master**, Michael draws from experience with gurus or with their senior students. His contact with astral gurus is rated. He walks you through the avenue of gurus showing what you should do and what you should not do, so as to gain proficiency in whatever area of spirituality the guru has proficiency.

sex you! is a masterpiece about the adventures of an individual spirit's passage through the parents' psyches. The conversion of a departed soul into a sexual urge is described. The transit from the afterlife to residency in the emotions of the parents is detailed. This is about sex and you. Learn about how much of you comprises the romantic energy of one's would-be parents!

Sleep Paralysis clears misconceptions so that one can see what sleep paralysis is and what frightening astral experience occurs while the paralysis is being experienced. This disempowerment has great value in giving you confidence that you can and do exist even if one is unable to operate the physical body. The implication is that one can exist apart from and will survive the loss of the material form.

Astral Projection details experiences Michael had even in childhood, where he assumed incorrectly that everyone was astrally conversant. He discusses the lifeForce psychic mechanism which operates the sleep-wake cycle of the physical form, and which budgets energy into the separated astral form which determines if the individual will have dream recall or no objective awareness during the projections. Astral travel happens on every occasion when the physical body sleeps. What is missing in awareness is the observer status while the astral body is separated.

Masturbation Psychic Details is a surprise presentation which relates what happens on the psychic plane during a masturbation event. This does not tackle moral issues or even addictions but shows the involvement of memory and the sure but hidden subconscious mind which operates many features of the psyche irrespective of the desire or approval of the self-conscious personality.

inVision Series

Yoga inVision 1
Yoga inVision 2
Yoga inVision 3
Yoga inVision 4
Yoga inVision 5
Yoga inVision 6
Yoga inVision 7
Yoga inVision 8
Yoga inVision 9
Yoga inVision 10
Yoga inVision 11
Yoga inVision 12
Yoga inVision 13
Yoga inVision 14
Yoga inVision 15
Yoga inVision 16
Yoga inVision 17
Yoga inVision 18
Yoga inVision 19
Yoga inVision 20

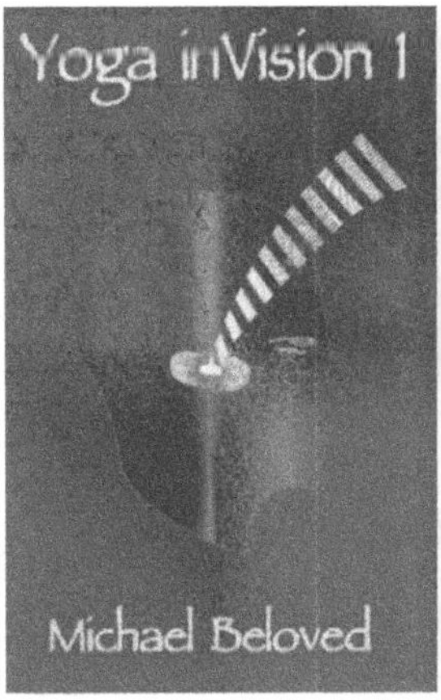
Yoga inVision 1
Michael Beloved

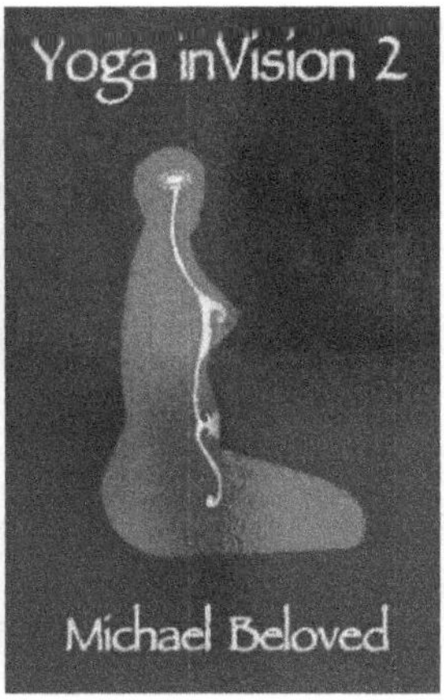
Yoga inVision 2
Michael Beloved

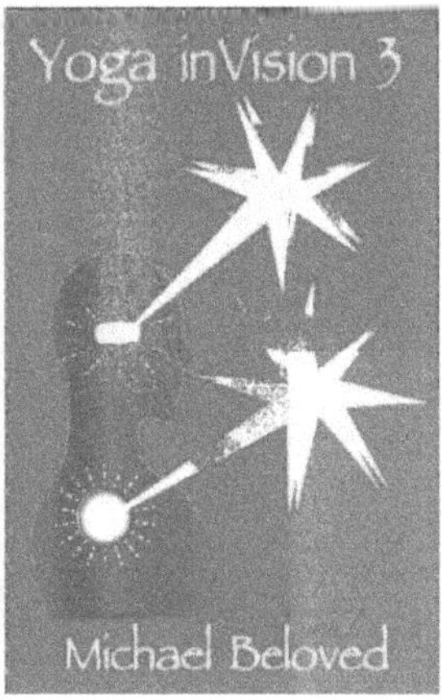
Yoga inVision 3
Michael Beloved

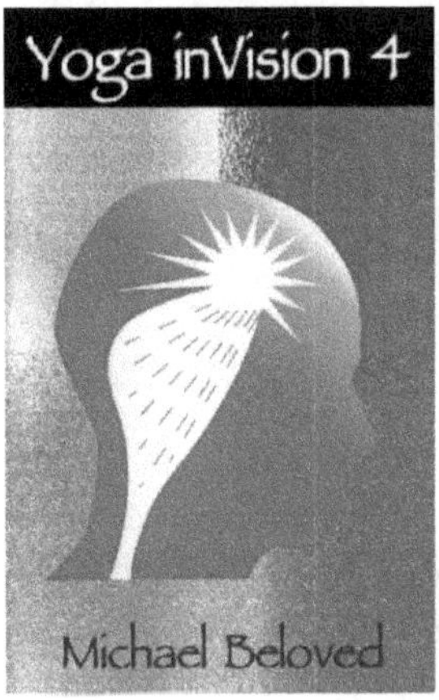
Yoga inVision 4
Michael Beloved

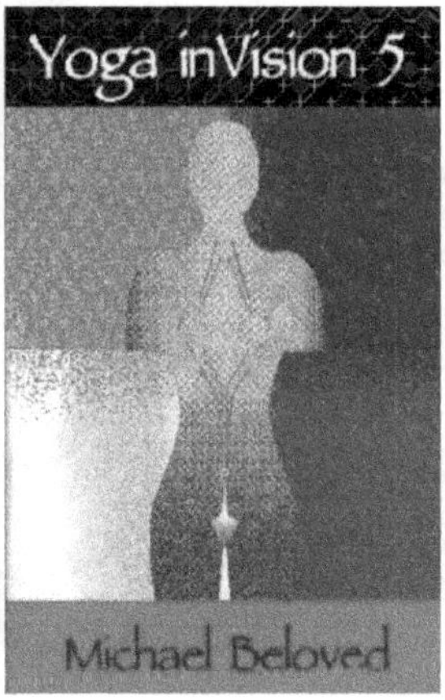
Yoga inVision 5
Michael Beloved

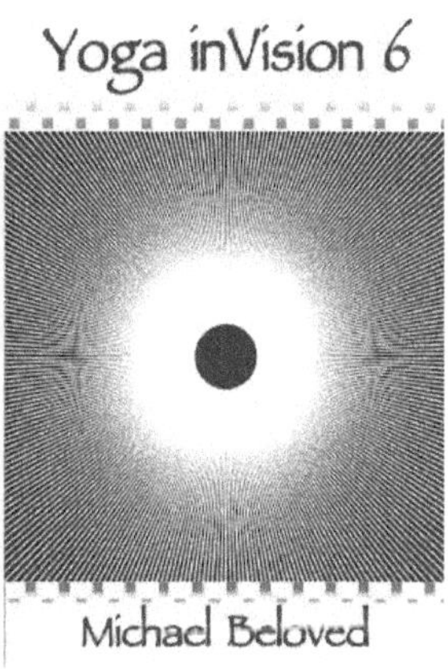
Yoga inVision 6
Michael Beloved

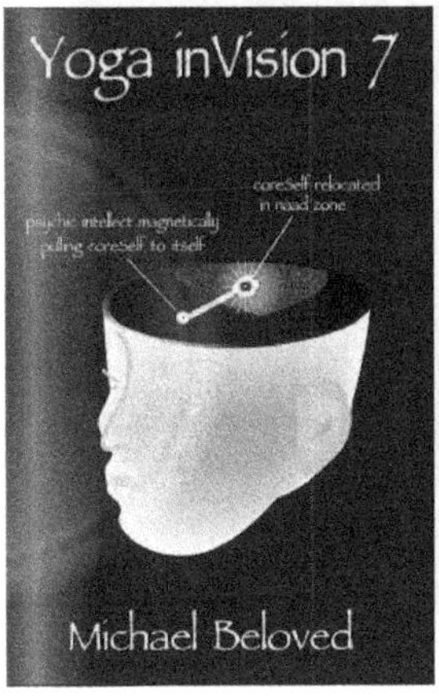
Yoga inVision 7
coreSelf relocated
in naad zone
Michael Beloved

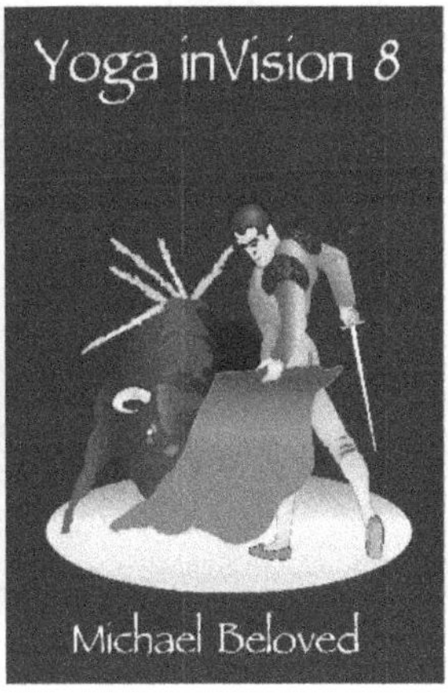
Yoga inVision 8
Michael Beloved

Yoga inVision 9
Michael Beloved

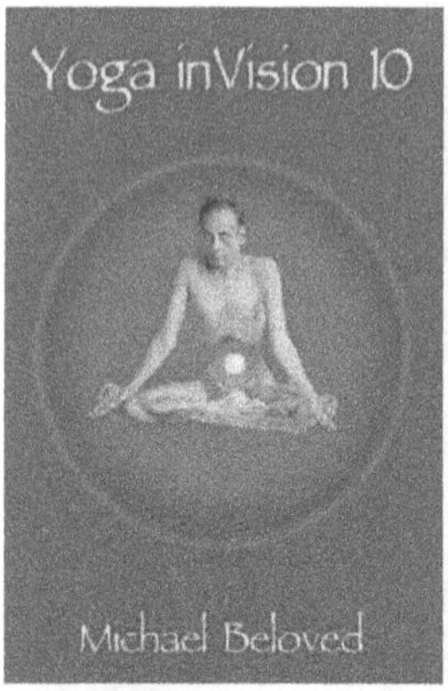
Yoga inVision 10
Michael Beloved

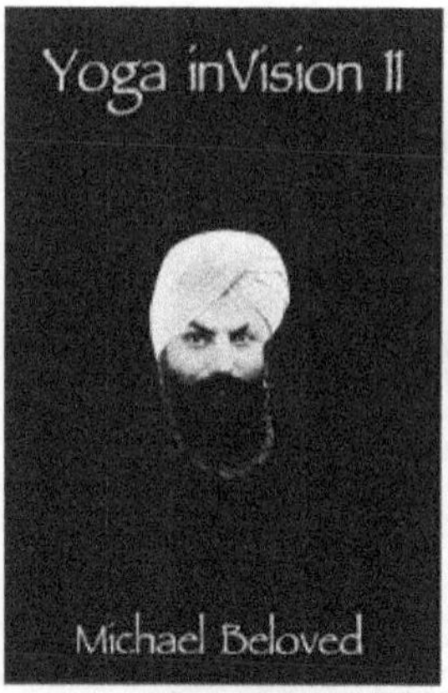
Yoga inVision 11
Michael Beloved

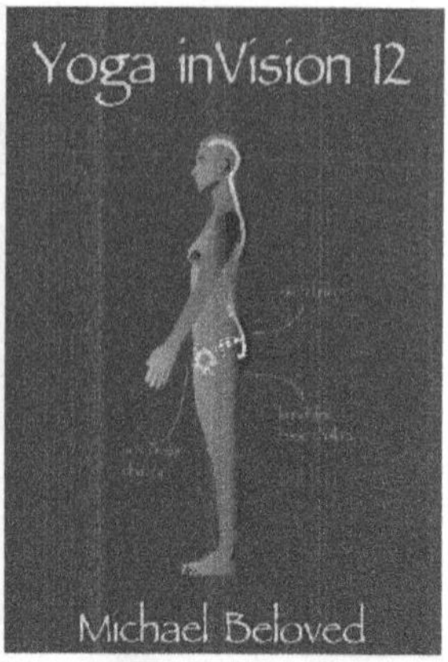
Yoga inVision 12
Michael Beloved

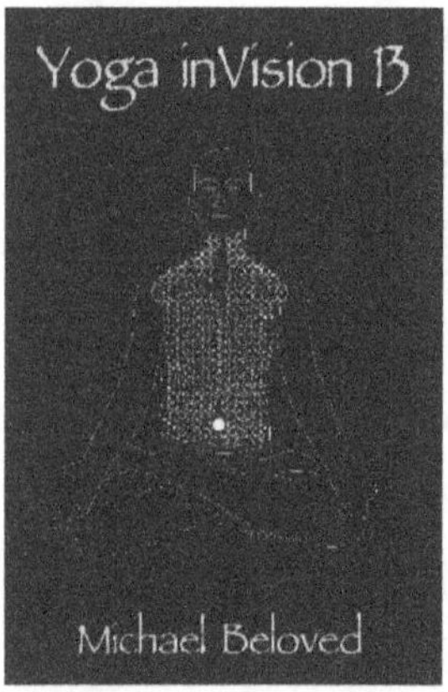
Yoga inVision 13
Michael Beloved

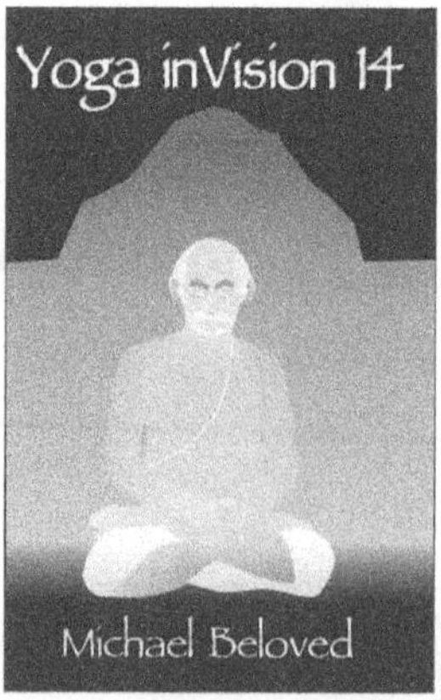
Yoga inVision 14
Michael Beloved

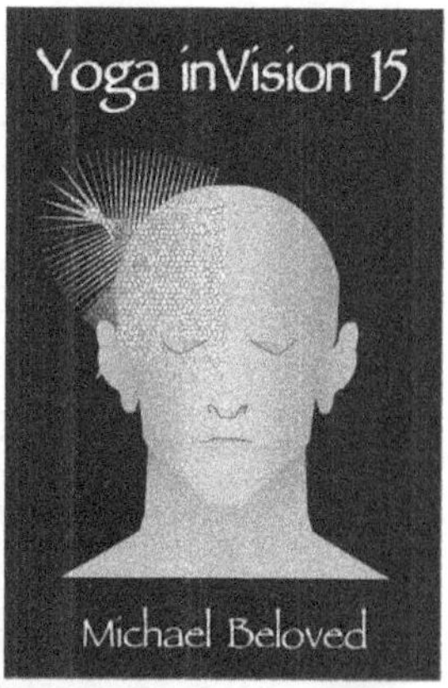
Yoga inVision 15
Michael Beloved

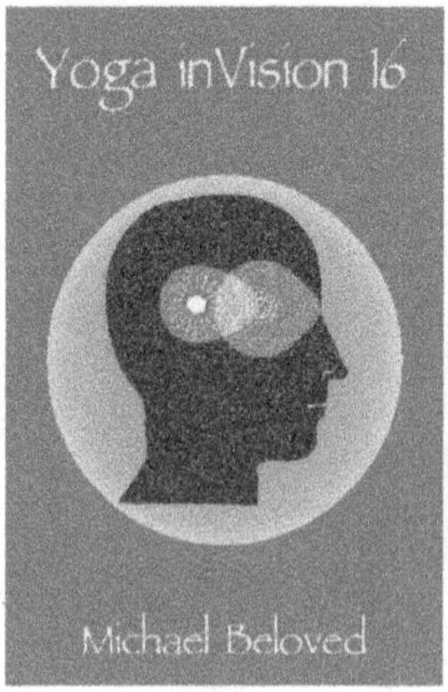
Yoga inVision 16
Michael Beloved

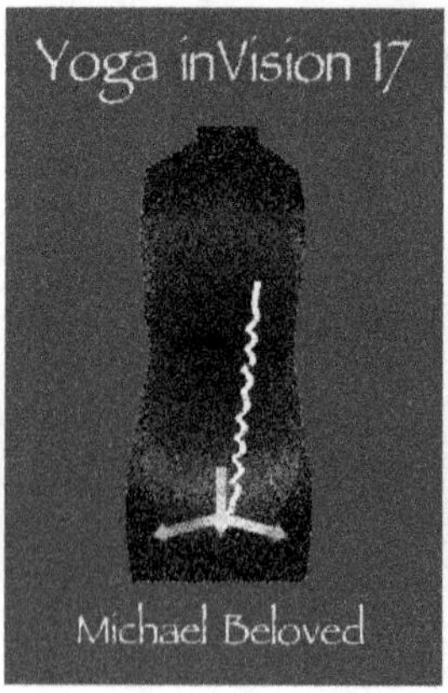
Yoga inVision 17
Michael Beloved

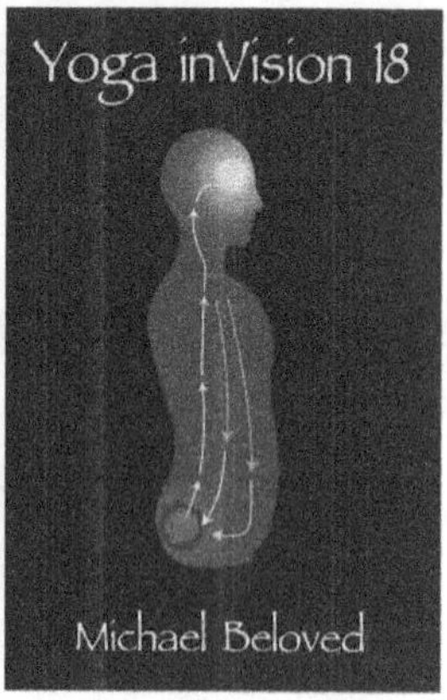
Yoga inVision 18
Michael Beloved

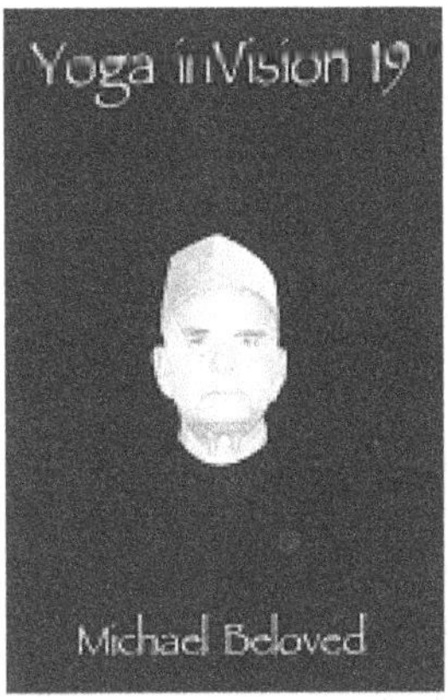

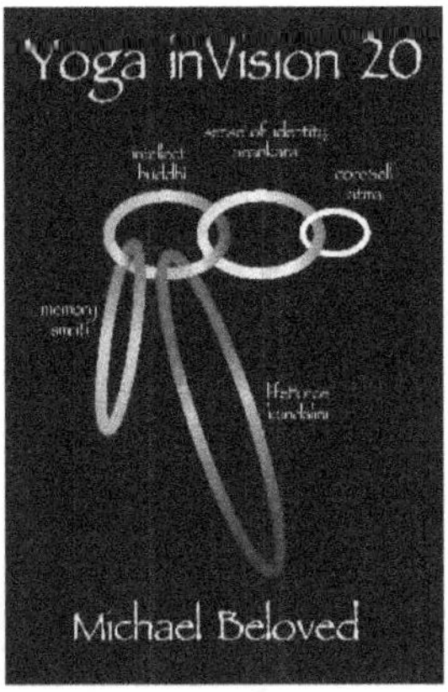

Yoga inVision 1, the first in this series, describes the breath infusion and meditation practices during the years of 1998 and 1999. There are unique, once in a lifetime as well as recurring insights which are elaborated. inFocus during breath infusion and the meditation which follows is an adventure for any yogi. This gives what happened to this particular ascetic.

Yoga inVision 2 reports on the author's experiences from 1999 to 2001. Each day the experience is unique, illustrating the vibrancy of practice. Many rare once-in-a-lifetime perceptions are described.

Yoga inVision 3 reports on the author's experiences from 2001 to 2003.

Yoga inVision 4 reports on the author's experiences from 2006 to 2009.

Yoga inVision 5 reports on the author's experiences from 2006 to 2008.

Yoga inVision 6 reports on the author's experiences in 2010.

Yoga inVision 7 reports on the author's experiences in 2011.

Yoga inVision 8 reports on the author's experiences in 2011.

Yoga inVision 9 reports on the author's experiences in 2012.

Yoga inVision 10 reports on the author's experiences in 2012.

Yoga inVision 11 reports on the author's experiences in 2012.

Yoga inVision 12 reports on the author's experiences in 2012-2013.

Yoga inVision 13 reports on the author's experiences in 2013-2014.

Yoga inVision 14 reports on the author's experiences in 2013-2014.

Yoga inVision 15 reports on the author's experiences in 2014.

Yoga inVision 16 reports on the author's experiences in 2014-2015.

Yoga inVision 17 reports on the author's experiences in 2016-2017.

Yoga inVision 18 reports on the author's experiences in 2017-2019.

Yoga inVision 19 reports on the author's experiences in 2019-2021.

Yoga inVision 20 reports on the author's experiences in 2021-2022.

Online Resources

Email: michaelbelovedbooks@gmail.com
axisnexus@gmail.com

Website: michaelbeloved.com

Forum: inselfyoga.com

Posters: zazzle.com/inself

www.ingramcontent.com/pod-product-compliance
Lightning Source LLC
Chambersburg PA
CBHW072134090426
42739CB00013B/3193
* 9 7 8 1 9 4 2 8 8 7 5 3 9 *